"Nolo's home page is worth bookmarking."
—WALL STREET JOURNAL

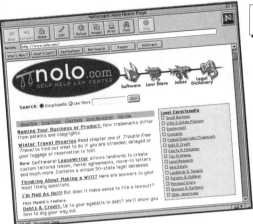

LEGAL INFORMATION ONLINE ANYTIME
24 hours a day
www.nolo.com

AT THE NOLO.COM SELF-HELP LAW CENTER ON THE WEB, YOU'LL FIND

- Nolo's comprehensive Legal Encyclopedia, with links to other online resources
- SharkTalk: Everybody's Legal Dictionary
- Auntie Nolo—if you've got questions, Auntie's got answers
- Update information on Nolo books and software
- The Law Store—over 250 self-help legal products including Downloadable Software, Books, Form Kits and E-Guides
- Discounts and other good deals, plus our hilarious Shark Talk game
- Our ever-popular lawyer jokes
- NoloBriefs.com, our monthly email newsletter

Quality LAW BOOKS & SOFTWARE FOR NON-LAWYERS

Nolo.com legal books and software are consistently first-rate because:

- A dozen in-house Nolo legal editors, working with highly skilled authors, ensure that our products are accurate, up-to-date and easy to use.
- We know our books get better when we listen to what our customers tell us. (Yes, we really do want to hear from you—please fill out and return the card at the back of this book.)
- We are maniacal about updating every book and software program to keep up with changes in the law.
- Our commitment to a more democratic legal system informs all of our work.

OUR "NO-HASSLE" GUARANTEE

Return anything you buy directly from Nolo for any reason and we'll cheerfully refund your purchase price. No ifs, ands or buts.

AN IMPORTANT MESSAGE TO OUR READERS

This product provides information and general advice about the law. But laws and procedures change frequently, and they can be interpreted differently by different people. For specific advice geared to your specific situation, consult an expert. No book, software or other published material is a substitute for personalized advice from a knowledgeable lawyer licensed to practice law in your state.

SECOND EDITION

Take Control
of Your

STUDENT
LOAN
DEBT

BY ATTORNEY ROBIN LEONARD

Second Edition Updated With Help from Deanne Loonin, Staff Attorney at
the National Consumer Law Center, Boston, Massachusetts

KEEPING UP TO DATE

To keep its books up-to-date, Nolo issues new printings and new editions periodically. New printings reflect minor legal changes and technical corrections. New editions contain major legal changes, major text additions or major reorganizations. To find out if a later printing or edition of any Nolo book is available, call Nolo at 510-549-1976 or check our website at www.nolo.com.

To stay current, follow the "Update" service at our website at www.nolo.com. In another effort to help you use Nolo's latest materials, we offer a 35% discount off the purchase of the new edition of your Nolo book when you turn in the cover of an earlier edition. (See the "Special Upgrade Offer" in the back of the book.) This book was last revised in: February 2000

SECOND EDITION	February 2000
EDITOR	Barbara Kate Repa
PRODUCTION	Lori Pacheco
COVER	Toni Ihara
PROOFREADER	Robert Wells
INDEX	Thérèse Shere
INSIDE CARTOON	Jimmy Margulies
PRINTING	Consolidated Printers, Inc.

Leonard, Robin.
    Take control of your student loan debt / by Robin Leonard-- 2nd ed.
      p. cm.
    Rev. ed. of: Take control of your student loans. 1st ed. 1997.
    Includes index.
    ISBN 0-87337-514-9
     1. Student aid--United States. 2. Payment--United States.
  I. Leonard, Robin. Take control of your student loans. III. Title.
LB2337.4.L46 1999
378.3'62--dc21   99-20334
                                       CIP

Quantity sales: For information on bulk purchases or corporate premium sales, please contact the Special Sales department. For academic sales or textbook adoptions, ask for Academic Sales, 800-955-4775, Nolo.com, Inc., 950 Parker St., Berkeley, CA 94710.

ACKNOWLEDGMENTS

I'd like to thank my original co-author, Shae Irving, for the insights, energy and creativity she brought to the first edition. Also, thanks to our editor, Barbara Kate Repa, who kept us going with her relentless questioning and great sense of humor.

For the second edition, I am most grateful to Deanne Loonin for sharing her vast well of knowledge with me and all of you readers.

CONTENTS

CHAPTER 1

THE WORLD OF STUDENT LOANS

CHAPTER 2

WHAT TYPES OF LOANS DO YOU HAVE?

CHAPTER 3

WHO HOLDS YOUR STUDENT LOANS?

CHAPTER 4

MAKING A BUDGET

CHAPTER 5

YOUR REPAYMENT OPTIONS

CHAPTER 6

STRATEGIES WHEN YOU CAN'T PAY

CHAPTER 7

CONSEQUENCES OF NOT PAYING YOUR LOANS

CHAPTER 8

GETTING OUT OF DEFAULT

CHAPTER 9

IF YOU ATTENDED A TRADE OR VOCATIONAL SCHOOL

CHAPTER 10

BANKRUPTCY AND STUDENT LOANS

CHAPTER 11

HELP BEYOND THE BOOK

GLOSSARY

APPENDIX

INDEX

The World of Student Loans

If you owe the government, your school or a private lender money you used to pay for your education, you're not alone. Nearly one-half of all undergraduates finance all or a part of their educations with student loans. The percentage is even greater for students who get advanced degrees: over 50% of all graduate students and 75% of professional students borrow money to attend school.

If your student loan debt is high, you may be overwhelmed with the thought of how you will ever repay it. Even if you owe a relatively small amount, you may be struggling. After all, it's harder for someone who earns $1,000 a month to lay out $100 than it is for someone who makes $5,000 a month to repay $500.

Millions of people leave the hallowed halls of colleges and universities with a diploma—and severe anxieties about how to pay off the loans that helped them get it. And if you withdrew from school before graduating, your woes may be worse: you owe money to repay the cost of a credential you never received.

A. Taking Control

If you are feeling overwhelmed by your student loans—whether you've recently left school and must start repaying soon or you've simply ignored your loan debt for many years—resolving to deal with them may be a hard step to take. But when you make a commitment to take control of the situation, you take the first step toward financial health.

1. Getting Started

When taking charge of your loans, be prepared to face a world that is complex and often frustrating. To get your bearings, you may need to sort through many different types of loans with names and terms that have changed over the years. You may not even know where your loans are being held—by your original lender, the Department of Education or some other institution. Even the language may seem strange and intimidating—grace periods, deferments, forbearances, defaults—and those are just a few of the terms you'll encounter. You may face a mountain of unsorted, confusing papers. And you are likely to have some exasperating conversations with government or loan company representatives. This book helps you handle all of these troubles and guides you through a number of additional pitfalls you may encounter.

MAINTAIN YOUR COOL, EVEN WHEN YOU'RE HOT

Taking charge of your student loans will mean that you'll have to get in touch with government or loan company representatives. You may become frustrated or angered by the person on the other end of the phone, who may be hostile or even suspicious if you want to make arrangements for paying or you request more time to pay.

Whatever the attitude of the person with whom you speak, you will only make matters worse if you meet hostility with hostility. Instead, be kind and polite. Grit your teeth and tell yourself that the other person is most likely overworked and underpaid.

Here are some specific suggestions.

- Have a good idea of what specific information you need before you call. Harried government or loan company representatives will quickly lose patience with you if you babble on or ask open-ended general questions. Be as succinct as possible.
- Get the names and direct phone numbers of all people with whom you speak. Take notes about the content of your conversations and write down the date of and time of the calls.

MAINTAIN YOUR COOL, EVEN WHEN YOU'RE HOT (continued)

- Be persistent. If the first person you speak with doesn't have the answer, ask that person for the name and phone number of someone who might. Remember that you are entitled to the benefits you are seeking.
- Don't despair. This book provides you with a wealth of information on student loans. If you speak with someone who has never heard of Federal Insured Student Loans, you can educate yourself *and* the person on the other end of the phone by explaining what you've learned.
- If you need only general information—not information about your specific loan—don't identify yourself as a person with a student loan problem. Government or loan company representatives may be more than happy to help you if you are gathering general information, for example, to write an article for your college newspaper on student loan problems.

2. Fighting Back

You may have turned to this book because you've already had some experiences with the people, institutions and paperwork associated with student loans. If you've neither made payments in a while nor arranged to postpone your payments, you may be facing some serious collection efforts. The Department of Education, working with the IRS, collects hundreds of thousands of dollars a year by intercepting the tax refunds of student loan defaulters. Thousands of others have their wages garnished by the government. And a growing number of souls wind up in court defending themselves against charges that they've reneged on their student loan debts.

Even if collections haven't reached any of these stages, you may have received nasty and threatening letters or phone calls. Perhaps no one is bothering you, but you're trying to buy a house and the student loans you neglected to pay have damaged your credit and now keep you from getting a loan. Or you may be a recent graduate worried about meeting the monthly loan payments you're supposed to make.

No matter what your situation, you are not alone. People of all ages and income brackets have student loan problems. Many people cannot afford the monthly payments. Throughout the 1970s and 1980s, the percentage of people who defaulted on their student loans grew each year at an alarming rate, peaking at 22.4% in 1990.

The default statistics horrified U.S. government officials. In response, Congress enacted several laws to control defaults. Much of the legislation limits the amount of loan money available to students who attend vocational or trade schools, where the default rate was high as 68% at individual schools and averaged 35%—several times more than the rate at two-year and four-year schools. But laws that provide for rigorous collection action and the opportunity to get out of default apply to all former students who are behind on their student loans, not just those who attended trade schools.

The laws appear to be working—at least from the government's point of view. The most recent statistics put the default rate at under 9%. In actual dollars, this represents an annual amount owed to the government of about $1 billion and a total amount due of about $26 billion.

These dollar amounts may depress you. But don't let them. There is much you can do to take control of your student loan situation if you have the right information, a little perseverance and a large amount of patience. Once you've organized your paperwork, made a budget, learned about your repayment options and contacted your loan holders, chances are good that you can create a strategy for dealing with your student loans that really works.

Ignoring your loans will not make them go away. Eventually, you will have to deal with them. Further delay just increases the amount you owe, as interest and fees and costs for collection mount up.

B. The Government's Role

The federal government has been helping students with education costs for over 50 years. After World War II, veterans were rewarded with student grants and loans for serving their country. In the 1960s, anti-poverty programs helped many low-income people go to college—again, by providing them with grants and loans.

BORROWING IS ON THE RISE

During the 1970s, 1980s and 1990s, the government expanded eligibility to help millions of people. By the late 1990s, the federal government was guaranteeing more nearly $50 billion in student loans each year, compared with less than $10 billion per year just a decade before. The average undergraduate borrows $14,000 during school; the average graduate student owes around $25,000 by the end of school and the typical borrower who attended professional school owes close to $50,000. Nearly one-half of the people who attended professional schools such as law or medical, have student loan debts in excess of their annual incomes. Most former students take more than ten years to repay their loans and often pay out over 12% of their income each month to do so.

1. Changing Programs

The federal student loan program is confusing. One reason is that it changes so often. Very few government programs that started in the 1960s and still exist today look anything like they did three decades ago. Government programs, including the student loan program, are altered, expanded and contracted to keep pace with government growth and with changing social and fiscal policies. Since 1965 alone, we've experienced student uprisings against the war in Vietnam, the energy crisis, high inflation, the savings and loan association crisis, the end of the cold war and military downsizing, corporate mergers, a huge budget deficit and a lengthy recession. Every one of these has had an influence on government lawmakers considering legislation dealing with how students should pay their higher education costs.

For example, when President Bush signed legislation in 1991 extending benefits to Americans experiencing prolonged periods of unemployment, that bill retroactively eliminated the time limit the government had to sue a former student to collect a student loan. As President Bush saw it, extending unemployment benefits would make the budget deficit worse. Collecting old student loans was one way to counter the problem.

Another reason for the confusion is that the system of student loans depends upon a complex web of moneylending institutions—banks, savings and loan associations, credit unions, finance companies that buy loans and collection agencies—and other unique institutions, such as guarantee agencies, student loan servicers and the federal Department of Education. The bank you borrowed from quite possibly hasn't handled your loan in years. Figuring out where your loan is held might take several phone calls and a strong store of tenacity.

Perhaps the most confusing gyration of all is that government programs change names when their purposes change. For example, Federal Insured Student Loans became Guaranteed Student Loans and National Defense Student Loans became National Direct Student Loans.

They also gain a new appellation when they gain a new champion in Congress. For instance, Guaranteed Student Loans became Stafford Loans and National Direct Student Loans became Perkins Loans after legislators Stafford and Perkins jumped on the student loan bandwagon.

One of the biggest changes in recent years occurred in 1994 when the federal government began a new federal direct loan program. The government hoped to make borrowing cheaper for students (and more lucrative for the government) by cutting out the middle people including banks and guarantee agencies. Direct loans are made directly from the government to the student.

All of these changes can lead to mass confusion. If you obtain current literature on student loans from the Department of Education, for example, you may have trouble locating the information concerning your loans. And once you locate the information, you may find that the rules today are far different than on the day you secured your loan. For example, the specifics on canceling your loan or postponing your payments, the interest rate or amount you can borrow are likely to have changed over time.

You're not the only one who is confused by it all. Unless the government or loan company representatives with whom you speak have been on the job many years or have received special training covering the student loan program in its many forms, they may not have heard of your loan or why you are entitled to postpone your payments.

Help may be on the way. Due to huge numbers of student complaints over the years, Congress finally responded in 1998 by creating a new student loan Ombudsman within the Office of Student Financial Assistance. This position was created specifically to help student borrowers resolve complaints with lenders, guarantee agencies and the Department of Education. As of November 1, 1999, the position was not yet filled, and so we cannot provide contact information. To find out more information, visit the website of the Department of Education's Office of Student Financial Assistance at http://www.ed.gov/offices/OSFAP.

2. The Anatomy of a Student Loan

Your confusion over your student loans may be compounded by your encounter with unfamiliar terminology. This book contains an extensive glossary—including words and phrases used by government and loan company representatives. And this section introduces you to the most common words and concepts you will come across.

a. Stage One

The first part of dealing with your student loans is to figure out who has it. As you read through the book, you will come across some terms with meanings that may not be obvious.

Guarantee agency. A state or private nonprofit company that is essentially an insurance company. Guarantee agencies insure your loans and pay off the holder if you default, and receive reinsurance money from the federal Department of Education.

Holder. The owner of your loan or company hired by the owner of your loan to service it—collect and process payments. This company or agency is entitled to receive your payments. Your loan holder may be your lender or a company that has purchased your loan from the lender. If you're in default, the holder would be a guarantee agency, the Department of Education or a collection agency working for the Department.

Lender. The institution from which you obtain your loan. This may be a bank, savings and loan, credit union, your school or the federal government.

b. Stage Two

Once you figure out who has your loans, you need to determine your options for paying or otherwise dealing with them. This section defines those options.

Cancellation. Relieving yourself of your obligation to repay your loan by meeting certain, carefully specified requirements.

Consolidation. Combining many loans into a single new loan or refinancing one loan. When you consolidate, you typically extend your repayment period and lower your monthly payments, increasing the overall cost of your loan.

Deferment. A temporary postponement of your loan payments. Sometimes, the federal government pays the interest that accrues during any authorized period of deferment. Other times, interest continues accruing, increasing the amount you owe.

Forbearance. A temporary postponement or reduction of your loan payments, or an extension of your time to pay. Forbearances are typically granted at the discretion of the holder of your loan. Interest continues to accrue during all forbearance periods.

Grace period. A period of time following your graduation or departure from school during which you are not required to make payments on your loan.

c. Stage Three

If you don't repay your loans or take any of the steps defined in Stage Two, your loans will officially be considered past due and collection efforts will begin.

Default. Failure to repay a loan according to the terms you agreed to when you signed your loan papers coupled with the holder of your loan concluding that you do not intend to repay. Default may also result from failure to submit timely requests for cancelation, deferment or forbearance.

C. Getting Help From This Book

There is no reason for you to read the entire book. You need only to scan the table of contents and read the chapters that apply to you.

- **Chapter 1—The World of Student Loans.** Everyone should read.

- **Chapter 2—What Types of Loans Do You Have?** Most of the repayment opportunities and collection techniques described in this book depend on the type of loans involved. Be sure to read Chapter 2 if you are unsure of what type of loans you have.

- **Chapter 3—Who Holds Your Student Loans?** You probably know who holds your loans if you are making payments, are in the grace period or are in a deferment or forbearance period. If you've defaulted, the institution that holds your loans may make itself known if it begins taking collection action. If you have no idea who holds your loans, however, read Chapter 3.

- **Chapter 4—Making a Budget.** Unless you are absolutely certain that your loans are eligible for cancelation or bankruptcy, you should read this chapter.

- **Chapter 5—Your Repayment Options.** Read if you think you will repay your loans now or sometime in the future.

- **Chapter 6—Strategies When You Can't Pay.** If you can't afford the payments on your loans or want to know if your loans are eligible for cancellation, read this chapter.

- **Chapter 7—Consequences of Not Paying Your Loans.** This chapter is a must for anyone in default. It's also good to read it if you're not in default but want to know what can happen to you if you get there.

- **Chapter 8—Getting Out of Default.** Read this chapter if you are in default and want to go back to school or clean up your credit.

- **Chapter 9—If You Attended a Trade or Vocational School.** Read this chapter if you are a former student of a trade or vocational school.

- **Chapter 10—Bankruptcy and Student Loans.** Read if you want to figure out if you can use bankruptcy to wipe out or help you repay your student loans.

- **Chapter 11—Help Beyond the Book.** If you need more information on your student loan problem than what is included in the first ten chapters, read this material.

Most readers of this book will fall into one of three categories, and should follow a similar path in proceeding through the book.

Situation 1. You have a very old loan on which you haven't made payments for years. The government informs you that it plans to take aggressive collection action.

Example: You got out of college many years ago and never gave much thought to repaying your loans. For many years you seemed to be lost in the government's bureaucracy. But just last month you received a notice that the Department of Education will take your tax refund and apply it toward your outstanding loans. You want to know if there is any way to avoid that, or better yet, get rid of the loans.

1. *Read Chapter 7 on collection efforts to find out what defenses are available when the government threatens to take your tax refund.*

2. *Read Chapter 10 to see if you can discharge the loans in bankruptcy.*

3. *If you can't discharge the loan in bankruptcy, re-read Chapter 7, and read Chapter 8 on getting out of default and Chapter 5 on new payment options.*

Situation 2. You stopped paying on your student loans a number of years ago, but want to return to school and need to come clean.

Example: You got out of college a number of years ago. You paid your loans for a while, but then lost your job. You stopped paying without notifying the holder. You want to go back to graduate school and need to borrow money, but have been told you can't get a new loan.

1. *Read Chapter 3 to find out who holds your loans.*
2. *Read Chapter 8 on getting out of default.*
3. *Read Chapter 7 on collection efforts in the event you don't get out of default.*

Situation 3. You need to start making payments soon—perhaps you recently finished school or were granted a postponement that will end soon—but you can't afford very much.

Example: You got out of college six months ago and are about to come out of your grace period. You can't afford the amount the bank wants each month.

1. *Read Chapter 4 to figure out how much you can afford to pay each month.*
2. *Read Chapter 5 to learn about loan consolidation and your various options for extended, flexible and income contingent repayments.*

ICONS USED IN THIS BOOK

 Books or organizations that give more information about the issue discussed in the text.

 Telephone resources that give more information about the issue discussed in the text.

 Slow down and consider potential problems.

 Lets you know when you need the advice of an attorney or other expert.

 You'll be alerted to a chance to skip some material you may not need to read.

What Types of Loans Do You Have?

In this chapter, you'll take the first step toward managing your student loans: understanding what types of loans you have. Many of you know plenty about your loans already. For example, you may know what your loans are called, who loaned you the money and when you must start making payments. You may know where to send your payments and the name of the person you should call if you're having difficulty meeting your obligations.

But many people don't know much at all about their loans. It's easy to go into denial when a burden feels too great. And former students often push aside their loan paperwork for so long that when it comes time to face what they owe, they no longer know what kinds of loans they took out, much less how to handle their monthly payments.

If you're not sure what kinds of loans you have, there's one good reason to identify them by name and learn about their basic terms: it's the only way to make informed decisions about how to handle them. Many of the factors you may need to consider, including repayment options, postponing your loan payments, handling collection efforts and getting out of default, depend on the kind of loan with which you're grappling.

TERMS TO KNOW

As you read this chapter, you may stumble across a few unfamiliar words or phrases. Here is a brief explanation of some terms you'll need to know. If you're looking for a definition of a word that's not listed here, check the glossary at the back of the book.

Cosigner. A cosigner is someone who has guaranteed your debt. If you fail to make payments on a cosigned loan, your cosigner must repay what you owe. Most student loans are not cosigned. Sometimes, however, a financial institution will offer special incentives—for example, reduced interest rates or fees—if someone cosigns your loan.

Cost of Attendance/Cost of Education. Your cost of attendance is the total amount it costs you to go to school each year. It typically includes tuition, fees, room and board, books, supplies, transportation, loan fees, dependent care, costs related to disability and miscellaneous expenses. Most lenders use your cost of attendance to determine how much money you can borrow under a loan program.

Deferment. A deferment is a temporary postponement of your loan payments. On some loans known as subsidized loans, the federal government pays the interest that accrues during any authorized period of deferment. (See Chapter 6.)

Forbearance. A forbearance is temporary postponement or reduction of your loan payments, or an extension of your time to pay. Interest continues to accrue during all forbearance periods. (See Chapter 6.)

Grace Period. A grace period is a period of time after you graduate from or leave school during which you are not required to make payments on your loan. If you have a subsidized loan, the federal government pays the interest that accrues during your grace period. Whether or not you have a grace period, and how long it lasts, depends on the type of loan you have.

Half-time Enrollment. Many lenders require that you begin repaying your loan within a short time after you leave school or drop below half-time enrollment. For schools that measure progress by credit hours and semesters, trimesters or quarters, half-time enrollment is at least six semester hours or quarter hours per term. For schools that measure progress by credit hours without using semesters, trimesters or quarters, half-time enrollment is at least 12 semester hours or 18 quarter

TERMS TO KNOW (continued)

hours per year. For schools measuring progress by clock hours, half-time enrollment is at least 12 hours per week. Schools may, however, choose to set higher requirements for half-time enrollment.

Independent Student. Some loans are available only to independent students. To be an independent student, you must be over 24 years of age or:

- married
- enrolled in a graduate a professional school program
- responsible for legal dependents other than a spouse
- either be an orphan or ward of the court or have been one until the age of 18, or
- a veteran of the U.S. Armed Forces.

This chapter provides you with basic information about the many types of student loans. You can learn about where your loans came from, how much you might have borrowed under any given program, and what each type of loan costs you in interest rates and fees. You'll also find information about when your loan payments first become due. (See Chapter 3 for guidance on who holds your loan and where to send your payments.)

Section A discusses federally guaranteed student loans. Student loans available from private loan programs are covered in Section B. And miscellaneous student loans, such as those made from state or university funds, are discussed in Section C. If, like many people, you have more than one type of loan, you'll need to read all the sections that apply.

INTEREST: SOME BASIC INFORMATION

If you have a loan of any type, you're probably familiar with the term interest. But it escapes an easy definition, complicated by different rates and the different ways it mounts up.

Interest is the commission you pay a bank, your school or the government for lending you money. For example, you may have a loan with an interest rate of 8%. This means that each year the holder of your loan adds 8% of your outstanding balance, also called your principal balance, to the total amount you owe.

But the method for adding interest to a loan is actually a bit more complex than that. Interest is calculated and added to your loan on a daily or monthly basis through a process called compounding. If your loan papers state that the interest on your loan will be compounded daily, your loan holder will add 1/365th of 8% to the balance of your loan each day. If the interest on your loan is compounded monthly, the holder will add 1/12th of 8% at the start of every month.

Interest that builds up on your loan over time is known as accrued interest. When you get your first bills for a student loan, you'll be paying off a little bit of your principal balance—that is, the money you originally borrowed—plus the interest that accrued since your last payment. If it's your very first payment, you'll be paying the interest that accrued since your loan entered the repayment period. Typically, you are responsible for paying all accrued interest. However, on some loans known as subsidized loans, the federal government pays any interest that accrues while you are in school and during any other authorized periods of deferment. If your loans are not subsidized, any interest that accrues and remains unpaid will be capitalized, which means that it is added to the principal balance of your loan. When this happens, you end up paying interest on interest, and the overall amount that you pay for your loan increases greatly.

The interest rate on your loans may be fixed or variable. A fixed interest rate remains the same for the life of your loan, while a variable interest rate changes slightly from time to time.

You may be discouraged by the amount of interest you have to pay on your loans over time. Unfortunately, there's not much you can do to

INTEREST: SOME BASIC INFORMATION (continued)

lower the rate. Occasionally, it is possible to do so by consolidating your loans. (See Chapter 5, Section C.) And some lenders will cut your interest rate slightly if you make your first payments on time or allow your payments to be deducted directly from your checking account. Beyond this, there's only one surefire way to control the amount of interest you pay, and that's to pay off your loans as quickly as you can.

You may be able to skip some material. If you already know what types of loans you have and you've got a good grasp on their essential terms—grace periods, interest rates and the like—you can skip this chapter.

A. Federal Student Loans

Most student loans are guaranteed by the federal government, meaning that the government will reimburse your lender if you don't pay what you owe. You may already know whether or not your loans are federally guaranteed. But that knowledge alone is of little help when tracing their identities. There are 15 different kinds of federally guaranteed student loans, falling into five broad categories. Furthermore, in 1993, the federal government initiated the William D. Ford Federal Direct Loan Program. Under this program, the government makes loans directly to students, eliminating the role of banks in many new loans. So if you've recently obtained a federally guaranteed loan, it may have come straight from the government, rather than through a financial institution.

FEDERAL DIRECT LOANS

The direct loan program provides government loans directly to students through their schools. The program was meant to help students by lowering the costs of borrowing and also help the government by getting rid of banks and other lenders who have been soaking up much of the profit of student loan borrowing over the years. As the increased competition from the government threatens to cut into lenders' profits, they have fought back. In recent congressional battles, banks and guarantee agency lobbyists have tried to limit the ways that the government is allowed to make direct loans more affordable for students. The government keeps trying to improve the direct loan program, but it is unclear whether it will be able to continue to compete with banks and other lenders.

Whether you have a direct loan or an institutional loan depends on which program your school used when you obtained it. The basic rules about interest rates, fees, grace periods and deferments are the same for both types of loans. You will find, however, that there are some differences in the repayment options available under the two programs. (See Chapter 5.) And of course, if you need to contact your lender—for example, to find out how much money you owe or to postpone your payments—you'll need to know whether you're dealing with a bank or whether you should contact the Department of Education directly.

ARE YOUR LOANS FEDERALLY GUARANTEED?

If your loans are federally guaranteed, it means that the government has promised to reimburse your lender if you default. This doesn't mean that the government will be content to hold the bag for you. If you don't pay what you owe on a federally guaranteed loan, the government will come after you—perhaps quite aggressively—to collect its due. (See Chapter 7.)

Federally guaranteed loans may bring unique benefits to borrowers. For example, the government may cover your interest payments during times when you are not required to make payments—such as while you are in school or when you have obtained a deferment.

Following is a list of federally guaranteed student loans. If the name of the loan is followed by an asterisk, it means that type of loan is no longer made, though you may still have one you must pay. If it's marked with an "x," it means the loan may have come directly from the federal government rather than through a financial institution.

Loan Name	Discussion in This Chapter
Stafford Loans^x	Section A.1
Guaranteed Student Loans (GSL)*	Section A.1
Federal Insured Student Loans (FISL)*	Section A.1
Perkins Loans	Section A.2
National Direct Student Loans (NDSL)*	Section A.2
National Defense Student Loans (NDSL)*	Section A.2
Parental Loans for Students (PLUS)^x	Section A.3.a
Supplemental Loans for Students (SLS)*	Section A.3.b
Auxiliary Loans to Assist Students*	Section A.3.b
Student PLUS Loans*	Section A.3.b
Health Education Assistance Loans (HEAL)*	Section A.4.a
Health Professions Student Loans (HPSL)	Section A.4.b
Loans for Disadvantaged Students (LDS)	Section A.4.c
Nursing Student Loans (NSL)	Section A.4.d
Federal Consolidation Loans^x	Section A.5

1. Stafford Loans, Guaranteed Student Loans and Federal Insured Student Loans

Most student loans are federal Stafford loans. Some older loans of this type are called Guaranteed Student Loans (GSLs) or Federal Insured Student Loans (FISLs). GSLs were made between 1966 and 1988; FISLs were made from 1966 to 1984. Since 1988, however, all loans of this type have been called Stafford loans—and for the sake of convenience, this book uses that term as well.

Stafford loans are made directly by the government or by a financial institution to help pay for your college or graduate school education. The amount you may have borrowed under the program varies—from $2,625 per year for first year, dependent undergraduate students, up to $18,500 per year for most graduate students. Medical students may borrow up to $45,167 per year under the program. A persevering student who finishes graduate school may come out owing as much as $138,500 in Stafford loans. The total may rise to as much as $189,125 for medical students.

If you have Stafford loans, they may be subsidized or unsubsidized, in part or in full. For example a graduate student who borrowed $18,500 in one academic year would have received a maximum of $8,500 in subsidized Stafford loans; the rest would have been unsubsidized. In general, subsidized loans are based on a student's financial need, while unsubsidized loans are available regardless of need. If your loans are subsidized, the government pays the interest on them while you are in school and during any authorized periods of deferment. On some older FISLs made during the 1960s, the government also paid a 3% interest subsidy while former students repaid their loans.

If a Stafford loan is unsubsidized, the government charges interest from the moment you obtain your loan until you pay it in full. If you are in school or you go back to school, you can keep paying the interest on your unsubsidized loan—and defer paying the principal—or you can let the interest accumulate. If you don't pay the interest, it will be added to the principal of your loan, so you'll pay more in the long run. If you want to find out exactly how much the balance of your loan—and your monthly payments—will increase if you let the interest accumulate, ask your loan holder to do the math for you. Stafford loan interest rates have fluctuated over the years, ranging from 6% to 8.25%.

When you obtained your Stafford loan, your lender deducted an origination or insurance fee of up to 5% of the total amount of your loan to cover the costs of making, administering and insuring your loan. You must pay back the full amount of the loan, including the fee.

If you are currently in school, you have no obligation to begin repaying your Stafford loans until you drop below half-time enrollment or have been out of school for six months, or nine months for loans made before 1981. This period between the end of your schooling and the beginning of repayment is called your grace period.

⚠ Don't be late! Before the end of your grace period, your loan holder should provide you with information about repaying your student loans. But even if you never hear a word, you're responsible for beginning repayment on time. If you're near the end of your grace period and you haven't heard from your loan holder, contact the federal Student Financial Assistance Program at 800-433-3243. You can also visit the website at http://www.ed.gov/finaid.html.

2. Perkins Loans, National Direct Student Loans and National Defense Student Loans

A Perkins loan is a low-interest loan for undergraduate or graduate students with very low incomes. These loans were known as National Direct Student Loans (NDSLs) from July 1, 1972, until October 17, 1986, and National Defense Student Loans (again, NDSLs) before then.

The federal government guarantees repayment of Perkins loans. But unlike other federal loans, Perkins loans were made by your school with a combination of federal and school funds, so your school—rather than the government or a bank—is considered your lender. You may have borrowed up to $20,000 under this program as an undergraduate—and up to an additional $40,000 as a graduate student.

The interest rate on Perkins loans has historically been very low— never more than 5%. And when you obtained your Perkins loans, you received the entire loan amount—that is, your school did not charge you an origination or insurance fee. Finally, Perkins loans are subsidized, so interest does not accrue while you are in school and during authorized periods of deferment. (See Chapter 6, Section C.)

If you are in school, your obligation to repay begins nine months after you leave or drop below half-time status.

3. Loans for Parents or Independent Students

You may have obtained either or both of the other common types of federal student loans, neither of which depend on financial need.

a. Loans for Parents

Loans for Parents (called PLUS loans—an acronym of their former name, Parental Loans for Students) are federally guaranteed loans made to credit-worthy parents so they can pay the education expenses of their dependent children. Your PLUS loans may have been made directly by the government or by a financial institution. You may have borrowed up to the cost of the student's education, minus any other financial aid received, such as grants or Stafford loans.

PLUS loans are not subsidized; the lender charges interest from the date a loan is issued until it is paid in full. Interest rates have fluctuated over the years, ranging from 8% to 14%. Currently, the rate is capped at 9%.

When you obtained your PLUS loan, your lender deducted an origination or insurance fee from the total amount—probably 4% or 5% of the principal. You must pay back the full amount of the loan, including the fee deducted by your lender. And there is no grace period for PLUS loans; you are obligated to begin repaying the loan within 60 days of receiving the money.

b. Independent Students

You may have one of the several types of loans for independent students: Supplemental Loans for Students (SLS), Auxiliary Loans to Assist Students (appropriately termed ALAS) or Student PLUS Loans. The government stopped making special loans to independent students on June 30, 1994. Before that, SLS loans were available to independent students with good credit histories or cosigners. Most students who obtained SLS loans were graduate or professional students, though in unusual circumstances undergraduate students were also eligible. A student who didn't qualify for sufficient aid under the Stafford program often took out SLS loans as a supplement.

You may have borrowed as much as $4,000 per year under the SLS program, at an interest rate as high as 12%. The origination or insurance fee was also steep—up to 8%. And SLS loans did not have an in-school deferment or a post-school grace period; first payments were due within 60 days of the final loan disbursements. But if you have both a Stafford loan and an SLS loan and are not in default, you can use the Stafford loan grace period and deferments for both loans.

Auxiliary Loans to Assist Students and Student PLUS loans were precursors to the SLS program. They were available in the 1980s under terms very similar to those for SLS loans.

More information about federal loans. If you need more information about the basic terms of a federal student loan, contact your lender or the Federal Student Aid Information Center. The Center offers a free booklet, *The Student Guide*, that explains many of the basic terms and rules governing federal loans. Call 800-433-3243 or visit the Center's website at http://www.ed.gov/prog_info/SFA/StudentGuide.

If you want to learn more about a federal direct student loan, contact the Direct Loan Servicing Center:

Borrower Services
Direct Loan Servicing Center
P.O. Box 4609
Utica, NY 13504
800-848-0979
800-848-0983 (TDD)

For general information about the federal student loan program, visit the website of the Department of Education at http://www.ed.gov.

4. Loans for Healthcare Professionals

Four types of loans have been created and funded by the federal government for students studying the healthcare professions. Unlike other federal loans, which are managed by the Department of Education, these loans are managed by the Department of Health and Human Services (HHS).

a. Health Education Assistance Loans

Health Education Assistance Loans are commonly known as HEAL loans. HEAL loans to first-time borrowers were discontinued as of October 1, 1995. You received a HEAL loan after that date only if you had already secured at least one other HEAL loan.

HEAL loans were made by financial and educational institutions to those studying medicine, osteopathy, dentistry, veterinary medicine, optometry, podiatry, public health, pharmacy, chiropractic, health administration or clinical psychology. You may have borrowed up to $20,000 per year under the program, depending on your area of study.

HEAL loans were not subsidized; your lender charged interest from the time you obtained your loan until it was paid in full. The interest rate on HEAL loans is based on the treasury bill rate and ranged widely—from a low of just 6% in the early 90s to a high of 18% in the mid-80s. When you obtained your loan, your lender deducted an origination or insurance fee of up to 8% from the total amount, but you must repay the full amount, including the amount deducted as insurance.

You must begin to repay a HEAL loan nine months after you leave school or drop below full-time enrollment. If, however, you become a resident or intern in an accredited program within nine months after leaving school, you may defer repayment for up to four years while you participate in the program (See Chapter 6, Section C.). The repayment period begins nine months after the end of your internship or residency.

More information about HEAL Loans. For more information about the basic terms of a HEAL loan, call your lender or the Department of Health and Human Services at 301-443-1540.

b. Health Professions Student Loans

Health Professions Student Loans (HPSLs) are loans made by schools to financially needy students pursuing degrees in medicine, osteopathy, dentistry, optometry, pharmacy, podiatry or veterinary medicine. You may have borrowed up to the cost of attendance, although until 1999, the maximum amount you could have borrowed was the amount of your tuition plus $2,500.

The interest rate on HPSLs has historically been very low—never more than 5%. And when you obtained your loan, your school did not charge you an origination-insurance fee. Furthermore, HPSLs are subsidized, so interest does not accrue while you are in school full-time.

Your obligation to begin repaying an HPSL begins 12 months after you leave school or drop below full-time enrollment. Deferments are available for periods of internship or residency. (See Chapter 6, Section C.)

Medicine and osteopathic medicine students who obtained their first HPSL after June 30, 1993, must agree to enter and complete residency training in primary care and then must practice primary care until their loans are paid off.

c. Loans for Disadvantaged Students

Loans for Disadvantaged Students (LDS) were available for only three years, by a very small number of schools for very low amounts. The loans were made available for the same purposes and under the same terms, as HPSLs. In this context, "disadvantaged" refers to students who have very low incomes.

d. Nursing Student Loans

Nursing Student Loans (NSLs) are loans made by schools to financially needy students pursuing a course of study leading to a diploma, associate, baccalaureate or graduate degree in nursing. You may have borrowed up to $2,500 per year during your first two years of nursing school and up to $4,000 per year your last two years. If you attended nursing school for more than five years, you were still limited to borrowing a maximum of $13,000. The interest rate on these loans has historically been very low—never more than 5%. There were no origination or insurance fees. And NSLs are subsidized, so interest does not accrue while you are in school full-time or during authorized deferment periods. If you are in school, your obligation to begin repaying an NSL begins nine months after you leave or drop below half-time enrollment.

More information about loans: HPSL, LDS or NSL. For more information about the basic terms of an HPSL, LDS or NSL, call your lender or the Department of Health and Human Services at 301-443-4776.

5. Federal Consolidation Loans

If you've combined several loans or refinanced one loan, you probably have a federal consolidation loan from either the government or a private loan consolidation company, such as Sallie Mae or the USA Group. You can get information about the terms of your consolidation loan from your lender. Basic information is also contained in your loan agreement. (See Chapter 5, Section C.)

B. Private Loans

Many former students have private loans—loans made by banks and other financial institutions without any direct financial backing from the federal government.

Private loans are closely linked with federal loans, however. Many graduate students and a few undergraduates apply for federally guaranteed loans and private loans with one application package. If you did this, you were awarded private loans to cover educational and living expenses that exceeded the amount of any federal loans you received. You probably had to pass a credit check before you obtained a private loan.

Private loans are not subsidized, which means that interest started to accrue when you obtained your loans and will continue to mount up until you pay them in full. If you're in school or have obtained a deferment, you can pay the interest on your private loans as it accrues or you can let it accumulate. If you don't pay the interest as it accrues, it will be added to the principal amount of your loans, so you will pay more for your loans in the long run. If you want to find out exactly how much the balance of your loan—and your monthly payments—will increase if you let the interest accumulate, ask your loan holder to do the math for you.

All lenders deduct guarantee fees, sometimes called origination or insurance fees, from private loans. Your guarantee fees may have been as high as 11%, depending on the type of loan you have. You must pay back the full amount of your loan, including any fees your lender charged. Your lender may even have loaned you the money to cover the cost of the origination fee. In this case, your loan check would have been for the stated amount of your loan, but your promissory agreement will indicate you borrowed more—the stated amount of your loan plus the origination fee.

Following, you'll find summaries of basic information about some of the major private loan programs. This information is divided into the following categories:

Name of Loan Program: What your loan is called.

Who Is Eligible: Who is permitted to obtain a loan under the program.

Maximum Annual Loan Amount: How much money you might have borrowed under the program each year.

Maximum Aggregate Loan Amount: The total amount you may have borrowed under the program for all the years you were in school.

Maximum Guarantee Fee: This tells you the percentage of your loan that your lender charged you to insure your loan.

Interest Rate: The range of interest rates on your loan.

Repayment Begins: When you must begin making payments on your loan.

We have not included information about private loans available through banks because most banks that make Stafford loans also offer their own, non-federally guaranteed loans. Some offer private loans for graduate and professional studies, such as Citibank's Assist Loans and Wells Fargo/Norwest's Med CAP, Law Student and MBA Tuition Loans. Some banks offer loans for undergraduate studies, such as Wells Fargo/Norwest's Collegiate Loans and Bank of America's Student Maximizer. To find out information about your private loans issued by a bank, contact the bank directly.

1. Medical and Dental Students

Many private companies make loans to assist medical, dental and other health care students with their school and residency-related expenses.

a. AAMC (Association of American Medical Colleges) MEDLOANS

Alternative Loan Program Loans (ALPs)

Who Is Eligible: Students enrolled at least half-time at an approved medical school who have also applied for a federal Stafford loan.

Dates of Loan Program: 1985-present.

Maximum Annual Loan Amount: $38,500.

Maximum Aggregate Loan Amount: $175,000 in student loans from all sources.

Maximum Guarantee Fee: 7% when the loan is made, plus 5% immediately before the repayment period begins.

Interest Rate: 7%-12%.

Repayment Begins: Nine months after you leave school or drop below half-time enrollment, or three to four years after your graduation if you enter a residency training program.

MEDEX Loans

Who Is Eligible: Students in the final year at an approved medical school who need to borrow money to assist with the residency application and relocation process.

Maximum Loan Amount: $8,000 one time only.

Maximum Guarantee Fee: 7% when the loan is made, plus 5% immediately before the repayment period begins.

Interest Rate: 7%-12%.

Repayment Begins: Three to four years after your graduation, depending on the length of residency training.

b. The Access Group

Medical Access Loans

Who Is Eligible: Students enrolled at least half-time at an approved medical school.

Maximum Annual Loan Amount: Cost of attendance minus any other financial aid received.

Maximum Aggregate Loan Amount: $195,000 in student loans from all sources.

Maximum Guarantee Fee: 6.5% when the loan is made, plus 2% immediately before the repayment period begins.

Interest Rate: Accrues at two different rates—one for the time when you are in school and a slightly higher rate once your loan enters the repayment period; these rates have ranged from 7%-10%.

Repayment Begins: Nine months after you leave school or drop below half-time enrollment, or nine months after you complete a required residency program, which may not exceed four years.

Medical Residency Loans

Who Is Eligible: Students in the final year at an approved medical school who need to borrow money to assist with the residency application and relocation process.

Maximum Annual Loan Amount: $8,000 one time only.

Maximum Aggregate Loan Amount: $195,000 in student loans from all sources.

Maximum Guarantee Fee: 6.5% when the loan is made, plus 2% immediately before the repayment period begins.

Interest Rate: Accrues at two different rates—one for the time when you are in school and a slightly higher rate once your loan enters the repayment period; these rates have ranged between 7%-10%.

Repayment Begins: Nine months after you complete a required residency program, which may not exceed four years.

Dental Access Loans

Who Is Eligible: Students enrolled at least half-time in an approved school of dentistry.

Maximum Annual Loan Amount: Cost of attendance minus any other financial aid received.

Maximum Aggregate Loan Amount: $195,000 in student loans from all sources.

Maximum Guarantee Fee: 8% when the loan is made, plus 2% immediately before the repayment period begins.

Interest Rate: Accrues at two different rates—one for the time when you are in school and a slightly higher rate once your loan enters the repayment period; these rates have ranged from 7%-10%.

Repayment Begins: Nine months after you leave school or drop below half-time enrollment.

Dental Residency/Dental Board Examination Loans

Who Is Eligible: Students in the final year at an approved dental school who need to borrow money to assist with the residency and board examination process.

Maximum Annual Loan Amount: $8,000 one time only.

Maximum Aggregate Loan Amount: $195,000 in student loans from all sources.

Maximum Guarantee Fee: 6.5% when the loan is made, plus 2% immediately before the repayment period begins.

Interest Rate: Accrues at two different rates—one for the time when you are in school and a slightly higher rate once your loan enters the repayment period; these rates have ranged between 7%-10%.

Repayment Begins: Nine months after you complete a required residency program, which may not exceed four years.

c. Nellie Mae (New England Loan Marketing Association)

MedDent•EXCEL Loans

Who Is Eligible: Students enrolled at least half-time at an approved medical or dental school.

Maximum Annual Loan Amount: $15,000 per year; more with a cosigner.

Maximum Aggregate Loan Amount: $150,000–$200,000 depending on the program.

Maximum Guarantee Fee: 10%.

Interest Rate: 7%-12%.

Repayment Begins:

- First payment due six months after you leave school or drop below half-time enrollment, or four and a half years after your first loan disbursement, whichever comes first.

- An additional fee of up to 2% is added if you don't make interest payments while you are in school.

Graduate Extension Loans

Who Is Eligible: Students in the final year at an approved medical or dental school who need to borrow money to assist with the residency application and relocation process—and who have at least one other loan from Nellie Mae.

Maximum Annual Loan Amount: $8,000 one time only.

Maximum Aggregate Loan Amount: $150,000–$200,000 depending on the program.

Maximum Guarantee Fee: 10%.

Interest Rate: 7%-12%.

Repayment Begins:

- First payment due six months after you leave school or drop below half-time enrollment, though you can defer your payments for an additional four years while you are completing your residency or internship.

- An additional fee of up to 2% is added if you don't make interest payments while you are in school or during your residency period.

d. Sallie Mae (Student Loan Marketing Association)

Signature Health Loans

Who Is Eligible: Students enrolled at least half-time at an approved school in graduate studies in dentistry, optometry, osteopathic medicine, pharmacy, podiatry or veterinary medicine and under-graduate and graduate students in allied health programs: nursing, nurse anethestist, nurse practitioner, occupational therapy, physical therapy, physician's assistant, pharmacy and dental hygienist.

Maximum Annual Loan Amount: Cost of attendance minus any other financial aid received.

Maximum Aggregate Loan Amount: $100,000 in private loans.

Maximum Guarantee Fee: 6% when the loan is made, plus 3% immediately before the repayment period begins; additional fee is waived if you have a cosigner.

Interest Rate: Approximately 8.5%.

Repayment Begins: Six months after you leave school or drop below half-time enrollment.

e. TERI (The Education Resources Insitute)

MedChoice Loans

Who Is Eligible: Students enrolled at least half-time studying health care as an undergraduate (acupuncture, nursing, occupational therapy, pharmacy, physical therapy or physician's assistant) or graduate or professional student (allopathic medicine, cell and molecular biology, cell and molecular pathogenesis & cancer, clinical psychology, dentistry, neurobiology, neuropharmacology, nurse anesthetist, nurse midwifery, nurse practitioner, nursing, nutrition, occupational therapy, optometry, osteopathic medicine, pharmacy, physical therapy, physician's assistant, podiatry, public health, vascular biology or veterinary medicine).

Maximum Annual Loan Amount: Undergraduate students may borrow up to the cost of attendance minus any other financial aid received. Graduate and professional students may borrow up to $20,000. Medical students may borrow an additional $10,000 for internship and residency costs.

Maximum Aggregate Loan Amount: None.

Maximum Guarantee Fee: 10%.

Interest Rate: 7%-12%.

Repayment Begins:

- If you are in school, you can defer payments of principal and interest until nine months after graduation.

- Medical students may request a second deferment to cover an internship or residency period—a maximum of four years.

2. MBA Students

A couple of companies currently make private loans to graduate business students. If you went to business school, you may have a private loan from any one of these companies.

a. The Access Group

Business Access Loans

Who Is Eligible: Students enrolled in approved graduate business programs.

Maximum Annual Loan Amount:

- Students who attended at least half-time may have borrowed up to the cost of attendance.

- Students who attended half-time or less are limited to the cost of tuition and fees plus a maximum of $500 for books and supplies.

Maximum Aggregate Loan Amount: $120,000 in student loans from all sources.

Maximum Guarantee Fee: 6.5% when the loan is made, plus 2% immediately before the repayment period begins.

Interest Rate: Accrues at two different rates—one for the time when you are in school and a slightly higher rate once your loan enters the repayment period; these rates have ranged from 7%-10%.

Repayment Begins: Nine months after you leave school or three years after you receive your first Business Access Loan, whichever comes first.

b. Nellie Mae (New England Loan Marketing Association)

MBA•EXCEL Loans

Who Is Eligible: Students enrolled at least half-time at an approved business school.

Maximum Annual Loan Amount: $15,000 per year; more with a cosigner.

Maximum Aggregate Loan Amount: $150,000–$200,000, depending on the program.

Maximum Guarantee Fee: 10%.

Interest Rate: 8%-10%.

Repayment Begins:

- Six months after you leave school or drop below half-time enrollment, or four and a half years after you receive your first MBA•EXCEL loan, whichever comes first.

- An additional fee of up to 2% is added to your loan if you defer your interest payments while you are in school.

3. Law Students

The two major providers of private loans for law students are Law Access Loans and LawEXCEL Loans.

a. The Access Group

Law Access Loans (LAL)

Who Is Eligible: Students pursuing a J.D., LL.M. or joint law degree program at an approved law school who are enrolled at least half-time.

Maximum Annual Loan Amount: Cost of attendance minus any other financial aid received.

Maximum Aggregate Loan Amount: $130,000 in student loans from all sources.

Maximum Guarantee Fee: 7% when the loan is made, plus 4% immediately before the repayment period begins.

Interest Rate: Accrues at two different rates—one for the time when you are in school and a slightly higher rate once your loan enters repayment; these rates have ranged from 7%-12%.

Repayment Begins: Nine months after you leave school or drop below half-time enrollment.

Bar Examination Loans (BEL)

Who Is Eligible: Students in the final year of law school who need to borrow money for bar study expenses, including living expenses.

Maximum Annual Loan Amount: $8,000 one time only.

Maximum Aggregate Loan Amount: $130,000 in student loans from all sources.

Maximum Guarantee Fee: 7% when the loan is made, plus 4% immediately before the repayment period begins.

Interest Rate: Accrues at two different rates—one for the time when you are in school and a slightly higher rate once your loan enters repayment; these rates have ranged from 7%-12%.

Repayment Begins: Nine months after you graduate.

b. Nellie Mae (New England Loan Marketing Association)

LawEXCEL Loans

Who Is Eligible: Students enrolled at least half-time at an approved law school.

Maximum Annual Loan Amount: $15,000 per year; more with a cosigner.

Maximum Aggregate Loan Amount: $150,000–$200,000 depending on the program.

Maximum Guarantee Fee: 10%.

Interest Rate: 8%-10%.

Repayment Begins: Six months after you leave school or drop below half-time enrollment, or four and a half years after you receive your first LawEXCEL loan, whichever comes first; an additional fee of 2% is added if you defer interest payments while you are in school.

Graduate Extension Loans

Who Is Eligible: Students in the final year at an approved law school who need to borrow money for bar study expenses—and who have at least one other loan from Nellie Mae.

Maximum Annual Loan Amount: $8,000 one time only.

Maximum Aggregate Loan Amount: $150,000–$200,000 depending on the program.

Maximum Guarantee Fee: 10%.

Interest Rate: 7%-12%.

Repayment Begins: First payment due six months after you leave school or drop below half-time enrollment.

4. Graduate Students

Most of the loans described in this section are made to graduate students in fields other than law, business, medicine and dentistry, although these students do qualify for the TERI PEP Loan.

a. The Access Group

Graduate Access Loans

Who Is Eligible: Students enrolled at least half-time in approved graduate programs other than medicine, dentistry, law or business.

Maximum Annual Loan Amount: Cost of attendance minus any other financial aid received.

Maximum Aggregate Loan Amount: $120,000 in student loans from all sources.

Maximum Guarantee Fee: 7% when the loan is made, plus 3% immediately before the repayment period begins.

Interest Rate: Accrues at two different rates—one for the time when you are in school and a slightly higher rate once your loan enters the repayment period; these rates have ranged from 7%-10%.

Repayment Begins: Nine months after you leave school or drop below half-time enrollment.

b. Nellie Mae (New England Loan Marketing Association)

GradEXCEL Loans

Who Is Eligible: Students enrolled at least half-time in approved graduate programs other than medicine, dentistry, law or business.

Maximum Annual Loan Amount: $15,000 per year; more with a cosigner.

Maximum Aggregate Loan Amount: $150,000–$200,000 depending on the program.

Maximum Guarantee Fee: 10%.

Interest Rate: 7%-12%.

Repayment Begins:

- If you are in school, you can defer payments of principal and interest or principal only until six months after you leave or drop below half-time enrollment, or four and a half years after you receive your first GradEXCEL loan, whichever comes first.
- An additional fee of up to 2% is added to your loan if you defer your interest payments while you are in school.

c. TERI (The Education Resources Institute)

Professional Education Plan (PEP)

Who Is Eligible: Students enrolled at least half-time in TERI - approved graduate or professional programs.

Maximum Annual Loan Amount: $15,000; more with a cosigner.

Maximum Aggregate Loan Amount: None.

Maximum Guarantee Fee: 10%.

Interest Rate: 7%-12%.

Repayment Begins:

- If you are in school, you can defer payments of principal and interest until six months after leaving school.
- Medical students may request a second deferment to cover an internship or residency period—a maximum of four years.

5. Undergraduates

Most undergraduate students finance their educations with job earnings, savings, grants, scholarships and federal student loans. Occasionally, however, an undergraduate—or his or her parents—turns to a private loan company for additional assistance.

a. Nellie Mae (New England Loan Marketing Association)

EXCEL Loans

Who Is Eligible: Parents, spouses and grandparents of undergraduate students enrolled at least half-time at an accredited college or university. Independent, creditworthy undergraduate students themselves may be eligible if they are enrolled at least half-time at an accredited college or university and work full-time.

Maximum Annual Loan Amount: Cost of attendance minus any other financial aid received.

Maximum Aggregate Loan Amount: None.

Maximum Guarantee Fee: 7%.

Interest Rate: 7%-12%.

Repayment Begins: Payment begins immediately after the loan was made; if the borrower is in school, however, the borrower can defer payments of principal until after leaving school.

b. TERI (The Education Resources Institute)

Alternative Loan Program

Who Is Eligible: Students enrolled at least half-time at a TERI-approved school.

Maximum Annual Loan Amount: Cost of attendance minus any other financial aid received.

Maximum Aggregate Loan Amount: None.

Maximum Guarantee Fee: 6.5%.

Interest Rate: 7%-12%.

Repayment Begins: First payment due 45 days after the loan was made; if you are in school, however, you can defer payments of principal until 45 days after you leave.

Degreed Undergraduate Alternative Loans (DUAL)

Who Is Eligible: Degreed undergraduate students seeking an additional undergraduate degree.

Maximum Annual Loan Amount: $15,000; more with a cosigner.

Maximum Aggregate Loan Amount: None.

Maximum Guarantee Fee: 10%.

Interest Rate: 7%-12%.

Repayment Begins: Six months after leaving school.

c. Sallie Mae (Student Loan Marketing Association)

Signature Student Loans

Who Is Eligible: Students enrolled at least half-time at an approved school.

Maximum Annual Loan Amount: Cost of attendance minus any other financial aid received.

Maximum Aggregate Loan Amount: $100,000 in private loans.

Maximum Guarantee Fee: 6% when the loan is made, plus 3% immediately before the repayment period begins; additional fee is waived if you have a cosigner.

Interest Rate: Approximately 8.5%.

Repayment Begins: Six months after you leave school or drop below half-time enrollment.

More information about private loans. If you need more information about any of the loans discussed in this section, contact the loan program's administrator.

Medical, Dental and Nursing Students

AAMC MEDLOANS	800-858-5050	http://www.aamc.org
Medical or Dental Access and Residency Loans	800-282-1550	http://www.accessgroup.org
Nellie Mae MedDent•EXCEL and Graduate Extension Loans	800-634-9308	http://www.nelliemae.com
Sallie Mae Signature Health Loans	800-222-7183	http://www.salliemae.com
TERI MedChoice Loans	800-255-8374	http://www.teri.org

Business Students

Business Access Loans	800-282-1550	http://www.accessgroup.org
Nellie Mae MBA•EXCEL Loans	800-634-9308	http://www.nelliemae.com

Law Students

Law Access and Bar Examination Loans	800-282-1550	http://www.accessgroup.org
Nellie Mae LawEXCEL and Graduate Extension Loans	800-634-9308	http://www.nelliemae.com

Graduate Students

Graduate Access Loans	800-282-1550	http://www.accessgroup.org
Nellie Mae GradEXCEL Loans	800-634-9308	http://www.nelliemae.com
TERI PEP Loans	800-255-8374	http://www.teri.org

Undergraduate Students

Nellie Mae EXCEL Loans	800-634-9308	http://www.nelliemae.com
Sallie Mae Signature Student Loans	800-222-7183	http://www.salliemae.com
TERI ALP and DUAL Loans	800-255-8374	http://www.teri.org

C. Other Loans

Most student loans are made by the federal government and private lenders. There are additional loan programs, however. If you weren't able to identify your loans in the first two sections of this chapter, they may fall into one of the following categories.

1. Loans From State Funds

Many states—including Alaska, Arkansas, Delaware, Florida, Iowa, Massachusetts, Minnesota, Mississippi, New Jersey, North Carolina, Ohio, Tennessee and Texas—have their own student loan programs. Most of these loans are for students who pursued degrees in teaching or the health professions and who pledge to teach or practice in the state granting the loans. Some states offer more general types of loans as well, but almost every state restricts loan programs to residents of that state who attend a state university. For information about a state loan program, contact the state office listed below.

STATE DEPARTMENTS OF HIGHER EDUCATION

ALABAMA

Commission on Higher
Education
P.O. Box 302000
Montgomery, AL 36130
334-242-1998
334-242-0268 (fax)
http://www.ache.state.al.us

ALASKA

Commission on
Postsecondary Education
3030 Vintage Boulevard
Juneau, AK 99801
907-465-2962
800-441-2962
907-465-3143 (TTY)
907-465-5316 (fax)
http://www.state.ak.us.acpe/
home.html

ARIZONA

Commission for
Postsecondary Education
2020 North Central Avenue,
Suite 275
Phoenix, AZ 85004
602-229-2591
602-229-2599 (fax)
http://www.acpe.asu.edu

ARKANSAS

Department of Higher
Education
114 East Capitol Street
Little Rock, AR 72201
501-371-2000
501-371-2003 (fax)
http://www.adhe.arknet.edu

CALIFORNIA

Postsecondary Aid
Commission
P.O. Box 419027
Rancho Cordova, CA 95741
916-526-7590
916-526-8002 (fax)
http://www.csac.ca.gov

COLORADO

Commission on Higher
Education
Colorado History Museum
1330 Broadway, 2nd Floor
Denver, CO 80203
303-866-2723
303-860-9750 (fax)
http://www.state.co.us/
cche_dir/hecche.html

CONNECTICUT

Department of Higher
Education
61 Woodland Street
Hartford, CT 06105
860-947-1833
860-947-1311 (fax)
http://ctdhe.commnet.edu

DELAWARE

Higher Education
Commission
820 North French Street,
Fifth Floor
Wilmington, DE 19801
302-577-3240
800-292-7935
302-577-6765 (fax)
http://www.doe.state.de.us/
high-ed

DISTRICT OF COLUMBIA

Office of Postsecondary
Education
2100 Martin Luther King, Jr.
Avenue SE, Suite 401
Washington, DC 20020
202-727-3688
http://dhs.washington.dc.us/
opera/opera.html

FLORIDA

Department of Education
Office of Student Financial
Assistance
1344 Florida Education
Center
Tallahassee, FL 32399-0400
904-488-6402
904-488-1492 (fax)
http://www.firn.edu/doe

GEORGIA

Student Finance Authority
2082 East Exchange Place,
Suite 200
Tucker, GA 30084
770-414-3200
800-776-6878
770-414-3162 (fax)
http://www.gsfc.org

HAWAII

State Postsecondary Education Commission
2444 Dole Street, Room 209
Honolulu, HI 96822
808-956-8213
808-956-5156 (fax)
http://www.hern.hawaii.edu/
hern

IDAHO

State Board of Education
P.O. Box 83720
Boise, ID 83720
208-334-2270
208-334-2632 (fax)
http://www.sde.state.id.us/
dept

ILLINOIS

Student Assistance
Commission
1755 Lake Cook Road
Deerfield, IL 60015
847-948-8500
800-899-4722
847-831-8326 (TTY)
847-948-5033 (fax)
http://www.isac-online.org

INDIANA

State Student Assistance
Commission
150 West Market Street,
Suite 500
Indianapolis, IN 46204
317-232-2350
317-232-3260 (fax)
http://www.state.in.us/ssaci/

IOWA

Student Aid Commission
200 Tenth Street,
Fourth Floor
Des Moines, IA 50309
515-281-3501
800-383-4222
515-242-5996 (fax)
http://www.state.ia.us/
collegeaid

KANSAS

Board of Regents
700 SW Harrison Street,
Suite 1410
Topeka, KS 66603
785-296-3421
785-296-0983 (fax)
http://www.ukans.edu/~kbor

KENTUCKY

Higher Education Assistance
Authority
1050 U.S. Highway 127
South
Frankfort, KY 40601
502-696-7200
800-928-8926
502-696-7496 (fax)
http://www.kheaa.com

LOUISIANA

Office of Student Financial
Assistance
P.O. Box 91202
Baton Rouge, LA 70821
504-922-1012
800-259-5626
504-922-0790 (fax)
http://www.osfa.state.la.us

MAINE

Finance Authority
Education Assistance Division
P.O. Box 949
83 Western Avenue
Augusta, ME 04332
207-623-3263
800-228-3734
207-626-2717 (TTY)
207-626-8208 (fax)
http://www.famemaine.com

MARYLAND

Higher Education
Commission
16 Francis Street
Annapolis, MD 21401
410-974-2971
800-974-0203 (in state only)
800-735-2258 (TTY)
410-974-3513 (fax)
http://www.mhec.state.md.us

MASSACHUSETTS

Board of Higher Education
One Ashburton Place,
Room 1401
Boston, MA 02108
617-727-9240
617-727-6397 (fax)
http://www.mass.edu

MICHIGAN

Higher Education Assistance
Authority
P.O. Box 30462
Lansing, MI 48909
517-373-3394
517-335-5984 (fax)
http://www.fafsa.ed.gov

MINNESOTA

Higher Education Services
Office
1450 Energy Park Drive,
Suite 350
St. Paul, MN 55108
651-642-0567
800-657-0866
800-627-3529 (TTY)
651-642-0675 (fax)
http://www.heso.state.mn.us

MISSISSIPPI

Postsecondary Education
Financial Assistance Board
3825 Ridgewood Road
Jackson, MS 39211
601-982-6663
800-327-2980 (in state only)
601-982-6527 (fax)
http://www.ihl.state.ms.us

MISSOURI

Department of Higher
Education
3515 Amazonas Drive
Jefferson City , MO 65109
573-751-2361
800-473-6757
573-751-6635 (fax)
http://www.mocbhe.gov

MONTANA

University System
2500 Broadway
Helena, MT 59620
406-444-6570
406-444-1469 (fax)
http://www.montana.edu/
wwwoche

NEBRASKA

Coordinating Committee for
Postsecondary Education
P.O. Box 95005
Lincoln, NE 68509
402-471-2847
402-471-2886 (fax)
http://nol.org/
NEpostsecondary

NEVADA

Department of Education
Fiscal Services
400 West King Street
Carson City, NV 89710
775-687-9228

NEW HAMPSHIRE

Postsecondary Education
Commission
2 Industrial Park Drive
Concord, NH 03301
603-271-2555
800-735-2964 (TTY)
603-271-2696 (fax)
http://www.state.nh.us/
postsecondary

NEW JERSEY

Higher Education Student
Assistance Authority
P.O. Box 540
4 Quakerbridge Plaza
Trenton, NJ 08625
609-588-3226
800-792-8670
609-588-2526 (TTY)
609-588-7389 (fax)
http://www.state.nj.us/
treasury/osa

NEW MEXICO

Commission on Higher
Education
1068 Cerrillos Road
Santa Fe, NM 87501
505-827-7383
800-279-9777
800-659-8331 (TTY)
505-827-4984 (fax)
http://www.nmche.org

NEW YORK

Higher Education Services
Corporation
99 Washington Avenue
Albany, NY 12255
518-473-7087
800-433-3243
518-474-2839 (fax)
http://www.hese.com

NORTH CAROLINA

State Education Assistance
Authority
P.O. Box 13663
Research Triangle Park,
NC 27709
919-549-8614
800-700-1775 (in state only)
919-549-8481 (fax)
http://www.ncseaa.edu

NORTH DAKOTA

Student Financial Assistance
Program
Department 215
600 East Boulevard
Bismarck, ND 58505
701-328-4114
701-328-2961 (fax)
http://www.nodak.edu

OHIO

Board of Regents
P.O. Box 182452
Columbus, OH 43218-2452
614-466-7420
888-833-1133
614-466-5866 (fax)
http://www.bor.ohio.gov/sgs

OKLAHOMA

State Regents for Higher
Education
P.O. Box 3000
Oklahoma City, OK 73101
405-858-4300
800-247-0420
405-858-4390 (fax)
http://www.osrhe.edu

OREGON

Higher Education Board
P.O. Box 3175
Eugene, OR 97401
541-346-5700
541-346-5741 (TTY)
541-346-5764 (fax)
http://www.ous.edu

PENNSYLVANIA

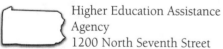

Higher Education Assistance
Agency
1200 North Seventh Street
Harrisburg, PA 17102
717-720-2850
800-629-7435
800-654-5988 (TTY)
717-720-3907 (fax)
http://www.pheaa.org

RHODE ISLAND

Higher Education Assistance
Authority
560 Jefferson Boulevard
Warwick, RI 02886
401-736-1100
800-922-9855
401-222-6195 (TTY)
401-732-3541 (fax)
http://www.uri.edu.ribog/
riche.htm

SOUTH CAROLINA

Commission on Higher
Education
1310 Lady Street, Suite 811
Columbia, SC 29201
803-734-1200
803-734-1426 (fax)
http://www.state.sc.us/
tuitiongrants

SOUTH DAKOTA

Board of Regents
207 East Capitol Avenue
Pierre, SD 57501
605-733-3455
605-733-5320 (fax)
http://www.ris.sdbor.edu

TENNESSEE

Higher Education
Commission
Parkway Towers, Suite 1900
404 James Robertson Park-
way
Nashville, TN 37243
615-741-3605
615-741-6230 (fax)
http://www.state.tn.us/thec/
index.htm

VERMONT

Student Assistance
Corporation
Champlain Mill
P.O. Box 2000
Winooski, VT 05404-2601
802-655-9602
800-642-3177
800-281-3341 (TTY)
802-654-3765 (fax)
http://www.vsac.org

TEXAS

Higher Education Coordinating Board
P.O. Box 12788
Capitol Station
Austin, TX 78711
512-483-6101
800-242-3062
512-483-6169 (fax)
http://www.thecb.state.tx.us

VIRGINIA

Council of Higher Education
James Monroe Building
101 North 14th Street,
9th Floor
Richmond, VA 23219
804-225-2137
804-371-8017 (TTY)
804-225-2604 (fax)
http://www.schev.edu

UTAH

State Board of Regents
3 Triad Center, Suite 550
Salt Lake City UT 84180
801-321-7100
801-321-7199 (fax)
http://www.utahsbr.edu

WASHINGTON

Higher Education Coordinating Board
P.O. Box 13430
917 Lakeridge Way
Olympia WA 98504
360-753-7800
360-753-7809 (TTY)
360-753-7808 (fax)
http://www.hecb.wa.gov

WEST VIRGINIA

State Colleges and University
Systems
1018 Kanawha Boulevard E.,
Suite 700
Charleston, WV 25301
304-558-2101
304-558-0259 (fax)
http://www.scusco.wvnet.edu

WYOMING

College Commission
2020 Carey Avnue,
Eighth Floor
Laramie, WY 82002
307-777-7763
307-777-6567 (fax)
http://commission.wcc.edu

WISCONSIN

Higher Educational Aid Board
1313 West Wilson Street
Madison, WI 53707
608-267-2206
608-267-2808 (fax)
http://heab.state.wi.us

2. Loans From University Funds

Many schools have their own loan programs. Schools set their own
interest rates and repayment terms. Contact your school's financial aid
office for information.

CHAPTER 3

Who Holds Your Student Loans?

When you borrow money, you usually know who to repay. You buy a car, for example, take the dealer's financing, and then send monthly payments to Ford Motor Credit for the next few years. Even if your loan is sold to another company or your lender hires a separate company to collect and process your payments, you are usually notified of the switch and told where to send your payments.

But student loan financing can be quite complex, involving the federal government in the form of the Department of Education or Department of Health and Human Services, colleges and universities, state agencies, banks and other lenders, the financial institutions with which lenders do business and collection agencies. Loans are frequently passed from one financial institution to another. If you've defaulted, your loans probably have moved from your lender to a state agency to the Department of Education and back to the state over the past few years.

A. Players in the World of Student Loan Financing

If you want to make arrangements for paying your loans, it may take you some time to track down the institution that has them. If you contact the wrong place, you probably won't get any information—or worse, you'll get wrong information.

If you're not in default, you need to know who holds your loans to send your payments or request help if you can't pay. If you're in default, you must know who holds your loans to defend against collection actions or to get out of default.

Your student loans may be held by any one of several different entities.

1. Lenders

Until 1994, virtually all federal student loans were issued by banks, savings and loan associations and credit unions. These lenders receive subsidies from the federal government to encourage them to make loans to college students. In 1994, the federal government began issuing federal loans along with financial institutions. As explained in Chapter 2, the program was meant to help lower the costs of borrowing.

The only federal loans not issued by financial institutions or the federal government are Perkins loans, which are made by colleges and universities. (See Section A.1.c.)

Private loan lenders are generally financial institutions, such as Citibank. And if you borrowed money from your state, your lender may have been a state agency.

a. Private Lenders

If you obtained your loans through a private lender, such as a bank, savings and loan association or credit union, your lender may still have them. This means that the lender makes money on the loan from the interest you pay, and is responsible for collecting and processing your payments. Private student loan lenders do not hold onto federal loans once they are in default, however; these loans will be with a guarantee agency or the Department of Education. And even if you have never been in default on your federal loans, your lender is likely to have them only if its basic policy is to collect its own loans. Banks rarely collect their own loans. But savings and loan associations and credit unions more frequently hang onto the loans they make. If you are unsure what institution holds your loans, it's a safe bet that it's not your lender.

b. Federal Government

Many federal student loans issued after 1993 were made by the U.S. Department of Education. The Department of Education will have your loans if you are not in default. If you've defaulted on loans obtained through the direct loan program, your loans will be with the Department of Education or possibly a collection agency working on its behalf.

c. Universities and Colleges

If you have Perkins loans and are not in default, your loans will be held by your school or a loan servicer hired by your school. (See Section 3.) If you are in default, the school may have passed the loans on to its legal department for collection, although it's more likely that the loans are with a guarantee agency, the Department of Education or a collection agency. (See Sections 4, 5 and 6.)

If you obtained your loans through college or university funds, the school you attended will have your loans if you are not in default. Even if you have defaulted, the school may still have your loans—or possibly have passed them on to a collection agency.

d. State Student Loan Agency

If you funded your education with money from state funds, such as the Alaska Student Loan Program, the state agency is your lender. In many instances, the state agency will hold onto the loan to try and collect even if you are in default. Some state agencies use guarantee agencies (see Section 4) or collection agencies (see Section 6) to collect for them.

2. Companies on the Secondary Market

The secondary market is a conglomeration of finance companies. It is where lenders sell loans that are not in default if they don't want to collect the loans themselves. Lenders make money by collecting interest on a loan and lose money if they have to put time and effort into collecting from you. So many lenders sell their loans and collect a fee from the company that buys them rather than risk losing money. A lender does not have to try to collect from you before selling your loans on the secondary market. In fact, it's probably likely that your loans were sold onto the secondary market while you were in school, before you were obligated to begin repayment. You should have been notified if this happened, but you may have misplaced the notice or may not have received it if you moved.

One secondary market company to which student loans are often sold is the Student Loan Marketing Association, or Sallie Mae. Sallie Mae is a private corporation initially established by Congress for the sole purpose of processing federal student loans.

3. Loan Servicers

A loan servicer will have your loan only if you have not defaulted. A loan servicer is a company hired by either your lender or a company on the secondary market, whichever one holds your loan. The loan servicers receive and process loan payments, process requests to have loan payments postponed or canceled, and handle other requests or correspondence. Lenders and companies on the secondary market frequently hire the Student Loan Servicing Center and EduServe.

4. Guarantee Agencies

Although the student loan program is a federal program, it is mostly administered through state or private nonprofit agencies, called guarantee agencies. A guarantee agency is essentially an insurance company: it insures your loans and pays off the holder of the loans if you don't pay, and it receives reinsurance money from the Department of Education. Not all defaulted loans are with guarantee agencies, however; some are held by the federal government or a collection agency. Most loans are sold to a guarantee agency from the original lender or secondary market company that bought the loan.

The federal government has encouraged every state to establish a guarantee agency, and most have done so. Some of these agencies do not collect defaulted student loans, however, as they play another role in the world of student loan financing—providing potential students with access to student loan money. In the states in which the guarantee agencies do not collect student loans, collection activities are handled by either a different state's guarantee agency or a private guarantee agency, such as United Student Aid Funds (USAF) or Educational Credit Management Corporation (ECMC). Until 1990, several states used the Higher Education Assistance Foundation (HEAF), which is now insolvent. Because a guarantee agency's sole function is to collect student loans, it pursues defaulters aggressively. (See Chapter 7.)

STATE AND PRIVATE NONPROFIT STUDENT LOAN GUARANTEE AGENCIES

ALABAMA

For loans in default prior to 12/1/95 U.S. Department of Education
800-621-3115
For loans in default beginning 12/1/95 Kentucky Higher Education Assistance Authority
1050 U.S. 127 South
Frankfurt, KY 40601-4323
800-928-8926
http://www.kheaa.state.ky.us

ALASKA

United Student Aid Funds
P.O. Box 6180
Indianapolis, IN 46206-6180
800-562-6872
http://www.usagroup.com

ARIZONA

United Student Aid Funds
P.O. Box 6180
Indianapolis, IN 46206-6180
800-562-6872
http://www.usagroup.com

ARKANSAS

Student Loan Guarantee Foundation
219 South Victory Street
Little Rock, AR 72201-1884
800-622-3446
http://www.slgfa.org

CALIFORNIA

California Student Aid Commission/EdFund
P.O. Box 419045
3300 Zinfandel Drive
Rancho Cordova, CA 95741-9045
916-526-7900
http://www.edfund.org

COLORADO

Colorado Student Loan Program
One Denver Place, South Terrace
999 18th Street, Suite 425
Denver, CO 80202-2440
303-294-5070
http://www.cslp.org

CONNECTICUT

 Connecticut Student Loan
Foundation
525 Brook Street
P.O. Box 1009
Rocky Hill, CT 06067
800-237-9721
http://www.cslf.com

DELAWARE

 Pennsylvania Higher Education Assistance Agency
1200 North Seventh Street
Harrisburg, PA 17102-1444
800-692-7392
http://www.pheaa.org

DISTRICT OF COLUMBIA

 American Student Assistance
330 Stuart Street
Boston, MA 02116-5292
800-999-9080
http://www.amsa.com

FLORIDA

 Department of Education
Office of Student Financial
Assistance
325 West Gaines Street
Collins Building, Room 255
Tallahassee, FL 32399-0400
904-488-4095
http://www.firn.edu/doe

GEORGIA

 Higher Education Assistance
Corporation
2082 East Exchange Place,
Suite 200
Tucker, GA 30084
800-776-6878
http://www.gsfc.org

HAWAII

 United Student Aid Funds
P.O. Box 6180
Indianapolis, IN 46206-6180
800-562-6872
http://www.usagroup.com

IDAHO

 **For loans in default prior to
1/1/95**
Student Loan Fund
P.O. Box 730
Fruitland, ID 83619
208-452-4058
208-452-5007 (fax)

**For loans in default begin-
ning 1/1/95**
Northwest Education Loan
Association
500 Colman Building
811 First Avenue
Seattle WA 98104
800-732-1077

ILLINOIS

Student Assistance Commission
50 West Monroe, Third Floor
Springfield, IL 62704-1876
800-899-4722
http://www.isac1.org

INDIANA

United Student Aid Funds
P.O. Box 6180
Indianapolis, IN 46206-6180
800-562-6872
http://www.usagroup.com

IOWA

College Student Aid Commission
200 10th Street, 4th Floor
Des Moines, IA 50309-3609
800-383-4222
http://www.state.ia.us/
government/icsac/index.htm

KANSAS

United Student Aid Funds
P.O. Box 6180
Indianapolis, IN 46206-6180
800-562-6872
http://www.usagroup.com

KENTUCKY

Higher Education Assistance
Authority
1050 U.S. 127 South
Frankfort, KY 40601-4323
800-928-8926
http://www.kheaa.com

LOUISIANA

Student Financial Aid
Commission
P.O. Box 91202
Baton Rouge, LA 70821-9202
800-259-5626
http://www.osfa.state.la.us

MAINE

Finance Authority
One Weston Court
State House Station 119
Augusta, ME 04333
207-626-8200
http://www.famemaine.com

MARYLAND

United Student Aid Funds
P.O. Box 6180
Indianapolis, IN 46206-6180
800-562-6872
http://www.usagroup.com

MASSACHUSETTS

American Student Assistance
330 Stuart Street
Boston, MA 02116-5292
800-999-9080
http://www.amsa.com

MICHIGAN

Higher Education Assistance
Authority
P.O. Box 30047
Lansing, MI 48909-7547
800-642-5626

MINNESOTA

Great Lakes Higher Education
Corporation
P.O. Box 7858
Madison, WI 53707-3192
800-236-5900
http://www.glhec.org

MISSISSIPPI

United Student Aid Funds
P.O. Box 6180
Indianapolis, IN 46206-6180
800-562-6872
http://www.usagroup.com

MISSOURI

Coordinating Board for
Higher Education
P.O. Box 6730
Jefferson City , MO 65102
800-473-6757
http://www.mocbhe.gov

MONTANA

Guaranteed Student Loan
System
P.O. Box 203101
Helena, MT 59620-3101
800-537-7508
http://www.mgslp.state.mt.us

NEBRASKA

Student Loan Program
P.O. Box 82507
Lincoln, NE 68501-2507
800-735-8778
http://www.nslp.com

NEVADA

United Student Aid Funds
P.O. Box 6180
Indianapolis, IN 46206-6180
800-562-6872
http://www.usagroup.com

NEW HAMPSHIRE

Higher Education Assistance
Foundation
P.O. Box 877
Concord, NH 03302-0877
800-525-2577
http://www.nhheaf.org

NEW JERSEY

Higher Education Assistance
Authority
4 Quakerbridge Plaza
CN 540
Trenton, NJ 08625
800-792-8670
http://www.nj.us/treasury/
osa/index.htm

NEW MEXICO

Student Loan Guarantee
Corporation
P.O. Box 92230
Albuquerque, NM
87199-2230
800-279-3070
http://www.nmslgc.org

NEW YORK

Higher Education Services
Corporation
99 Washington Avenue
Albany, NY 12255
518-473-7087
800-433-3243
518-474-2839 (fax)
http://www.hese.com

NORTH CAROLINA

State Education Assistance
Authority
P.O. Box 2688
Chapel Hill, NC 27515-2688
800-544-1644
http://www.ncseaa.edu

NORTH DAKOTA

Student Loans of North
Dakota
P.O. Box 5524
Bismarck, ND 58506-5524
800-472-2166
http://www.banknd.com/slnd

OHIO

Great Lakes Higher Educa-
tion Corporation
P.O. Box 7858
Madison, WI 53707-3192
800-236-5900
http://www.glhec.org

OKLAHOMA

Guaranteed Student Loan
Program
P.O. Box 3000
Oklahoma City, OK
73101-3000
800-247-0420
http://www.ogslp.org

OREGON

State Scholarship
Commission
1500 Valley River Drive,
Suite 100
Eugene, OR 97401-2130
800-452-8807
http://www.teleport.com/~ossc

PENNSYLVANIA

Pennsylvania Higher Education Assistance Agency
1200 North Seventh Street
Harrisburg, PA 17102-1444
800-692-7392
http://www.pheaa.org

RHODE ISLAND

Pennsylvania Higher Education Assistance Agency
1200 North Seventh Street
Harrisburg, PA 17102-1444
800-692-7392
http://www.pheaa.org

SOUTH CAROLINA

Student Loan Corporation
P.O. Box 21487
Columbia, SC 29221
803-798-0916
http://www.slc.sc.edu

SOUTH DAKOTA

Education Assistance
Corporation
115 First Avenue, SW
Aberdeen, SD 57401
800-592-1802
http://www.eac.easci.org

TENNESSEE

Student Assistance
Corporation
Parkway Towers, Suite 1950
404 James Robertson Parkway
Nashville, TN 37243-0820
615-741-1346

TEXAS

Guaranteed Student Loan
Corporation
P.O. Box 201725
Austin, TX 78720-1725
800-252-9743
http://www.tgslc.org

UTAH

Higher Education Assistance
Authority
P.O. Box 45202
Salt Lake City, UT 84145-
0202
800-418-8757
http://www.uheaa.org

VERMONT

Student Assistance
Corporation
P.O. Box 2000, Champlain Mill
Winooski, VT 05404-2601
800-642-3177
http://www.vsac.org

WISCONSIN

Great Lakes Higher Education
Corporation
P.O. Box 7858
Madison, WI 53707-3192
800-236-5900
http://www.glhec.org

VIRGINIA

Educational Credit
Management Corporation
411 East Franklin Street,
Suite 300
Richmond, VA 23219
888-775-3262
http://www.ecmc.org

WYOMING

United Student Aid Funds
P.O. Box 6180
Indianapolis, IN 46206-6180
800-562-6872
http://www.usagroup.com

WASHINGTON

Northwest Education Loan
Association
500 Colman Building
811 First Avenue
Seattle WA 98104
800-732-1077
http://www.nela.net

WEST VIRGINIA

Pennsylvania Higher Education Assistance Agency
1200 North Seventh Street
Harrisburg, PA 17102-1444
800-692-7392
http://www.pheaa.org

5. Federal Government

If you have defaulted on a federal loan you obtained from a private lender or from your school—that is, other than through the direct loan program—it is possible that your loans are held by the federal Department of Education. The Department of Education regulates and oversees the entire federal student loan program. The Department of Education doesn't hold onto all defaulted loans, however, preferring to pass them on to a guarantee agency or a collection agency. Guarantee and collection agencies are fully authorized to take aggressive collection actions to collect your loans, including intercepting your tax refund, garnishing your wages or suing you.

6. Collection Agencies

Collection agencies are hired by the federal Department of Education, guarantee agencies and private loan lenders to collect defaulted student loans. The amount you will owe can increase quickly if your loans are with a collection agency. The fees charged to you by the collection agency are based on the amount the Department pays the collection agency as commission. Sometimes, collection fees as high as 43% are tacked on to what you owe on your loan. Until recently, collection agencies and the Department of Education would routinely charge this much even if your promissory note limited the amount of collection fees to a lower amount. After being sued for this practice, the Department agreed that it was wrong to charge everyone 43% collection costs when some borrowers' promissory notes limited collection costs to 25%. Until they can straighten out exactly who can be charged which amount, the Department has agreed to limit fees for everyone to no more than 25%.

THE LONG AND WINDING ROAD

The below example highlights who might hold a student loan at any given time.

Example: In the spring of 1987, Sue was accepted into college to begin that fall. Included in her acceptance package was information on financial aid. Sue filled out the financial aid packet and her school determined that she was eligible for what was then known as a Guaranteed Student Loan (GSL), today's Stafford Loan. Sue filled out a GSL application at a local bank. She sent it to her school, which filled out its portion and sent the application back to the bank. The bank contacted the state guarantee agency, which verified that Sue was eligible for the money and agreed to guarantee the loan. The bank sent Sue a promissory note, which she signed and returned to the bank. The bank then issued the check in both names so that both Sue and her school could endorse it. Here's what happened once Sue began school.

1988	The bank sold Sue's loan to the Student Loan Marketing Association (Sallie Mae). Sue took out three more loans while she was in school, which were all sold to Sallie Mae.
1992	The grace period ended and Sue's loans entered repayment; Sue sent monthly checks to Sallie Mae.
1995	Sallie Mae hired the Student Loan Servicing Center to process Sue's loans.
1997	Sue had hard times and defaulted on her loans. The Student Loan Servicing Center notified Sallie Mae.
1998	Sallie Mae immediately sold Sue's loans to the Department of Education. The Department of Education passed the loans on to the guarantee agency for the state where Sue obtained the loan and attended college.
2000	The guarantee agency contacted Sue about paying. Sue ignored all efforts.
2001	The guarantee agency passed the loans on to a collection agency. Sue's loan balance immediately increased by 28%.

B. Figuring Out Who Holds Your Student Loans

The Higher Education Act requires that the holder of your federal loans notify you any time there is a change in where you must send your payments—that is, if the holder of your loans sells them to a company on the secondary market or uses a loan servicer to collect and process your payments. This law applies only if you are not in default. Once you are in default, the holder of your loans is under no obligation to let you know if your loans change hands, so it may be harder for you to track down the information.

If you are not in default on your federal loans, you probably know who holds your loans. It's where you send your payments or where you applied for a deferment, forbearance or cancellation. (See Chapter 6.)

If you don't know who holds your federal loans—whether or not you are in default—contact the Department of Education's Debt Collection Services for Student Loans at 800-621-3115. Or call one of the Department of Education's collection centers at 404-331-2501 (Atlanta), 312-353-6874 (Chicago), 415-556-7918 (San Francisco). Do not assume that the office nearest to your home or where you went to school has your loan. Although it defies logic, a midwesterner who moved to California after college may very well have his loan held by the Atlanta collection center, for example.

If you are in default, keep in mind some general rules. Student loans older than ten years are usually held by the Department of Education and serviced by a collection agency. Student loans taken out within the past six years are usually held and serviced by a guarantee agency. Loans that fall in between may be in either place.

For other types of loan, you may need to do more sleuth work. For example, for:

- private student loans, contact your lender
- student loans made from state funds, contact the appropriate state agency (see Chapter 2, Section C.1), and
- loans made from university funds, contact your school.

THE PERILS OF BEING IN DEFAULT

If you are not in default, be sure to notify the holder of your loans when you move and *always* send a change of address. And do what you can to avoid default. If you default, the guarantee agency, Department of Education or collection agency hired will put substantial effort into collecting. You will encounter extreme aggression in the collecting of your loans. The tactics are described in Chapter 7, but be aware that they include intercepting your tax refunds, garnishing up to 10% of your net wages and suing you. If the Department of Education doesn't know where you are, it can request the records of other government departments to find your address, phone number, dependents, employment history and other relevant information.

In addition, if you don't notify the holder of your Perkins loans or loans made from school funds that you have moved and you go into default, your school can—and probably will—prohibit you from re-enrolling or using any of the school's alumni services, such as the placement office. It is also likely to withhold your grades, diploma and transcript.

Making a Budget

Once you've figured out what kind of loans you have and who your loan holders are, it's time to organize your loan materials and make a budget. This is true no matter what your situation. A realistic budget is an important stepping stone on the way to choosing repayment options, negotiating with stubborn loan holders or collection agencies, making responsible decisions about postponing your loan payments and many other actions you may have to take. You'll be a better money manager and a better advocate for yourself if you know how much money you owe and what amount you can put toward your loan payments each month.

You may be sorely tempted to skip this chapter. Making a budget can be a mind numbing chore even when there's enough money to go around—and when times are bad, it can be downright scary. But be assured that getting your papers in order and figuring out where your money is going is well worth the effort. This chapter shows you how to make a budget using simple steps to make the process easier.

Often, the scariest thing about a facing a mountain of debt is *not* knowing exactly what you owe or how much money you have; it's feeling like you're spinning toward some terrible end that's out of your control. When you sit down to sort through your loan papers and begin to track your income and expenses, you'll combat this feeling of hurtling toward certain disaster. You may not like what you find out about your financial situation, but if you're serious about mastering your debts, having accurate information in hand and taking steps to gain control of a scary situation will almost certainly make you feel better, not worse. And don't give up hope—you may yet find some surprises, some options you never knew you had.

If you're in way over your head. Many people come out of school having to repay not only their student loans, but also credit card bills. In fact, most people leave school with credit card debt in excess of student loan debt. The number of students who were unable to cover their school expenses with loans and grants increases every year; about 25% used credit cards to help pay for tuition. For help with paying your credit cards and other non-student loan debts, see *Money Troubles: Legal Strategies to Cope With Your Debts,* by Robin Leonard (Nolo).

A. Get Organized

If you have just one student loan, you'll have plenty of paperwork to handle. If, like most people, you have an assortment of loans, you may feel as though you're drowning in all the applications, forms, notices and statements with which you're expected to keep up.

Every person responds differently to an onslaught of paper. Some of you may already have meticulous recordkeeping systems firmly in place. On the other hand, many of you probably have your records stuffed in a drawer or filing cabinet—well, somewhere. And others may have tossed all, or most, of your paperwork into the trash. Whatever your response has been in the past, it is possible and important to pull together whatever records you have—and even contact your loan servicers to get what's missing—and keep your records organized. Doing so will help you figure out what you owe, to whom you owe it and when your payments are due. And knowing these things is essential before you can create a loan management strategy that will work for you. Also, keeping accurate records will make your job much easier when you have to communicate with the holders of your loans.

1. Recordkeeping Basics

To get organized, start a file folder for each type of student loan or for each loan account you have. In these folders, keep copies of any of the following information that you have:

- summary of basic information about your loan (see the form below)

- copies of your loan application forms

- promissory notes—the documents you signed agreeing to repay the money you've borrowed

- account statements

- disbursement and disclosure statements—notices about your loan and its costs that you receive when your loan is made

- any other correspondence from your school's financial aid office, lender, loan holder, loan servicer, a guarantee agency or the Department of Education, and

- phone log, on which you can jot down the date of any phone calls to or from your loan holders, the subject of each call and the name of the person with whom you spoke; keeping these names on file will help you follow up on conversations and clarify any future misunderstandings (a sample phone log is provided below).

As suggested above, if you can't locate important information about your loan—for example, you've misplaced your promissory note or you don't have enough information to fill in the Student Loan Information form below—call your loan servicer and ask for help. Your servicer can probably send you copies of important documents and tell you what you need to know to fill in the blanks. (If you're not sure who holds or services your loan, see Chapter 3.)

⚠ **Keep your documents until you've paid off your loans.** Keep all documents related to your student loans until your last student loan has been repaid and you've received notice from your loan holder that your loan is paid in full. After that, you can toss everything except the final documents from your loan holders showing that your loans are paid off. Sometimes the Department of Education will try to collect a loan that's already been paid. Should this happen to you, these papers will act as proof that you don't owe anything.

Use the following forms to keep track of basic information about your loans and any phone conversations you have regarding them. (See the Appendix for blank forms.)

STUDENT LOAN INFORMATION

Stafford
_____
(Type of Loan)

60000-53659644-01
_____
(Account Number)

Repayment Information

Amount Borrowed: $16,400
Interest Rate: 5%
Payment Amount: $173.95 monthly
Repayment Start Date: 12/28/XX
Payment Due Date: 28th of the month

Loan Holder

Name: Big Bank of Wisconsin
Address: 2000 Debtors Road
    Wakashaw, WI 60000

Telephone: 999-555-1213
Fax: 999-555-1214

Loan Servicer

Name: EduServ Technologies
Address: P.O. Box 2901
    Winston Salem, NC 55164-0974

Telephone: 910-607-2351
Fax: 910-607-2352

Notes: Unemployment deferment granted 2/7/XY
    Deferment ends 8/7/XY — recertify in July!

STUDENT LOAN PHONE LOG

Stafford
(Type of Loan)

60000-536596444-01
(Account Number)

EduServ Technologies
(Loan Holder/Servicer's Name)

916-607-2351
(Loan Holder/Servicer's Phone Number)

Date	Subject of Conversation	Contact Person	Advice Given	Action Taken
1/3/XY	request unemployment deferment	David Weston	complete & return forms	forms submitted 1/20/XY
				deferment granted 2/7/XY
7/7/XY	recertify unemployment deferment	Anna Soto	complete & return forms	forms submitted 7/23/XY

2. Keeping Up to Date

The second part of organizing and managing your debts is keeping your records current. To do this, you'll need to stay in contact with the holders of your loans. Even if you're having trouble making payments, keep in touch with your loan holders; they will help you keep your accounts in good standing.

Take the following steps.

- Open and read all mail about your loans. If you don't, you may miss important information about the terms or administration of your loans, including where your payments should be sent and when they are due.

- If you are making payments on your loans, mail the payments at least five days before the due date, even if you don't receive a bill. Keep a record of your payment due date, such as the fifteenth of each month, on your Student Loan Information form.

- If you can't make a loan payment, immediately call the holder of your loans to discuss your options for postponing your payments or obtaining a flexible payment plan. (See Chapters 5 and 6.)

- If you change your name or other personal information, or if you move, notify the holder of your loans as soon as possible.

- If you have any questions about a billing statement or other loan document, call the holder of your loans and ask for clarification.

- Always include your account number and Social Security number on correspondence with the holder of your loans.

KNOW YOUR RIGHTS AND RESPONSIBILITIES AS A BORROWER

Borrowers of federal student loans have certain legal rights and responsibilities. You can find a detailed statement of these in your application materials or promissory note. The basics are summarized here.

Rights

- The holder of your loans must provide you with a repayment schedule before your repayment period begins.
- The holder of your loans must notify you in writing if your loans change hands—for example, if your lender sells or transfers them to a company on the secondary loan market, or contracts them out to a servicing agency. (See Chapter 3.) You lose this right, however, if you default on your loan payments.
- You have the right to pay off your loans at any time without penalty.
- You have the right to postpone repayment if you qualify for a deferment or forbearance. (See Chapter 6.)
- You may have your loans canceled under very limited circumstances. (See Chapter 6.)

Responsibilities

- You must notify the holder of your loans if you:
  —move
  —change your name
  —graduate or withdraw from school, or drop to less than half-time enrollment
  —fail to enroll in school for the period of time for which you obtained your loan
  —want to defer your payments, or
  —are unable to repay your loan.
- You must make payments on your loans even if you don't receive a bill or repayment notice. Statements and coupon books are sent to you as a convenience, but you're required to make payments even if you never receive reminders from the holders of your loans.

KNOW YOUR RIGHTS AND RESPONSIBILITIES AS A BORROWER (continued)

- You must repay your loans according to the terms described in your promissory note. If you fail to meet the terms and conditions of your note, you will be declared in default, and any or all of the following may result:

  —your default will be reported to national credit bureaus

  —your federal and possibly state income tax refunds may be intercepted

  —your wages may be garnished

  —you may be sued for the amount you owe plus collection costs and attorneys' fees

  —you may not be eligible for additional federal student aid, and

  —the entire unpaid balance of your defaulted loan, plus interest, will become due immediately.

B. How Much Can You Afford to Pay?

Perhaps the most important part of setting up a strategy to take control of your loans is understanding how much money you can afford to put toward your debts each month. With that information in hand, you can make responsible choices about how to handle your loans, including how to pick a repayment option and how to intelligently negotiate with loan collectors. This section first shows you how to track your income and expenses—including what you now spend on student loan payments. It then explains how to use your income and expense information to make a budget that works for you.

If you need help with your budget. At least one software program is specifically designed to teach student loan borrowers about repayment options and help them make budgets. USA Group's Student Loan Counseling Software was created for school financial aid administrators, but individuals can use it as well. With this program, you can key in your financial data to create a basic budget using several repayment options. Call 800-428-9250 for information.

Other computer programs, such as Quicken (Intuit), can help you keep track of your expenses, particularly those you pay by check or credit card. Many of these programs have budget features as well. Be sure you have an opportunity to record your cash outlays, however, before relying on these budgeting features. Most commercial budgeting programs have you analyze your expenses paid primarily by check, and overlook the most obvious source of payment: cash. You can get additional help with the calculators on Nolo's website. See http://www.nolo.com/calculator/index.html.

Finally, if you'd rather not create a budget yourself, you can contact a debt or counseling agency such as Debt Counselors of America (http://www.dca.org) or Consumer Credit Counseling Service (http://www.nfcc.org). These nonprofit organizations, which primarily help debtors negotiate with creditors, can also help you set up a budget.

1. Keep Track of Your Expenses

To create a realistic budget, you must figure out where your money goes. To help you keep track, use the Daily Expense form (below and in the Appendix) on which you can record everything you spend over the course of a week, paying special attention to cash outlays.

Here's how to make it work.

1. Make eight copies of the form so you can record your expenses. It's best to track for two months to avoid creating a monthly budget based on a week or a month of unusually high or low expenses. If

you are married or live with someone with whom you share expenses, make 16 copies so you each can record your outlays.

2. Select a Sunday to begin recording your expenses.

3. Record that Sunday's date in the blank at the top of one copy of the form.

4. Carry the week's form with you at all times.

5. Record every expense you for pay by cash or cash equivalent—that is, check or debit. Be sure to include bank fees. Also, don't forget savings and investments, such as deposits into savings accounts, certificates of deposit or money market accounts, or purchases of investments such as stocks or bonds.

    Do not record credit card charges, as your goal is to get a picture of where your cash goes. When you make a payment on a credit card bill, however, list the actual items covered by the payment. To do this, look at your statement and find older charges that total a little less than the amount of your payment and list these on your form. List the rest of the payment amount as interest.

Example: On Sunday night, you pay your bills for the week and make a $100 payment toward your $500 credit card bill. The $500 includes a $150 balance from the previous month, a $250 airline ticket, a few restaurant meals and accrued interest. On your Daily Expense form for Sunday, you list $100 in the second column. In the first column, you identify corresponding expenses—and attribute some of it to interest.

6. At the end of the week, put away the form and take out another copy. Go back to Step 3, in which you begin recording anew, starting with Sunday.

7. At the end of the eight weeks, under the category Other Expenses, list seasonal, annual, semi-annual or quarterly expenses you incur but did not pay during your two-month recording period. The most common are property taxes, car registration, magazine subscriptions, tax preparation fees, insurance payments, summer vacation and holiday gift expenses. Be creative and thorough.

When it comes time to make your budget, you'll divide up these occasional expenses to find out how much they cost you each month. For large expenses, such as property taxes or quarterly car insurance payments, it makes sense to save some money each month so you can cover the payments when they come due. For smaller expenses, such as magazines and newspapers, be aware of when the payments are due so you can adjust your monthly budget accordingly.

IF YOU DON'T KNOW WHICH BILLS TO PAY

It's a budgeter's nightmare: a stack of bills that have just come due, or are already past due, and not enough money to go around. Deciding which bills to pay and which to put off for another month or so can be difficult.

Here are some tips.

Pay your essential debts first. Essential debts are those that are likely to cause severe consequences in your life if you can't pay them. Ultimately, which debts are essential will be dictated by your own situation, but some debts are generally more important than others. For example, you probably won't want to let the following bills slide, even a teeny bit:

- rent or mortgage
- utility bills
- child support
- car payments
- unpaid taxes, and
- any loan for which you have pledged a specific item of property as collateral—meaning that if you don't pay what you owe, your creditor can take the property.

IF YOU DON'T KNOW WHICH BILLS TO PAY (continued)

Some debts straddle the line between essential and nonessential. Failing to pay these debts might not cause unbearable strife, but could cause plenty of inconvenience or embarrassment. Some of these debts include:

- auto insurance
- medical insurance
- items your children need
- court judgments, and
- student loans.

Rank your nonessential debts. A nonessential debt is one that will inflict no immediate or devastating consequences if you fail to pay. Paying these debts is a desirable goal, but not a top priority. You may be able to let these bills slide for a month or two without any adverse consequences at all—particularly those at the bottom of the list:

- credit or charge cards
- department store and gasoline charges
- loans from friends and relatives
- newspaper and magazine subscriptions
- legal, medical and accounting bills, and
- other unsecured loans.

Don't pay nonessential debts before essential ones. Always pay your essential debts first, even if your nonessential creditors are breathing down your neck. This advice may sound obvious, but when pressured by bill collectors, many people forget the obvious. Don't risk being evicted or having your heat turned off just because the collector from the local department store is loudest or most persistent. Keep your head cool and your priorities straight.

DAILY EXPENSES

Sunday's Expenditures	Cost	Monday's Expenditures	Cost	Tuesday's Expenditures	Cost	Wednesday's Expenditures	Cost
Daily Total:		Daily Total:		Daily Total:		Daily Total:	

Thursday's Expenditures	Cost	Friday's Expenditures	Cost	Saturday's Expenditures	Cost	Other Expenditures	Cost
Daily Total:		Daily Total:		Daily Total:		Weekly Total:	

2. Total Your Income

Your expenses account for only half of the picture in your budget. You also need to add up your monthly income. You can do this using the form, Monthly Income From All Sources (below and in the Appendix). If you have a spouse or partner with whom you share expenses and income, include information for both of you.

Column 1: Source of income. In Part A, list the jobs for which you receive a salary or wages. In Part B, list all self-employment for which you receive income, including sales commissions. In Part C, list any other sources of income. Here are some examples of the kinds of income that make up the nebulous Other Sources category.

- **Bonus pay.** All regular bonuses you receive, such as an annual commission bonus.

- **Dividends and interest.** All sources of dividends or interest—for example, bank accounts, security deposits or stocks.

- **Alimony or child support.** Support you receive for yourself, such as alimony, spousal support or maintenance—or money you get on behalf of your children, such as child support.

- **Pension or retirement income.** Any pension, annuity, IRA, Keogh or other retirement payments you receive.

- **Public assistance.** Any public benefits, such as welfare, SSI, public assistance, disability payments, veterans' benefits, unemployment compensation, workers' compensation or any other government benefit you receive.

- **Other.** Other sources of income, such as a tax refund you received within the past year or expect to receive within the next year, or payments you receive from friends or relatives. If, within the past 12 months, you received any one-time lump sum payment—such as the proceeds from an insurance policy or from the sale of a valuable asset—don't list it at all.

Column 2: Amount of each payment. For each source of income you listed in Parts A and B of Column 1, enter the amount you receive each pay period. If you don't receive the same amount each period, average the last 12 payments. Then enter your deductions for each pay period. Again, if these amounts vary, enter an average of the last 12 months. For the income you listed in Part A, you probably need to get out a paystub to see how much is deducted from your paycheck. Subtract the deductions and enter your net income in the Subtotal blank in Column 2.

In Part C, enter the amount of each payment for each source of income.

Column 3: Period covered by each payment. For each source of income, enter the period covered by each payment—such as weekly, twice monthly (24 times a year), every other week (26 times a year), monthly, quarterly (common for royalties), or annually (common for farm income).

Column 4: Amount per month. Multiply or divide the subtotals— or amounts in Part C—in Column 2 to determine the monthly amount. For example, if you are paid twice a month, multiply the Column 2 amount by two. If you are paid every other week, multiply the amount by 26—for the annual amount—and divide by 12. The shortcut is to multiply by 2.167.

When you are done, total Column 4. This is your total average monthly income.

MONTHLY INCOME FROM ALL SOURCES

1 Source of Income		2 Amount of each payment	3 Period covered by each payment	4 Amount per month
A. Wages or Salary				
Job 1:	Gross Pay, including overtime			
	Subtract:			
	Federal taxes			
	State taxes			
	Self-employment taxes			
	Other mandatory deductions (specify):			
	_____			
	Subtotal	$_____	_____	_____
Job 2:	Gross Pay, including overtime			
	Subtract:			
	Federal taxes			
	State taxes			
	Self-employment taxes			
	Other mandatory deductions (specify):			
	_____			
	Subtotal	$_____	_____	_____
Job 3:	Gross Pay, including overtime			
	Subtract:			
	Federal taxes			
	State taxes			
	Self-employment taxes			
	Other mandatory deductions (specify):			
	_____			
	Subtotal	$_____	_____	_____

MONTHLY INCOME FROM ALL SOURCES (continued)

1 Source of income		2 Amount of each payment	3 Period covered by each payment	4 Amount per month
B. Self-Employment Income				
Job 1:	Gross Pay, including overtime			
_____	Subtract:			
	Federal taxes			
	State taxes			
	Self-Employment taxes			
	Other mandatory deductions (specify):			
	_____			
	Subtotal	$_____	_____	_____
Job 2:	Gross Pay, including overtime			
_____	Subtract:			
	Federal taxes			
	State taxes			
	Self-employment taxes			
	Other mandatory deductions (specify):			
	_____			
	Subtotal	$_____	_____	_____
C. Other Sources				
	Bonuses			
	Dividends and interest			
	Rent, lease or license income			
	Royalties			
	Note or trust income			
	Alimony or child support you receive			
	Pension or retirement income			
	Social Security			
	Other public assistance			
	Other (specify):			
	_____			
	_____			
	_____			
	Total monthly income			$_____

3. Make Your Budget

After you've kept track of your expenses and income for a couple of months, you're ready to make a first pass at your budget. Your primary goal in making a budget is to get your spending in line with your income and establish a pool of money that you can put toward your loans each month. You may have to revise your budget many times over the coming months as you learn more about such factors as the level of austerity with which you are comfortable and the loan repayment options that are actually available to you.

At first, this process may seem a bit like the chicken and the egg. You can't make a final budget until you've chosen your repayment options, but you can't make wise choices about your repayment options until you know how much you can reasonably afford to pay toward your loans each month. You have to start somewhere—and making an initial budget will tell you how much money you currently have available for your loan payments.

Use the figures you entered on your expense and income forms as the basis for your budget. Follow these steps.

1. On a blank piece of paper—ruled paper works best—write down the categories into which your expenses fall. The list below includes suggested categories. Also, total your two months of expenses and your estimated seasonal, annual, semi-annual or quarterly expenses for the categories you create.

2. Using a second piece of paper or a copy of the Monthly Budget form in the Appendix, list your categories of expenses down the left side of the page. Use as many sheets as you need to list all categories. These are your budget sheets. (See the sample, below.)

3. On your budget sheets, make 13 columns. Label the first one Projected and the remaining 12 with the months of the year. Unless today is the first of the month, start with next month.

4. Using your total actual expenses for the two months you tracked or your estimated seasonal, annual, semi-annual or quarterly expenses, project your monthly expenses for the categories you've listed. To find your projected monthly expenses, divide your actual two months of expenses by two, divide your total seasonal or annual expenses by 12, divide your semi-annual expenses by six and divide your quarterly expenses by three.

   As mentioned earlier, after you've divided up your seasonal or annual expenses, you might want to include only the major expenses—such as quarterly loan payments or tax bills—in your monthly budget projections. This will enable you to set aside money for these bills so they won't be such a shock when they come due. Just make a note of when smaller expenses, such as magazine subscriptions, are due so you can adjust your budget for that month. These temporary adjustments make more sense than trying to save $1.23 each month so you can pay for your newspaper subscription once a year.

5. Enter your projected monthly expenses into the Projected column of your budget sheets.

6. Add all projected monthly expenses and enter the total in the Total Expenses category at the bottom of the projected column.

7. Enter your projected monthly income below your total projected expenses.

8. Figure out the difference.

   If your income exceeds your expenses, including your monthly student loan payments, congratulations! You may want to consider putting more money toward your loan payments each month so you'll pay less in the long run. (See Chapter 5, Section B.)

If your expenses exceed your income, as will be the case for many who read this book, you will have to tinker with your budget until you come up with a plan that works. You can do this by:

- earning more money

- reducing your spending on expenses other than student loans, or

- exploring alternative repayment options to find out whether you can lower your monthly loan payments. (See Chapter 5.)

You may not be able to find a higher paying job, take on a second job or make significant money by selling assets. Or you may be committed to keeping your low-paying job because the work is meaningful to you. If earning more money isn't feasible, adjust your budget by finding ways to cut expenses without depriving yourself of items or services you truly need. Rather than cutting out categories completely, look for items you can comfortably reduce slightly. Assume, for example, that you need to cut $150 from your budget. You had planned on spending $65 per month to eat dinner at restaurants, but are willing to decrease that to $30, saving $35. You had planned to spend $25 on music each month, but you can easily reduce it by $10 or more. Keep looking for ways to make similar, small adjustments.

If you still come up short, you may need to consider some larger changes. For example, you might sell your newer car for an older used car to free yourself from car payments. As you make adjustments to your budget, give careful thought to your priorities. Everyone has different ideas about what luxury is, and different feelings about what they're willing to give up and what they just can't live without. Think about what you value, and be honest with yourself.

EASY WAYS TO CUT YOUR EXPENSES

Here is a handful of tips that can help you reduce your monthly expenses.

- Shrink food costs by clipping coupons, buying sale items, purchasing generic brands, buying in bulk and shopping at discount outlets.
- Improve your gas mileage by tuning up your car, checking the air in the tires and driving less—form a carpool, work at home, ride your bicycle, take the bus or train and combine trips.
- Conserve gas, water and electricity.
- Discontinue cable—or at least the premium channels.
- Instead of buying books and CDs, borrow them from the public library. Read magazines and newspapers there, too, instead of subscribing to them.
- Make long distance calls only when necessary and then only at off-peak hours. Also, compare programs offered by the various long distance carriers to make sure you are getting the best deal.
- Carry your lunch to work; eat dinner at home, not at restaurants.
- Buy secondhand clothing, furniture and appliances.
- Spend less on gifts and vacations.

You may have to sacrifice some things that feel important to you, but don't expect to stick to your budget if you've taken away funds for almost everything beyond food, shelter and bills for your mundane necessities. Try making a list of things you feel you can't live without, and whittle your other expenses down to accommodate them. For example, you may be willing to live in a small, inexpensive apartment or with roommates if that allows you to take classes in a subject that interests you. Or you may decide to give up most of your magazine and newspaper subscriptions, but you'd go nuts if you didn't get to see a movie once a week. If you make room for at least some of the things you love most, you're much more likely to succeed at your plan.

Don't short yourself on savings. When we're facing hard times financially, money for savings is often the first thing to go. Think carefully before you cut savings out of your budget. Even if you can only save $25 or $50 per month, you'll be relieved to have something to fall back on if an emergency arises.

If you've pared down your expenses as far as you can, and you still can't make your loan payments under your current repayment plan, investigate whether there's a way for you pay less for your student loans each month. (See Chapter 5.) Even if you can make your payments, you may want to learn about the various repayment plans in case you stumble across one that works even better for you. Keep in mind that if you do lower your payments, you'll pay more—perhaps much more—for your loans in the long run. But you may decide it's the only way to keep your head above water, or that it's what you need to do to keep life bearable.

CATEGORIES OF EXPENSES

Using a blank piece of paper, make a list of categories into which your expenses fall. You'll need these categories to complete your budget. The following categories are suggestions to help you create your own list.

Home
rent/mortgage
property taxes
insurance (renter's or
homeowner's)
homeowner's association
dues
maintenance & repairs
telephone
gas & electric
water & sewer
cable TV
garbage
household supplies
housewares
furniture & appliances
cleaning
yard or pool care

Food
groceries
breakfast out
lunch out
dinner out
coffee/tea
snacks

Wearing Apparel
clothing & accessories
laundry, dry cleaning &
mending

Self Care
toiletries & cosmetics
haircuts
massage
health club membership
donations

Healthcare
insurance
doctors
dentist
eyecare
therapy
medications
vitamins

Transportation
insurance
registration
gasoline
maintenance & repairs

CATEGORIES OF EXPENSES (continued)

Transportation (cont.)
road service club
car wash
parking & tolls
public transit & cabs
parking tickets

Entertainment
music
movies & video rentals
concerts, theater & ballet
museums
sporting events
hobbies & lessons
club dues or membership
film development
books, magazines &
newspapers
software
online services

Dependent Care
child care
clothing
allowance
school expenses
toys & entertainment

Pet Care
vet
grooming
food, toys & supplies

Education
tuition or loan payments
books & supplies

Travel

Gifts & Cards
holidays
birthdays & anniversaries
weddings & showers

Personal Business
supplies
photocopying
postage
bank & credit card fees
interest payments
lawyer
accountant

Taxes

Insurance

Savings & Investments

SAMPLE MONTHLY BUDGET

EXPENSE CATEGORY	proj.	Aug.	Sept.	Oct.	Nov.	Dec.	Jan.	Feb.	Mar.	April	May	June	July
HOME													
rent	510	510	510										
renter's insurance	12	0	24										
phone	30	28	40										
gas & electric	25	21	24										
cable	25	25	25										
household supplies	20	35	28										
furniture & appliances	30	0	0										
maintenance & repairs	35	0	0										
FOOD													
groceries	200	250	197										
breakfast out	10	19	0										
lunch out	25	25	40										
dinner out	60	35	55										
coffee/tea	10	8	8										
snacks	10	15	12										
EDUCATION													
Stafford loans	350	350	350										
Perkins loans	45	45	45										
private loans	200	200	200										
WEARING APPAREL													
clothing & access.	20	30	0										
laundry	15	14	21										
SELF CARE													
toiletries & cosmetics	15	9	17										
haircuts	30	30	30										
donations	40	40	40										

SAMPLE MONTHLY BUDGET (continued)

EXPENSE CATEGORY	proj.	Aug.	Sept.	Oct.	Nov.	Dec.	Jan.	Feb.	Mar.	April	May	June	July
HEALTHCARE													
medications & prescriptions	10	5	0										
vitamins	15	15	15										
insurance	100	100	100										
dentist	10	0	0										
eyecare	10	0	0										
TRANSPORTATION													
car insurance	80	80	80										
registration	15	180	0										
gasoline	35	35	34										
maintenance & repairs	20	0	12										
parking & tolls	30	30	25										
public transit & cars	10	0	15										
ENTERTAINMENT													
music	15	16	25										
movies & video rentals	20	10	7										
books, magazines & newspapers	25	20	35										
online services	10	10	10										
GIFTS & CARDS	20	25	5										
PERSONAL BUSINESS													
supplies	20	30	0										
postage	15	14	21										
bank & credit card fees	25	12	18										
SAVINGS	35	35	35										
total expenses	35	35	35										
total income	2260	2260	2195										
difference	32	–39	178										

Your Repayment Options

The phrase "student loans" is laden with meaning for many people. Mutter it when you walk into a room full of people and you're likely to hear a chorus of groans. Most people who have student loans are full of tales about the hardships their loans have wrought upon them. And nobody likes paying them back—even if they can do so comfortably. For those who can't afford it, however, repayment is more than unpleasant or uncomfortable; it can be downright oppressive and even terrifying. You may not know what to do, for example, if you have some money to put toward loan payments, but you know you can't make ends meet if you pay as much as required by the standard repayment plan offered by your loan holders. And you'll probably feel even worse if you don't have any money at all to put toward your loans.

But if you're struggling to repay your loans, you have many good reasons to feel hopeful. Many lenders, daunted by the number of students defaulting on their loans, have pitched in to create new, flexible repayment options for student loan borrowers. And there are several other creative repayment options to consider. For example, most lenders now offer graduated or flexible payment plans geared to borrowers' incomes. If these repayment plans still put too much strain on your finances, consider consolidating multiple loans—combining them into one packaged loan and reducing your monthly payments by extending your repayment period. You might also consider paying back some of your loans while postponing payments on others.

This chapter explains the many methods you may use to pay off your student loans. It provides you with information about traditional ways to repay, new and flexible repayment plans offered by many lenders, creative strategies for raising cash on your own and information about special repayment incentives and repayment assistance plans. You may choose just one of the repayment methods discussed here, or you may combine several different options to create an overall payment plan that works for your situation.

WHY YOU CAN'T BE AN OSTRICH

Once upon a time, a former student who ignored loans might hear from the government several years later, if at all—and usually after the time limit the government had to collect, called the statute of limitations, had expired. Many student loan debtors thought that if they stayed out of sight for long enough, the government would forget all about them and the money they owed—and often this strategy worked.

But times have changed. Today, if you let your loan payments slip, you'll probably hear from the loan holder right away. Your federal and state income tax refunds may be intercepted, a portion of your paycheck may be withheld, and you may eventually be sued. If you still don't pay your debt, the government will probably put a lien on your property and take a larger portion of your wages. And there is no longer any deadline on how long the government has to track you down and collect from you. All outstanding student loans—even those handed out in the 1960s during the early days of the student loan program—are subject to collections.

Shirking your loans may also cost you a bundle. Collection agencies typically add a hefty collection fee when they take on the job of tracking you down. This fee is added to the principal, interest and any other collection fees you owe.

Worse yet, the government—in the guise of the Department of Education and any agency collecting on its behalf—is a very tough negotiator. You're not likely to succeed in having collection or late fees dropped or negative remarks removed from your credit report by simply trying to strike a deal.

All this isn't meant to upset or frustrate you if your student loan debt feels unmanageable. It is, however, meant to show you that you'll be wise to do everything you can to pay your loans when they're due—or to contact the holder of your loans and get authorization to postpone your payments. This chapter and Chapter 6 will help you find your way.

A. Repayment Plans

When it comes time to repay your loans, you'll be relieved to know that many lenders offer a variety of repayment plans—some of them quite flexible—from which you can pick and choose. Which plans are available to you will depend on the types of loans you have, when you obtained them and the identity of your original lenders.

DO YOU HAVE TO PAY YOUR LOANS?

Most likely you will be required to pay off your student loans. But in certain limited circumstances, you may be able to do away with your loans altogether. (See Chapters 6, 9 and 10.) Or you may be able to postpone your payments for a time. You may want to consider postponing repayment if you can't presently make payments on some or all of your loans, but you think your financial situation will improve in the future. (See Chapter 6.)

If you have a federal loan, you'll probably be able to choose from several repayment plans designed to make your life less stressful: graduated plans where your payments start out low and step up over time, extended plans that lower your monthly payment by lengthening the time you have to repay, plans that are geared to your income and consolidation plans that allow you to combine several loans into just one loan with a lower monthly payment. You may pick just one method or, if you have several loans, you may use a combination.

Private loans, on the other hand, offer fewer repayment options. This book introduces the many types of repayment plans available for all types of student loans. But to learn exactly which options apply to your loans, check with the appropriate official—your lender, a company on the secondary market, a loan servicer, your school financial aid office, the Department of Education or a guarantee agency.

As with your budget, you're best off reviewing your repayment options with a careful eye on your income and your priorities. If you have a good, steady income and you're not swamped by your monthly payments, you'll probably want to pay off your loans quickly, at the lowest cost. Your wisest choice may be the standard plan or even accelerated payment plan in which you pay off your loans ahead of schedule. (See Section B.) If you have a low salary now, but expect your income to increase substantially in the coming years, consider a graduated payment plan. Or if you have an enormous debt and need long-term payment relief, consider an extended payment plan or perhaps loan consolidation. (See Section C.) Choose the plan that will help you keep to your budget. (See Chapter 4.)

CHANGING REPAYMENT PLANS

If you're eligible for more than one repayment plan, keep in mind that you aren't locked in to the method you choose. The holder of your loan must let you change repayment at least annually, but you must repay your loans within the maximum amount of time permitted under the repayment option you choose. For example, assume that you start out with the standard repayment plan to reduce your loan balance as quickly as possible. Two years later, things get tough financially, and you switch to a plan that allows you to make lower payments stretched over a longer time. Your situation improves after 18 months. You switch back to the standard plan, but must pay off your remaining balance within the shorter time period associated with that plan—typically ten years from the date your loan originally came due. This could cause your payments to shoot way up. An alternative to switching back is to pay off your loans more quickly, and pay less in the long run, by sending additional payments of principal under your existing plan.

Just below, you'll find a Loan Payments chart that can help you figure out your best repayment choice. On this chart, you can record information for each of your loans—the type of loan, the amount you borrowed, the monthly payment, the amount of interest you will pay and the total—principal plus interest—you will pay back over the life of the loan. Your loan holders can help you figure out these amounts for each type of loan and payment plan. You'll probably want to make several copies of this form so you can compare the costs of paying back your loans under the different programs available to you. For example, you can fill out the form once for the standard plan, again for a graduated or extended plan, and yet again if you are thinking of consolidating your loans. This will allow you to see exactly what each option will cost you each month and over time.

Compare monthly payment amounts to see which plans are feasible. Compare overall costs to learn what a payment plan will cost you over the long haul. Some of those low monthly payments may look great until you realize that lowering your payments may get you on the hook for two or three times more than the amount you borrowed in the first place.

There's no one right answer when it comes to choosing a repayment plan. Some people might counsel you to choose the plan with the lowest overall cost; they might tell you to put your nose to the grindstone and find a way to make the highest monthly payments no matter how miserable it makes you. And they'd be right about one thing: choosing a plan with low long-term costs makes eminent financial sense. But for many people, other things take priority.

Try to find a balance: a plan that allows you some breathing room in your daily life, but that won't wipe out all hope of future financial security. For example, you may consent to pay more for your loans in the long run, but try to take advantage of the lower monthly payments by creating a safety net for yourself, even if that means setting aside a tiny amount as savings each month or making a small monthly investment in a 401(k) plan at work. And make a commitment that if your income increases, you will use some of the money to pay off your loans more quickly.

STUDENT LOAN PAYMENTS

Federal Loans	Amount Borrowed	Monthly Payments	Total Interest Paid	Total Loan Payments	Number of Payments
Totals for Federal Loans					
Private Loans	**Amount Borrowed**	**Monthly Payments**	**Total Interest Paid**	**Total Paid**	
Totals for Private Loans					
Other Loans	**Amount Borrowed**	**Monthly Payments**	**Total Interest Paid**	**Total Paid**	
Totals for Other Loans					
	Amount Borrowed	**Monthly Payments**	**Total Interest Paid**	**Total Paid**	
Grand Totals for all Loans					

1. Standard Repayment Plan

If you can afford the monthly payments, you'll probably want to stick with the original repayment plan offered by your lenders. These plans are known as standard plans. A standard plan carries the highest monthly payment, but costs less in the long haul because you pay less interest than you would under a plan with a lower monthly payment. With a standard plan, you pay a fixed amount each month for up to ten years, although payments on variable interest rate loans—that is, loans for which the interest rate changes slightly over time—may increase or decrease over the life of the loan. Your actual payment amount and repayment period will depend on your loan balance. The standard plan is what you will get if you don't select another plan. And quite surprisingly, despite the existence of several other repayment options, the standard plan is selected by approximately 90% of all former students.

ESTIMATING YOUR PAYMENT AMOUNT

You may already know what you owe under your loan's standard repayment plan. If not, contact your loan holder and find out that amount. Or use the following chart to estimate what you'll owe. As a very general guide, plan on shelling out $125 per month for every $10,000 you borrowed.

Interest Rate		6%			7%			8%	
Amount Borrowed	Monthly Payment	Months	Total Interest	Monthly Payment	Months	Total Interest	Monthly Payment	Months	Total Interest
$3,000	$50	71	$571	$50	75	$703	$50	77	$844
$6,000	$67	120	$1,993	$70	120	$2,360	$73	120	$2,736
$10,000	$111	120	$3,322	$116	120	$3,993	$123	120	$4,559
$20,000	$222	120	$6,644	$232	120	$7,866	$243	120	$9,119
$50,000	$555	120	$16,612	$581	120	$19,665	$607	120	$22,797
$100,000	$1,110	120	$33,225	$1,161	120	$39,330	$1,213	120	$45,593

Example: You owe $10,000 at 6% interest. Your payments would be approximately $111 per month for 120 months (ten years) for a total of approximately $13,320.

2. Graduated Repayment Plan

Under a graduated plan, your payments start out low and increase every two to three years. This plan may be your best option if you are just starting a career or business and you have an income that's low but likely to increase steadily over time.

Under the federal direct loan program, for example, your payments may start out as low as half of what they would be under the standard plan (there is no minimum amount, but your payment can never be less than the monthly interest amount), and then increase every two years over a period of time ranging from ten to 30 years. Obviously, you'll pay much more this way, but your monthly payments will never rise to more than 150% of the amount you'd owe under the standard plan.

Other lenders' plans vary. Some may require that you pay only the interest on your loans for a few years. Then you'll switch to payments of principal and interest until your loan is paid off. Your repayment period will always depend on the amount you owe; in extreme cases, it may stretch to 30 years.

With any graduated repayment plan, you'll pay more for your loan over time than you would under a standard plan. This happens for two reasons: First, because interest charges are based on your unpaid balance each month, if you keep a higher balance in the early years of your loan you will pay higher interest charges. Second, because you're likely to extend your repayment period to keep your payments from becoming too high toward the end of the loan, you'll be paying more interest over the life of your loan. The two examples that follow show you how your loan costs may increase under two different types of graduated payment plans.

Example: *You owe $10,000 at 8% interest, and you choose a four-year, interest-only plan. Your payments would be approximately $67 per month for four years and $175 per month for the rest of your ten-year repayment period, for a total of about $15,816. Under the standard plan, you'd pay about $14,559 total.*

Example: *You choose a graduated plan and extend your payments from ten to 15 years. Your schedule looks something like this: $67 per month for four years, $82 per month in your fifth year, $100 per month in your sixth year and $122 for the rest of your repayment period. Your total cost would be $18,568—versus $14,559 under the standard plan.*

Graduated repayment plans are available for most Stafford, SLS, PLUS, HEAL and consolidation loans. (See Section C.2 for more on repaying consolidation loans.) Graduated repayment is also available for some private loans. For more information, call your loan holder or servicer.

3. Extended Repayment Plan

Under an extended repayment plan, you stretch your repayment over a period of 12 to 30 years, depending on your loan amount. Your fixed monthly payment is lower than it would be under the standard plan, but you'll pay more interest because the repayment period is longer. If you need long-term lower payments, you might consider this type of plan.

Example: You owe $10,000 at 8% interest. You extend your payments from ten to 15 years and reduce your monthly payment to approximately $96 per month. Your total cost for the loan will be about $17,204—compared with the $14,559 you'd pay under the standard plan.

The federal government and many other lenders allow you to combine the extended plan with graduated payments, which will lower your payments even further—and increase your overall costs even more.

Extended repayment plans are available for most federal loans, including direct loans, PLUS loans, and Stafford loans. Most federal lenders must offer an extended repayment plan of up to 25 years to borrowers who took out loans after October 7, 1998, and who accumulate student loans totaling more than $30,000.

4. Income Contingent or Income Sensitive Repayment Plan

Under an income contingent or income sensitive repayment plan, your monthly loan payment is based on your annual income, family size and loan amount. If you are married and file a joint federal tax return, your joint income is used to calculate the required monthly payment. As your income rises or falls, so do your payments. If your income is low or unstable, this plan may be right for you.

If you sign up for an income contingent or income sensitive plan, you'll need to reapply every year so that your payments can be adjusted based on your current income.

a. Federal Direct Student Loans

If you have a federal direct Stafford or consolidation loan, you can choose an income contingent repayment plan. You may also be able to get this type of plan for your HEAL loans. PLUS loans are not eligible. The amount you pay annually will vary, but it will never exceed 20% of your discretionary income—that is, your annual gross income less an amount based on the poverty level for your family size, as determined by the Department of Health and Human Services. To learn what your maximum payment will be, call the direct loan servicing center at 800-848-0979. To qualify for an income contingent plan, you must authorize the IRS to release your income information to the Department of Education. The direct loan servicing center will send you a form to sign and return. After you do, it will get the necessary information from the IRS.

If your income is very low, you may not be required to pay anything under an income contingent plan—or the amount you pay each month will be less than the amount of interest that is accumulating. This may feel like a relief, but be aware that as time goes on, your loan balance will continue to increase—and eventually it may seem as if you'll never get out from under.

But the current law provides some hope: if you have any balance remaining on your loans after 25 years, the government will forgive what you owe. Your slate won't be wiped completely clean, however, because current IRS rules require you to report the amount forgiven as income and pay taxes on it unless you can prove that you are insolvent. These taxes may be high, but you won't have to fork over nearly as much as you would have without the loan forgiveness plan. For example, if you're in the 28% tax bracket and you have a forgiven balance of $10,000, you'll owe the IRS $2,800. In most states, you'll also owe state income taxes.

Example: To go to law school, you borrowed $55,000 at an interest rate of 8.25%. After graduation, you take a public interest job with a salary of $24,000 per year. Under an income contingent plan, your initial payments drop from $603 per month to just $271 per month. By the end of your 25-year repayment period, your payments have returned to $603 per month, but you still owe $10,806. The government forgives the balance of the loan, leaving you with a tax bill of nearly $3,025. By choosing this plan, you paid about $149,000 in principal and interest plus the taxes—for a grand total of almost $146,000. Under the standard plan, you would have paid about $75,000.

b. Federal Loans From Financial Institutions

If you obtained a federal Stafford, SLS, PLUS, HEAL or consolidation loan from a financial institution, your lender or other loan holder may offer an income sensitive plan. Such plans are similar to the government's income contingent plan, with one important difference: there is no provision for loan forgiveness as there is under the government's plan. Because you must pay your loans in full, your monthly payments may be slightly higher.

Example: Same facts as above—you borrowed $55,000 at 8.25% to go to law school and take a public interest job with a salary of $24,000 per year. Your loans are held by a nongovernment lender, and you choose an income sensitive plan. Under this plan, your initial payments drop from $675 to $378 per month. At the end of your 30-year repayment period, you're paying $434 per month for your loans. Paying off your loans in full costs $152,783, versus about $75,000 under a standard repayment plan.

IF YOU CAN'T FIND A PLAN THAT WORKS FOR YOU

As you read through the repayment options discussed in this chapter, you may feel frustrated if it turns out that a plan you like isn't available for your type of loan. If you have private student loans, for example, your repayment choices will be limited. Your lender may offer just one, standard repayment plan with high monthly payments. But don't despair. You can probably lower your overall monthly payments by choosing an alternative plan for your federal loans. And if things get really tough, you can ask your private lender for a forbearance (see Chapter 6, Section E) or try to negotiate a lower payment amount (see this chapter, Section E.3).

Furthermore, if you obtained your federally guaranteed loans from a financial institution and you aren't happy with its repayment plans, you might try asking your lender to sell your loans to a secondary company that offers more flexible payment options, such as the Student Loan Marketing Association (Sallie Mae) or USA Group. Or you can consider consolidating your loans with the federal government or a private company, which may give you more payment options. (See Section C.)

In addition, the 1998 amendments to the Higher Education Act could offer you a glimmer of hope. A new provision allows a guarantee agency to develop "voluntary and flexible payment agreements" with borrowers. The purpose of the law is to encourage creativity on the part of the guarantee agencies to increase the chances that borrowers will repay their loans. No one knows exactly what these agreements will look like, but if none of the repayment plans described in this chapter will work for you, you have nothing to lose by asking about a voluntary and flexible payment agreement.

B. Accelerated Payment

If you get a higher paying job or come up with some extra cash, you may want to pay more than the monthly minimum on your loans. By doing this, you can greatly reduce the overall cost of your loans because you'll pay much less interest. And there are no penalties for paying off your loans early.

But give some thought to what you do with your surplus cash. If you have more than one student loan, you'll want to pay down those with high interest rates first. And keep an eye on your other debts. For example, if you have credit card balances with higher interest rates than your student loans, tackle those first. And always make sure you pay your high priority debts first. Debts that are secured by something you want to keep, such as a home or a car, are always highest priority debts.

WHAT TO DO WITH YOUR EXTRA CASH

If you find yourself with a little cash to spare each month, think about investment opportunities that may work to your advantage. Rather than paying off loans early, some enterprising borrowers continue to make their minimum monthly loan payments and invest their extra income in stocks, bonds, mutual funds or other money-making ventures. Beware, however, that you don't invest more than you can afford—and that the return on your investment is likely to be greater than the interest you're paying on your student loans. If you're paying interest of 7% on your student loans, for example, you'll be better off making payments on those loans than selecting an investment opportunity that promises a yield of just 5%.

But you may find some good investments out there. For example, consider sinking your extra income into a retirement savings plan, especially if your contributions are made with pretax dollars and your employer matches your contribution. Your retirement investment may provide a greater return than paying down your student loans—and increase your feelings of security about the future.

Recommended reading. If you want to learn more about investing your money, consider these books:

- *The Under 40 Financial Planning Guide,* by Cornelius P. McCarthy (Merritt Publishing). A guide to taking care of yourself financially that covers everything from the basic concepts of investing to information about specific kinds of investments: stocks, bonds, mutual funds, retirement accounts and the like.
- *Wall Street Journal: Guide to Understanding Money and Investing,* by Kenneth Morris and Alan Siegal (Lightbulb Press). An easy-to-understand book that explains the nitty gritty details of how all basic investments work.
- *Personal Finance for Dummies,* by Eric Tyson (IDG Books). A book that takes a long-term, commonsense approach to investing. Particularly good information on picking high-quality, low cost mutual funds.

C. Loan Consolidation

With loan consolidation, you can lower your monthly payments by combining several loans into one packaged loan and extending your repayment period. Most consolidation lenders won't accept your application unless you have an outstanding balance of at least $7,500 on your eligible loans. As with the other low-payment options described above, consolidating your loans will greatly increase the amount of interest you pay over the life of your loan. You may also be able to refinance several loans, or just one loan, to secure a lower interest rate. Despite the potential for high costs to borrowers, the popularity of loan consolidation is steadily increasing as students graduate from college ever deeper in debt.

There are a number of situations in which you may want to consider consolidating your loans.

- You can't afford the monthly payments on your federal student loans, don't qualify for a postponement and aren't eligible for any of the low-payment plans described above. This may be true, for example, if you have older federal loans.

- You qualify for some of the low-payment plans described above, but you are so deep in debt that you still can't afford your monthly payments. This may be true if you have many federal loans, or if you have private loans—which typically aren't eligible for flexible payment plans or consolidation—in addition to your federal loans.

- You can afford substantial monthly payments and intend to pay off your loans under a standard ten-year plan, but you want to refinance at a lower interest rate.

1. Loans That Are Eligible for Consolidation

The vast majority of student loans may be consolidated, but there are some important restrictions. You probably won't be able to consolidate your private loans because these loans aren't accepted into federal loan consolidation programs.

But a few private lenders, moved by the increasing demand, have set up consolidation plans for private loans. For example, The Access Group, a maker of private loans for graduate and professional students, has a consolidation program for former law students who have Law Access Loans. If you have private loans, ask your lender what it offers. Emphasize that you want a consolidation plan, and ask whether it intends to develop one.

Most federal loans, including Perkins loans and most loans for healthcare professionals, can be consolidated without too much trouble. HEAL loans, however, may present some problems. The federal direct loan program allows you to consolidate HEAL loans with other federal loans, and the Department of Health and Human Services offers information about several HEAL-only consolidation plans. Other lenders take varying approaches. Citibank, for example, accepts HEAL loans for consolidation with other federal loans. Sallie Mae will refinance your HEAL loans separately from your other federal loans, but sends you one statement each month, so you have only one payment to make for both accounts. If you have HEAL loans, explore your options carefully before you choose a consolidation lender.

Also, in most situations, you cannot consolidate loans if the holder of the loan has obtained a judgment against you or has a wage garnishment order on the loan. This requirement does not apply, however, if you seek to consolidate under the federal direct loan consolidation program.

If your loan is in default. Under the direct loan program, even loans in default qualify for consolidation. Some nongovernment lenders will consolidate defaulted loans as well, though they are often reluctant to do so. To have a shot at qualifying for consolidation with a nongovernment lender, you will have to make at least three consecutive, reasonable and affordable repayments toward your loan or ask for an income sensitive repayment plan. The consolidation lender may still refuse your application if it thinks you are likely to default again. Keep in mind that consolidating defaulted loans may not be the best strategy for getting out of default. For example, the default notation will continue to appear on your credit report. For a full discussion of getting out of default, see Chapter 8.

2. Repayment Options

Many different lenders, including the federal government, offer consolidation loans. Your repayment options will vary slightly depending on the lender you choose. To consolidate under the federal direct loan program, you must meet one of two conditions:

- *You have a federal direct student loan.* If you took out a Stafford loan after the direct loan program began on July 1, 1994, and don't know if yours is a direct loan, check your loan documents or call your school.

- *You have tried and failed to obtain a consolidation loan with terms as good as those offered by the government.* If you've already consolidated with a nongovernment lender, you may be able to reconsolidate under the federal program if the government program didn't exist or you didn't know about it when you consolidated, and the government offers better terms than you're now getting.

Private companies that offer consolidation loans have their own requirements. You can contact them to find out whether your loans qualify. (See Section C.6 for contact information.)

All consolidation lenders allow you to stretch the term of your loan from its original length—typically, ten years—to between 12 to 30 years, depending on how much money you owe. You can choose a fixed monthly payment for the life of the loan or a graduated payment plan in which your payments start out low and increase over time. (See Section A.2.)

If lengthening the repayment period doesn't bring down your monthly payment enough, you can choose a payment plan based on your income level. Income contingent and income sensitive plans are available for most consolidation loans. (See Section A.4.) If you have PLUS loans, however, they cannot be included in a government income contingent plan, although they are eligible for private income sensitive plans.

Talk to the lenders. Consolidation lenders are happy to help you figure out what your costs will be under various repayment options. Ask potential lenders to help you calculate your payment amounts and overall costs before you make the decision to consolidate. (See Section C.6 for contact information.)

3. Lowering Your Interest Rate

It may be possible to lower your interest rate by consolidating your loans. The direct loan consolidation program offers a variable interest rate that will never exceed 8.25%. On PLUS loans, the maximum is 9%. If your loans carry a higher interest rate, it may be to your advantage to consolidate them or refinance. You can save money by paying off your loans quickly under a standard ten-year schedule—or you can extend your payment period if you can't make the payments even at the lower interest rate.

If you consolidate your loans with a nongovernment lender, you'll get only a small interest rate reduction, at best. Your new loan will carry a fixed rate, based on the average rate of all the loans you consolidate. But ask your lender about other ways to reduce the rate. For example, Sallie Mae—one of the largest private loan consolidators—will cut your interest rate by .25% if you authorize automatic payments from your checking account, and will knock off 1% if you make your loan payments on time for 48 consecutive months. (For more information about repayment incentives, see Section E.2 below.)

4. When You Shouldn't Consolidate

Loan consolidation may sound great—and it may turn out to be the best option for repaying your loans. But there are plenty of reasons to think twice before signing up.

If you can find a sane way to make your current monthly payments, consolidation is probably not wise—unless you do it solely to lower your interest rate and you quickly repay your loans. If your income is low and you want to go back to school, getting a consolidation loan with an income contingent repayment plan may be a very good choice for you.

If you have old loans, however, your interest rate will probably go up, not down, if you consolidate. If you extend your repayment period, the amount of interest you'll pay may shock you. Read the fine print in the application materials and quiz potential lenders to find how much your consolidation loan will cost you in the long run.

Example: *You borrowed $49,000 at an interest rate of 8.25% to get a graduate degree in engineering. Understandably, you feel daunted by your payments, which amount to $600 per month. You turn to a loan consolidation program for help with your federal loans and find that you'll be able to lower your payments to about $411 per month. This sounds terrific—until you calculate the overall costs of the loan. If you paid back that $49,000 in ten years, you'd pay about $90,000 in total costs. But by lowering your payments and lengthening your repayment term to 25 years, you'll wind up paying close to $123,400.*

As you can see, consolidation is a pricey option. But if you really need that lower monthly payment, it may still be your best choice.

HOW TO SIMPLIFY RECORDKEEPING

Some borrowers find loan consolidation attractive because it simplifies recordkeeping; you can combine many loans into one account and avoid the hassle of writing several checks each month. But if you choose consolidation for this reason, be sure to stick to the traditional repayment term so you don't raise your costs. You may also want to look for other ways of simplifying your loan management tasks, without consolidation.

- Give your lenders permission to withdraw monthly payments directly from your checking account.
- Ask one lender to purchase all of your loans and combine the payments without changing the terms. This can often be accomplished at no cost.
- If your loans come due at different times of the month or don't coincide with your paydays, ask your loan servicer to coordinate your payment due dates.

If you decide that you do need to consolidate your loans, proceed with care. You may not want to include all of your federal loans in one consolidation package. Here are some pitfalls to consider, depending on the types of loans you have.

Unsubsidized Stafford or SLS Loans. If you have subsidized Stafford loans and higher-rate SLS loans or unsubsidized Stafford loans, you might not want to include them in the same consolidation package. You'll lose your special Stafford loan subsidies if you do. For example, the government won't pay the interest on your subsidized Stafford loans if you go back to school or during other authorized deferment periods if those loans are consolidated with SLS or unsubsidized Stafford loans. (This rule doesn't apply to loans consolidated with the federal government; you won't lose your subsidies under that program.) Consider consolidating your subsidized Stafford loans through one program and the high-interest-rate or non-subsidized loans through another. If you do this, you'll also have the option of choosing a faster payoff option for your SLS or unsubsidized Stafford loans.

Perkins Loans. There are a couple of things to consider if you're thinking of consolidating your Perkins loans.

• You may want to keep Perkins loans out of your loan consolidation plan altogether so that you don't lose the low 5% interest rate. On the other hand, including them may cause the interest rate on your consolidation loan to drop substantially. Talk with potential lenders and calculate your overall costs both ways before you decide what to do.

- If you consolidate Perkins loans with other loans—even subsidized Stafford loans—you'll lose the government subsidies on all of your loans. This may seem illogical, but a quirk in the law makes it so.

If you are married. You can consolidate your loans jointly, but you and your spouse must both agree to repay the entire loan if you later divorce. Given the current divorce rate, this is an unwise risk to take. Also, you may lose certain benefits if you consolidate jointly. For example, most student loans held individually are canceled if the borrower dies. In the case of a joint consolidation loan, however, if one spouse dies, the other is responsible for the entire remaining debt.

5. Applying for Consolidation

Typically, you cannot apply for consolidation until after you leave school. The exception is the federal direct loan program, which allows you to consolidate while you're still in school.

Once you've consolidated, you may still add old loans to the consolidation package, but only within 180 days following the making of the consolidation loan. During this same 180 day period, you may also make new loans and add these to the package. You will need to get a new consolidation loan if you later decide to consolidate loans made after the 180-day period.

Until the consolidation process is complete, keep making payments under your existing repayment plan—or get a postponement. (See Chapter 6.) The lender is required to give you a 60-day forbearance while your loan consolidation application is pending. It takes some lenders more than 60 days to deal with consolidation paperwork, so if you don't keep your accounts up to date, your loans might slip into default. This may ruin your consolidation application and cost you a lot of money in collection fees to boot. The federal government and some guarantee agencies will consolidate defaulted loans, but nongovernment lenders are generally reluctant to do so. Sallie Mae, for example, won't consolidate any loan that's more than 150 days past due. (See Section C.1, above.)

Again, think carefully before you consolidate. After your consolidation loan comes through, you can't undo it. If you become dissatisfied, your only options are to pay off the loan as quickly as possible or to attempt to reconsolidate under a plan that offers better terms.

6. When Your Lender Doesn't Want to Let You Go

If you want to consolidate your loans under the government's direct loan program, you may have some trouble getting nongovernment lenders to transfer your loans to the program. Private lenders stand to lose a lot of money if many borrowers transfer loans to the government for consolidation. But if you qualify for the government's plan and you want to make the move, your lender cannot stop you.

Nongovernment lenders may conjure up problems with your paperwork, or try to dissuade you from consolidating by telling you that the government's plan is failing, that its payment plans aren't flexible or that you can't consolidate defaulted loans under the program. Nonsense.

You'll succeed if you're thorough when filling out your papers and persistent about transferring your loans. If you have questions about the government program, call a federal consolidation loan counselor at 800-848-0982.

More information about loan consolidation. Because of the complexity of servicing federal student loans, only a few nongovernment lenders offer consolidation programs. Here's how to contact the largest of them.

- **Sallie Mae**
  800-524-9100
  http://www.salliemae.com
  To qualify for Sallie Mae's consolidation plan, at least one of the loans you want to consolidate (or a HEAL loan) must be serviced by Sallie Mae, unless your loan holder does not offer loan consolidation. At the site, you'll find calculators to help you determine your monthly payments under Sallie Mae's different repayment options and online access to your Sallie Mae accounts.

- **USA Group**
  800-448-3533
  http://www.usagroup.com
  To qualify for USA Group's consolidation program, at least one of your loans must be guaranteed by USA Group. Check your promissory note or call USA Group for more information. USA Group's site features an online calculator to help you figure out what your payments and overall costs will be if you consolidate your loans under USA Group's plan.

- **Citibank**
  800-967-2400
  800-845-1298 (TDD)
  To qualify for Citibank's consolidation program, you must have one loan serviced by Citibank or your current lenders must not offer a consolidation program.

- **Federal Direct Consolidation Loan Information Center**
  800-557-7392
  http://www.ed.gov/offices/OPE/DirectLoan
  To qualify for a Federal Direct Consolidation Loan, you must meet strict requirements. (See Section C.2.)

- **Department of Health and Human Services (for information about HEAL consolidation plans)**
  301-443-1540

D. Raising Cash

One way to help make your student loan payments is to raise cash or borrow money from a person or institution other than those involved directly in student loan financing. Here are a few suggestions.

1. Sell a Major Asset

One of the best ways you can raise cash and keep associated costs to a minimum is to sell a major asset, such as a house or car, in which you have substantial equity. Equity is the market value less the debts owed. With the proceeds of the sale, you'll have to pay off what you still owe on the asset and also pay any other secured creditor to whom you pledged the asset as collateral. Then you'll have to pay off any liens placed on the property by your creditors. You can use what's left to pay all or a part of your student loans. But be careful about making this decision if you need this asset, such as a car to go to work. Always first consider the repayment, deferment and cancellation options discussed in this book.

2. Withdraw Money From a Tax-Deferred Account

If you have an IRA or other tax-deferred account into which you've deposited money, consider cashing it in if you have other substantial retirement funds. You'll have to pay the IRS a penalty—10% of the money you withdraw—and you'll owe income taxes on the money you take out. But paying these penalties to the IRS may be worth it if you can substantially reduce your student loan balances.

Example: *You currently owe $8,000 on your student loans. When you got out of school, you worked for a company that did not have a retirement plan. You deposited $2,000 a year into an IRA to build toward your retirement. Your IRA has a little over $5,500 in it: two and one-half years of deposits plus interest. If you use the money to pay down your student loans, you'll owe $550 to the IRS in penalties—and you'll have to pay taxes on the money, but you'll be able to reduce your student loans substantially.*

You may also be able to tap your 401(k) plan. Again, you'll owe taxes on the money withdrawn and a 10% penalty if you're under age 59-1/2. But there is a bit of good news: Not only can you withdraw money to cover your expenses, but you can also withdraw enough to cover the taxes and penalty.

3. Obtain a Home Equity Loan

Many banks, savings and loans, credit unions and other lenders offer home equity loans or lines of credit. Lenders who make home equity loans establish how much you can borrow by starting with a percentage of the market value of your house—usually between 50% and 80%. Then, they deduct what you still owe on it.

In most cases, you will not want to risk losing your home in order to pay back your student loans. The government is limited in what it can do to collect your student loan, and as discussed throughout this book, you have many repayment, deferment and cancellation options to use to avoid the worst debt collection tactics. Getting a home equity loan means risking your home if you can't pay back the loan. You are also likely to run into one of the many high-rate lenders out there just waiting to rip you off.

If you still want to consider a home equity loan, be sure you understand all the terms—and the pros and cons—before signing up.

Advantages of Home Equity Loans

- You can borrow a fixed amount of money and repay it in equal monthly installments for a set period. Or you can borrow as you need the money, drawing against the amount granted when you opened the account. You'll pay off this type of loan as you would a credit card bill.

- Most likely, you will be able to deduct the interest you pay on your income tax return.

- You can look for a loan with a fixed or adjustable rate interest. If you take out a home equity loan with an adjustable interest rate, federal law requires that the lender must cap the rate. This means that the rate will never be allowed to go above a certain percentage. Your lender can tell you the exact amount of the cap.

Disadvantages of Home Equity Loans

- Your student loans are unsecured debts; your property cannot be taken away if you don't pay. By turning the debt into a home equity loan, it becomes secured. If you are unable to pay, you may have to sell your house, or even worse, face the possibility of foreclosure— the procedure in which the lender forces a sale of your house to pay off what you owe.

- While interest is deductible and capped for adjustable rate loans, it's often high—up to 19% per year, which is much higher than the interest rate on your student loans.

- You may have to pay an assortment of fees up front for an appraisal, credit report, title insurance and points. These fees can run close to $1,000. In addition, for giving you an open line of credit, many lenders charge a yearly fee of $25 to $100.

4. Borrow From Family or Friends

Some people are lucky enough to have friends or relatives who can and will help out in times of financial need. But before you ask your former college roommate, Uncle Paul or some other soul who's not tapped out, consider the following.

- *Can the lender really afford to help you?* If the person is on a fixed income and needs the money to get by, look elsewhere for a loan.

- *Do you want to owe this person money?* If the loan comes with emotional strings attached, be sure you can handle the situation before taking the money.

- *Will you have to repay the loan now or will the lender let you wait until you're back on your feet?* If you have to make payments now, can you afford them?

- *If the loan is from your parents, can you treat it as part of your eventual inheritance?* If so, you won't ever have to repay it. If your siblings get angry that you're getting some of mom and dad's money, be sure they understand that your inheritance will be reduced.

E. Additional Help With Repayment

In addition to the repayment strategies described above, you may want to consider the following sources and options when looking for ways to ease the burdens of repayment.

1. Tax Deduction for Student Loan Interest

Beginning in 1998, student loan borrowers became eligible to deduct up to $1,000 per year of the interest paid on student loans. The $1,000 limit will go up $500 each year to a maximum of $2,500 in 2001.

The deduction is available only for payments made during the first 60 months in which the interest is due. It applies not only to your federally guaranteed loans, but also to any loan you took out while enrolled in a school and eligible to participate in federal student aid programs.

Not everyone can take this tax deduction—there are income restrictions that limit the use of the deduction for people with high incomes. To claim the maximum deduction, your income must be $40,000 or less—$60,000 for married taxpayers filing jointly. If you have a higher income, you are still eligible for a pro rata refund, as long as your income is less than $55,000 if you are single and $75,000 if you are married and filing jointly.

2. Lender Incentives

Many of the largest makers of federal student loans, including Sallie Mae, Nellie Mae and Citibank, offer incentives to borrowers who pay on time or have their payments electronically deducted from their checking accounts. The Department of Education intends to offer similar incentives in early 2000.

For example, all three lenders offer an interest rate reduction of up to 2% if you make the first 48 loan payments on time. Sallie Mae's plan applies to loans obtained after January 1, 1993; Citibank's is for loans obtained after January 1, 1995; and Nellie Mae's is available for loans obtained after January 1, 1996. Under Nellie Mae's plan, if you don't opt for the interest rate reduction, you may be able to get your final six monthly payments waived if you make the first 48 payments on time.

In addition, there's an incentive repayment program for Perkins loans. That program allows interest rate reductions of no more than 1% if you make 48 consecutive monthly payments, or no more than 5% on the balance owed on a loan that you pay back early.

If you arrange to have your payments automatically deducted from your bank account each month, your lender may reduce your interest rate even more—.25% in most cases.

Ask your lender, loan holder or loan servicer if these or similar incentives are available.

3. Repayment Assistance and Loan Forgiveness

A number of organizations sponsor repayment assistance or loan forgiveness plans for former students who agree to do public service work for a certain length of time. Here are two examples.

- **Repayment Assistance for Community Service Workers.** The Corporation for National and Community Service (AmeriCorps) provides educational awards in exchange for community service work in education, public safety, human needs and the environment. In addition to a small stipend for living expenses and healthcare benefits, you can earn an education credit of up to $4,725 for full-time work (1,700 hours per year) or up to $2,362 for part-time work (900 hours per year). You can use your credit to pay current educational costs or to repay federal student loans. Furthermore, if your loans qualify for forbearance (a postponement of payments but interest accrues) while you do your AmeriCorps service, AmeriCorps may pay for the interest for you.

For more information, contact AmeriCorps as follows:

Corporation for National and Community Service
1201 New York Avenue, NW
Washington, DC 20525
800-942-2677
http://www.cns.gov

• **Repayment Assistance for Healthcare Professionals.** The National
Health Service Corps (NHSC) may help you repay your healthcare
professions loans if you agree to work in an area where healthcare
workers are seriously needed. For more information, contact NHSC
at the address or phone number listed below.

Physicians
2070 Chain Bridge Road
Suite 450
Vienna, VA 22182
800-221-9393

Nurses
4350 East West Highway
10th Floor
Bethesda, MD 20814
800-435-6464

In addition, many states sponsor repayment assistance or loan
forgiveness programs. Under these programs, the state will pay all or
part of what you owe if you agree to perform a designated public service
for a specified length of time. Loan forgiveness plans are typically offered
to former students working in the health or teaching professions, and
are sometimes restricted to loans obtained from state student loan funds.
To find out if your state offers a loan forgiveness or repayment assistance
program that applies in your situation, call the state's financial aid office.
(See Chapter 2, Section C.1, for contact details.)

Some schools offer loan forgiveness programs as well; requirements vary widely from school to school. Check with your school's financial aid office to see if it sponsors a loan forgiveness plan that can help you.

Typically, repayment assistance and loan forgiveness plans cover only federal, state or university funded student loans. Commercial or private loans are not considered.

4. Negotiating With the Holder of Your Loan

Many loans, including private loans and federal Perkins loans, come with just one repayment option. But you can try asking your loan holder to reduce or temporarily suspend your payments if:

- you can't afford your payments

- you don't qualify for a deferment or forbearance (see Chapter 6), and

- consolidation is unavailable or won't help you.

If your loan is held by your school, as is the case with most Perkins loans, take a deep breath and understand that colleges and universities often extend a lot of flexibility to their former students. You should have little trouble contacting someone from your school's financial aid office and explaining your situation. A financial aid officer who sees that you are earnestly trying but unable to pay may agree to suspend or lower your payments until your financial situation improves. Of course, if you don't stay in touch with your school, it will likely begin collection efforts. (See Chapter 4, Section A.2.)

Private lenders are apt to be more difficult when it comes to negotiations, but the same rules apply. Show that you are willing but unable to pay, and keep in touch.

Below is a sample letter from a borrower trying to work out an affordable repayment schedule.

SAMPLE LETTER TO LOAN HOLDER

1818 Jane Street
New York, NY 10000
December 1, 20XX

Donald Havana
Student Loan Department
The Randolph Institute
Alexandria and Peanut Streets
Oxnard, MS 34567

Dear Mr. Havana:

I graduated from The Randolph Institute last June. While there, I borrowed $15,000 in Perkins loans. I know that my grace period is nearly over and that I must begin making payments soon.

In your letter of November 11, you stated that I must repay a minimum of $159 per month. Recently, however, I took a job as a dancer for Equinox (a small avant-garde improvisational dance troupe) and my income barely covers my expenses. Nevertheless, I do not want to avoid my obligation to repay.

Consequently, I am able and wish to make payments of $50 a month at this time. Should my income increase, I will try to raise my payments. Please contact me at once so that we may discuss this matter.

Very truly yours,

Miki Campbell
212-555-9876

TIPS ON NEGOTIATING WITH CREDITORS

You are most vulnerable when pleading for more time to pay off a debt. Try to follow these suggestions.

- Get outside help negotiating from an organization such as Debt Counselors of America (http://www.dca.org) or Consumer Credit Counseling Service (http://www.nfcc.org).
- If any of your requests are refused, politely ask to speak with a supervisor.
- Adopt a plan and stick with it. If you can't afford to pay more than $100 a month, don't agree to pay more.
- Try to identify the lender's bottom line. For example, if a loan holder offers to reduce your payments by $75 a month, perhaps the loan holder will actually reduce the amount by $150. If you need to, push it.

If you send letters to the holder of your loans, try to adhere to the following guidelines.

- Type your letters, if possible.
- Keep a copy of all correspondence for yourself.
- Send all communications by certified mail, return receipt requested.
- If you are enclosing money, use a cashier's check or money order if possible. Otherwise, the recipient of the check could pass your account number on to any debt collector which will make it easier for the collector to grab your assets to collect if you later default.

Above all, be persistent. If you want something from your loan holders or servicers, whether it be a change in repayment option, a new payment due date, a postponement of your payments or a compromise, keep after them until you get what you need. These companies and agencies are swamped with calls and paperwork, so you may have to work extra hard to avoid getting lost in the shuffle. Get the names of the people with whom you talk on the phone; keep a phone log. (See Chapter 4, Section A.1.) Make follow-up phone calls to be sure the proper action has been taken. If the holder of your loan agrees to any change, follow up all your phone calls with letters confirming what you've discussed. Don't assume your loan holder or servicer has processed any request until you get confirmation in writing.

CHAPTER 6

Strategies When You Can't Pay

I f you're in over your head and you can't make payments on one or more of your student loans, don't panic. And don't just give up and invite default. If you default on your student loans, your credit will be damaged and your loan balance will increase dramatically as collection fees are added to the pot. In the worst scenario, your loan holder will take aggressive action to get the loan money from you, such as taking a portion of your paycheck, nabbing any tax refund to which you are entitled or suing you.

Even if you are unable to make your loan payments and worried about default, all is not lost. But you must act quickly to find out your options. In certain limited circumstances, you may be able to cancel your student loans—meaning that you are completely absolved from repaying them. You face no negative consequences if you cancel your student loans; however, it is not easy to qualify. You will have to meet specific conditions that depend on what type of loans you have and when you borrowed the money. In some situations, you may be able to cancel only a portion of your loans.

If you can't cancel your student loans, you can probably find a way to postpone making payments by obtaining a deferment or forbearance. A deferment is a delay based on a specific condition—such as returning to school or being unemployed—that excuses you from making payments for a set period of time. For some types of loans, the government pays the interest during the deferment period, so your loan balance will not increase. In other situations, you can defer principal only, which means that interest continues to accrue and your balance goes up during the deferment period. Like cancellation, deferment depends on what type of loans you have and when you obtained them—and you can never obtain a deferment if you are in default.

If you don't qualify for a deferment, you may be able to postpone your payments through a forbearance. When you obtain a forbearance, your loan holder gives you permission to reduce or stop making payments for a set period of time. Interest always continues to accrue during a forbearance, which generally makes forbearance less attractive than deferment. But forbearances are easier to obtain because they are not tied to the type of loans you have or the date you obtained them—and they aren't governed by the picayune rules that make cancellations and deferments so hard to come by.

This chapter helps you figure out if you qualify for cancellation, deferment or forbearance. Skim the table of contents and see if you fit into any of the conditions listed under Section A. If you don't, jump ahead to Section E to read about forbearances.

A. Conditions for Canceling or Deferring Student Loans

You may be able to cancel or defer a federal student loan if your circumstances match any of those described below. Section 1 explains the circumstances that allow you to cancel your loans, Section 2 the cases in which you may be able to cancel or defer the loans, and Section 3 the circumstances in which you only can defer your loans.

1. Loan Cancellation

If you meet the conditions described in this section, you may be able to cancel your loans.

a. Death of the Borrower

If a former student borrower dies, the executor—the person who collects and distributes the property left at death—can cancel any federal student loan. In addition, PLUS loans may be cancelled if the former student for whom the parent borrowed the money has died, but only if the death occurred after July 22, 1992.

b. Permanent Total Disability

You can cancel any federal student loan if you are unable to work or go to school because of an injury or illness that is expected to continue indefinitely or result in your death. In most cases, to qualify for this cancellation, you cannot have had the injury or illness at the time you signed up for the loan. There is an exception to this rule if your condition or injury substantially deteriorated after you took out the loan.

To qualify for a disability cancellation, you will need a statement from your treating physician on a form provided by the holder of your loan. Once you get a disability cancellation, you will not be eligible for student assistance again in the future unless your doctor later certifies that you can work and you certify that you will not cancel the loan due to a medical condition unless that condition substantially deteriorates.

Parents who took out PLUS loans together cannot both get disability cancellation unless both are disabled. If only one parent is disabled and both parents took out the loan, the non-disabled parent is still obligated to pay.

Amendments to the Higher Education Act passed in 1998 include a new provision to make it easier for disabled veterans to get cancellations of their loans. Eventually, Department of Veterans Affairs physicians will be able to certify and document that a disabled veteran is eligible for a cancellation of his or her loan. Contact the DVA for more information.

c. Attended a Trade School

Many former students were lulled into taking out student loans to attend a trade school, only to have the school doors close before they could finish the program. Other students were falsely certified by school officials as being able to benefit from the loan. If this happened to you, you can probably cancel 100% of a Stafford, PLUS or SLS loan made after December 31, 1986. (See Chapter 9.)

d. Filing for Bankruptcy

If you meet certain requirements, you may be able to cancel your student loans in bankruptcy. (See Chapter 10.)

2. Loan Cancellation or Deferment

The conditions in this section allow you to either defer or cancel your loans depending on the specific requirements of the program.

WILL THE GOVERNMENT PAY YOUR INTEREST CHARGES?

Whether the government pays the interest on your loans during deferment depends on the type of loans you have and when you obtained them. Here are the rules.

- **Stafford, Perkins, PLUS, SLS and consolidation loans obtained after June 30, 1993.** The government pays the interest on Perkins and Stafford loans. On PLUS and SLS loans, interest continues to accrue. If you have a consolidation loan, whether the government pays the interest depends on the types of loans you consolidated.

- **Stafford, SLS and consolidation loans obtained before July 1, 1993.** The government pays the interest on subsidized or need-based Stafford loans. If your Stafford loan is unsubsidized, interest continues to accrue. The same is true on SLS loans. If you have a consolidation loan, whether the government pays the interest depends on the types of loans you consolidated.

- **PLUS loans obtained before July 1, 1993.** You can defer principal, but not interest.

- **Perkins loans obtained before July 1, 1993.** You can defer principal and interest.

- **HEAL, HPSL, LDS and NSL loans.** You can defer principal and interest.

a. Membership in a Uniformed Service

For reasons known only to Congress, former students who currently serve the U.S. government wearing a uniform are grouped together for purposes of loan cancellation and deferment. If you serve in the U.S. military, the National Oceanic and Atmospheric Corps or the U.S. Public Health Service, the situations in which you may cancel or defer your loans are described in this section.

•   If you are on active duty in the U.S. military in an area of hostility or are in imminent danger, the Defense Department will repay up to half of a Perkins loan. The military will pay off your loan at the rate of 12.5% for each year that you serve. In addition, you may defer your payments on your Perkins loans while you are waiting for your cancellation benefits to come through. You must submit a postponement request form, available from the holder of your loan, to be eligible for this deferment.

•   You can defer the payments on Perkins loans for up to three years if you meet any of the following requirements.

    —You are on active duty in the U.S. military and obtained your loans before July 1, 1993.

    —You are serving full-time as a commissioned officer in the U.S. Public Health Service and obtained your loans after September 30, 1980.

    —You are serving in the National Oceanic and Atmospheric Administration Corps and obtained your loans after June 30, 1987.

•   You can defer the payments on Stafford, SLS, consolidation or PLUS loans obtained before August 15, 1983, if you are on active duty in the U.S. military or serving full-time as a commissioned officer in the U.S. Public Health Service. If you obtained a Stafford or SLS loan after June 30, 1987, you can also defer your payments if you are serving in the National Oceanic and Atmospheric Administration Corps.

- You can defer your payments on any NSL, HPSL and LDS loans if you are on sustained full-time active duty in the U.S. military, U.S. Public Health Service or National Oceanic and Atmospheric Administration Corps. The deferment is for a maximum total of three years.

- You can defer the payments on HEAL loans if you are on active duty in the U.S. military. The deferment is for a maximum of three years.

- If you have a PLUS loan, you may be eligible for repayment assistance if the student for whom you borrowed is serving in the military. Technically, this is not considered cancellation, but it may have the same effect. For more information, contact the student's recruiting officer.

- If you are in the Armed Forces Reserves and are called or ordered to active duty for a period of more than 30 days, you can exclude this period of service from your initial grace period (see Chapter 2) up to a maximum of three years.

b. Teaching Needy Populations

Teachers who serve certain needy populations—including low-income or disabled students—may be able to have their student loans cancelled or the payments deferred. For loan purposes, a teacher is defined as a professional employee of a school or school system who provides classroom instruction or related services as part of an educational program.

You are eligible for cancellation or deferment if you fall into one of the following categories.

- If you are a full-time elementary or secondary school teacher serving low-income students, you can cancel up to 100% of your Perkins loans and eligible federal direct loans. You must work in a designated public or nonprofit private elementary or secondary school with a high concentration of students from low-income families. These schools are listed in the *Directory of Designated Low-Income Schools for Teacher Cancellation Benefits,* published annually by the Department of Education. Call your school's financial aid office or the holder of your loan to find out whether your school is listed.

- If you are a full-time public or other nonprofit elementary or secondary school teacher of children with disabilities, you can cancel up to 100% of your Perkins loans. You must teach in a class where the majority of the students are disabled.

- If you are a full-time teacher of math, science, foreign languages, bilingual education, or another field designated by the Department of Education as a teacher shortage area, you can cancel up to 100% of your Perkins or federal direct loans. Perkins loans may be cancelled regardless of when made; however, if your loan was made before July 23, 1992, you can get credit only for teaching service on or after October 7, 1998. For direct loans, cancellation applies only for loans made on or after July 23, 1992.

- If you are a recent borrower—that is, you had no student loans outstanding as of October 7, 1998—you are not in default on your loans and you have been employed as a full-time teacher for five consecutive years in a school that qualifies for loan cancellation under the Perkins program described just above, you can have cancelled up to $5,000 of the total amount still outstanding after you have completed the fifth year of teaching.

- If you are a full-time public or nonprofit private elementary school teacher in a geographic region, grade level or academic discipline that the Department of Education has designated as a teacher shortage area, you can defer payments on Stafford, SLS or consolidation loans obtained after June 30, 1987, for a maximum of three years. In either situation, you can get a list of your state's shortage areas from your school's financial aid office or from your loan holder.

If your loans qualify for cancellation, the Department of Education will wipe them out at the rate of:

- 15% after each of your first two years of teaching

- 20% after each of your third and fourth years, and

- 30% after your fifth year.

You may defer your payments while you are waiting for your cancellation application to be approved. You must submit a postponement request form, available from the holder of your loan, to be eligible for this interim deferment.

c. Providing Services Other Than Teaching to Needy Populations

People who do not teach but who serve certain needy populations may be able to have their student loans cancelled, depending on the type of loan and population served.

The workers and loans eligible for cancellation are as follows.

- Full-time educators, therapists, nurses and nutritionists who work in public or other nonprofit programs under public supervision and provide inexpensive or free services for disabled toddlers or infants can cancel up to 100% of their Perkins loans obtained after July 22, 1992.

- Full-time employees of public or nonprofit agencies providing services to low-income, high-risk children and their families can cancel up to 100% of Perkins loans obtained after July 22, 1992. If you work for an agency that provides services to needy populations, contact your loan holder to find out whether your work qualifies you for loan cancellation.

- Full-time staff members in the educational component of a Head Start program can cancel up to 100% of their Perkins loans.

If you qualify, the Department of Education will wipe out your loans at the rate of:

- 15% after each of your first two years of teaching

- 20% after each of your third and fourth years, and

- 30% after your fifth year.

- Full-time child care providers who work in a child care facility, including a licensed home facility, located in a low income community may be eligible for loan cancellation. You must be a recent borrower—that is, you had no student loans outstanding as of October 7, 1998—and have a degree in early childhood education. Awards are limited and will be made on a first come first served basis. the Department of Education will wipe out your loans at the rate of 20% after each of your second and third years of work and 30% after each of your fourth and fifth years.

Also, you can postpone your loan payments while you wait for your cancellation benefits to come through. Call your loan holder and ask for a postponement request form.

d. Performing Community Service

In many situations, you can partially cancel your student loans or defer your payments in exchange for performing community service. There are several different programs, all with very different rules, so be sure to read carefully. Opportunities range from serving in the Peace Corps to volunteering your time with an organization that assists low-income people in your community.

Here are the programs available.

- The Corporation for National and Community Service (AmeriCorps) provides money for your tuition or loans in exchange for community service work. You may, for example, work in the public schools, assist families in need or help to preserve the environment. You can earn up to $4,725 annually for full-time work (1,700 hours per year) or up to $2,362 for part-time work (900 hours per year). You can use the money you earn to repay your federal student loans—in effect, obtaining a partial cancellation. For more information, contact AmeriCorps at:

  Corporation for National and Community Service
  1201 New York Avenue, NW
  Washington, DC 20525
  800-942-2677
  http://www.cns.gov

- Under a number of loan forgiveness programs, your state or former school will pay all or part of your loans if you agree to perform a designated public service for a specified length of time. These programs are typically offered to former students working in the health or teaching professions, and are sometimes restricted to loans obtained from state student loan funds. To find out if your state or school offers a loan forgiveness program that applies to you, contact both your school's financial aid office and your state's Office of Higher Education. (See Chapter 2, Section C.1, for contact details.)

- Peace Corps and VISTA volunteers can cancel up to 70% of a Perkins loan. The Department of Education will cancel your loans at the rate of 15% after each of your first two years of service and 20% after each or your third and fourth years. You can also defer your payments while you are waiting for your cancellation application to be approved. Call your loan holder and ask for a postponement request form.

- Peace Corps and ACTION program volunteers can defer their payments for up to three years on Stafford, SLS, consolidation or PLUS loans obtained before August 15, 1983. Peace Corps volunteers who do not qualify for the special Peace Corps deferment can still apply for economic hardship deferments. The paperwork requirements are less restrictive for those volunteers choosing to apply for hardship deferments.

- Peace Corps volunteers can defer payments on HEAL, NSL, HPSL and LDS loans for up to three years.

- VISTA and National Health Service Corps volunteers can defer payments on HEAL loans for up to three years.

- Full-time paid volunteers in tax-exempt organizations can defer payments for up to three years on Stafford, SLS, consolidation and PLUS loans obtained before August 15, 1983—and on Perkins loans obtained after September 30, 1980. You must:

   —provide assistance to low-income people

   —agree to serve full-time for at least one year

   —not receive compensation that exceeds the federal minimum wage—currently $5.15 an hour, and

   —not teach religion or engage in religious activities as part of your work.

e. Working in the Healthcare Professions

Healthcare professionals, including nurses and physicians in their residency, sometimes can cancel their student loans or defer their loan payments. Several programs are available.

- If you are a full-time nurse or medical technician, you can cancel up to 100% of Perkins loans obtained after July 22, 1992. The Department of Education will cancel your loans at the rate of 15% after each of your first two years of service, 20% after each of your third and fourth years and 30% after your fifth year. If you obtained your loan after June 30, 1993, you are allowed to postpone your payments while you are waiting for your cancellation benefits to come through. To be eligible for the postponement, you must complete a postponement request form, available from the holder of your loan.

- The National Health Service Corps (NHSC) may help you repay your healthcare loans if you agree to work in an area where healthcare workers are seriously needed. To find out whether your area qualifies, contact NHSC at the address or phone number listed below.

  Nurses
  4350 East West Highway
  10th Floor
  Bethesda, MD 20814
  800-435-6464

  Physicians
  2070 Chain Bridge Road
  Suite 450
  Vienna, VA 22182
  800-221-9393

- If you are a healthcare professional completing an internship or residency program, you can defer the payments on your Perkins loans obtained after September 30, 1980, for a maximum of two years. Your program must:

—require that you hold at least a bachelor's degree before being accepted, and

—be required before you can be certified for professional practice or service.

You must get a letter from your state licensing agency stating that your program meets the above requirements. Also, you must provide a letter from the institution or organization with which you are completing your residency stating that a bachelor's degree is required before being admitted to the program and that you have been accepted into it. The letter must also set out the anticipated starting and ending dates of the program.

- If you are a healthcare professional completing a professional internship or residency, you can defer the payments on Stafford, SLS, consolidation and PLUS loans obtained before August 15, 1983, for up to two years. If the internship is at an institution of higher education, hospital or healthcare facility, the program must:

    —be a supervised training program

    —lead to a degree or certificate, and

    —require that you hold at least a bachelor's degree.

    At any other institution or organization, the internship must:

    —be a supervised training program

    —be required before you can be certified for professional practice or service as shown by a letter from your state licensing agency, and

    —require that you hold at least a bachelor's degree.

- If you are a healthcare professional completing a professional internship or residency, you can defer the payments on HEAL loans for up to four years.

- If you are a healthcare professional enrolled in a full-time program of advanced professional training, you can defer the payments on HPSL and LDS loans for as long as you participate in the training. Advanced professional training includes:

    —internship and residency programs, and

    —full-time academic training programs that last at least one academic year.

- If you graduated from a chiropractic school, you can defer your HEAL loan payments for up to one year following graduation.

- If you are a primary care physician who has completed an internship or residency training program in osteopathic general practice, family medicine, general internal medicine, preventative medicine or general pediatrics, you can defer the payments on your HEAL loans for up to three years.

f. Working in Law Enforcement

Full-time law enforcement and corrections officers can cancel up to 100% of their Perkins loans obtained after November 29, 1990. The Department of Education will cancel your loans at the rate of:

- 15% after each of your first two years of law enforcement or corrections service

- 20% after each of your third and fourth years, and

- 30% after your fifth year.

If you obtained your loan after June 30, 1993, you can postpone your payments while you are serving as a law enforcement officer and waiting for your cancellation benefits to come through. Call your loan holder to request the necessary paperwork.

⚠️ **If you have a consolidation loan.** If you consolidated your loans, you may have lost some cancellation options. Under the terms of most consolidation loans, lenders will wipe out a debt only if a borrower dies or becomes disabled. This means, for example, that if you included a federal Perkins loan in your consolidation package, you lost the cancellation options that were unique to Perkins loans and are limited to those offered by the consolidation lender.

3. Loan Deferment

The final set of conditions in this section allow you to defer your loans. Deferment, unlike cancellation, means that you will still have to pay the loans back, but you will be able to postpone these payments for a while. Most importantly, in many cases, interest on the loans will not accrue during this deferral period.

a. Enrollment in School

If you return to school to study at least half-time, you can almost always defer the payments on your student loans. There are several programs available, and you'll have to read through a long list to find one that might apply. Of course, if the result is that you can defer your student loan payments, it's well worth the effort.

- If you are a full-time student, you can defer loan payments on any federal student loan. You must provide a certification from your school on a form obtained from your loan holder. For all types of loans except Perkins loans, you must resume your payments as soon as you leave school. For Perkins loans, repayment begins nine months after your schooling ends.

• If you are enrolled at least half-time, you can defer loan payments on Stafford, SLS, consolidation and PLUS loans obtained after June 30, 1987, and on all Perkins loans. You must provide a certification from your school on a form obtained from your loan holder. For all types of loans except Perkins loans, you must resume your payments as soon as you leave school. For Perkins loans, repayment obligations begin nine months after your schooling ends.

• If you are enrolled in an approved graduate fellowship program, you can defer Stafford, Perkins, SLS, consolidation and PLUS loans obtained after June 30, 1993, if you hold at least a bachelor's degree, and a college or university accepts you into its full-time program. The deferment lasts until the schooling ends, and the program must:

—provide sufficient financial support to allow for full-time study for at least six months

—require a written statement from you explaining your study goals prior to any award of financial support

—require that you submit periodic reports, projects or other evidence of your progress, and

—if you are studying at a foreign university, be a course accepted by the American university in which you are enrolled.

• If you are a full-time student at an institution that participates in the HEAL or Stafford loan program, you can defer your HEAL loan payments. The deferment lasts for as long as you are in school. You can also defer your HEAL loans if you are a medical student enrolled in an approved fellowship or educational training program. This deferment lasts for up to two years. Contact your loan holder to find out if your program qualifies and to obtain the necessary paperwork.

- If you are a full-time student who obtained an HPSL or LDS loan after November 3, 1988, you can defer your payments. The deferment lasts for as long as you are in school. In addition, you can defer HPSL or LDS loans obtained after October 21, 1985, if you are participating in an approved fellowship or educational training program. This deferment lasts for up to two years. You must begin this program within 12 months after completing your internship or residency training. If you leave school to participate in an educational training program, you must intend to return to school after completing the activity. Your loan holder will tell you whether your program qualifies and send you the necessary paperwork.

- If you are a nursing student enrolled at least half-time, you can defer your NSL payments for a maximum of ten years. You must be studying for a nursing degree, pursuing other advanced training in nursing or training to be a nurse anesthetist.

b. Temporary Total Disability

If you, your spouse or one of your dependents are temporarily totally disabled, you can defer the payments on Stafford, SLS, consolidation and PLUS loans obtained before July 1, 1993, for up to three years. For Perkins loans, you can defer your payments if you or a spouse is disabled and you obtained your loan after September 30, 1980—or if your dependent is disabled and you obtained your loan after June 30, 1987. To qualify for this deferment, the sickness or injury must make you unable to attend school or hold a job for at least 60 days. If your spouse or dependent is sick or injured, you must be unable to hold a job because he or she needs your caretaking for at least three months.

c. Unemployment

You can defer the payments on any Stafford, SLS, consolidation or PLUS loan—and on Perkins loans obtained after June 30, 1993. You can get a deferment for up to three years if you are unemployed but looking for work; the period is two years for loans obtained before July 1, 1993. To show that you are unemployed, you need only submit evidence that you are eligible for unemployment insurance benefits. You do not have to be actually receiving the benefits in order to qualify. If you are not eligible for unemployment insurance, you will need to submit other written evidence of your attempts to find a job. Adequate documentation of your job search includes the name of an employment agency with which you've registered; agency registration is mandatory if there is one within 50 miles of your home. You must also provide the names of companies where you've applied for work.

d. Economic Hardship

You can defer payments on federal loans obtained after June 30, 1993, for up to three years if you are suffering an economic hardship. You are automatically entitled to this deferment if you receive public assistance, such as welfare or SSI. If you don't receive public benefits, qualifying is based on a complex formula that's a mix of your income, the federal minimum wage, the federal poverty level and your monthly or annual federal student loan payments. You will have to provide documentation of your income, such as pay stubs.

Under this formula, you will qualify if you meet one of three conditions based on your work status and income level.

- You work full-time and your total monthly gross income—that is, the total amount you earn before taxes or other legal deductions are withheld—is no more than the poverty level for a family of two listed in the chart below.

Example: Angela is having trouble making her Stafford loan payment of $50 per month. She lives in Pennsylvania and must earn less than $863.33 per month, the state poverty level, to qualify for an economic hardship deferment. She works full-time at a coffee shop where she makes $830 a month, including tips. Angela clearly qualifies.

- You work full-time and your total annual federal student loan payments are at least 20% of your adjusted gross annual income— that is, the amount of your total annual income plus or minus any adjustments recorded on your federal income tax return. In addition, after you deduct your total annual federal student loan payments, your income must be less than 220% of the annual amount listed in the chart below.

Example: Jonathan graduated from business school two years ago, and is struggling to make $700 in federal student loan payments each month. His annual student loan payments total $8,400, and he makes $28,000 working full-time for a small nonprofit organization in Honolulu. Jonathan's annual student loan payments amount to slightly more than 36% of his annual income, well more than the required 20%. In addition, after deducting his annual federal student loan payments from his annual income, it falls to $19,600, less than 220% of the maximum annual income amount listed for Hawaii (220% of $11,920 is $26,224). Jonathan qualifies for an economic hardship deferment.

- You neither work full-time nor receive a total monthly gross income that exceeds two times the monthly amount listed in the chart below. In addition, after you deduct your total monthly federal student loan payments, your income from all sources must not exceed the monthly amount listed below.

Example: Toni and her partner live together in Mississippi, and are raising two young children together. Toni earns about $650 per month working part-time as a freelance accountant. In addition, she receives $400 per month in child support from her ex-husband, bringing her total monthly income to approximately $1,100, less than twice the maximum monthly amount for her state ($863.22 times two is $1,726.66). Toni's student loans cost her $250 per month. After deducting this amount from her monthly income, it falls to $850, less than the $863.33 maximum for Mississippi. Toni is entitled to an economic hardship deferment.

Poverty Level for a Family of Two	Monthly Income	Annual Income
Alaska	1,078.33	12,940.00
Hawaii	993.33	11,920.00
All Other States	863.33	10,360.00

Economic hardship deferments for older loans. If you qualify for an economic hardship deferment, but you obtained your federal student loans before July 1, 1993, you may not be out of luck. First, check to see if you qualify for any other deferments. If you don't, and you're certain you need to defer your loan payments, consider consolidating your loans. If you combine all of your outstanding federal loans into one packaged loan, your loan will be considered new and you will be eligible for the economic hardship deferment, as well many of the other deferments. There are a number of caveats about consolidating, however. (See Chapter 5, Section C.)

e. Enrollment in Rehabilitation Program for the Disabled

If you are enrolled in a rehabilitation training program for the disabled, you can defer payments on any Stafford, SLS, consolidation or PLUS loan—and on Perkins loans obtained after June 30, 1993. You must begin making payments six months after your training ends. To qualify, the program must:

- be licensed, approved, certified or recognized as providing rehabilitation training to disabled individuals by the Department of Veterans' Affairs or a state agency responsible for vocational rehabilitation, drug abuse treatment, mental health services or alcohol abuse treatment

- provide services under a written, individualized plan that specifies the date services are expected to end, and

- require substantial time and effort that would normally prevent you from working full-time.

f. Parents With Young Children

Working mothers and mothers and fathers on parental leave can defer their student loan payments in two situations.

- If you are a working mother, you can defer your Stafford, SLS or Perkins loans obtained after June 30, 1987, for up to one year if you:

    —have preschool-age children

    —enter or reenter the workforce, and

    —earn no more than $1 per hour above the federal minimum wage—currently $5.15 per hour.

Your application for a deferment must include documentation of your rate of pay and the age of your children as shown on their birth or baptismal certificates.

• If you are on parental leave, you can defer your Stafford, SLS or Perkins loans obtained before July 1, 1993, for up to six months if you are pregnant, or caring for a newborn or newly adopted child. You cannot be working full-time or attending school, but you must have been enrolled in school at least half-time during the six months preceding the deferment. You'll need to give your loan holder a school official's certification of your recent enrollment plus one of the following documents:
—a letter from your physician stating that you are pregnant
—a copy of your newborn child's birth certificate, or
—a letter from an adoption agency documenting your newly adopted child's placement.

CANCELING AND DEFERRING PRIVATE, STATE AND UNIVERSITY LOANS

Generally, you can defer payments on a private loan while you are completing the educational program for which you borrowed the money and during a grace period, usually six to nine months, after you leave school or drop below half-time enrollment. But once your loan becomes due, you cannot obtain another deferment. The notable exception to this rule is for medical students, who can usually defer payments while completing an internship or residency.

Cancellation and deferment provisions for state and university loans vary from program to program. If you have one of these loans, contact the state office listed in Chapter 2 (for state loans) or your school's financial aid office (for college and university loans) and ask if there are any circumstances under which you can defer your loan payments.

If you have any other type of student loan, contact your loan holder and ask for information about canceling your loans or deferring payments.

B. Applying for a Cancellation

To cancel a student loan, or to determine if you qualify for cancellation, call your loan holder or the Department of Education's Debt Collection Services Office at 800-621-3115. A customer service representative will send you a cancellation application, which you will have to complete and return with any necessary documentation, such as a statement from a physician describing your disability.

More information when you can't pay. The Department of Education publishes a free booklet entitled *The Student Guide*. Though it's geared toward students now applying for financial assistance, it contains important information on cancelling student loans and obtaining deferments. You can order the guide by calling the Federal Student Aid Information Center at 800-433-3243, or through the Department of Education's website (http://www.ed.gov).

C. Applying for a Deferment

Deferments are never automatic. You must apply for them. You can defer repayment of a student loan if you meet one of the conditions described above and you are not in default—that is, you have made your payments on time, are in the grace period after graduation or have been granted other deferments or forbearances. Occasionally, you may qualify for retroactive deferment—a deferment that will cover past due payments short of default.

To obtain a deferment, you must obtain the appropriate paperwork from the holder of your loan, complete it carefully and follow up to make sure your request is processed correctly. This may sound like a lot of work, but if you're having trouble making your loan payments, it's worth the effort. A deferment can buy you some time when you need it most.

Start by contacting the holder of your loan. Tell your loan holder which deferment you think you qualify for and ask for the proper form. The holder's representative will generate the form, including your name, address and account information, and should note in your file that you've requested the form. This may help you keep the loan holder off your back if your payments are past due; the representatives are likely to be friendlier and more patient if it's clear that you're applying for a deferment.

When you receive your deferment form, read it carefully and fill it out thoroughly. You will probably need to attach additional documentation or required certifications. For example, if you're requesting an economic hardship deferment, include the proper evidence of your income, such as pay stubs or tax returns. If you're in school, take the form to your school's financial aid office to obtain the necessary certification and signature. A deferment form may look like a lot of small print to you, but it sets out everything you need to do to get and keep your deferment. If you don't follow the directions exactly, your loan holder will likely to send the application back to you—or even ignore it altogether—and this could cost you valuable time. Before submitting your application, make a copy of it for your records.

Follow up on your application a couple of weeks after you submit it. Call your loan holder to make sure that it has received your form and is processing it. Many borrowers are surprised to find that their paperwork was never received or was processed incorrectly. Don't assume your deferment request has been granted until you receive written confirmation from your loan holder. The process can take as long as six weeks.

CALLING ALL LOAN HOLDERS

A week or so after you submit your deferment application, call your loan holder to make sure the application arrived and reached the proper hands for processing. Pull out the copy of the application you kept for your records. Look it over carefully to find your loan holder's phone number. If it's not on the application, it should be on the coupon book or other payback materials you received from your loan holder.

When you call, tell the person who answers the phone that you are calling about your deferment application. You will be connected with the repayment division. Don't be afraid to give your name and Social Security number; after all, they've got you on file. Ask about the status of your application. Emphasize that you are anxious to make arrangements to avoid being in default. Ask for a specific date on which you can expect your application to be approved.

If your loan is not past due and you can continue to make payments while you're waiting for your deferment to come through, do so. Making payments will ensure that you don't slip into default while you're trying to get the official sanction to postpone your loan payments. You can also request a forbearance for up to 60 days while you are waiting for a response to your deferment application.

If you're curious about what a deferment form looks like, take a peek at the sample forms below. These are deferment requests for federal direct loans or federal loans obtained from a financial institution when the student is enrolled in school.

IN-SCHOOL DEFERMENT REQUEST

Federal Family Education Loan Program

OMB No. 1845-0005
Form Approved
Exp. Date 06/30/2002

SCH

WARNING: Any person who knowingly makes a false statement or misrepresentation on this form or on any accompanying documents shall be subject to penalties which may include fines, imprisonment or both, under the U.S. Criminal Code and 20 U.S.C. §1097.

SECTION 1: BORROWER IDENTIFICATION

Please correct or, if information is missing, enter below. If a correction, check this box: ❏

SSN | | | | – | | | – | | | | |

Name _____

Address _____

City, State, Zip _____

Telephone - Home ( ) _____

Telephone - Other ( ) _____

SECTION 2: DEFERMENT REQUEST

Before answering any questions, carefully read the entire form, including the instructions and other information in Sections 5 and 6.

■ I meet the qualifications for the deferment checked below and request that my loan holder defer repayment of my loan(s):

❏ While I am enrolled at an eligible school as a **FULL-TIME STUDENT**. (For borrowers with any FFEL Program loan.)

❏ While I am enrolled at an eligible school as a **LESS THAN FULL-TIME BUT AT LEAST HALF-TIME STUDENT**. (For borrowers who, on the date they signed the promissory note, did not have an outstanding balance on a FFEL Program loan made before July 1, 1987.)

NOTE: Your promissory note or other loan documents may state that a borrower with an outstanding balance on a FFEL Program loan made prior to July 1, 1993 must receive another loan in order to qualify for a half-time student deferment. This requirement was eliminated by the Higher Education Amendments of 1998. Effective October 1, 1998, no FFEL Program borrower who is eligible for a deferment based on enrollment as at least a half-time student is required to receive another loan in order to qualify for this deferment.

SECTION 3: BORROWER UNDERSTANDINGS AND CERTIFICATIONS

■ **I understand that: (1)** Principal payments will be deferred, but if I have an unsubsidized loan, I am responsible for paying the interest that accrues. **(2)** I have the option of making interest payments on my unsubsidized loan(s) during my deferment. I may choose to make interest payments by checking the box below; unpaid interest that accrues will be capitalized by my loan holder.

❏ I wish to make interest payments on my unsubsidized loan(s) during my deferment.

(3) My deferment will begin on the date the deferment condition began, but no more than six months before the date my loan holder receives this request. **(4)** My deferment will end on the earlier of the date that the condition that establishes my deferment eligibility ends or the certified deferment end date. **(5)** My loan holder will not grant this deferment request unless all applicable sections of this form are completed and any required additional documentation is provided. **(6)** If my deferment does not cover all my past due payments, my loan holder may grant me a forbearance for all payments due before the begin date of my deferment or — if the period for which I am eligible for a deferment has ended — a forbearance for all payments due at the time my deferment request is processed. **(7)** If I am eligible for a post-deferment grace period on loans made before October 1, 1981, my loan holder may grant me a forbearance on my other loans for this period so that I can begin repayment of all my loans at the same time. I understand that my loan holder may capitalize the interest that accrues on my other loans during the six-month period and that this will increase the principal balance of my other loans. **(8)** My loan holder may grant me a forbearance on my loans for up to 60 days, if necessary, for the collection and processing of documentation related to my deferment request. Interest that accrues during the forbearance will not be capitalized.

■ **I certify that: (1)** The information I provided in Sections 1 and 2 above is true and correct. **(2)** I will provide additional documentation to my loan holder, as required, to support my deferment status. **(3)** I will notify my loan holder immediately when the condition(s) that qualified me for the deferment ends. **(4)** I have read, understand, and meet the eligibility criteria of the deferment for which I have applied.

Borrower's Signature _____ Date _____

SECTION 4: AUTHORIZED OFFICIAL'S CERTIFICATION

NOTE: As an alternative to completing this section, the school may attach its own enrollment certification report listing the required information.

I certify, to the best of my knowledge and belief, that the borrower named above:

(1) is/was enrolled as (check the appropriate box)   ❏ a full-time student   ❏ at least a half-time student

during the academic period from | | – | | – | | | | to | | – | | – | | | | and

(2) is reasonably expected to complete his/her program requirements on | | – | | – | | | | .

Name of Institution _____   OPE-ID _____

Address _____   City, State, Zip _____

Name/Title of Authorized Official _____   Telephone ( ) _____

Authorized Official's Signature _____   **Date** _____

Page 1 of 2

SECTION 5: INSTRUCTIONS FOR COMPLETING THE FORM

Type or print using dark ink. Report dates as month-day-year (MM-DD-YYYY). For example, 'January 1, 1999' = '01-01-1999'. An authorized school official must either (A) complete Section 4, or (B) attach the school's own enrollment certification report listing the required information. If you need help completing this form, contact your loan holder.

Return the completed form and any required documentation to the address shown in Section 7.

SECTION 6: DEFINITIONS FOR IN-SCHOOL DEFERMENT REQUEST

Definitions

■ The **Federal Family Education Loan (FFEL) Program** includes Federal Stafford Loans (both subsidized and unsubsidized), Federal Supplemental Loans for Students (SLS), Federal PLUS Loans, and Federal Consolidation Loans.

■ A **deferment** is a period during which I am entitled to postpone repayment of the principal balance of my loan(s). The federal government pays the interest that accrues during an eligible deferment for all subsidized Federal Stafford Loans and for Federal Consolidation Loans for which the Consolidation loan application was received by my loan holder **(1)** on or after January 1, 1993 but before August 10, 1993, **(2)** on or after August 10, 1993, if it includes *only* Federal Stafford Loans that were eligible for federal interest subsidy, or **(3)** on or after November 13, 1997, for that portion of the Consolidation loan that paid a subsidized Federal Stafford Loan or a Federal Direct Stafford/Ford (Direct Subsidized) Loan. I am responsible for the interest that accrues during this period on all other FFEL Program loans.

■ **Forbearance** means permitting the temporary cessation of payments, allowing an extension of time for making payments, or temporarily accepting smaller payments than previously scheduled. I am responsible for paying the interest on my loan(s) during a forbearance.

■ The **holder** of my FFEL Program loan(s) may be a lender, guaranty agency, secondary market, or the U.S. Department of Education.

■ **Capitalization** is the addition of unpaid interest to the principal balance of my loan. This will increase the principal and the total cost of my loan.

■ An **authorized certifying official** for an In-School Deferment is an authorized official of the school where I am/was enrolled as a full-time or at least half-time student.

SECTION 7: WHERE TO SEND THE COMPLETED DEFERMENT REQUEST

RETURN THE COMPLETED DEFERMENT REQUEST AND ANY REQUIRED DOCUMENTATION TO:
(IF NO ADDRESS IS SHOWN, RETURN TO YOUR LOAN HOLDER)

SECTION 8: IMPORTANT NOTICES

Privacy Act Disclosure Notice

The Privacy Act of 1974 (5 U.S.C. §552a) requires that we disclose to you the following information:

The authority for collecting this information is §421 *et seq.* of the Higher Education Act of 1965, as amended (the HEA) (20 U.S.C. §1071 to 1087-2). The principal purpose for collecting this information is to determine whether you are eligible for a deferment on your loan(s) under the Federal Family Education Loan (FFEL) Program.

We ask that you provide the information requested on this deferment request on a voluntary basis. However, you must provide all of the requested information so that the holder(s) of your loan(s) can determine whether you qualify for a deferment.

The information in your file may be disclosed to third parties as authorized under routine uses in the Privacy Act notices called "Title IV Program Files" (originally published on April 12, 1994, *Federal Register*, Vol. 59, p. 17351) and "National Student Loan Data System" (originally published on December 20, 1994, *Federal Register*, Vol. 59, p. 65532). Thus, this information may be disclosed to parties that we authorize to assist us in administering the federal student aid programs, including contractors that are required to maintain safeguards under the Privacy Act. Disclosures may also be made for verification of information, determination of eligibility, enforcement of conditions of the loan or grant, debt collection, and the prevention of fraud, waste, and abuse and these disclosures may be made through computer matching programs with other federal agencies. Disclosures may be made to determine the feasibility of entering into computer matching agreements. We may send information to members of Congress if you ask them in writing to help you with federal student aid questions. If we are involved in litigation, we may send information to the Department of Justice (DOJ), a court, adjudicative body, counsel, or witness if the disclosure is related to financial aid and certain other conditions are met. If this information, either alone or with other information, indicates a potential violation of law, we may send it to the appropriate authority for consideration of action and we may disclose to DOJ to get its advice related to the Title IV, HEA programs or questions under the Freedom of Information Act. Disclosures may be made to qualified researchers under Privacy Act safeguards. In some circumstances involving employment decisions, grievances, or complaints or involving decisions regarding the letting of a contract or making of a grant, license, or other benefit, we may send information to an appropriate authority. In limited circumstances, we may disclose to a federal labor organization recognized under 5 U.S.C. Chapter 71.

Because we request your social security number (SSN), we must inform you that we collect your SSN on a voluntary basis, but section 484(a)(4) of the HEA (20 U.S.C. §1091(a)(4)) provides that, in order to receive any grant, loan, or work assistance under Title IV of the HEA, a student must provide his or her SSN. Your SSN is used to verify your identity, and as an account number (identifier) throughout the life of your loan(s) so that data may be recorded accurately.

Paperwork Reduction Notice

According to the Paperwork Reduction Act of 1995, no persons are required to respond to a collection of information unless it displays a currently valid OMB control number. The valid OMB control number for this information collection is 1845-0005. The time required to complete this information collection is estimated to average 0.16 hours (10 minutes) per response, including the time to review instructions, search existing data resources, gather and maintain the data needed, and complete and review the information collection. *If you have any comments concerning the accuracy of the time estimate(s) or suggestions for improving this form, please write to:*

U.S. Department of Education, Washington, DC 20202-4651.

If you have any comments or concerns regarding the status of your individual submission of this form, write directly to the address shown in Section 7.

ECONOMIC HARDSHIP DEFERMENT REQUEST

HRD

Federal Family Education Loan Program

USE THIS FORM ONLY IF **ALL** OF YOUR OUTSTANDING FEDERAL FAMILY EDUCATION LOAN PROGRAM LOANS WERE MADE ON OR AFTER JULY 1, 1993.

WARNING: Any person who knowingly makes a false statement or misrepresentation on this form or on any accompanying documents shall be subject to penalties which may include fines, imprisonment or both, under the U.S. Criminal Code and 20 U.S.C. §1097.

OMB No. 1845-0716
Form Approved
Exp. Date 06/30/2002

SECTION 1: BORROWER IDENTIFICATION

Please correct or, if information is missing, enter below. If a correction, check this box: ☐

SSN |___|___|___| – |___|___| – |___|___|___|___|

Name _____

Address _____

City, State, Zip _____

Telephone - Home ( ) _____

Telephone - Other ( ) _____

SECTION 2: DEFERMENT REQUEST

Before answering any questions, carefully read the entire form, including the instructions and other information in Sections 4, 5, and 6.

■ I meet the qualifications stated in Section 6 for the Economic Hardship Deferment checked below and request that my loan holder defer repayment of my loan(s) beginning |___|___| – |___|___| – |___|___|___|___|. To qualify, I must meet **one** of the conditions listed below and must provide the required documentation, as described in Section 6, for only that condition. *Check one:*

(1) ☐ I have been granted an economic hardship deferment under the William D. Ford Federal Direct Loan (Direct Loan) Program or the Federal Perkins Loan Program for the same period of time for which I am requesting this deferment. **I have attached documentation of the deferment.**

(2) ☐ I am receiving or received payments under a federal or state public assistance program, such as Aid to Families with Dependent Children (AFDC), Supplemental Security Income (SSI), Food Stamps, or state general public assistance. **I have attached documentation of these payments.**

(3) ☐ I am serving as a Peace Corps volunteer. **I have attached documentation certifying my period of service in the Peace Corps.**

(4) ☐ I work full-time **and** my total monthly gross income does not exceed the **larger of** (A) the Federal Minimum Wage Rate, or (B) the Poverty Line income for a family of two for my state (regardless of my actual family size), as listed below. **I have attached documentation of this income.**

My total monthly gross income is $ _____

   (A) Federal Minimum Wage Rate (monthly amount, based on $5.15 an hour) $ 892.66

   (B) Poverty Lines for a Family of Two (monthly amounts)
     • All states and the District of Columbia (except Alaska and Hawaii) $ 921.67
     • Alaska $1,153.33
     • Hawaii $1,060.83

(5) ☐ I do **not** work full-time **and** my total monthly gross income does not exceed the **larger of** (A) **two times** the Federal Minimum Wage Rate, or (B) **two times** the Poverty Line income for a family of two for my state (regardless of my actual family size), as listed above under condition (4). In addition, after deducting the total monthly payments that I am making on all of my federal education debts from my total monthly gross income, the amount remaining does not exceed the **larger of** (A) the Federal Minimum Wage Rate, or (B) the Poverty Line income for a family of two for my state, as listed above under condition (4). My total monthly federal education debt payments must be adjusted, if necessary, to reflect a minimum 10-year repayment period. **I have attached documentation of my total monthly gross income and my federal education loan debt.**

NOTE: A worksheet to help you determine whether you meet this condition is available from your loan holder. Completion of the worksheet is optional. Your loan holder will determine whether you qualify based on the income and education debt information that you provide below.

My total monthly gross income is $ _____

The total amount I borrowed for all of my federal education loans now in repayment (including loans for which I am requesting this deferment) is $ _____

(6) ☐ I work full-time **and** the total amount of my annual payments on all of my federal education loans in repayment is equal to or larger than 20% of my adjusted gross income. In addition, after deducting the total amount of my annual payments on my federal education loans in repayment from my adjusted gross income, the amount remaining must be less than 220% of the **larger of** (A) the Federal Minimum Wage rate, or (B) the Poverty Line income for a family of two for my state (regardless of my actual family size), as listed below. My total annual federal education loan payments must be adjusted, if necessary, to reflect a minimum 10-year repayment period. **I have attached documentation of my adjusted gross income and my federal education loan debt.**

NOTE: A worksheet to help you determine whether you meet this condition is available from your loan holder. Completion of the worksheet is optional. Your loan holder will determine whether you qualify based on the income and education debt information that you provide below.

My adjusted gross income is $ _____

The total amount I borrowed for all of my federal education loans now in repayment (including loans for which I am requesting this deferment) is $ _____

   (A) Federal Minimum Wage Rate (annual amount, based on $5.15 an hour) $10,712.00

   (B) Poverty Lines for a Family of Two (annual amounts)
     • All states and the District of Columbia (except Alaska and Hawaii) $11,060.00
     • Alaska $13,840.00
     • Hawaii $12,730.00

SECTION 3: BORROWER INTEREST SELECTION AND CERTIFICATION

■ Principal payments will be deferred, but if I have an unsubsidized loan, I am responsible for paying the interest that accrues. I have the option of making interest payments on my unsubsidized loan(s) during my deferment. I may choose to make interest payments by checking the box below; unpaid interest that accrues will be capitalized by my loan holder.

   ☐ I wish to make interest payments on my unsubsidized loan(s) during my deferment.

■ **I certify that** the information I provided in Sections 1 and 2 above is true and correct, and that I have read, understand, and meet the terms and conditions and eligibility criteria of the deferment for which I have applied, as explained in Section 6.

Borrower's Signature _____ **Date** _____

Page 1 of 3

SECTION 4: INSTRUCTIONS FOR COMPLETING THE FORM

Type or print using dark ink. Report dates as month-day-year (MM-DD-YYYY). For example, 'January 1, 1999' = '01-01-1999'. Include your name and social security number (SSN) on any documentation that you are required to submit with this form. If you need help completing this form, contact your loan holder.

Return the completed form and any required documentation to the address shown in Section 7.

SECTION 5: DEFINITIONS

■ The **Federal Family Education Loan (FFEL) Program** includes Federal Stafford Loans (both subsidized and unsubsidized), Federal Supplemental Loans for Students (SLS), Federal PLUS Loans, and Federal Consolidation Loans.

■ The **William D. Ford Federal Direct Loan (Direct Loan) Program** includes Federal Direct Stafford/Ford (Direct Subsidized) Loans, Federal Direct Unsubsidized Stafford/Ford (Direct Unsubsidized) Loans, Federal Direct PLUS (Direct PLUS) Loans, and Federal Direct Consolidation (Direct Consolidation) Loans.

■ The **holder** of my FFEL Program loan(s) may be a lender, guaranty agency, secondary market, or the U.S. Department of Education.

■ A **deferment** is a period during which I am entitled to postpone repayment of the principal balance of my loan(s). The federal government pays the interest that accrues during an eligible deferment for all subsidized Federal Stafford Loans and for Federal Consolidation Loans for which the Consolidation loan application was received by my loan holder **(1)** on or after January 1, 1993 but before August 10, 1993, **(2)** on or after August 10, 1993, if it includes **only** Federal Stafford Loans that were eligible for federal interest subsidy, or **(3)** on or after November 13, 1997, for that portion of the Consolidation loan that paid a subsidized Federal Stafford Loan or a Federal Direct Stafford/Ford (Direct Subsidized) Loan. I am responsible for the interest that accrues during this period on all other FFEL Program loans.

■ **Monthly gross income** is the amount of my monthly income from my employment (either full-time or part-time) or any other source before taxes and other deductions.

■ **Adjusted gross income** means the amount recorded on my Federal Income Tax Return as adjusted gross income.

■ **Full-time** employment is defined as working at least 30 hours per week in a position expected to last at least three consecutive months.

■ Eligible **federal education loans** that may be included in determining the total amount I borrowed for deferment conditions (5) and (6) in Section 2 are listed below. I may include defaulted loans only if I have made satisfactory repayment arrangements with the holder of those loans.

• All **FFEL Program** loans listed above	• National Direct Student Loans (NDSL)	• Health Professions Student Loans (HPSL)
• All **Direct Loan Program** loans listed above	• National Defense Student Loans (NDSL)	• Loans for Disadvantaged Students (LDS)
• Guaranteed Student Loans (GSL)	• Auxiliary Loans to Assist Students (ALAS)	• Primary Care Loans (PCL)
• Federal Insured Student Loans (FISL)	• Parent Loans for Undergraduate Students (PLUS)	• Nursing Student Loans (NSL)
• Federal Perkins Loans	• Health Education Assistance Loans (HEAL)	

■ **Minimum 10-year repayment period** (for deferment conditions (5) and (6) in Section 2) refers to the period that is 10 years from the date I entered repayment, regardless of the actual length of my repayment schedule. If the length of my repayment schedule is more than 10 years, my payment amounts must be adjusted to show the estimated monthly or annual amount that I would owe if my loan were scheduled to be repaid in fixed installments within a 10-year period.

■ **Forbearance** means permitting the temporary cessation of payments, allowing an extension of time for making payments, or temporarily accepting smaller payments than previously scheduled. I am responsible for paying the interest on my loan(s) during a forbearance.

■ **Capitalization** is the addition of unpaid interest to the principal balance of my loan. This will increase the principal and the total cost of my loan.

SECTION 6: ELIGIBILITY CRITERIA / TERMS AND CONDITIONS FOR ECONOMIC HARDSHIP DEFERMENT

■ If **ALL** of my outstanding FFEL Program loans were made **on or after July 1, 1993**, I may defer repayment of my loan(s) while I meet one of the economic hardship conditions listed in Section 2.

■ If my economic hardship deferment eligibility is based on condition (1), as described in Section 2, I must provide my loan holder with documentation of the deferment that has been granted under the Direct Loan Program or the Federal Perkins Loan Program (for example, correspondence from my loan holder showing that I have been granted a deferment).

■ If my economic hardship deferment eligibility is based on condition (2), as described in Section 2, I must provide my loan holder with documentation confirming that I am receiving or received payments under a federal or state public assistance program.

■ If my economic hardship deferment eligibility is based on condition (3), as described in Section 2, I must provide my loan holder with documentation which certifies the beginning and anticipated ending dates of my service in the Peace Corps and which is signed and dated by an authorized Peace Corps official.

■ If my economic hardship deferment eligibility is based on condition (4), as described in Section 2, I must provide my loan holder with documentation of my most recent monthly gross income from all sources, such as pay stubs.

■ If my economic hardship deferment eligibility is based on condition (5) or condition (6), as described in Section 2, I must provide my loan holder with:

• documentation of my most recent total monthly gross income from all sources, such as pay stubs (for condition 5 only);

• documentation of my adjusted gross income (a copy of my Federal Income Tax Return — for condition 6 only); and

• documentation of the total amount I borrowed for all federal education loans that are now in repayment, such as disclosure statements or current repayment schedules. This must include the monthly payment amount, beginning loan balance, and repayment terms.

• If my total federal education loan debt includes defaulted loans, I must provide documentation that I have made satisfactory repayment arrangements with the holder of the defaulted loans.

■ If my economic hardship deferment eligibility is based on conditions (4), (5), or (6), as described in Section 2, and I am applying for an additional period of economic hardship deferment that begins less than one year after the end of my previous period of economic hardship deferment, I must provide my loan holder with a copy of my latest federal income tax return (if one was filed within the preceding eight months), in addition to the other documentation required for these conditions.

■ If my economic hardship deferment eligibility is based on conditions (4), (5), or (6), as described in Section 2, and I am not currently residing in the United States, I will use the Poverty Line amounts for my last state of residence in the United States.

Section 6 continued on Page 3.

Page 2 of 3

SECTION 6 (Continued)

■ I will provide additional documentation to my loan holder, as required, to support my deferment status.

■ I will notify my loan holder immediately when the condition that qualified me for the deferment ends.

■ My deferment will begin on the date the deferment condition began, but no more than six months before the date my loan holder receives this request.

■ My deferment will end on the earlier of the date that the condition that establishes my deferment eligibility ends or the certified deferment end date.

■ My maximum cumulative eligibility for an economic hardship deferment is 36 months. Except for a deferment based on condition (3), as described in Section 2, I must reapply every 12 months if I continue to meet the criteria for an economic hardship deferment.

■ My loan holder will not grant this deferment request unless all applicable sections of this form are completed and any additional required documentation is provided.

■ If my deferment does not cover all my past due payments, my loan holder may grant me a forbearance for all payments due before the begin date of my deferment. If the period for which I am eligible for a deferment has ended, my loan holder may grant me a forbearance for all payments due at the time my deferment request is processed.

■ My loan holder may grant me a forbearance on my loans for up to 60 days, if necessary, for the collection and processing of documentation related to my deferment request. Interest that accrues during the forbearance will not be capitalized.

SECTION 7: WHERE TO SEND THE COMPLETED DEFERMENT REQUEST

RETURN THE COMPLETED DEFERMENT REQUEST AND ANY REQUIRED DOCUMENTATION TO:
(IF NO ADDRESS IS SHOWN, RETURN TO YOUR LOAN HOLDER)

SECTION 8: IMPORTANT NOTICES

Privacy Act Disclosure Notice

The Privacy Act of 1974 (5 U.S.C. §552a) requires that we disclose to you the following information:

The authority for collecting this information is §421 *et seq.* of the Higher Education Act of 1965, as amended (the HEA) (20 U.S.C. §1071 to 1087-2). The principal purpose for collecting this information is to determine whether you are eligible for a deferment on your loan(s) under the Federal Family Education Loan (FFEL) Program.

We ask that you provide the information requested on this deferment request on a voluntary basis. However, you must provide all of the requested information so that the holder(s) of your loan(s) can determine whether you qualify for a deferment.

The information in your file may be disclosed to third parties as authorized under routine uses in the Privacy Act notices called "Title IV Program Files" (originally published on April 12, 1994, *Federal Register*, Vol. 59, p. 17351) and "National Student Loan Data System" (originally published on December 20, 1994, *Federal Register*, Vol. 59, p. 65532). Thus, this information may be disclosed to parties that we authorize to assist us in administering the federal student aid programs, including contractors that are required to maintain safeguards under the Privacy Act. Disclosures may also be made for verification of information, determination of eligibility, enforcement of conditions of the loan or grant, debt collection, and the prevention of fraud, waste, and abuse and these disclosures may be made through computer matching programs with other federal agencies. Disclosures may be made to determine the feasibility of entering into computer matching agreements. We may send information to members of Congress if you ask them in writing to help you with federal student aid questions. If we are involved in litigation, we may send information to the Department of Justice (DOJ), a court, adjudicative body, counsel, or witness if the disclosure is related to financial aid and certain other conditions are met. If this information, either alone or with other information, indicates a potential violation of law, we may send it to the appropriate authority for consideration of action and we may disclose to DOJ to get its advice related to the Title IV, HEA programs or questions under the Freedom of Information Act. Disclosures may be made to qualified researchers under Privacy Act safeguards. In some circumstances involving employment decisions, grievances, or complaints or involving decisions regarding the letting of a contract or making of a grant, license, or other benefit, we may send information to an appropriate authority. In limited circumstances, we may disclose to a federal labor organization recognized under 5 U.S.C. Chapter 71.

Because we request your social security number (SSN), we must inform you that we collect your SSN on a voluntary basis, but section 484(a)(4) of the HEA (20 U.S.C. §1091(a)(4)) provides that, in order to receive any grant, loan, or work assistance under Title IV of the HEA, a student must provide his or her SSN. Your SSN is used to verify your identity, and as an account number (identifier) throughout the life of your loan(s) so that data may be recorded accurately.

Paperwork Reduction Notice

According to the Paperwork Reduction Act of 1995, no persons are required to respond to a collection of information unless it displays a currently valid OMB control number. The valid OMB control number for this information collection is 1845-0716. The time required to complete this information collection is estimated to average 0.16 hours (10 minutes) per response, including the time to review instructions, search existing data resources, gather and maintain the data needed, and complete and review the information collection. *If you have any comments concerning the accuracy of the time estimate(s) or suggestions for improving this form, please write to:*

U.S. Department of Education, Washington, DC 20202-4651.

If you have any comments or concerns regarding the status of your individual submission of this form, write directly to the address shown in Section 7.

ECONOMIC HARDSHIP DEFERMENT
WORKSHEET A

Use this worksheet to determine if you are eligible for an economic hardship deferment based on condition (5) in Section 2 of the Economic Hardship Deferment Request form. Completion of this worksheet is optional — if you check condition (5), your loan holder will determine your eligibility based on the income and federal education debt documentation that you provide.

DO NOT RETURN THIS WORKSHEET WITH THE DEFERMENT REQUEST — KEEP IT FOR YOUR RECORDS.

STEP 1

Are you working full-time?

❏ Yes   You do not qualify for an economic hardship deferment based on condition (5). Do not continue with this worksheet.

❏ No   Go to Step 2.

STEP 2

(1) Line 1. Enter the amount listed below for your state: $ _____

(2) Line 2. $ ____1,785.32____

(3) Line 3. Enter the **larger** of Line 1 or Line 2: $ _____

(4) Line 4. Enter your **TOTAL MONTHLY GROSS INCOME**: $ _____

(5) Is the amount on Line 4 **larger** than the amount on Line 3?

❏ Yes   You do not qualify for an economic hardship deferment based on condition (5). Do not continue with this worksheet.

❏ No   Go to Step 3.

Amounts for Line 1, above:

$1,843.34   (if you live in any state or the District of Columbia, *except* Alaska or Hawaii)

$2,306.66   (if you live in Alaska)

$2,121.66   (if you live in Hawaii)

NOTE: *If you are not currently living in the United States, use the amount for your last state of residence in the United States.*

STEP 3

Determine the total amount you borrowed in federal education loans that are now in repayment by adding together the amounts owed for the federal education loans listed below. You may include defaulted loans only if you have made satisfactory repayment arrangements with the holder of the loans.

Loan Type	Total Amount You Owed When Your Loans Entered Repayment
Federal Stafford Loans (subsidized and unsubsidized)	$ _____
Direct Subsidized and Direct Unsubsidized Loans	+ $ _____
Federal PLUS Loans	+ $ _____
Direct PLUS Loans	+ $ _____
Federal SLS Loans	+ $ _____
Federal Consolidation Loans	+ $ _____
Direct Consolidation Loans	+ $ _____
Federal Perkins Loans and/or National Direct Student Loans	+ $ _____
Other eligible federal education loans listed in Section 5	+ $ _____
TOTAL AMOUNT BORROWED:	= $ _____

Worksheet A continued on Page 2.

Worksheet A
Page 1 of 2

ECONOMIC HARDSHIP DEFERMENT

WORKSHEET A (Continued)

STEP 4

(1) Circle the current interest rate for your FFEL Program loan(s) in the chart below. If your exact interest rate is not listed, choose the next highest interest rate. If you have loans with different interest rates, circle the rate for the loan with the highest interest rate.

Interest Rate	7.0%	7.25%	7.43%	7.5%	7.75%	8.0%	8.25%	8.38%	8.5%	8.75%	9.0%
Constant Multiplier	.0116108	.0117401	.0118337	.0118702	.0120011	.0121328	.0122653	.0123345	.0123986	.0125237	.0126676

(2) Multiply the **TOTAL AMOUNT BORROWED** from Step 3 by the constant multiplier listed directly below the interest rate that you circled in the chart above:

TOTAL AMOUNT BORROWED (from Step 3)		**Constant multiplier** (from the chart above)		**ESTIMATED MONTHLY PAYMENT***
$ _____	X	_____	=	$ _____

* This is an estimate of the amount that you would pay each month on your federal education loans if all of your loans were scheduled to be repaid in fixed installments over a 10-year period, regardless of the actual repayment period for your loans.

STEP 5

(1) Line 1. Enter your **TOTAL MONTHLY GROSS INCOME** (from Step 2): $ _____

(2) Line 2. Enter your **ESTIMATED MONTHLY PAYMENT** (from Step 4): $ _____

(3) Line 3. Subtract Line 2 from Line 1: $ _____

(4) Line 4. Enter the amount listed below for your state: $ _____

(5) Line 5. $ 892.66

(6) Line 6. Enter the **larger** of Line 4 or Line 5: $ _____

(7) Line 7. Enter the amount from Line 3: $ _____

(8) Is the amount on Line 7 larger than the amount on Line 6?

    ☐   Yes   You do not qualify for an economic hardship deferment based on condition (5).

    ☐   No   You meet the qualifications for an economic hardship deferment based on condition (5). Check the box for condition (5) in Section 2 of the deferment request.

Amounts for Line 4, above:

$ 921.67   (if you live in any state or the District of Columbia, *except* Alaska or Hawaii).

$1,153.33   (if you live in Alaska)

$1,060.83   (if you live in Hawaii)

NOTE: *If you are not currently living in the United States, use the amount for your last state of residence in the United States.*

ECONOMIC HARDSHIP DEFERMENT
WORKSHEET B

Use this worksheet to determine if you are eligible for an economic hardship deferment based on condition (6) in Section 2 of the Economic Hardship Deferment Request form. Completion of this worksheet is optional — if you check condition (6), your loan holder will determine your eligibility based on the income and federal education debt documentation that you provide.

DO NOT RETURN THIS WORKSHEET WITH THE DEFERMENT REQUEST — KEEP IT FOR YOUR RECORDS.

STEP 1

Are you working full-time?

❒ Yes   Go to Step 2.

❒ No   You do not qualify for an economic hardship deferment based on condition (6). Do not continue with this worksheet.

STEP 2

Determine the total amount you borrowed in federal education loans that are now in repayment by adding together the amounts owed for the federal education loans listed below. You may include defaulted loans only if you have made satisfactory repayment arrangements with the holder of the loans.

Loan Type	Total Amount You Owed When Your Loans Entered Repayment
Federal Stafford Loans (subsidized and unsubsidized)	$ _____
Direct Subsidized and Direct Unsubsidized Loans	+ $ _____
Federal PLUS Loans	+ $ _____
Direct PLUS Loans	+ $ _____
Federal SLS Loans	+ $ _____
Federal Consolidation Loans	+ $ _____
Direct Consolidation Loans	+ $ _____
Federal Perkins Loans and/or National Direct Student Loans	+ $ _____
Other eligible federal education loans listed in Section 5	+ $ _____
TOTAL AMOUNT BORROWED:	= $ _____

STEP 3

(1) Circle the current interest rate for your FFEL Program loan(s) in the chart below. If your exact interest rate is not listed, choose the next highest interest rate. If you have loans with different interest rates, circle the rate for the loan with the highest interest rate.

Interest Rate	7.0%	7.25%	7.43%	7.5%	7.75%	8.0%	8.25%	8.38%	8.5%	8.75%	9.0%
Constant Multiplier	.0116108	.0117401	.0118337	.0118702	.0120011	.0121328	.0122653	.0123345	.0123986	.0125237	.0126676

(2) Multiply the **TOTAL AMOUNT BORROWED** from Step 3 by the constant multiplier listed directly below the interest rate that you circled in the chart above:

TOTAL AMOUNT BORROWED (from Step 3)		**Constant multiplier** (from the chart above)		**Estimated monthly payment**
$ _____	X	_____	=	$ _____

(3) Multiply the estimated monthly payment (from the line above) by 12:

Estimated monthly payment				**ESTIMATED ANNUAL PAYMENT** *
$ _____	X	12	=	$ _____

* This is an estimate of the amount that you would pay each year on your federal education loans if all of your loans were scheduled to be repaid in fixed installments over a 10-year period, regardless of the actual repayment period for your loans.

Worksheet B continued on Page 2.

Worksheet B
Page 1 of 2

ECONOMIC HARDSHIP DEFERMENT
WORKSHEET B (Continued)

STEP 4

(1) Line 1. Enter your adjusted gross income: $ _____

(2) Line 2. Multiply the amount on Line 1 by .20 (= 20%): $ _____

(3) Line 3. Enter your **ESTIMATED ANNUAL PAYMENT** (from Step 3): $ _____

(4) Is the amount on Line 3 **equal to or larger than** the amount on Line 2?

    ❐ Yes   Go to Step 5.

    ❐ No   You do not qualify for an economic hardship deferment based on condition (6). Do not continue with this worksheet.

STEP 5

(1) Line 1. Enter your adjusted gross income: $ _____

(2) Line 2. Enter your **ESTIMATED ANNUAL PAYMENT** (from Step 3): $ _____

(3) Line 3. Subtract Line 2 from Line 1: $ _____

(4) Line 4. Enter the amount listed below for your state: $ _____

(5) Line 5. $ ___23,566.00___

(6) Line 6. Enter the **larger** of Line 4 or Line 5: $ _____

(7) Line 7. Enter the amount from Line 3: $ _____

(8) Is the amount on Line 7 **less than** the amount on line 6?

    ❐ Yes   You meet the qualifications for an economic hardship deferment based on condition (6). Check the box for condition (6) in Section 2 of the deferment request.

    ❐ No   You do not qualify for an economic hardship deferment based on condition (6).

Amounts for Line 4, above:

$24,332.00 (if you live in any state or the District of Columbia, *except* Alaska or Hawaii)

$30,448.00 (if you live in Alaska)

$28,006.00 (if you live in Hawaii)

NOTE: *If you are not currently living in the United States, use the amount for your last state of residence in the United States.*

Worksheet B
Page 2 of 2

EDUCATION RELATED DEFERMENT REQUEST

Federal Family Education Loan Program

OMB No. 1845-0005
Form Approved
Exp. Date 06/30/2002

EDU

WARNING: Any person who knowingly makes a false statement or misrepresentation on this form or on any accompanying documents shall be subject to penalties which may include fines, imprisonment or both, under the U.S. Criminal Code and 20 U.S.C. §1097.

SECTION 1: BORROWER IDENTIFICATION

Please correct or, if information is missing, enter below. If a correction, check this box: ❑

SSN |___|___|___| – |___|___| – |___|___|___|___|

Name _____

Address _____

City, State, Zip _____

Telephone - Home ( ) _____

Telephone - Other ( ) _____

SECTION 2: DEFERMENT REQUEST

Before answering any questions, carefully read the entire form, including the instructions and other information in Sections 5 and 6.

■ I meet the qualifications stated in Section 6 for the deferment checked below and request that my loan holder defer repayment of my loan(s):

For all FFEL Program borrowers:

❑ While I am engaged in a full-time course of study in a **GRADUATE FELLOWSHIP** program.

❑ While I am engaged in a full-time **REHABILITATION TRAINING** program.

For borrowers with an outstanding balance on at least one FFEL Program loan that was made before July 1, 1993:

❑ While I am engaged in an **INTERNSHIP/RESIDENCY*** program at the following type of institution (check the appropriate box):

   ❑ Institution of higher education, hospital, or health care facility.

   ❑ Any other institution or organization. Name of Internship/Residency program _____ .

* Federal PLUS Loans qualify for INTERNSHIP/RESIDENCY deferments only if they were made **before August 15, 1983**.

❑ While I am teaching in a designated **TEACHER SHORTAGE AREA.****

Only Federal Stafford and SLS borrowers whose first loans were made **on or after July 1, 1987 and before July 1, 1993 are eligible for TEACHER SHORTAGE AREA deferments.

SECTION 3: BORROWER UNDERSTANDINGS AND CERTIFICATIONS

■ **I understand that: (1)** Principal payments will be deferred, but if I have an unsubsidized loan, I am responsible for paying the interest that accrues. **(2)** I have the option of making interest payments on my unsubsidized loan(s) during my deferment. I may choose to make interest payments by checking the box below; unpaid interest that accrues will be capitalized by my loan holder.

❑ I wish to make interest payments on my unsubsidized loan(s) during my deferment.

(3) My deferment will begin on the date the deferment condition began, but no more than six months before the date my loan holder receives this request. **(4)** My deferment will end on the earlier of the date that the condition that establishes my deferment eligibility ends or the certified deferment end date. **(5)** My loan holder will not grant this deferment request unless all applicable sections of this form are completed and any required additional documentation is provided. **(6)** If my deferment does not cover all my past due payments, my loan holder may grant me a forbearance for all payments due before the begin date of my deferment or — if the period for which I am eligible for a deferment has ended — a forbearance for all payments due at the time my deferment request is processed. **(7)** If I have used all 24 months allowed for an INTERNSHIP/RESIDENCY Deferment, I can apply for a forbearance for up to 12 months at a time for the remainder of my internship/residency program. **(8)** If I am eligible for a post-deferment grace period on loans made before October 1, 1981, my loan holder may grant me a forbearance on my other loans for this period so that I can begin repayment of all my loans at the same time. I understand that my loan holder may capitalize the interest that accrues on my other loans during the six-month period and that this will increase the principal balance of my other loans. **(9)** My loan holder may grant me a forbearance on my loans for up to 60 days, if necessary, for the collection and processing of documentation related to my deferment request. Interest that accrues during the forbearance will not be capitalized.

■ **I certify that: (1)** The information I provided in Sections 1 and 2 above is true and correct. **(2)** I will provide additional documentation to my loan holder, as required, to support my deferment status. **(3)** I will notify my loan holder immediately when the condition(s) that qualified me for the deferment ends. **(4)** I have read, understand, and meet the eligibility criteria of the deferment for which I have applied, as explained in Section 6.

Borrower's Signature _____ **Date** _____

SECTION 4: AUTHORIZED OFFICIAL'S CERTIFICATION

I certify, to the best of my knowledge and belief, that the borrower named above is/was engaged in the program/teaching service indicated in Section 2, and that the borrower and the borrower's program/teaching service meet all of the eligibility requirements specified in Section 6. The borrower's program/teaching service begins/began on |___|___| – |___|___| – |___|___|___|___| and is expected to end/ended on |___|___| – |___|___| – |___|___|___|___| .

Teacher Shortage Area Deferment Only

The borrower is/was teaching in (area/curriculum) _____, which is a shortage area designated by the U.S. Secretary of Education for the state of _____ for the school year beginning on |___|___| – |___|___| – |___|___|___|___| and ending on |___|___| – |___|___| – |___|___|___|___| . The borrower is/was teaching grade level _____ .

Name of Institution _____ OPE-ID (if applicable) _____

Address _____ City, State, Zip _____

Name/Title of Authorized Official _____ Telephone ( ) _____

Authorized Official's Signature _____ **Date** _____

Page 1 of 3

SECTION 5: INSTRUCTIONS FOR COMPLETING THE FORM

Type or print using dark ink. Report dates as month-day-year (MM-DD-YYYY). For example, 'January 1, 1999' = '01-01-1999'. An authorized official must complete Section 4. If you need help completing this form, contact your loan holder.

Return the completed form and any required documentation to the address shown in Section 7.

SECTION 6: DEFINITIONS / ELIGIBILITY CRITERIA FOR EDUCATION RELATED DEFERMENT REQUEST

Definitions

■ The **Federal Family Education Loan (FFEL) Program** includes Federal Stafford Loans (both subsidized and unsubsidized), Federal Supplemental Loans for Students (SLS), Federal PLUS Loans, and Federal Consolidation Loans.

■ A **deferment** is a period during which I am entitled to postpone repayment of the principal balance of my loan(s). The federal government pays the interest that accrues during an eligible deferment for all subsidized Federal Stafford Loans and for Federal Consolidation Loans for which the Consolidation loan application was received by my loan holder **(1)** on or after January 1, 1993 but before August 10, 1993, **(2)** on or after August 10, 1993, if it includes *only* Federal Stafford Loans that were eligible for federal interest subsidy, or **(3)** on or after November 13, 1997, for that portion of the Consolidation loan that paid a subsidized Federal Stafford Loan or a Federal Direct Stafford/Ford (Direct Subsidized) Loan. I am responsible for the interest that accrues during this period on all other FFEL Program loans.

■ **Forbearance** means permitting the temporary cessation of payments, allowing an extension of time for making payments, or temporarily accepting smaller payments than previously scheduled. I am responsible for paying the interest on my loan(s) during a forbearance.

■ The **holder** of my FFEL Program loan(s) may be a lender, guaranty agency, secondary market, or the U.S. Department of Education.

■ **Capitalization** is the addition of unpaid interest to the principal balance of my loan. This will increase the principal and the total cost of my loan.

■ **Authorized certifying officials**:

  • Authorized Graduate Fellowship Program Official

  • Rehabilitation Training Program Official

  • Internship/Residency Program Official (for all internships and residencies)

  • State Licensing Official (for internships required to begin professional practice or service)*

  • Chief School Administrator (for borrowers teaching in teacher shortage areas; additional certification may be required if the Chief State School Office has not provided a list of approved shortage areas to school administrators)

  * **NOTE**: Certification by a state licensing official, if required, must be provided on a separate statement attached to this form.

Eligibility Criteria

GRADUATE FELLOWSHIP and **REHABILITATION TRAINING** Deferments

I may defer repayment of my loan(s) while I am:

■ Engaged in a full-time course of study in a **GRADUATE FELLOWSHIP** program. To qualify: **(1)** My graduate fellowship program must **(a)** provide sufficient financial support to allow for full-time study for a period of at least six months; **(b)** require, prior to the awarding of financial support, a written statement from each applicant which explains the applicant's objectives; **(c)** require a graduate fellow to submit periodic reports, projects, or other evidence of the graduate fellow's progress, and **(d)** in the case of a course of study at a foreign university, accept the course of study for completion of the fellowship program. **(2)** I must **(a)** hold at least a Bachelor's Degree conferred by an institution of higher education, and **(b)** have been accepted or recommended by an institution of higher education for acceptance into the graduate fellowship program on a full-time basis. **(3)** If I am in a medical internship or residency program, I am not eligible for this deferment.

■ Engaged in a full-time **REHABILITATION TRAINING** program. To qualify, **(1)** My training program must: **(a)** be licensed, approved, certified or recognized as providing rehabilitation training to disabled individuals by the Department of Veterans Affairs or a state agency responsible for vocational rehabilitation, drug abuse treatment, mental health services, or alcohol abuse treatment programs; **(b)** provide services under a written individualized plan that specifies the date the services are expected to end; and **(c)** be structured in a way that requires a substantial commitment by me to my rehabilitation. ("Substantial commitment" means a commitment of time and effort that would normally prevent a person from being employed 30 or more hours per week in a position expected to last at least three months.) **(2)** I must be either receiving, or scheduled to receive, these rehabilitation services.

INTERNSHIP/RESIDENCY and **TEACHER SHORTAGE AREA** Deferments

To qualify:

■ I must have an outstanding balance on at least one FFEL Program loan which was made **before July 1, 1993**. If I am a Federal PLUS Loan borrower, **(1)** I am eligible for the INTERNSHIP/RESIDENCY Deferment only on PLUS loans made **before August 15, 1983**, and **(2)** I am not eligible for the TEACHER SHORTAGE AREA Deferment. I am eligible for the TEACHER SHORTAGE AREA deferment only if I am a Federal Stafford or SLS loan borrower whose first FFEL Program loan was made **on or after July 1, 1987 and before July 1, 1993**.

I may defer repayment of my loan(s) while I am:

■ Engaged in an **INTERNSHIP/RESIDENCY** program. (Maximum eligibility is two years; borrowers may request forbearance for the remainder of a medical or dental internship/residency program. Dental Interns/Residents are encouraged to apply for an IN-SCHOOL Deferment.) To qualify: **(1)** I must have been accepted into a medical or dental internship/residency program which must **(a)** be a supervised training program, and **(b)** require that I hold at least a Bachelor's Degree before acceptance into the program. **(2)** In addition, my program must either **(a)** lead to a degree or certificate from an institution of higher education, a hospital, or a health care facility that offers postgraduate training, or **(b)** be required before I may be certified for professional practice or service. **(3) If my program does not lead to a degree or certificate, but is required before I may be certified for professional practice or service, I must also provide (attached to this form) a separate statement from the appropriate state licensing agency certifying this requirement, in addition to the Authorized Official's Certification in Section 4.**

■ Teaching in a designated **TEACHER SHORTAGE AREA**. (Maximum eligibility is three years; borrowers must reapply each school year.) To qualify, I must teach full-time in a public or non-profit private elementary or secondary school in a geographic region, grade level, academic, instructional subject matter or discipline classified shortage area as defined by the U.S. Department of Education. (I will contact my Chief School Administrator or Chief State School Officer for a list of my state's shortage areas.) I may reapply for a continuation of this deferment even if my teaching area is no longer classified as a shortage area.

SECTION 7: WHERE TO SEND THE COMPLETED DEFERMENT REQUEST

RETURN THE COMPLETED DEFERMENT REQUEST AND ANY REQUIRED DOCUMENTATION TO:
(IF NO ADDRESS IS SHOWN, RETURN TO YOUR LOAN HOLDER)

SECTION 8: IMPORTANT NOTICES

Privacy Act Disclosure Notice

The Privacy Act of 1974 (5 U.S.C. §552a) requires that we disclose to you the following information:

The authority for collecting this information is §421 *et seq.* of the Higher Education Act of 1965, as amended (the HEA) (20 U.S.C. §1071 to 1087-2). The principal purpose for collecting this information is to determine whether you are eligible for a deferment on your loan(s) under the Federal Family Education Loan (FFEL) Program.

We ask that you provide the information requested on this deferment request on a voluntary basis. However, you must provide all of the requested information so that the holder(s) of your loan(s) can determine whether you qualify for a deferment.

The information in your file may be disclosed to third parties as authorized under routine uses in the Privacy Act notices called "Title IV Program Files" (originally published on April 12, 1994, *Federal Register*, Vol. 59, p. 17351) and "National Student Loan Data System" (originally published on December 20, 1994, *Federal Register*, Vol. 59, p. 65532). Thus, this information may be disclosed to parties that we authorize to assist us in administering the federal student aid programs, including contractors that are required to maintain safeguards under the Privacy Act. Disclosures may also be made for verification of information, determination of eligibility, enforcement of conditions of the loan or grant, debt collection, and the prevention of fraud, waste, and abuse and these disclosures may be made through computer matching programs with other federal agencies. Disclosures may be made to determine the feasibility of entering into computer matching agreements. We may send information to members of Congress if you ask them in writing to help you with federal student aid questions. If we are involved in litigation, we may send information to the Department of Justice (DOJ), a court, adjudicative body, counsel, or witness if the disclosure is related to financial aid and certain other conditions are met. If this information, either alone or with other information, indicates a potential violation of law, we may send it to the appropriate authority for consideration of action and we may disclose to DOJ to get its advice related to the Title IV, HEA programs or questions under the Freedom of Information Act. Disclosures may be made to qualified researchers under Privacy Act safeguards. In some circumstances involving employment decisions, grievances, or complaints or involving decisions regarding the letting of a contract or making of a grant, license, or other benefit, we may send information to an appropriate authority. In limited circumstances, we may disclose to a federal labor organization recognized under 5 U.S.C. Chapter 71.

Because we request your social security number (SSN), we must inform you that we collect your SSN on a voluntary basis, but section 484(a)(4) of the HEA (20 U.S.C. §1091(a)(4)) provides that, in order to receive any grant, loan, or work assistance under Title IV of the HEA, a student must provide his or her SSN. Your SSN is used to verify your identity, and as an account number (identifier) throughout the life of your loan(s) so that data may be recorded accurately.

Paperwork Reduction Notice

According to the Paperwork Reduction Act of 1995, no persons are required to respond to a collection of information unless it displays a currently valid OMB control number. The valid OMB control number for this information collection is 1845-0005. The time required to complete this information collection is estimated to average 0.16 hours (10 minutes) per response, including the time to review instructions, search existing data resources, gather and maintain the data needed, and complete and review the information collection. *If you have any comments concerning the accuracy of the time estimate(s) or suggestions for improving this form, please write to:*

U.S. Department of Education, Washington, DC 20202-4651.

If you have any comments or concerns regarding the status of your individual submission of this form, write directly to the address shown in Section 7.

TEMPORARY TOTAL DISABILITY DEFERMENT REQUEST
Federal Family Education Loan Program

USE THIS FORM ONLY IF YOU HAVE AN OUTSTANDING BALANCE ON A FEDERAL FAMILY EDUCATION LOAN PROGRAM LOAN THAT WAS MADE BEFORE JULY 1, 1993.

WARNING: Any person who knowingly makes a false statement or misrepresentation on this form or on any accompanying documents shall be subject to penalties which may include fines, imprisonment or both, under the U.S. Criminal Code and 20 U.S.C. §1097.

TDIS

OMB No. 1845-0005
Form Approved
Exp. Date 06/30/2002

SECTION 1: BORROWER IDENTIFICATION

Please correct or, if information is missing, enter below. If a correction, check this box: ☐

SSN ⎵⎵⎵ – ⎵⎵ – ⎵⎵⎵⎵

Name _____

Address _____

City, State, Zip _____

Telephone - Home ( ) _____

Telephone - Other ( ) _____

SECTION 2: DEFERMENT REQUEST

Before answering any questions, carefully read the entire form, including the instructions and other information in Sections 5 and 6. A representative may complete and sign this form on your behalf if you are unable to do so because of your disability.

■ I meet the qualifications stated in Section 6 on the following page for a Temporary Total Disability Deferment and request that my loan holder defer repayment on my loans while I am **TEMPORARILY TOTALLY DISABLED** or while I am unable to secure employment because I am caring for a spouse or dependent who is **TEMPORARILY TOTALLY DISABLED.** Check the appropriate box:

☐ I am disabled.   ☐ I am taking care of my spouse or dependent who is disabled. (For spouse or dependent disability, provide the information requested below.)

Name of Spouse or Dependent _____ Relationship to Borrower _____

SECTION 3: BORROWER AUTHORIZATION, UNDERSTANDINGS AND CERTIFICATIONS

■ **I authorize** any physician, hospital, or other institution having records about the disability for which I am requesting a deferment of loan payments to make information from these records available to the holder of my loans.

■ **I understand that: (1)** Principal payments will be deferred, but if I have an unsubsidized loan, I am responsible for paying the interest that accrues. **(2)** I have the option of making interest payments on my unsubsidized loan(s) during my deferment. I may choose to make interest payments by checking the box below; unpaid interest that accrues will be capitalized by my loan holder.

☐ I wish to make interest payments on my unsubsidized loan(s) during my deferment.

(3) My deferment will begin on the date the deferment condition began, but no more than six months before the date my loan holder receives this request. **(4)** My deferment will end on the earlier of the date that the condition that establishes my deferment eligibility ends or the certified deferment end date. **(5)** My deferment will last no more than six months after the date my physician certifies this request. **(6)** My loan holder will not grant this deferment request unless all applicable sections of this form are completed. **(7)** If my deferment does not cover all my past due payments, my loan holder may grant me a forbearance for all payments due before the begin date of my deferment or — if the period for which I am eligible for a deferment has ended — a forbearance for all payments due at the time my deferment request is processed. **(8)** If I am eligible for a post-deferment grace period on loans made before October 1, 1981, my loan holder may grant me a forbearance on my other loans for this period so that I can begin repayment of all my loans at the same time. I understand that my loan holder may capitalize the interest that accrues on my other loans during the six-month period and that this will increase the principal balance of my other loans. **(9)** My loan holder may grant me a forbearance on my loans for up to 60 days, if necessary, for the collection and processing of documentation related to my deferment request. Interest that accrues during the forbearance will not be capitalized. **(10)** If I am a veteran, the certification by a physician on this form is only for the purposes of establishing my eligibility to receive a deferment of a FFEL Program loan and is not for purposes of determining my eligibility for or the extent of my eligibility for Department of Veterans Affairs benefits.

■ **I certify that: (1)** The information I provided in Sections 1 and 2 above is true and correct. **(2)** I will provide additional documentation to my loan holder, as required, to support my deferment status. **(3)** I will notify my loan holder immediately when the condition(s) that qualified me for the deferment ends. **(4)** I have read, understand, and meet the eligibility criteria of the deferment for which I have applied, as explained in Section 6.

Signature of Borrower or Borrower's Representative _____ Date _____

Name of Borrower's Representative (if applicable) _____ Relationship to Borrower _____

Address of Borrower's Representative _____

SECTION 4: PHYSICIAN'S CERTIFICATION

Instructions for physician: You are being asked to complete and sign this form to certify that the borrower or the borrower's spouse or dependent identified in Section 2 is temporarily totally disabled. You may complete this form **only** if you are a **doctor of medicine or osteopathy** legally authorized to practice. Sign the certification only if the disabled person's condition meets the definition of Temporary Total Disability in Section 6. Provide all requested information (you may attach additional pages). Report dates as month-day-year (MM-DD-YYYY).

■ The disabled person became unable to work and earn money or attend school, or required continuous nursing or similar care on ⎵⎵ – ⎵⎵ – ⎵⎵⎵⎵ . The disabling condition or care is expected to continue until ⎵⎵ – ⎵⎵ – ⎵⎵⎵⎵ .

■ Diagnosis of the disabled person's present medical condition: _____

■ If different from the date provided above, when did the disabled person's injury or illness begin? ⎵⎵ – ⎵⎵ – ⎵⎵⎵⎵

■ I certify that, in my best professional judgment, the borrower identified in Section 2 is unable to work and earn money or attend school for at least 60 days because of a medically determinable impairment, or the borrower's spouse or dependent identified in Section 2 requires continuous nursing or similar care for a period of at least 90 days. I am a **doctor of medicine or osteopathy** legally authorized to practice.

Physician's Signature _____ Date _____

Physician's Name (printed) _____ Telephone ( ) _____

Address _____ City, State, Zip _____

Page 1 of 3

SECTION 5: INSTRUCTIONS FOR COMPLETING THE FORM

Type or print using dark ink. Report dates as month-day-year (MM-DD-YYYY). For example, 'January 1, 1999' = '01-01-1999'. A doctor of medicine or osteopathy legally authorized to practice must complete Section 4. If you need help completing this form, contact your loan holder.

Return the completed form and any required documentation to the address shown in Section 7.

SECTION 6: DEFINITIONS / ELIGIBILITY CRITERIA FOR TEMPORARY TOTAL DISABILITY DEFERMENT REQUEST

Definitions

■ The **Federal Family Education Loan (FFEL) Program** includes Federal Stafford Loans (both subsidized and unsubsidized), Federal Supplemental Loans for Students (SLS), Federal PLUS Loans, and Federal Consolidation Loans.

■ A **deferment** is a period during which I am entitled to postpone repayment of the principal balance of my loan(s). The federal government pays the interest that accrues during an eligible deferment for all subsidized Federal Stafford Loans and for Federal Consolidation Loans for which the Consolidation loan application was received by my loan holder **(1)** on or after January 1, 1993 but before August 10, 1993, **(2)** on or after August 10, 1993, if it includes *only* Federal Stafford Loans that were eligible for federal interest subsidy, or **(3)** on or after November 13, 1997, for that portion of the Consolidation loan that paid a subsidized Federal Stafford Loan or a Federal Direct Stafford/Ford (Direct Subsidized) Loan. I am responsible for the interest that accrues during this period on all other FFEL Program loans.

■ **Forbearance** means permitting the temporary cessation of payments, allowing an extension of time for making payments, or temporarily accepting smaller payments than previously scheduled. I am responsible for paying the interest on my loan(s) during a forbearance.

■ The **holder** of my FFEL Program loan(s) may be a lender, guaranty agency, secondary market, or the U.S. Department of Education.

■ **Capitalization** is the addition of unpaid interest to the principal balance of my loan. This will increase the principal and the total cost of my loan.

■ The **physician** who completes Section 4 of this form must be a doctor of medicine or osteopathy legally authorized to practice.

■ **Temporary Total Disability**: The disabled borrower must, because of injury or illness, be unable to work and earn money or go to school for at least 60 days in order to recover. If the disabled person is the borrower's spouse or dependent, the disabled person must require at least 90 days of continuous nursing or similar care from the borrower. An uncomplicated pregnancy is **not** a qualifying condition for a pregnant borrower, or for a borrower caring for a spouse or dependent with an uncomplicated pregnancy.

Eligibility Criteria

■ To qualify for a Temporary Total Disability Deferment, I must have an outstanding balance on at least one FFEL Program loan which was made **before July 1, 1993**.

■ I may defer repayment of my loan(s) while I am, or my spouse or dependent is, **TEMPORARILY TOTALLY DISABLED**. (Maximum eligibility is three years. Eligibility must be recertified every six months). To qualify:

(1) I must be unable to work and earn money or go to school for at least 60 days in order to recover from an injury or illness.

(2) I must not be requesting this deferment based on a condition that existed before I applied for my loan(s) (underlying loan(s) in the case of a Consolidation loan), unless my condition has since substantially deteriorated, and I am now temporarily totally disabled.

(3) I must not be requesting this deferment based on an uncomplicated pregnancy (either my pregnancy, or my spouse's or dependent's uncomplicated pregnancy).

(4) If I am requesting this deferment based on the disability of my spouse or dependent, my spouse or dependent must have an injury or illness that requires at least 90 days of continuous nursing or similar care from me, which prevents me from securing full-time employment of at least 30 hours per week in a position expected to last at least three months.

(5) I understand that my physician (or my spouse's or dependent's physician) must recertify this condition every six months to continue this deferment.

SECTION 7: WHERE TO SEND THE COMPLETED DEFERMENT REQUEST

RETURN THE COMPLETED DEFERMENT REQUEST AND ANY REQUIRED DOCUMENTATION TO:
(IF NO ADDRESS IS SHOWN, RETURN TO YOUR LOAN HOLDER)

SECTION 8: IMPORTANT NOTICES

Privacy Act Disclosure Notice

The Privacy Act of 1974 (5 U.S.C. §552a) requires that we disclose to you the following information:

The authority for collecting this information is §421 *et seq.* of the Higher Education Act of 1965, as amended (the HEA) (20 U.S.C. §1071 to 1087-2). The principal purpose for collecting this information is to determine whether you are eligible for a deferment on your loan(s) under the Federal Family Education Loan (FFEL) Program.

We ask that you provide the information requested on this deferment request on a voluntary basis. However, you must provide all of the requested information so that the holder(s) of your loan(s) can determine whether you qualify for a deferment.

The information in your file may be disclosed to third parties as authorized under routine uses in the Privacy Act notices called "Title IV Program Files" (originally published on April 12, 1994, *Federal Register*, Vol. 59, p. 17351) and "National Student Loan Data System" (originally published on December 20, 1994, *Federal Register*, Vol. 59, p. 65532). Thus, this information may be disclosed to parties that we authorize to assist us in administering the federal student aid programs, including contractors that are required to maintain safeguards under the Privacy Act. Disclosures may also be made for verification of information, determination of eligibility, enforcement of conditions of the loan or grant, debt collection, and the prevention of fraud, waste, and abuse and these disclosures may be made through computer matching programs with other federal agencies. Disclosures may be made to determine the feasibility of entering into computer matching agreements. We may send information to members of Congress if you ask them in writing to help you with federal student aid questions. If we are involved in litigation, we may send information to the Department of Justice (DOJ), a court, adjudicative body, counsel, or witness if the disclosure is related to financial aid and certain other conditions are met. If this information, either alone or with other information, indicates a potential violation of law, we may send it to the appropriate authority for consideration of action and we may disclose to DOJ to get its advice related to the Title IV, HEA programs or questions under the Freedom of Information Act. Disclosures may be made to qualified researchers under Privacy Act safeguards. In some circumstances involving employment decisions, grievances, or complaints or involving decisions regarding the letting of a contract or making of a grant, license, or other benefit, we may send information to an appropriate authority. In limited circumstances, we may disclose to a federal labor organization recognized under 5 U.S.C. Chapter 71.

Because we request your social security number (SSN), we must inform you that we collect your SSN on a voluntary basis, but section 484(a)(4) of the HEA (20 U.S.C. §1091(a)(4)) provides that, in order to receive any grant, loan, or work assistance under Title IV of the HEA, a student must provide his or her SSN. Your SSN is used to verify your identity, and as an account number (identifier) throughout the life of your loan(s) so that data may be recorded accurately.

Paperwork Reduction Notice

According to the Paperwork Reduction Act of 1995, no persons are required to respond to a collection of information unless it displays a currently valid OMB control number. The valid OMB control number for this information collection is 1845-0005. The time required to complete this information collection is estimated to average 0.16 hours (10 minutes) per response, including the time to review instructions, search existing data resources, gather and maintain the data needed, and complete and review the information collection. *If you have any comments concerning the accuracy of the time estimate(s) or suggestions for improving this form, please write to:*

U.S. Department of Education, Washington, DC 20202-4651.

If you have any comments or concerns regarding the status of your individual submission of this form, write directly to the address shown in Section 7.

UNEMPLOYMENT DEFERMENT REQUEST

Federal Family Education Loan Program

UNEM

OMB No. 1845-0005
Form Approved
Exp. Date 06/30/2002

WARNING: Any person who knowingly makes a false statement or misrepresentation on this form or on any accompanying documents shall be subject to penalties which may include fines, imprisonment or both, under the U.S. Criminal Code and 20 U.S.C. §1097.

SECTION 1: BORROWER IDENTIFICATION

Please correct or, if information is missing, enter below. If a correction, check this box: ❏

SSN |___|___|___| – |___|___| – |___|___|___|___|

Name _____

Address _____

City, State, Zip _____

Telephone - Home ( ) _____

Telephone - Other ( ) _____

SECTION 2: DEFERMENT REQUEST

Before answering any questions, carefully read the entire form, including the instructions and other information in Sections 4, 5, and 6.

■ I meet the qualifications stated in Section 6 for an Unemployment Deferment and request that my loan holder defer repayment of my loan(s).
To document eligibility, complete the following:

(A) TO BE COMPLETED BY ALL BORROWERS:

I became unemployed or began working less than 30 hours per week on |___|___| – |___|___| – |___|___|___|___| . My deferment begins on this date (but no more than 6 months before the date my loan holder receives this request) unless I request my deferment to begin on the following later date: |___|___| – |___|___| – |___|___|___|___| .

(B) IF YOU ARE ELIGIBLE FOR UNEMPLOYMENT BENEFITS, CHECK THIS BOX AND ATTACH THE REQUIRED DOCUMENTATION:

❏   I am eligible for unemployment benefits. I have attached documentation of my eligibility for these benefits. The documentation includes my name, address, social security number, and the effective dates of my eligibility to receive unemployment benefits.

If you checked this box, skip to Section 3 ("Borrower Interest Selection and Certification"). Do not complete items (C) and (D).

(C) IF YOU ARE NOT ELIGIBLE FOR UNEMPLOYMENT BENEFITS, OR IF YOUR ELIGIBILITY HAS EXPIRED, CHECK THE APPROPRIATE BOX BELOW AND PROVIDE THE REQUESTED INFORMATION:

❏   I registered with the following public or private employment agency on |___|___| – |___|___| – |___|___|___|___| .

Name of Employment Agency _____

Address (Street, City, State, Zip Code) _____ Telephone ( ) _____

NOTE: School placement offices and "temporary" agencies do not qualify as public or private employment agencies.

❏   I am not registered with an employment agency because there is not one within 50 miles of my permanent or temporary address. If I am not residing at my permanent address, my temporary address is:

Street, City, State, Zip Code _____ Telephone ( ) _____

(D) COMPLETE THIS ITEM ONLY IF (1) YOU ARE REQUESTING AN EXTENSION OF AN EXISTING UNEMPLOYMENT DEFERMENT AND (2) YOU ARE NOT ELIGIBLE FOR UNEMPLOYMENT BENEFITS. IF THIS IS YOUR FIRST UNEMPLOYMENT DEFERMENT REQUEST, OR IF YOU ARE ELIGIBLE FOR UNEMPLOYMENT BENEFITS, SKIP TO SECTION 3 ("BORROWER INTEREST SELECTION AND CERTIFICATION").

In the last six months, I have attempted to secure full-time employment (see Section 5: Definitions) with the following six employers:

1. Employer _____	2. Employer _____	3. Employer _____
Street _____	Street _____	Street _____
City _____ State ___ Zip ___	City _____ State ___ Zip ___	City _____ State ___ Zip ___
Contact (Name or Title) _____	Contact (Name or Title) _____	Contact (Name or Title) _____
Telephone ( ) _____	Telephone ( ) _____	Telephone ( ) _____
4. Employer _____	5. Employer _____	6. Employer _____
Street _____	Street _____	Street _____
City _____ State ___ Zip ___	City _____ State ___ Zip ___	City _____ State ___ Zip ___
Contact (Name or Title) _____	Contact (Name or Title) _____	Contact (Name or Title) _____
Telephone ( ) _____	Telephone ( ) _____	Telephone ( ) _____

SECTION 3: BORROWER INTEREST SELECTION AND CERTIFICATION

■ Principal payments will be deferred, but if I have an unsubsidized loan, I am responsible for paying the interest that accrues. I have the option of making interest payments on my unsubsidized loan(s) during my deferment. I may choose to make interest payments by checking the box below; unpaid interest that accrues will be capitalized by my loan holder.

❏ I wish to make interest payments on my unsubsidized loan(s) during my deferment.

■ I certify that the information I have provided in Sections 1 and 2 above is true and correct, and that I have read, understand, and meet the eligibility criteria and terms and conditions of the deferment for which I have applied, as explained in Section 6.

Borrower's Signature _____ Date _____

SECTION 4: INSTRUCTIONS FOR COMPLETING THE FORM

Type or print using dark ink. Report dates as month-day-year (MM-DD-YYYY). For example, 'January 1, 1999' = '01-01-1999'. If you need more space to provide any of the information requested in Section 2, continue on separate sheets of paper attached to this form. Indicate the number of the item for which you are providing information, and include your name and social security number (SSN) on all attached sheets. If you need help completing this form, contact your loan holder.

Return the completed form and any required documentation to the address shown in Section 7.

SECTION 5: DEFINITIONS

■ The **Federal Family Education Loan (FFEL) Program** includes Federal Stafford Loans (both subsidized and unsubsidized), Federal Supplemental Loans for Students (SLS), Federal PLUS Loans, and Federal Consolidation Loans.

■ A **deferment** is a period during which I am entitled to postpone repayment of the principal balance of my loan(s). The federal government pays the interest that accrues during an eligible deferment for all subsidized Federal Stafford Loans and for Federal Consolidation Loans for which the Consolidation loan application was received by my loan holder **(1)** on or after January 1, 1993 but before August 10, 1993, **(2)** on or after August 10, 1993, if it includes *only* Federal Stafford Loans that were eligible for federal interest subsidy, or **(3)** on or after November 13, 1997, for that portion of the Consolidation loan that paid a subsidized Federal Stafford Loan or a Federal Direct Stafford/Ford (Direct Subsidized) Loan. I am responsible for the interest that accrues during this period on all other FFEL Program loans.

■ **Forbearance** means permitting the temporary cessation of payments, allowing an extension of time for making payments, or temporarily accepting smaller payments than previously scheduled. I am responsible for paying the interest on my loan(s) during a forbearance.

■ The **holder** of my FFEL Program loan(s) may be a lender, guaranty agency, secondary market, or the U.S. Department of Education.

■ **Capitalization** is the addition of unpaid interest to the principal balance of my loan. This will increase the principal and the total cost of my loan.

■ **Full-time** employment is defined as working at least 30 hours per week in a position expected to last at least three months.

SECTION 6: ELIGIBILITY CRITERIA / TERMS AND CONDITIONS FOR UNEMPLOYMENT DEFERMENT

■ I may defer (postpone) repayment of my loans while I am unemployed. I must reapply every six months. If my first loans were made **before July 1, 1993**, my maximum cumulative eligibility for Unemployment Deferments is 24 months. If my first loans were made **on or after July 1, 1993**, my maximum cumulative eligibility is 36 months.

■ To qualify:

(1) I must be conscientiously seeking but unable to find full-time employment in the United States in any field or at any salary or responsibility level. (The United States includes the 50 states, the District of Columbia, Puerto Rico, American Samoa, Guam, the Trust Territory of the Pacific Islands, the Virgin Islands, the Commonwealth of the Northern Mariana Islands, and U.S. military bases and embassy compounds in a foreign country.)

(2) I must provide documentation establishing that I am eligible for unemployment benefits. This documentation must include my name, address, social security number, and the effective dates of my eligibility to receive unemployment benefits.

OR

(3) If I am not eligible for unemployment benefits, I must be registered with a private or public employment agency if there is one within 50 miles of my permanent or temporary address (school placement offices and "temporary" agencies do not qualify as public or private employment agencies). If I am not eligible for unemployment benefits and I am requesting an extension of an existing unemployment deferment, I must provide my loan holder with documentation of my conscientious search for full-time employment in the preceding six months by completing Item (D) in Section 2 of this form.

■ I will provide additional documentation to my loan holder, as required, to support my deferment status.

■ I will notify my loan holder immediately when the condition(s) that qualified me for the deferment ends.

■ **My deferment will begin on the date the deferment condition began, but no more than six months before the date my loan holder receives this request.**

■ My deferment will end on the earlier of the date that the condition that establishes my deferment eligibility ends or the certified deferment end date.

■ My deferment will last for no more than six months after the date I sign the deferment request.

■ My loan holder will not grant this deferment request unless all applicable sections of this form are completed and any required additional documentation is provided.

■ If my deferment does not cover all my past due payments, my loan holder may grant me a forbearance for all payments due before the begin date of my deferment or — if the period for which I am eligible for a deferment has ended — a forbearance for all payments due at the time my deferment request is processed.

■ If I am eligible for a one-time post-deferment grace period on loans made before October 1, 1981, my loan holder may grant me a forbearance on my other loans for this period so that I can begin repayment of all my loans at the same time. I understand that my loan holder may capitalize the interest that accrues on my other loans during the six-month period and that this will increase the principal balance of my other loans.

■ My loan holder may grant me a forbearance on my loans for up to 60 days, if necessary, for the collection and processing of documentation related to my deferment request. Interest that accrues during the forbearance will not be capitalized.

SECTION 7: WHERE TO SEND THE COMPLETED DEFERMENT REQUEST

RETURN THE COMPLETED DEFERMENT REQUEST AND ANY REQUIRED DOCUMENTATION TO:
(IF NO ADDRESS IS SHOWN, RETURN TO YOUR LOAN HOLDER)

SECTION 8: IMPORTANT NOTICES

Privacy Act Disclosure Notice

The Privacy Act of 1974 (5 U.S.C. §552a) requires that we disclose to you the following information:

The authority for collecting this information is §421 *et seq.* of the Higher Education Act of 1965, as amended (the HEA) (20 U.S.C. §1071 to 1087-2). The principal purpose for collecting this information is to determine whether you are eligible for a deferment on your loan(s) under the Federal Family Education Loan (FFEL) Program.

We ask that you provide the information requested on this deferment request on a voluntary basis. However, you must provide all of the requested information so that the holder(s) of your loan(s) can determine whether you qualify for a deferment.

The information in your file may be disclosed to third parties as authorized under routine uses in the Privacy Act notices called "Title IV Program Files" (originally published on April 12, 1994, *Federal Register*, Vol. 59, p. 17351) and "National Student Loan Data System" (originally published on December 20, 1994, *Federal Register*, Vol. 59, p. 65532). Thus, this information may be disclosed to parties that we authorize to assist us in administering the federal student aid programs, including contractors that are required to maintain safeguards under the Privacy Act. Disclosures may also be made for verification of information, determination of eligibility, enforcement of conditions of the loan or grant, debt collection, and the prevention of fraud, waste, and abuse and these disclosures may be made through computer matching programs with other federal agencies. Disclosures may be made to determine the feasibility of entering into computer matching agreements. We may send information to members of Congress if you ask them in writing to help you with federal student aid questions. If we are involved in litigation, we may send information to the Department of Justice (DOJ), a court, adjudicative body, counsel, or witness if the disclosure is related to financial aid and certain other conditions are met. If this information, either alone or with other information, indicates a potential violation of law, we may send it to the appropriate authority for consideration of action and we may disclose to DOJ to get its advice related to the Title IV, HEA programs or questions under the Freedom of Information Act. Disclosures may be made to qualified researchers under Privacy Act safeguards. In some circumstances involving employment decisions, grievances, or complaints or involving decisions regarding the letting of a contract or making of a grant, license, or other benefit, we may send information to an appropriate authority. In limited circumstances, we may disclose to a federal labor organization recognized under 5 U.S.C. Chapter 71.

Because we request your social security number (SSN), we must inform you that we collect your SSN on a voluntary basis, but section 484(a)(4) of the HEA (20 U.S.C. §1091(a)(4)) provides that, in order to receive any grant, loan, or work assistance under Title IV of the HEA, a student must provide his or her SSN. Your SSN is used to verify your identity, and as an account number (identifier) throughout the life of your loan(s) so that data may be recorded accurately.

Paperwork Reduction Notice

According to the Paperwork Reduction Act of 1995, no persons are required to respond to a collection of information unless it displays a currently valid OMB control number. The valid OMB control number for this information collection is 1845-0005. The time required to complete this information collection is estimated to average 0.16 hours (10 minutes) per response, including the time to review instructions, search existing data resources, gather and maintain the data needed, and complete and review the information collection. *If you have any comments concerning the accuracy of the time estimate(s) or suggestions for improving this form, please write to:*

U.S. Department of Education, Washington, DC 20202-4651.

If you have any comments or concerns regarding the status of your individual submission of this form, write directly to the address shown in Section 7.

PUB

PUBLIC SERVICE DEFERMENT REQUEST

Federal Family Education Loan Program

USE THIS FORM ONLY IF YOU HAVE AN OUTSTANDING BALANCE ON A FEDERAL FAMILY EDUCATION LOAN PROGRAM LOAN THAT WAS MADE BEFORE JULY 1, 1993.

WARNING: Any person who knowingly makes a false statement or misrepresentation on this form or on any accompanying documents shall be subject to penalties which may include fines, imprisonment or both, under the U.S. Criminal Code and 20 U.S.C. §1097.

OMB No. 1845-0005
Form Approved
Exp. Date 06/30/2002

SECTION 1: BORROWER IDENTIFICATION

Please correct or, if information is missing, enter below. If a correction, check this box: ☐

SSN | | | | – | | | – | | | | |

Name _____

Address _____

City, State, Zip _____

Telephone - Home ( ) _____

Telephone - Other ( ) _____

SECTION 2: DEFERMENT REQUEST

Before answering any questions, carefully read the entire form, including the instructions and other information in Sections 5 and 6.

■ I meet the qualifications stated in Section 6 for the deferment checked below and request that my loan holder defer repayment of my loan(s) while I am:

☐ On active duty in the **ARMED FORCES** of the United States.*

☐ Serving full time as an officer in the Commissioned Corps of the **PUBLIC HEALTH SERVICE.***

☐ Serving in the **PEACE CORPS.***

☐ A full-time paid volunteer in the **ACTION PROGRAMS.***

☐ A full-time paid volunteer for a **TAX-EXEMPT ORGANIZATION.***

* Federal PLUS Loans made **on or after August 15, 1983** do **not** qualify for the Armed Forces, Public Health Service, Peace Corps, ACTION Programs, and Tax-Exempt Organization Deferments.

☐ On active duty in the **NATIONAL OCEANIC AND ATMOSPHERIC ADMINISTRATION (NOAA).****

** The NOAA Deferment is available **only** to Federal Stafford and SLS loan borrowers whose first loans were made **on or after July 1, 1987 and before July 1, 1993.**

SECTION 3: BORROWER UNDERSTANDINGS AND CERTIFICATIONS

■ **I understand that: (1)** Principal payments will be deferred, but if I have an unsubsidized loan, I am responsible for paying the interest that accrues. **(2)** I have the option of making interest payments on my unsubsidized loan(s) during my deferment. I may choose to make interest payments by checking the box below; unpaid interest that accrues will be capitalized by my loan holder.

☐ I wish to make interest payments on my unsubsidized loan(s) during my deferment.

(3) My deferment will begin on the date the deferment condition began, but no more than six months before the date my loan holder receives this request. **(4)** My deferment will end on the earlier of the date that the condition that establishes my deferment eligibility ends or the certified deferment end date. **(5)** My loan holder will not grant this deferment request unless all applicable sections of this form are completed and any required additional documentation is provided. **(6)** If my deferment does not cover all my past due payments, my loan holder may grant me a forbearance for all payments due before the begin date of my deferment or — if the period for which I am eligible for a deferment has ended — a forbearance for all payments due at the time my deferment request is processed. **(7)** If I am eligible for a post-deferment grace period on loans made before October 1, 1981, my loan holder may grant me a forbearance on my other loans for this period so that I can begin repayment of all my loans at the same time. I understand that my loan holder may capitalize the interest that accrues on my other loans during the six-month period and that this will increase the principal balance of my other loans. **(8)** My loan holder may grant me a forbearance on my loans for up to 60 days, if necessary, for the collection and processing of documentation related to my deferment request. Interest that accrues during the forbearance will not be capitalized.

■ **I certify that: (1)** The information I provided in Sections 1 and 2 above is true and correct. **(2)** I will provide additional documentation to my loan holder, as required, to support my deferment status. **(3)** I will notify my loan holder immediately when the condition(s) that qualified me for the deferment ends. **(4)** I have read, understand, and meet the eligibility criteria of the deferment for which I have applied, as explained in Section 6.

Borrower's Signature _____ Date _____

SECTION 4: AUTHORIZED OFFICIAL'S CERTIFICATION

I certify, to the best of my knowledge and belief, that the borrower named above is/was engaged in the service indicated in Section 2, and that the borrower and the borrower's service meet all the eligibility requirements specified in Section 6.

The borrower's service began on | | | – | | | – | | | | | and is expected to end/ended on | | | – | | | – | | | | | .

Name of Organization _____

Address _____ City, State, Zip _____

Name/Title of Authorized Official _____ Telephone ( ) _____

Authorized Official's Signature _____ **Date** _____

Page 1 of 3

SECTION 5: INSTRUCTIONS FOR COMPLETING THE FORM

Type or print using dark ink. Report dates as month-day-year (MM-DD-YYYY). For example, 'January 1, 1999' = '01-01-1999'. An authorized official must complete Section 4. If you need help completing this form, contact your loan holder.

Return the completed form and any required documentation to the address shown in Section 7.

SECTION 6: DEFINITIONS / ELIGIBILITY CRITERIA FOR PUBLIC SERVICE DEFERMENT REQUEST

Definitions

- The **Federal Family Education Loan (FFEL) Program** includes Federal Stafford Loans (both subsidized and unsubsidized), Federal Supplemental Loans for Students (SLS), Federal PLUS Loans, and Federal Consolidation Loans.

- A **deferment** is a period during which I am entitled to postpone repayment of the principal balance of my loan(s). The federal government pays the interest that accrues during an eligible deferment for all subsidized Federal Stafford Loans and for Federal Consolidation Loans for which the Consolidation loan application was received by my loan holder **(1)** on or after January 1, 1993 but before August 10, 1993, **(2)** on or after August 10, 1993, if it includes *only* Federal Stafford Loans that were eligible for federal interest subsidy, or **(3)** on or after November 13, 1997, for that portion of the Consolidation loan that paid a subsidized Federal Stafford Loan or a Federal Direct Stafford/Ford (Direct Subsidized) Loan. I am responsible for the interest that accrues during this period on all other FFEL Program loans.

- **Forbearance** means permitting the temporary cessation of payments, allowing an extension of time for making payments, or temporarily accepting smaller payments than previously scheduled. I am responsible for paying the interest on my loan(s) during a forbearance.

- The **holder** of my FFEL Program loan(s) may be a lender, guaranty agency, secondary market, or the U.S. Department of Education.

- **Capitalization** is the addition of unpaid interest to the principal balance of my loan. This will increase the principal and the total cost of my loan.

- **Authorized certifying officials:**
  - Commanding or Personnel Officer (Armed Forces Deferment)
  - Authorized Official of the U.S. Public Health Service (Public Health Service Deferment)
  - Authorized Official of the Peace Corps (Peace Corps Deferment)
  - Authorized Official of the ACTION Program (ACTION Program Deferment)
  - Authorized Official of the Volunteer Program (Tax-Exempt Organization Deferment)
  - Authorized Official of the NOAA Corps (NOAA Deferment)

Eligibility Criteria

- To qualify for any of the deferments listed in Section 2 of this form:
  - I must have an outstanding balance on at least one FFEL Program loan which was made **before July 1, 1993**. If I am a Federal PLUS Loan borrower, **(1)** I am not eligible for the NOAA Deferment, and **(2)** I am eligible for the Armed Forces, Public Health Service, Peace Corps, ACTION Programs, and Tax-Exempt Organization Deferments only if my first loan was made **before August 15, 1983**. I am eligible for the NOAA Deferment only if I am a Federal Stafford or SLS loan borrower whose first loan was made **on or after July 1, 1987 and before July 1, 1993**.

- I may defer repayment of my loan(s) while I am:
  - On active duty in the **ARMED FORCES** of the United States. (Maximum eligibility is three years; this is a combined limit with Public Health Service and NOAA deferments.) To qualify, I must: **(1)** be on active duty in the Army, Navy, Air Force, Marine Corps or Coast Guard, and **(2)** provide my loan holder with copies of my military identification and orders or have my commanding or personnel officer certify Section 4 on the front of this form. **NOTE:** Borrowers enlisted in a reserve component of the Armed Forces or the National Guard (while on active duty status in the Army or Air Force Reserves) may qualify for this deferment only if: (1) serving full-time for a period expected to last at least one year, or (2) serving under an order for national mobilization.
  - Serving full-time as an officer in the Commissioned Corps of the **PUBLIC HEALTH SERVICE**. (Maximum eligibility is three years; this is a combined limit with Armed Forces and NOAA deferments.)
  - Serving in the **PEACE CORPS**. (Maximum eligibility is three years.) To qualify, I must have agreed to serve for a period of at least one year.
  - A full-time paid volunteer in the **ACTION PROGRAMS**. (Maximum eligibility is three years.) To qualify, I must have agreed to serve for a period of at least one year.
  - A full-time paid volunteer for a **TAX-EXEMPT ORGANIZATION**. (Maximum eligibility is three years.) To qualify, I must: **(1)** be serving full-time in an organization that has a tax exemption under Section 501(c)(3) of the Internal Revenue Code of 1986; **(2)** assist low income people and their communities in eliminating poverty and poverty-related human, social, and environmental conditions; **(3)** not earn more than the federal minimum wage; however, I may receive fringe benefits like those received by other employees of the organization; **(4)** not engage in religious instruction, proselytizing, fund-raising to support religious activities, or conduct worship services as part of my duties; and **(5)** have agreed to serve for a period of at least one year.
  - On active duty in the **NATIONAL OCEANIC AND ATMOSPHERIC ADMINISTRATION (NOAA)**. (Maximum eligibility is three years; this is a combined limit with Armed Forces and Public Health Service Deferments.)

SECTION 7: WHERE TO SEND THE COMPLETED DEFERMENT REQUEST

RETURN THE COMPLETED DEFERMENT REQUEST AND ANY REQUIRED DOCUMENTATION TO:
(IF NO ADDRESS IS SHOWN, RETURN TO YOUR LOAN HOLDER)

SECTION 8: IMPORTANT NOTICES

Privacy Act Disclosure Notice

The Privacy Act of 1974 (5 U.S.C. §552a) requires that we disclose to you the following information:

The authority for collecting this information is §421 *et seq.* of the Higher Education Act of 1965, as amended (the HEA) (20 U.S.C. §1071 to 1087-2). The principal purpose for collecting this information is to determine whether you are eligible for a deferment on your loan(s) under the Federal Family Education Loan (FFEL) Program.

We ask that you provide the information requested on this deferment request on a voluntary basis. However, you must provide all of the requested information so that the holder(s) of your loan(s) can determine whether you qualify for a deferment.

The information in your file may be disclosed to third parties as authorized under routine uses in the Privacy Act notices called "Title IV Program Files" (originally published on April 12, 1994, *Federal Register*, Vol. 59, p. 17351) and "National Student Loan Data System" (originally published on December 20, 1994, *Federal Register*, Vol. 59, p. 65532). Thus, this information may be disclosed to parties that we authorize to assist us in administering the federal student aid programs, including contractors that are required to maintain safeguards under the Privacy Act. Disclosures may also be made for verification of information, determination of eligibility, enforcement of conditions of the loan or grant, debt collection, and the prevention of fraud, waste, and abuse and these disclosures may be made through computer matching programs with other federal agencies. Disclosures may be made to determine the feasibility of entering into computer matching agreements. We may send information to members of Congress if you ask them in writing to help you with federal student aid questions. If we are involved in litigation, we may send information to the Department of Justice (DOJ), a court, adjudicative body, counsel, or witness if the disclosure is related to financial aid and certain other conditions are met. If this information, either alone or with other information, indicates a potential violation of law, we may send it to the appropriate authority for consideration of action and we may disclose to DOJ to get its advice related to the Title IV, HEA programs or questions under the Freedom of Information Act. Disclosures may be made to qualified researchers under Privacy Act safeguards. In some circumstances involving employment decisions, grievances, or complaints or involving decisions regarding the letting of a contract or making of a grant, license, or other benefit, we may send information to an appropriate authority. In limited circumstances, we may disclose to a federal labor organization recognized under 5 U.S.C. Chapter 71.

Because we request your social security number (SSN), we must inform you that we collect your SSN on a voluntary basis, but section 484(a)(4) of the HEA (20 U.S.C. §1091(a)(4)) provides that, in order to receive any grant, loan, or work assistance under Title IV of the HEA, a student must provide his or her SSN. Your SSN is used to verify your identity, and as an account number (identifier) throughout the life of your loan(s) so that data may be recorded accurately.

Paperwork Reduction Notice

According to the Paperwork Reduction Act of 1995, no persons are required to respond to a collection of information unless it displays a currently valid OMB control number. The valid OMB control number for this information collection is 1845-0005. The time required to complete this information collection is estimated to average 0.16 hours (10 minutes) per response, including the time to review instructions, search existing data resources, gather and maintain the data needed, and complete and review the information collection. *If you have any comments concerning the accuracy of the time estimate(s) or suggestions for improving this form, please write to:*

U.S. Department of Education, Washington, DC 20202-4651.

If you have any comments or concerns regarding the status of your individual submission of this form, write directly to the address shown in Section 7.

PARENTAL LEAVE / WORKING MOTHER
DEFERMENT REQUEST

Federal Family Education Loan Program

USE THIS FORM ONLY IF YOU HAVE AN OUTSTANDING BALANCE ON A FEDERAL FAMILY EDUCATION LOAN PROGRAM LOAN
THAT WAS MADE BEFORE JULY 1, 1993.
WARNING: Any person who knowingly makes a false statement or misrepresentation on this form or on any accompanying documents
shall be subject to penalties which may include fines, imprisonment or both, under the U.S. Criminal Code and 20 U.S.C. §1097.

PLWM

OMB No. 1845-0005
Form Approved
Exp. Date 06/30/2002

SECTION 1: BORROWER IDENTIFICATION

Please correct or, if information is missing, enter below. If a correction,
check this box: ☐

SSN ⌷⌷⌷ – ⌷⌷ – ⌷⌷⌷⌷

Name _____

Address _____

City, State, Zip _____

Telephone - Home ( ) _____

Telephone - Other ( ) _____

SECTION 2: DEFERMENT REQUEST

Before answering any questions, carefully read the entire form, including the instructions and other information in Sections 5 and 6.

■ I meet the qualifications stated in Section 6 for the deferment checked below and request that my loan holder defer repayment of my loan(s) beginning

⌷⌷ – ⌷⌷ – ⌷⌷⌷⌷ while I am (check one):

☐ On **PARENTAL LEAVE**.

NOTE: For a Parental Leave Deferment, the beginning deferment date listed above must be within six months of the date you were last enrolled in school at least half-time. **Federal PLUS Loan borrowers are not eligible for Parental Leave Deferments.**

☐ A **WORKING MOTHER**.

NOTE: Federal PLUS Loan borrowers are not eligible for Working Mother Deferments. Additional conditions apply — see Section 6.

SECTION 3: BORROWER UNDERSTANDINGS AND CERTIFICATIONS

■ **I understand that: (1)** Principal payments will be deferred, but if I have an unsubsidized loan, I am responsible for paying the interest that accrues.
(2) I have the option of making interest payments on my unsubsidized loan(s) during my deferment. I may choose to make interest payments by checking the box below; unpaid interest that accrues will be capitalized by my loan holder.

☐ I wish to make interest payments on my unsubsidized loan(s) during my deferment.

(3) My deferment will begin on the date the deferment condition began, but no more than six months before the date my loan holder receives this request. **(4)** My deferment will end on the earlier of the date that the condition that establishes my deferment eligibility ends or the certified deferment end date. **(5)** My loan holder will not grant this deferment request unless all applicable sections of this form are completed and any required additional documentation is provided. **(6)** If my deferment does not cover all my past due payments, my loan holder may grant me a forbearance for all payments due before the begin date of my deferment or — if the period for which I am eligible for a deferment has ended — a forbearance for all payments due at the time my deferment request is processed. **(7)** If I am applying for a Parental Leave Deferment and am in my grace period, I agree to waive up to one month of my grace period so that my deferment begins within six months of the date I was last enrolled in school at least half-time. **(8)** If I am eligible for a post-deferment grace period on loans made before October 1, 1981, my loan holder may grant me a forbearance for all my other loans for this period so that I can begin repayment of all my loans at the same time. I understand that my loan holder may capitalize the interest that accrues on my other loans during the six-month period and that this will increase the principal balance of my other loans. **(9)** My loan holder may grant me a forbearance on my loans for up to 60 days, if necessary, for the collection and processing of documentation related to my deferment request. Interest that accrues during the forbearance will not be capitalized.

■ **I certify that: (1)** The information I provided in Sections 1 and 2 above is true and correct. **(2)** I will provide additional documentation to my loan holder, as required, to support my deferment status. **(3)** I will notify my loan holder immediately when the condition(s) that qualified me for the deferment ends. **(4)** I have read, understand, and meet the eligibility criteria of the deferment for which I have applied, as explained in Section 6.

Borrower's Signature _____ **Date** _____

SECTION 4: AUTHORIZED OFFICIAL'S CERTIFICATION

Required for Parental Leave Deferments only.

I certify, to the best of my knowledge and belief, that the borrower named above was last enrolled at least half-time on:

⌷⌷ – ⌷⌷ – ⌷⌷⌷⌷ .

Name of Institution _____ OPE-ID _____

Address _____ City, State, Zip _____

Name/Title of Authorized Official _____ Telephone ( ) _____

Authorized Official's Signature _____ **Date** _____

Page 1 of 3

SECTION 5: INSTRUCTIONS FOR COMPLETING THE FORM

Type or print using dark ink. Report dates as month-day-year (MM-DD-YYYY). For example, 'January 1, 1999' = '01-01-1999'. If you are applying for a Parental Leave Deferment, an authorized official must complete Section 4. If you need help completing this form, contact your loan holder.

Return the completed form and any required documentation to the address shown in Section 7.

SECTION 6: DEFINITIONS / ELIGIBILITY CRITERIA FOR PARENTAL LEAVE / WORKING MOTHER DEFERMENT REQUEST

Definitions

■ The **Federal Family Education Loan (FFEL) Program** includes Federal Stafford Loans (both subsidized and unsubsidized), Federal Supplemental Loans for Students (SLS), Federal PLUS Loans, and Federal Consolidation Loans.

■ A **deferment** is a period during which I am entitled to postpone repayment of the principal balance of my loan(s). The federal government pays the interest that accrues during an eligible deferment for all subsidized Federal Stafford Loans and for Federal Consolidation Loans for which the Consolidation loan application was received by my loan holder **(1)** on or after January 1, 1993 but before August 10, 1993, **(2)** on or after August 10, 1993, if it includes *only* Federal Stafford Loans that were eligible for federal interest subsidy, or **(3)** on or after November 13, 1997, for that portion of the Consolidation loan that paid a subsidized Federal Stafford Loan or a Federal Direct Stafford/Ford (Direct Subsidized) Loan. I am responsible for the interest that accrues during this period on all other FFEL Program loans.

■ **Forbearance** means permitting the temporary cessation of payments, allowing an extension of time for making payments, or temporarily accepting smaller payments than previously scheduled. I am responsible for paying the interest on my loan(s) during a forbearance.

■ The **holder** of my FFEL Program loan(s) may be a lender, guaranty agency, secondary market, or the U.S. Department of Education.

■ **Capitalization** is the addition of unpaid interest to the principal balance of my loan. This will increase the principal and the total cost of my loan.

■ **Full-time** employment is defined as working at least 30 hours per week in a position expected to last at least three months.

■ An **authorized certifying official** for the Parental Leave Deferment is an authorized official from the school where I was enrolled at least half-time within the six-month period preceding this deferment.

Eligibility Criteria

■ To qualify for a Parental Leave / Working Mother Deferment:
   • I must have an outstanding balance on at least one FFEL Program loan which was made **before July 1, 1993**. If I am a Federal PLUS Loan borrower, I am not eligible for the Parental Leave or Working Mother Deferments. I am eligible for the Working Mother Deferment only if I am a Federal Stafford or SLS loan borrower whose first FFEL Program loan was made **on or after July 1, 1987 and before July 1, 1993**.

■ I may defer repayment of my loan(s) while I am:
   • On **PARENTAL LEAVE**. (Maximum eligibility is six months per occurrence.) To qualify:

   (1) I must:
       (a) be pregnant, caring for my newborn child (a child less than six months of age), or caring for my newly adopted child;
       (b) not be working full-time or attending school during the deferment period; and
       (c) have been enrolled in school at least half-time within the six-month period preceding this deferment (an authorized school must certify my enrollment in Section 4).

   (2) I must provide my loan holder with:
       (a) a statement from my physician documenting my pregnancy, if I am requesting this deferment due to my pregnancy; or
       (b) a copy of my newborn child's birth certificate; or
       (c) a statement from the adoption agency documenting my newly adopted child's placement and the placement date.

   • A **WORKING MOTHER**. (Maximum eligibility is 12 months).) To qualify:

   (1) I must:
       (a) have entered or reentered the workforce within one year preceding this deferment;
       (b) be working full-time in a position earning not more than $1 per hour above the federal minimum wage; and
       (c) be the mother of a preschool-age child who has not yet enrolled in the first grade or a higher grade in elementary school.

   (2) I must provide my loan holder with documentation of:
       (a) my rate of pay, such as a pay stub; and
       (b) the age of my preschool-age child, such as a birth certificate.

SECTION 7: WHERE TO SEND THE COMPLETED DEFERMENT REQUEST

RETURN THE COMPLETED DEFERMENT REQUEST AND ANY REQUIRED DOCUMENTATION TO:
(IF NO ADDRESS IS SHOWN, RETURN TO YOUR LOAN HOLDER)

SECTION 8: IMPORTANT NOTICES

Privacy Act Disclosure Notice

The Privacy Act of 1974 (5 U.S.C. §552a) requires that we disclose to you the following information:

The authority for collecting this information is §421 *et seq.* of the Higher Education Act of 1965, as amended (the HEA) (20 U.S.C. §1071 to 1087-2). The principal purpose for collecting this information is to determine whether you are eligible for a deferment on your loan(s) under the Federal Family Education Loan (FFEL) Program.

We ask that you provide the information requested on this deferment request on a voluntary basis. However, you must provide all of the requested information so that the holder(s) of your loan(s) can determine whether you qualify for a deferment.

The information in your file may be disclosed to third parties as authorized under routine uses in the Privacy Act notices called "Title IV Program Files" (originally published on April 12, 1994, *Federal Register*, Vol. 59, p. 17351) and "National Student Loan Data System" (originally published on December 20, 1994, *Federal Register*, Vol. 59, p. 65532). Thus, this information may be disclosed to parties that we authorize to assist us in administering the federal student aid programs, including contractors that are required to maintain safeguards under the Privacy Act. Disclosures may also be made for verification of information, determination of eligibility, enforcement of conditions of the loan or grant, debt collection, and the prevention of fraud, waste, and abuse and these disclosures may be made through computer matching programs with other federal agencies. Disclosures may be made to determine the feasibility of entering into computer matching agreements. We may send information to members of Congress if you ask them in writing to help you with federal student aid questions. If we are involved in litigation, we may send information to the Department of Justice (DOJ), a court, adjudicative body, counsel, or witness if the disclosure is related to financial aid and certain other conditions are met. If this information, either alone or with other information, indicates a potential violation of law, we may send it to the appropriate authority for consideration of action and we may disclose to DOJ to get its advice related to the Title IV, HEA programs or questions under the Freedom of Information Act. Disclosures may be made to qualified researchers under Privacy Act safeguards. In some circumstances involving employment decisions, grievances, or complaints or involving decisions regarding the letting of a contract or making of a grant, license, or other benefit, we may send information to an appropriate authority. In limited circumstances, we may disclose to a federal labor organization recognized under 5 U.S.C. Chapter 71.

Because we request your social security number (SSN), we must inform you that we collect your SSN on a voluntary basis, but section 484(a)(4) of the HEA (20 U.S.C. §1091(a)(4)) provides that, in order to receive any grant, loan, or work assistance under Title IV of the HEA, a student must provide his or her SSN. Your SSN is used to verify your identity, and as an account number (identifier) throughout the life of your loan(s) so that data may be recorded accurately.

Paperwork Reduction Notice

According to the Paperwork Reduction Act of 1995, no persons are required to respond to a collection of information unless it displays a currently valid OMB control number. The valid OMB control number for this information collection is 1845-0005. The time required to complete this information collection is estimated to average 0.16 hours (10 minutes) per response, including the time to review instructions, search existing data resources, gather and maintain the data needed, and complete and review the information collection. *If you have any comments concerning the accuracy of the time estimate(s) or suggestions for improving this form, please write to:*

U.S. Department of Education, Washington, DC 20202-4651.

If you have any comments or concerns regarding the status of your individual submission of this form, write directly to the address shown in Section 7.

PLUS BORROWER WITH DEPENDENT STUDENT DEFERMENT REQUEST

OMB No. 1845-0005
Form Approved
Exp. Date 06/30/2002

Federal Family Education Loan Program

PLUS

USE THIS FORM ONLY IF YOU HAVE AN OUTSTANDING BALANCE ON A FEDERAL FAMILY EDUCATION LOAN PROGRAM LOAN THAT WAS MADE BEFORE JULY 1, 1993.

WARNING: Any person who knowingly makes a false statement or misrepresentation on this form or on any accompanying documents shall be subject to penalties which may include fines, imprisonment or both, under the U.S. Criminal Code and 20 U.S.C. §1097.

SECTION 1: BORROWER IDENTIFICATION

Please correct or, if information is missing, enter below. If a correction, check this box: ☐

SSN | | | | – | | | – | | | | |

Name _____

Address _____

City, State, Zip _____

Telephone - Home ( ) _____

Telephone - Other ( ) _____

SECTION 2: DEFERMENT REQUEST

Before answering any questions, carefully read the entire form, including the instructions and other information in Sections 5 and 6.

■ I meet the qualifications stated in Section 6 for this deferment and request that my loan holder defer repayment of my loan(s) while the student (named below) for whom I borrowed a PLUS loan is dependent and is (check one):

☐ Enrolled full-time at an eligible school.

☐ Enrolled at least half-time at an eligible school (additional conditions apply — see Section 6).

☐ Engaged full-time in a rehabilitation training program.

Student's Name _____ Student's SSN | | | | – | | | – | | | | |

SECTION 3: BORROWER UNDERSTANDINGS AND CERTIFICATIONS

■ **I understand that:** (1) Principal payments will be deferred. I am responsible for paying the interest that accrues. (2) I have the option of making interest payments during my deferment. I may choose to make interest payments by checking the box below; unpaid interest that accrues will be capitalized by my loan holder.

☐ I wish to make interest payments on my loan(s) during my deferment.

(3) My deferment will begin on the date the deferment condition began, but no more than six months before the date my loan holder receives this request. (4) My deferment will end on the earlier of the date that the condition that establishes my deferment eligibility ends or the certified deferment end date. (5) My loan holder will not grant this deferment request unless all applicable sections of this form are completed and any required additional documentation is provided. (6) If my deferment does not cover all my past due payments, my loan holder may grant me a forbearance for all payments due before the begin date of my deferment or — if the period for which I am eligible for a deferment has ended — a forbearance for all payments due at the time my deferment request is processed. (7) If I am eligible for a post-deferment grace period on loans made before October 1, 1981, my loan holder may grant me a forbearance on my other loans for this period so that I can begin repayment of all my loans at the same time. I understand that my loan holder may capitalize the interest that accrues on my other loans during the six-month period and that this will increase the principal balance of my other loans. (8) My loan holder may grant me a forbearance on my loans for up to 60 days, if necessary, for the collection and processing of documentation related to my deferment request. Interest that accrues during the forbearance will not be capitalized.

■ **I certify that:** (1) The information I provided in Sections 1 and 2 above is true and correct. (2) I will provide additional documentation to my loan holder, as required, to support my deferment status. (3) I will notify my loan holder immediately when the condition(s) that qualified me for the deferment ends. (4) I have read, understand, and meet the eligibility criteria of the deferment for which I have applied, as explained in Section 6.

Borrower's Signature _____ **Date** _____

SECTION 4: AUTHORIZED OFFICIAL'S CERTIFICATION

I certify, to the best of my knowledge and belief, that the dependent student named above is/was enrolled at an eligible institution or engaged in the program indicated in Section 2, and that the dependent student and (if applicable) the dependent student's program meet all the eligibility requirements specified in Section 6 on the following page.

☐ Is/was enrolled as (check the appropriate box) ☐ a full-time student ☐ at least a half-time student

during the academic period from | | | – | | | – | | | | | to | | | – | | | – | | | | |

and is reasonably expected to complete his/her program requirements on | | | – | | | – | | | | | .

☐ Is/was engaged full-time in a rehabilitation training program that began on | | | – | | | – | | | | |

and will end/ended on | | | – | | | – | | | | | .

Name of Institution/Facility _____ OPE-ID (if applicable) _____

Address _____ City, State, Zip _____

Name/Title of Authorized Official _____ Telephone ( ) _____

Authorized Official's Signature _____ **Date** _____

Page 1 of 3

SECTION 5: INSTRUCTIONS FOR COMPLETING THE FORM

Type or print using dark ink. Report dates as month-day-year (MM-DD-YYYY). For example, 'January 1, 1999' = '01-01-1999'. An authorized school/program official must complete Section 4. If you need help completing this form, contact your loan holder.

Return the completed form and any required documentation to the address shown in Section 7.

SECTION 6: DEFINITIONS / ELIGIBILITY CRITERIA FOR PLUS BORROWER WITH DEPENDENT STUDENT DEFERMENT REQUEST

Definitions

- The **Federal Family Education Loan (FFEL) Program** includes Federal Stafford Loans (both subsidized and unsubsidized), Federal Supplemental Loans for Students (SLS), Federal PLUS Loans, and Federal Consolidation Loans.

- A **deferment** is a period during which I am entitled to postpone repayment of the principal balance of my loan(s). The federal government pays the interest that accrues during an eligible deferment for all subsidized Federal Stafford Loans and for Federal Consolidation Loans for which the Consolidation loan application was received by my loan holder **(1)** on or after January 1, 1993 but before August 10, 1993, **(2)** on or after August 10, 1993, if it includes *only* Federal Stafford Loans that were eligible for federal interest subsidy, or **(3)** on or after November 13, 1997, for that portion of the Consolidation loan that paid a subsidized Federal Stafford Loan or a Federal Direct Stafford/Ford (Direct Subsidized) Loan. I am responsible for the interest that accrues during this period on all other FFEL Program loans.

- **Forbearance** means permitting the temporary cessation of payments, allowing an extension of time for making payments, or temporarily accepting smaller payments than previously scheduled. I am responsible for paying the interest on my loan(s) during a forbearance.

- The **holder** of my FFEL Program loan(s) may be a lender, guaranty agency, secondary market, or the U.S. Department of Education.

- **Capitalization** is the addition of unpaid interest to the principal balance of my loan. This will increase the principal and the total cost of my loan.

- **Authorized certifying officials**:
  - Authorized School Official (for dependent students enrolled full-time or at least half-time at an eligible institution)
  - Authorized Rehabilitation Training Program Official

Eligibility Criteria

To qualify:

- To receive a deferment based on my dependent student's full-time or at least half-time enrollment at an eligible school, I must have an outstanding balance on a Federal Stafford, SLS, FISL, PLUS, or Consolidation loan made **on or after July 1, 1987 and before July 1, 1993**. To receive a deferment based on my dependent student's full-time engagement in a rehabilitation training program, I must have had an outstanding balance on a Federal Stafford, SLS, FISL, PLUS, or Consolidation loan **on June 30, 1993**.

- I may defer repayment of my loan(s) while the student for whom I borrowed a Federal PLUS Loan is dependent and is:
  - Enrolled full-time at an eligible school.
  - Enrolled at least half-time at an eligible school. In addition, the dependent student must have an outstanding balance on a Federal Stafford, SLS, FISL, PLUS, or Consolidation loan made **on or after July 1, 1987**.
  - Engaged full-time in a rehabilitation training program. To qualify: **(1)** The training program must **(a)** be licensed, approved, certified or recognized as providing rehabilitation training to disabled individuals by the Department of Veterans Affairs or a state agency responsible for vocational rehabilitation, drug abuse treatment, mental health services, or alcohol abuse treatment programs; **(b)** provide services under a written individualized plan that specifies the date the services are expected to end; and **(c)** be structured in a way that requires a substantial commitment by the student to his/her rehabilitation. ("Substantial commitment" means a commitment of time and effort that would normally prevent a person from being employed 30 or more hours per week in a position expected to last at least three months.) **(2)** The dependent student must be either receiving, or scheduled to receive, these rehabilitation services.

SECTION 7: WHERE TO SEND THE COMPLETED DEFERMENT REQUEST

RETURN THE COMPLETED DEFERMENT REQUEST AND ANY REQUIRED DOCUMENTATION TO:
(IF NO ADDRESS IS SHOWN, RETURN TO YOUR LOAN HOLDER)

SECTION 8: IMPORTANT NOTICES

Privacy Act Disclosure Notice

The Privacy Act of 1974 (5 U.S.C. §552a) requires that we disclose to you the following information:

The authority for collecting this information is §421 *et seq.* of the Higher Education Act of 1965, as amended (the HEA) (20 U.S.C. §1071 to 1087-2). The principal purpose for collecting this information is to determine whether you are eligible for a deferment on your loan(s) under the Federal Family Education Loan (FFEL) Program.

We ask that you provide the information requested on this deferment request on a voluntary basis. However, you must provide all of the requested information so that the holder(s) of your loan(s) can determine whether you qualify for a deferment.

The information in your file may be disclosed to third parties as authorized under routine uses in the Privacy Act notices called "Title IV Program Files" (originally published on April 12, 1994, *Federal Register*, Vol. 59, p. 17351) and "National Student Loan Data System" (originally published on December 20, 1994, *Federal Register*, Vol. 59, p. 65532). Thus, this information may be disclosed to parties that we authorize to assist us in administering the federal student aid programs, including contractors that are required to maintain safeguards under the Privacy Act. Disclosures may also be made for verification of information, determination of eligibility, enforcement of conditions of the loan or grant, debt collection, and the prevention of fraud, waste, and abuse and these disclosures may be made through computer matching programs with other federal agencies. Disclosures may be made to determine the feasibility of entering into computer matching agreements. We may send information to members of Congress if you ask them in writing to help you with federal student aid questions. If we are involved in litigation, we may send information to the Department of Justice (DOJ), a court, adjudicative body, counsel, or witness if the disclosure is related to financial aid and certain other conditions are met. If this information, either alone or with other information, indicates a potential violation of law, we may send it to the appropriate authority for consideration of action and we may disclose to DOJ to get its advice related to the Title IV, HEA programs or questions under the Freedom of Information Act. Disclosures may be made to qualified researchers under Privacy Act safeguards. In some circumstances involving employment decisions, grievances, or complaints or involving decisions regarding the letting of a contract or making of a grant, license, or other benefit, we may send information to an appropriate authority. In limited circumstances, we may disclose to a federal labor organization recognized under 5 U.S.C. Chapter 71.

Because we request your social security number (SSN), we must inform you that we collect your SSN on a voluntary basis, but section 484(a)(4) of the HEA (20 U.S.C. §1091(a)(4)) provides that, in order to receive any grant, loan, or work assistance under Title IV of the HEA, a student must provide his or her SSN. Your SSN is used to verify your identity, and as an account number (identifier) throughout the life of your loan(s) so that data may be recorded accurately.

Paperwork Reduction Notice

According to the Paperwork Reduction Act of 1995, no persons are required to respond to a collection of information unless it displays a currently valid OMB control number. The valid OMB control number for this information collection is 1845-0005. The time required to complete this information collection is estimated to average 0.16 hours (10 minutes) per response, including the time to review instructions, search existing data resources, gather and maintain the data needed, and complete and review the information collection. *If you have any comments concerning the accuracy of the time estimate(s) or suggestions for improving this form, please write to:*

U.S. Department of Education, Washington, DC 20202-4651.

If you have any comments or concerns regarding the status of your individual submission of this form, write directly to the address shown in Section 7.

D. Recertifying Your Deferment

After you've obtained a deferment, you may have to reapply every so often to keep it. This is called recertification. Although most deferments last for a certain number of years, they are often doled out in six- or 12-month intervals. For example, you may keep an economic hardship deferment for up to three years, but you have to prove your eligibility every 12 months. Your deferment form will tell you how often you must reapply. If you don't have a copy of your form, call the holder of your loan and ask. In reapplying, you will have to provide evidence showing that the condition upon which your deferment was based still exists. For example, unemployment deferments are granted to borrowers who are unemployed but looking for work. To recertify this deferment, you will have to provide the names of companies with which you applied for a job during the previous six months.

Not all deferments require recertification. In-school and public service deferments, for example, are determined by the dates provided by the person who completes your initial certification form. But if these dates change—say, you graduate earlier or later than expected—you'll need to contact your loan holder and recertify your deferment so that it matches the new date.

A month or so before the end of your deferment period, your loan holder should send you a notice that payments will become due if you don't recertify your current deferment or set up some other plan for postponing repayment. This is the time to recertify. If you don't, and you're unable to resume your payments, you will have to deal with late payment notices and phone calls when your deferment lapses. Even if you never hear from your loan holder, keep a record of when your deferment period ends and start the recertification process well in advance of that date. Call at least four weeks before the deferment period ends and ask for the recertification paperwork. Complete it and return it promptly.

E. Obtaining a Forbearance

If you don't qualify for a deferment, but are facing hard times financially, your loan holder may still allow you to postpone payment on your loans or temporarily reduce your payments. An arrangement of this sort is called a forbearance. Forbearances are easier to obtain than deferments—for example, you may be able to obtain a forbearance even if your loan is in default. But forbearance is often the less attractive option because interest will continue to accrue when you are not making payments, no matter what type of loan you have. This means that your loan balance will increase during a forbearance period. But if you can't make your loan payments, the advantage of a forbearance is that it will keep you out of default. And in the long run, the cost of default is a much more expensive than the extra interest that accrues during a forbearance.

Think first about obtaining forbearances on some, but not all, of your loans. Arranging for partial forbearance may be enough to give you some breathing room while you catch up financially. Ask for forbearances on your low interest loans first. If you can keep making payments on your high interest loans, it will cost you less in the long run.

Or, your loan holder may send you a form to fill out and require that you document your income and expenses. Your loan holder must give you a forbearance on a federal student loan if your student loan payments exceed 20% of your gross monthly income. Forbearances are also mandatory in cases of local or national emergencies or disasters. In most other circumstances, your loan holder may use its discretion when deciding whether or not to grant a forbearance. Congress encourages loan holders to grant forbearances when poor health or other personal problems make it difficult for a borrower to meet loan obligations. Sometimes, the holder of your loan will grant you a forbearance based on your simply asking, without requiring you to complete any paperwork. But your forbearance agreement must be in writing, clearly spelling out the terms.

If you qualify for a forbearance, you may be able to keep it for up to three years. To find out the maximum forbearance period for your loan, ask your loan holder.

Help! I still can't manage my loans. If you've carefully explored the repayment and postponement options described in the last two chapters, and you still can't manage one or more of your loans, read Chapter 7 to learn about what you can expect if you default on your loans, and Chapter 10 to find out whether bankruptcy might be an option for you.

Consequences of Not Paying Your Loans

If you haven't made any payments on your student loans for quite some time and haven't arranged for a cancellation, deferment or forbearance, your loans have no doubt been placed in default. Being in default on your loans generally means that you haven't paid for nine months or more and the holder of your loan has concluded that you do not intend to pay. It also means that the Department of Education or guarantee agency holding your loan will put a lot of time and effort into finding you and trying to collect what you owe.

If you've missed only a payment or two, your loans are considered delinquent, not in default, but the holder of your loan will still contact you to make payment arrangements.

This chapter describes the precise steps that student loan holders can take when loans are delinquent or in default—and what you can do to avoid having your money or property taken and to avoid getting sued. Chapter 8 explains the steps you can take to get out of default.

A. Initial Collection Attempts

If you are delinquent or have defaulted on a student loan, you will probably first receive a series of collection or dunning letters and perhaps some phone calls. The holder of your loans will demand payment and describe to you the horrors that might occur if you don't pay—such as having your wages garnished or losing any tax refunds to which you are entitled. You are likely to be called if your loan is held by a collection agency or aggressive guarantee agency. Holders of loans prefer sending collection letters to maintain a paper history, however. If you don't pay up or enter into a repayment agreement after receiving the dunning letters, you may be subjected to more serious collection tactics. (See Section B.)

1. Dunning Letters

If you are delinquent on a student loan, expect to receive dunning letters quickly—sometimes in as few as ten days after a payment is past due. Once you are in default and your loans are held by a guarantee agency, Department of Education regulations state that the agency must contact you in writing to demand payment. (59 C.F.R. §682.410.) There is often a gap between what Department of Education regulations require and what occurs, however, so you may never actually receive letters demanding payment. This is especially true if the guarantee agency has lost track of you.

If you receive letters, they are likely to come in intervals.

- **One to 45 days after default.** During this period, you will be sent a notice stating that if you do not make payment arrangements, the agency will either garnish your wages (see Section B.3) or sue you (see Section B.4).

- **46 to 180 days after default.** During this period, the regulations require that you be sent a minimum of three notices demanding that you immediately begin repaying the loan and informing you that your delinquency has been reported to the national credit bureaus if it has been. The final notice is supposed to state that the agency will take more forceful action, including intercepting your tax refund (see Section B.2), garnishing your wages (see Section B.3) or suing you (see Section B.4).

If you are sent these notices and any of them are returned to the guarantee agency because it does not have your correct address, within ten days of receiving the returned notice, the agency must attempt to locate you through skip-tracing methods.

Here are the primary resources a guarantee agency may use to find you.

Information on your loan application. The Department of Education file contains your loan application, which includes your address, phone number, nearest living relative and some credit and employment information. If you've moved, someone listed on a credit application—such as a past employer—may know where you are.

Relatives, friends and neighbors. A guarantee agency collector may call your relatives, friends or neighbors for information on your whereabouts.

Your former landlord. A guarantee agency collector may call the county property tax office and find the name, address and phone number of your old landlord.

WHEN YOUR AUNT SALLY GETS A CALL FROM A COLLECTOR

Collectors know that they walk a thin line between ethical and unethical behavior when they call around trying to find you. Most, however, don't care about behaving ethically. They just want to find you to collect what you owe. One of the most common tactics used by collectors when they call your relatives is to pose as a long-lost friend desperate to contact you. When they call your friends, employer, neighbors or former landlord they may pose as a long-lost cousin to try to get your forwarding address or phone number. The collector may claim to be in some kind of a bind which needs your immediate attention. Most people want to be helpful and readily give out the information, not realizing that your alleged prodigal cousin or friend is really one of your worst nightmares.

Post office. The guarantee agency collector may check the post office for a forwarding address and is likely to examine several regional phone books. And guarantee agencies are likely to get a post office employee to give out the street address associated with a post office box.

State motor vehicle department. The guarantee agency collector will most likely contact your state's motor vehicle department. Although a few states restrict access to motor vehicle records to only people with a legitimate reason for requesting the information, state guarantee agencies often have muscle here. In fact, federal regulations encourage guarantee agencies to seek information from state motor vehicle departments to help locate student debtors.

Voter registration records. Some guarantee agency collectors check voter registration records in the county where you live. If you've moved out of a county and registered in the new place, your new county would have forwarded cancellation information to your old county, and the registrar may make that information available.

Utility companies. Although it is difficult, a guarantee agency collector may be able to find you through the electric or phone company, especially if you have remained in the same service area for a while. Even if you move out of the area, the company may have your new address as a place to send your final bill.

Banks. If you move but leave your old bank account open—even if you don't continue to do business with the bank—the bank will probably have your new address and may provide it to a guarantee agency.

Credit bureaus. For a small fee, a guarantee agency collector can place your name on a credit bureau locate list. (See Section 2.) In theory at least, if you apply for credit—even if you've moved hundreds or thousands of miles from where you previously lived—your name will be forwarded to the guarantee agency. Guarantee agencies are encouraged to contact credit bureaus to obtain location information on student debtors.

Federal government records. Social Security, unemployment, disability, census and most other government records are not public documents, so collectors can't get them. The one exception is IRS records. Under federal regulations guarantee agencies looking for student debtors have access to their IRS files.

AVOIDING A GUARANTEE AGENCY

If you have reason to avoid the guarantee agency, you may want to take steps to avoid being found. Here are a few ideas.

- Don't reveal your new address, city or state to anyone except a few trusted people who won't tell anyone else.

- Don't send the post office a change of address form; instead, write directly to the people who need your new address.

- Keep your new phone number unlisted.

- Don't register to vote if you are required to provide a previous address.

- Close your old bank accounts; open new ones at different banks—not at the banks nearest to where you work or live. It's best to pick a bank clear across town.

- Don't, under any circumstance, apply for new credit.

2. Reporting Default to Credit Bureaus

Credit bureaus are profit-making companies that gather and sell information about individual credit histories. They sell credit files to banks, mortgage lenders, credit unions, credit card companies, department stores, insurance companies, landlords and even a few employers. These companies and individuals use the files to supplement applications for credit, insurance, housing and employment.

Credit bureaus may also provide identifying information concerning a consumer—including name, address, former address, place of employment and former place of employment—to government agencies, including the Department of Education. Credit bureaus may also be key players in keeping tabs on you and your student loan debt.

If you haven't been making payments on your student loans or been granted a deferment or forbearance, your default will be reported to national credit bureaus. This means that if you apply for credit—and possibly for rental housing, a job or an insurance policy—the place where you submitted your application will find the default if it does a credit check and may reject your application because of it. Before a credit bureau can add your default to your credit report, however, the holder of your loans must send you a notice about your right to enter into a repayment plan. You also have the right to look at your loan file and request a hearing if you think there is a problem. For example, you might owe less than what is being reported to the credit bureau.

If you're delinquent on your student loans and the holder has reported the delinquency to the credit bureaus, you probably won't be able to remove the late payment notation from your credit file. Nevertheless, it is wise to contact the holder of your loans to make arrangements for a payment schedule you can afford or to see if you qualify to postpone your payments. (See Chapters 5 and 6.)

If you are in default, the negative notation in your credit file will be virtually impossible to remove unless you take steps to get out of default. (See Chapter 8, Section A.)

There are three major credit bureaus—Equifax, Experian and Trans Union. There are also thousands of smaller credit bureaus. These smaller companies buy their information from the big three.

There are several types of information collected and kept in your credit report.

- **Personal information.** A credit file usually includes your name and any former names, past and present addresses, Social Security number and employment history including salary. If you're married, information about your spouse may be in your file as well.

- **Accounts reported monthly.** The bulk of information in your credit file is your credit history. Certain creditors provide monthly reports to credit bureaus showing the status of your accounts with them. On these accounts, your credit report will contain the name of the creditor, type of account, account number, date the account was opened, your payment history, your credit limit or loan amount and your current balance. Creditors that provide monthly reports generally include banks, savings and loans and credit unions; credit and charge card issuers; large department stores; oil and gas companies; and other creditors receiving regular monthly installments, such as mortgage and auto finance companies.

- **Accounts reported when in default.** Landlords and property managers, utility companies, local retailers, insurance companies, magazines and newspapers, hospitals and people you hire to work for you such as accountants, doctors and lawyers generally provide information to credit bureaus only when an account is past due or the creditor has attempted to collect from you. In these situations, your credit report will generally include the name of the creditor, type of account, account number and your delinquency status.

- **Public records.** Public records are maintained by government agencies and anyone can get access to them. Local, state and federal court filings are public records. So is the data kept at land records offices. Credit bureaus use private companies to search public records for information such as lawsuits—including divorces—court judgments and judgment liens, foreclosures, bankruptcy filings and tax liens.

- **Inquiries.** The final items in your credit report are called inquiries. These are the names of creditors and others, such as a potential employer, who requested a copy of your report during the previous six months—although credit bureaus may report inquiries for up to two years.

If the amount outstanding is $100 or more, the Department or guarantee agency is supposed to report your default to credit bureaus before proceeding with a tax intercept. (See Section B.2.) In truth, your default may be reported at any time, by any holder of your loan. When the Department of Education or a guarantee agency reports your default to a credit bureau, the report is supposed to include the total amount you borrowed, the total balance you owe and the collection and repayment status.

With the exception of Perkins loans, however, there is a time limit on how long the holder of your loan can report a default to the credit bureaus. For most loans, defaults may be listed in your credit report for seven years from the date that the loan holder first reported the account to the reporting agency. The clock stops running during periods when you make payments, but starts again if you go back into default.

More information on credit bureaus. You can find an explanation of the inner workings of credit bureaus and credit files, and information on cleaning up and correcting error in a credit file, in *Credit Repair*, by Robin Leonard (Nolo).

B. More Serious Collection Efforts

If you're in default on your student loans and ignore the loan holder's attempts to contact you, expect more serious action. At a minimum, your balance will begin to rise quickly as collection fees are added. In addition, the Department of Education will probably grab your tax refunds. If you're one of the truly unlucky, your wages may be garnished or you may be sued.

1. Assessing Collection Fees

Defaulting on federal student loans can cost you a bundle—far in excess of the amount you borrowed originally. The precise amount may depend on who is attempting to collect the debt.

a. Guarantee Agency

The Higher Education Act requires a guarantee agency to assess reasonable collection costs against a borrower who has defaulted on student loans. Department of Education regulations authorize a fee of as much as 43%, clearly not reasonable. Until 1996, guarantee agencies often added the full 43%, even though some student loan promissory notes limit collection fees to 25%. Today, however, rather than read each note to determine when they can charge 43% and when they are limited to 25%, guarantee agencies simply cap the fee at 25%.

This 25% limit is a temporary arrangement while the Department of Education tries to figure out a system to sort through the different types of loans. Eventually the Department would like to cap fees to 25% only for those loans that specifically require this lower amount.

The collection is added to the balance of what you already owe—principal, interest, penalties and other collection fees. The penalty is assessed at an annual rate of 6% of the amount past due whenever you do not make at least a partial payment within 90 days of receiving a demand for payment from the Department of Education. Other collection fees may include mail and phone costs, fees for reporting information to or requesting information from credit bureaus, bank charges and computer maintenance charges.

Common sense dictates that borrowers in default are not likely to contact a guarantee agency when collection fees pump up their loan balances. To combat this reality, the Department of Education has created fee reduction incentives. If you take steps to get out of default—

such as entering into a repayment plan (see Chapter 8, Section A.1) or consolidating your loans (see Chapter 5, Section C)—the guarantee agency will reduce the collection fee to 18.5%. In addition, the Department has authorized the guarantee agencies to compromise or waive such fees in extreme cases. (See Chapter 8, Section A.3.) Your offer to repay your balance in a lump sum or over a few months may be all the incentive the guarantee agency needs to dispense with the collection fee.

b. Collection Agencies

Collection agencies charge the Department of Education a commission—usually around 28%. The Department will authorize the collection agency to pass that commission on to you—meaning you have to pay both the money you owe on the loan and the commission. For every $100 you owe, you will have to pay the collection agency both the $100 and collection agency's commission. After a quick mental calculation, you might conclude that you would have to pay $128 for every $100 you owe; but in fact, the collection agency's commission is calculated on the amount you owe the Department of Education and the commission combined. So, for every $100 you owe, you'll have to pay $140 as 28% of $140 (the commission) is $40, leaving $100 to go to the Department of Education or the guarantee agency.

2. Losing Your Income Tax Refund

The IRS can intercept your income tax refund until your defaulted student loans are paid in full. The Department of Education refers to this as the tax offset program. It is one of the most popular methods of collecting defaulted student loans.

The IRS can intercept a refund only if the loan is held by a guarantee agency, the Department of Education or a collection agency working for the Department of Education. If your school, the lender, a loan servicer or a company on the secondary market has your loan—even if you are behind on your payments—your tax refund is protected from the clutches of the IRS.

Here is how the intercept program works.

1. Each tax year, the guarantee agency or collection agency working for the Department of Education must review your account to verify that:

   • the Department of Education or a guarantee agency holds your loan

   • the balance owed is $25 or more, and

   • you have made no payments on your loan within the previous 90 days.

2. Once it verifies this information, the guarantee or collection agency notifies the IRS that your loan is in default.

3. The IRS determines whether or not you're entitled to a tax refund.

4. If you are entitled to a refund, the guarantee or collection agency will notify you that the IRS proposes to keep all or some of it. The notice must include the name of the guarantee or collection agency, the amount of your refund that may be taken and how you can obtain more information or file an objection. The Department of Education encourages guarantee and collection agencies to include on their notices as much other information as possible—such as the loan amount, the date of the loan, the lender's name, where you attended school, the payments you've made, the principal owed, the interest owed and when the loan was turned over to the agency. The agencies are under no obligation to include this other information, however, which means that the notice can be very confusing if you have more than one loan. You will not get separate notices for each loan in default.

5. Within 20 days of the date on the notice, you can make a written request for copies of the loan documents, including the promissory note and your record of payments. You can also file a written objection to the intercept, request a repayment schedule or request a review of your file within 65 days of receiving the notice. The notice will include a Request for Review form. (See the Appendix for a copy.) The review will be based on your documents alone—your file and the other documentation you submit—unless you request an oral hearing. If you feel that you are better able to explain your situation by speaking than by writing, request an oral hearing. If you do not live near or cannot easily get to the city in which the agency is located, you can request a telephone hearing.

To stop the intercept, you must present written evidence showing any of the following:

- You've repaid the loan.

- You are making payments under a repayment agreement you reached with the guarantee agency, Department of Education or collection agency, or you've been granted a cancellation, deferment or forbearance.

- You have filed for bankruptcy and your case is still open. This means that the bankruptcy automatic stay—the order that prohibits creditors from trying to collect—bars the IRS from intercepting your tax refund.

- The loan was discharged in bankruptcy. (See Chapter 10.)

- The debtor has died.

- You are totally and permanently disabled, meaning that you are unable to work or go to school because of an injury or illness that is expected to continue indefinitely or result in your death.

- It is not your loan. This would be unusual; however, it could come up if you were being pursued for example, on a deceased spouse's loan.

- The loan is not legally enforceable for any other reason—for example, your signature on the loan papers was forged.

- You dropped out and the school owes you a refund.

- You borrowed the money to attend a trade school and were either unable to complete your education because the school closed or you were falsely certified by the school as eligible for the loan. (See Chapter 9.)

6. The guarantee or collection agency considers your evidence. It is really important that you send in all papers you have supporting your claim that the IRS should not grab your refund.

7. If the guarantee or collection agency decides against you—which is likely to happen if your documents do not support your claim—it notifies the IRS, which intercepts your tax refund. The IRS can also deduct the costs, such as a collections fee, incurred in trying to collect from you. Unfortunately, you have no right to appeal the decision. If you later find additional documentation to support your claim, however, you can contact the guarantee or collection agency and plead your case anew.

a. Avoiding an Intercept

You can avoid having your income tax refunds intercepted by figuring out how much you'll owe in taxes and making sure your employer withholds the minimum amount necessary to cover it. If you try this strategy, be careful not to underpay, or the IRS could hit you with a penalty of 0.25% per month.

Also, if you are married and file a joint tax return, your non-debtor spouse can obtain a partial payment of a refund slated to be intercepted by filing with the IRS an Injured Spouse form. (You can download the form from the IRS at http://www.irs.ustreas.gov.) If you're concerned about a likely tax intercept, however, your spouse may be better off filing a separate return.

b. Getting Your Money Back

If the IRS proceeds with the intercept but you later convince the guarantee or collection agency that the offset should not have happened, or if the IRS takes your entire refund which is more than the amount you owe, you must request a full or partial reimbursement from the agency. It is the agency's responsibility to refund your money and then seek reimbursement from the Department of Education. You can also get the money back if you went to a trade school and are able to qualify for a loan cancellation. (See Chapter 9.)

If you get grief from the agency representative, ask to speak with a supervisor. In the unlikely event that the supervisor won't process your request for a refund, you may need to play hardball. Tell him or her that the action is required by the U.S. Department of Education's *Addendum to the Agreement with a State or Private Nonprofit Institution or Organization for Coverage of its Student Loan Insurance Program*. You may even need to read chapter and verse of the law. Paragraph 3.4 of that document reads:

If the agency determines that the offset should not have been made, the agency should refund the offset amount to the borrower. If the offset was for a joint return, the refund must be made payable to both taxpayers. The agency should then seek reimbursement from [the Department of Education] for that amount....

c. Losing State Tax Refunds

A growing number of states assist the federal government by intercepting state tax refunds and turning them over to the Department of Education. And if your loan is from a public college which has turned it over to the state for collection, the state may try to collect by intercepting your state income tax refund.

Losing other state entitlements. Your state tax refund may not be the only benefit at risk if you default on your student loans. In some states, licenses necessary to practice certain professions, such as medicine, dentistry, law and accountancy, may be withheld from people who default on a student loan guaranteed by a state guarantee agency. In Illinois, for example, the Department of Professional Regulation can deny or refuse to renew a license to run a collection agency to any person who is in default on a loan guaranteed by the Illinois State Scholarship Commission. (225 ILCS §425/9.)

3. Having Your Wages Garnished

The Department of Education and guarantee agencies are authorized to garnish, or take, 10% of the wages of a student loan debtor who is in default. If you act quickly and raise recognized objections discussed below, however, you may be able to stop this from happening.

For virtually all other debts, a creditor can garnish your wages only if it first sues you and obtains a court judgment—and in that situation, it can garnish up to 25% of your wages. But the holder of your student loans does not have to sue you first. In fact, if the Department of Education or a guarantee agency sues you and obtains a court judgment (see Section B.4), it cannot garnish 25% of your wages. It is limited to garnishing only 10% to pay what you owe.

At least 30 days before the garnishment is set to begin, the guarantee agency or Department must notify you in writing of:

- the amount you owe

- how you can obtain a copy of records relating to the debt

- how to enter into a repayment schedule, and

- how to request a hearing on the proposed garnishment.

To stop the garnishment before it begins, you must respond to the notice in writing within 15 days of receiving it. You are presumed to receive the notice five days after it is postmarked. If you do not respond, the Department or guarantee agency will send a wage garnishment order to your employer within 20 days of when you receive the notice. Your employer must comply with the order or be subject to penalties.

Here's a timeline showing how the wage garnishment procedure works.

May 1	**May 6**	**May 21**	**May 26**
Notice is mailed.	You are presumed to have received it.	Deadline for responding to notice.	If you do not respond garnishment begins

You can object to the garnishment if you returned to work within the past 12 months after being fired or laid off and have not yet been back on the job for a full year. A number of guarantee agencies have been known to claim that you must have received unemployment compensation to qualify; there is no such legal requirement. Object vigorously if the agency makes this claim. If you have been continually employed for the previous 12 months, raise one of the objections permitted when the IRS seeks to intercept your tax refund. (See Section B.2.)

You can also object to the garnishment if you'd be left with a weekly take-home pay of less than 30 times the federal minimum wage, which is currently $5.15 per hour. That amount is $154.50. Federal laws prohibit wage garnishments in such a situation. State laws limiting wage garnishments, such as Alaska's law requiring that you be left with at least $350 per week or Florida's requiring that you take home a minimum of $500 per week, don't apply in the cases of student loan garnishments.

To avoid the wage garnishment, you can simply request a repayment schedule. To do so, you must call the Department of Education or the collections department of the guarantee agency that sent you the notice of the wage garnishment.

To object to the garnishment, you must complete and return a Request for Hearing or Exemption form. (See the Appendix for a copy.)

4. Getting Sued

The Department of Education has forever to sue you to collect your student loans. This wasn't always the case. But on April 9, 1991, President Bush signed the Higher Education Technical Amendments which retroactively did away with the statute of limitations—a six-year time limit during which the holder of a loan could sue—as a defense on any student loan lawsuit. The retroactive application goes back to 1965, when student loans were first disbursed.

More information if you are sued. Nolo publishes three excellent resources for people who are sued.

- *Represent Yourself in Court,* by Paul Bergman and Sara Berman-Barrett, contains detailed information on representing yourself in any court, in most kinds of cases.
- *Money Troubles: Legal Strategies to Cope With Your Debts,* by Robin Leonard, devotes an entire chapter to what happens if you are sued.
- *How to Sue for Up to $25,000...and Win,* by Judge Roderic Duncan, gives Californians all the forms and instructions they need to sue or defend themselves in civil court.

a. When You Aren't Likely to Be Sued

The guarantee agency or Department of Education or its collection agency probably won't sue you if it determines that:

- the cost would exceed any amount it could get from you; litigation is expensive, so this might be the case if you owe a relatively small amount, or

- you have no assets that could be taken to satisfy all or a substantial portion of the debt; this is called being judgment proof (see Section B.4.b.ii).

THE LIKELIHOOD OF GETTING SUED

Department of Education regulations state that the civil lawsuit *shall* be initiated by the 545th day following default. It took the Department quite some time to begin using this collection practice, however. In 1993 it was used only rarely. For the 12-month period ending September 30, 1995, only about 200 student loan defaulters had been sued. During the next three months, however, the government sued over 700 defaulters, an increase of 250%.

And they have begun these suits in full force. There was a 55% increase in student loan lawsuits filed by the Justice Department from 1997 to 1998. By 1998, the government had filed over 14,000 of these cases in the federal court system. The Department of Education expects the numbers to grow as it gets more and more aggressive in trying to collect defaulted student loans.

b. When There's a Judgment Against You

A judgment is a piece of paper issued by the court stating that the person or agency that filed the lawsuit, or plaintiff, won and is entitled to a certain sum of money. Once a judgment against you is entered into the court records, you and the person who sued you get new legalistic names: the plaintiff is referred to as a judgment creditor and you are a judgment debtor. Judgment creditors usually take a judgment debtor's property to satisfy the judgment.

i. Common Collection Techniques

What property the judgment creditor can take varies from state to state. Usually, the creditor can go after your bank and other deposit accounts, your valuable personal property such as cars and antiques and a portion of your wages. Most judgment creditors can go after 25% of your net wages, but the Department of Education or a guarantee agency is limited to a 10% garnishment. (See Section B.3.) The most common methods of collection are property liens, property levies and assignment orders.

Property liens. One collection technique often used by judgment creditors is to record or file the judgment with the county records office. This creates a property lien—a public notice that the person who recorded the lien claims you owe him or her money. In some states, a judgment entered against you automatically creates a lien on the home and land you own in the county where the judgment was obtained. In other states, the creditor must record the judgment with the county, and then the recorded judgment creates a lien on your real property. A judgment creditor can also get a lien on personal property by recording the judgment with the Secretary of State. This lien usually applies to property that is registered or titled, such as a car or stock.

A judgment creditor who has a lien on your property will likely be paid, even though the process may be a slow one. When you sell or refinance your property, title will have to be cleared—that is, all liens must be removed, usually by paying the lienholder—before the deal can close.

Instead of waiting for you to sell your property, the judgment creditor can execute on the lien—that is, have a sheriff seize your property, arrange for a public sale and take the proceeds. This is unusual, however, because public sales are time-consuming and expensive. Furthermore, the judgment creditor may not get very much money by selling your property at this kind of sale, called a distress sale. Any lender you still owe, such as a mortgage holder or car dealer, government taxing authority or other creditor who has placed a lien on your property before the judgment creditor, will be paid first. Then you get any exemption to which you are entitled. (See Section B.4.b.ii.) Only then does the judgment creditor get a share.

Property levies. A judgment creditor can seize, or levy, some of your personal property. If you have money in a bank account or safe deposit box, the judgment creditor can present a copy of the judgment to a sheriff, who can usually take the money. Or if you own valuable personal property such as a car or antique, the judgment creditor could send the sheriff to take the property, sell it at a public auction and apply the proceeds toward the debt. You do not have to let the sheriff into your home, however, unless he or she has a special court order authorizing entry. The judgment creditor won't be interested in property that has little value.

Assignment orders. A third collection method is called an assignment order. This lets judgment creditors go after property you own that cannot be levied on, such as an anticipated tax refund, the loan value of an unmatured life insurance policy or an annuity policy. Independent contractors and other self-employed people who have no regular wages that can be garnished are particularly susceptible to an assignment order against the accounts owed but not yet paid to them. In some states, retirement funds such as IRAs, Keoghs or 401(k) deposits may be taken by assignment.

An assignment order works simply. The judgment creditor applies to the court for an order prohibiting you from disposing of money you have a right to receive. You are given the date and time of the court hearing and an opportunity to appear and object. A judgment creditor who gets such an order serves it on whomever holds your money. When payment to you comes due, the money is sent to the judgment creditor instead of you.

ii. Stopping Judgment Collection Efforts

Having your property taken can be devastating. It's miserable enough to owe money; it's worse to have a judgment creditor take what little property you may have left.

Don't be a victim. Although you may doubt it, you still can fight. The process of trying to grab property to pay a judgment can be time-consuming and burdensome for a judgment creditor. Furthermore, just because a judgment creditor levies on your property doesn't mean that he or she is entitled to take it. Every state exempts certain property from creditors. This means that creditors cannot take that property, even if you owe $100,000 and have no other resources. In addition, you may be able to keep property that isn't exempt if you can show a judge, in a simple court hearing where you can represent yourself, that you need it to support yourself or your family.

All public benefits—Social Security, unemployment benefits, workers' compensation benefits and welfare—are off limits to most creditors. The government can, however, get to your Social Security and other federal benefits to collect defaulted student loans. Up to $9,000 of your benefits are exempt, but any amount higher than the $9,000 limit can be taken to pay off student loans.

In most states, your clothing, furniture, appliances, books and personal effects can't be taken to pay a debt. Nor can a portion of the equity in your car or house, most insurance policies and most retirement pensions. The chart below summarizes the main exemptions for each state.

- **Equity in your house.** Equity is the market value minus the value of debts against the property, such as mortgages, home equity loans and liens. In most states, your creditors cannot reach at least some of the equity in your home.

- **Equity in your car.** Equity is the car's current book value less the amount you still owe on it or owe on any property for which you've pledged your car as collateral. In most states, you'll be able to keep an inexpensive car or a car on which you still owe a lot.

- **Work tools.** Most states bar your creditors from taking the equipment you need to carry out your livelihood, such as computer equipment, work tools and reference books.

- **Wildcard.** About half the states have a wildcard exemption—an amount you can apply toward any item of property.

More information on exemptions. You can find a detailed list of what's exempt in each state in *Money Troubles: Legal Strategies to Cope With Your Debts,* by Robin Leonard (Nolo).

IF YOU'RE SUED: PROPERTY YOU GET TO KEEP

State	Equity In Your House	Equity In Your Car	Work Tools	Wildcard (to be used on any property)
Alabama	5,000	0	0	3,000
Alaska	62,000	3,450	3,220	0
Arizona	100,000	1,500	2,500	0
Arkansas	unlimited	1,200	750	500
California	50,000-125,000	1,900	5,000	0
Colorado	30,000	1,000	1,500	0
Connecticut	75,000	1,500	necessary	1,000
Delaware	0	0	50-75	500
Dist. of Col.	0	0	200-500	0
Florida	unlimited	1,000	0	1,000
Georgia	5,000	1,000	500	400
Hawaii	30,000	1,000	necessary	0
Idaho	50,000	1,500	1,000	0
Illinois	7,500	1,200	750	2,000
Indiana	7,500	0	0	4,000
Iowa	unlimited	5,000	10,000	100
Kansas	unlimited	20,000	7,500	0
Kentucky	5,000	2,500	1,000-3,000	1,000
Louisiana	15,000	0	necessary	0
Maine	25,000-60,000	2,500	5,000	400
Maryland	0	0	2,500	5,550
Massachusetts	100,000-200,000	750	500	0
Michigan	3,500	0	1,000	0
Minnesota	200,000-500,000	3,400	8,500-13,000	0
Mississippi	75,000	0	0	10,000
Missouri	8,000	1,000	2,000	400-1,250
Montana	60,000	1,200	3,000	0
Nebraska	12,500	0	2,400	2,500
Nevada	125,000	4,500	4,500	0

IF YOU'RE SUED: PROPERTY YOU GET TO KEEP (contined)

State	Equity In Your House	Equity In Your Car	Work Tools	Wildcard (to be used on any property)
New Hampshire	30,000	4,000	5,000	1,000
New Jersey	0	0	0	0
New Mexico	30,000	4,000	1,500	500
New York	10,000	2,400	600	0
North Carolina	10,000	1,500	750	500
North Dakota	80,000	1,200	1,000	2,500
Ohio	5,000	1,000	750	400
Oklahoma	unlimited	3,000	5,000	0
Oregon	25,000	1,700	3,000	400
Pennsylvania	0	0	0	300
Rhode Island	0	0	500	0
South Carolina	5,000	1,200	750	0
South Dakota	unlimited	0	300	4,000
Tennessee	5,000	0	1,900	4,000
Texas	unlimited	one vehicle (part of 30,000 personal property exemption)	what's needed (part of 30,000 personal property exemption)	0
Utah	10,000	2,500	3,500	0
Vermont	75,000	2,500	5,000	400
Virginia	5,000	2,000	10,000	0
Washington	30,000	2,500	5,000	1,000
West Virginia	15,000	2,400	1,500	800
Wisconsin	40,000	1,200	7,500	0
Wyoming	10,000	2,400	2,000	0

Any time a judgment creditor attempts to take your property, you'll be notified by a court paper the sheriff sends to you. If the property is exempt or you need nonexempt property to live on, you can request a hearing called a claim of exemption, or something similar, to argue that it will be a financial hardship on you if the property is taken, or that your property is exempt under state law. Here is an overview of how a claim of exemption hearing normally works. You don't need a lawyer to fill out the papers or to represent yourself at the hearing.

1. When you are notified of a property levy or assignment order, you will be told in writing how to file a claim of exemption—that is, how to tell the judgment creditor you consider the property unavailable.

2. Complete and send a copy of your claim of exemption to the judgment creditor, who will probably file a challenge to your claim. He or she may decide not to challenge you, however, if it's too expensive or time-consuming. If the creditor drops the property levy or assignment order, any property taken will be returned to you.

3. If the creditor doesn't drop the property levy or assignment order, he or she will schedule a hearing before a judge. If you don't attend, you'll probably lose.

4. At the hearing, you'll have to explain to the judge that your property is exempt or that you need it to support yourself or your family. This is your opportunity to defend yourself from having your property taken. You must prepare well for this hearing if you want to keep your property.

   For example, if the creditor tries to take your work tools, which are exempt to a certain value in your state, bring along someone who works in your occupation to briefly testify at the hearing. A supervisor, union boss or shop leader can verify that you use the items in your job. You'll need to add the fact that the value of the item does not exceed the exemption amount.

5. The judge will listen to both you and the judgment creditor. Some-times the judgment creditor relies on the papers filed with the court and opts not to attend the hearing. The judge may make a ruling, or may set up an arrangement for you to pay the judgment in install-ments.

c. Defenses

There are very few defenses you can raise to get out of paying your student loans if you are sued by the Department of Education, a collec-tion agency or a guarantee agency.

i. Violations of the Fair Debt Collection Practices Act

Collection agencies and private guarantee agencies, such as USA Funds, must adhere to the federal Fair Debt Collection Practices Act, or FDCPA, in attempting to collect your loan. (15 U.S.C. §1692 and following.) This law bars private companies that collect debts for another person or business from lying, harassing, misleading and otherwise abusing debtors. Because the law does not apply to public entities, neither the Department of Education nor a state guarantee agency must adhere to its provisions.

Some private guarantee agencies claim that the FDCPA doesn't apply to them because they are not collection agencies—that is, they are not collecting for another, but are seeking reimbursement for a debt paid to the lender. The argument against this is that the FDCPA does apply to guarantee agencies because they devote most of their resources to debt collection and they regularly collect debts originally owed others.

If your student loans are held by a collection agency or private guarantee agency, keep reading. The collector violates the FDCPA if it acts in specific ways that might annoy, harass or embarrass you. By explaining the behavior to the court, you might win money damages against the collector, which you can put toward your student loans.

Here's a summary of what the FDCPA prohibits.

Communications with others. A collector cannot contact third parties, such as your employer or neighbors, except to locate you. A collector who contacts any third person must first identify himself or herself—and is strictly limited to confirming or correcting information about your whereabouts.

Communications with you. As mentioned above, a collector must state at the outset that he or she is attempting to collect a debt. In addition, the collector cannot contact you at an unusual or inconvenient time or place: calls before 8 a.m. and after 9 p.m. are prohibited as are calls at work if you tell the collector that your employer prohibits you from receiving collections calls there. If you have hired an attorney, he or she serves as a buffer between you and the collector—who must not contact you unless you give permission, or your attorney doesn't respond on your behalf.

Harassment or abuse. A collector cannot harass, oppress or abuse you—that is, use or threaten to use violence, harm or threaten to harm you or another person, use obscene or profane language, call you repeatedly or place telephone calls to you without identifying himself or herself as a bill collector.

False or misleading representations. A collector can't lie. For instance, he or she cannot falsely represent the amount you owe or the amount of money to be collected. And a collector cannot claim to be a law enforcement officer or suggest a connection with the government, claim to be an attorney, use a false business name or threaten to take action that isn't intended or can't be taken—for example, send a letter stating that it is a final notice, then write to you again demanding payment.

Unfair practices. A collector cannot use any unfair or outrageous method to collect a debt. For example, he or she can't add interest, fees or charges not authorized in the original agreement or by state law, accept a check postdated by more than five days unless you are notified between three and ten days in advance of when the check will be deposited, deposit a postdated check prior to the date on the check, solicit a postdated check by threatening you with criminal prosecution or call you collect or otherwise cause you to incur communications charges.

COLLECTION LAW AND REALITY: THE GAP

Bill collectors aren't supposed to engage in any of the untoward practices described here. But more than a few do. Low income and non-English-speaking debtors are especially targeted. So are non-U.S. citizens. Here are some of the illegal acts in which bill collectors often engage:

- Asserting that you must pay a minimum amount each month to obtain a repayment plan. (See Chapter 8, Section A.1.)

- Claiming that a wage garnishment may be accomplished without legal action—implying that you have no right to a notice before the garnishment occurs or a hearing to object to the garnishment.

- Sending fake legal papers and then pretending to be sheriffs, threatening that you will lose your personal possessions if you don't pay at once.

- Using vulgarity and profanity.

- Harassing your parents.

- Soliciting a postdated check, depositing it early and threatening you with prosecution for writing a bad check.

- Suggesting that you take up prostitution or some other illegal activity to increase your income.

- Threatening to report you to the Immigration and Naturalization Service if you do not appear to be a native-born American.

You also have the right to sue a collection agency or private guarantee agency for harassment. You can represent yourself in small claims court or hire an attorney. You may be able to claim attorneys' fees and court costs if you win. You're entitled to any actual damages, including pain and suffering, and up to $1,000 in punitive damages. To win, you'll probably need to have a witness who can testify about the illegal activities and you'll need to document repeated abusive behavior. If the collector calls five times in one day and then you don't hear back again, you probably don't have a case.

In truly outrageous cases, consider hiring a lawyer to represent you in regular court. This route is wise in those rare cases in which you suffer severe mental abuse and you have reports from therapists and doctors documenting your suffering.

COMPLAINING ABOUT COLLECTION AGENCY HARASSMENT

If your loan is held by the Department of Education and you are being harassed, abused, threatened or lied to by an agency collecting on its behalf, contact the Deputy Director of Debt Collection Services for the U.S. Department of Education. Include your name, Social Security number, the name of the collection agency, the name of the particular collector and the dates of the illegal acts. Fax your complaint letter to 202-708-4954. You can call the office to make sure it received your letter and to find out what action may be taken at 202-708-4766.

Another possible place to go for help is the new student loan Ombudsman within the Office of Student Financial Assistance. This position was created specifically to help student borrowers resolve complaints with lenders, guarantee agencies, the Department of Education and these agencies' collection agencies. To find out more information, visit the website of the Department of Education's Office of Student Financial Assistance at http://www.ed.gov/offices/OSFAP or call toll-free 877-557-2575.

If your loan is held by a private nonprofit guarantee agency, you must voice your complaint with the agency itself. If your loan is held by a state guarantee agency, you can complain about the collection harassment to the state department of education, any public body that oversees the agency or your elected representative. Also, consider whether a state debt collection law applies to the acts of the guarantee agency. (See Section B.4.c.ii.) If you are repeatedly harassed by a state or private guarantee agency, consider contacting the Policy Development Division, Loans Branch of the U.S. Department of Education. You can send a fax to 202-205-0786 or call 202-708-8242. Guarantee agencies are fairly independent of the Department of Education and the Department may not take any action. Nevertheless, Department workers should be interested to learn about systematic problems with guarantee agencies.

ii. State Fair Debt Collection Practices Act

Several states have enacted laws prohibiting unfair debt collection practices. A few laws are similar to the federal legislation. Some, however, prohibit additional collection actions. As with the federal Fair Debt Collection Practices Act, state debt collection laws do not apply to government agencies. Unfortunately, at least one court has held that state debt collection laws are pre-empted by federal laws for all guaranteed student loans. (*Brannan v. U.S.A. Funds*, 94 F.3d 1260 (9th Cir. 1996).) This means that in states covered by the 9th Circuit—Alaska, Arizona, California, Hawaii, Idaho, Oregon and Washington—you cannot assert your state's debt collection law against collection agencies and private guarantee agencies.

Two other cases on this matter, however, have come out the other way. (*McComas v. Financial Collection Agencies*, S.D.W.V. 1997, and *Student Loan Fund of Idaho, Inc. v. Duerner*, Supreme Court of Idaho, 1998.) So, in West Virginia and Idaho at least, collection agencies and private guarantee agencies must adhere to the state law. In other states, it's anyone's guess how a court would rule.

STATE PROTECTIONS AGAINST UNFAIR COLLECTIONS		
STATE	**CODE SECTION**	**LEGAL REQUIREMENTS**
ARIZONA	Ariz. Admin. Code R20-4-1512	Collection agency cannot contact debtor at work unless agency has made reasonable attempt to contact debtor at home and has failed.
	Ariz. Admin. Code R20-4-1514	In the first contact, collection agency must disclose name of original creditor, time and place debt was incurred, merchandise or service purchased and date account was turned over to agency. Debtor has right to see agency's books and records concerning debt and right to copies of all relevant documents in agency's possession.
ARKANSAS	Ark. Code Ann. §17-21-307	Collection agency cannot contact debtor at work unless agency has made good faith attempt to contact debtor at home and has failed.
COLORADO	Code of Colo. Regs. 4-903-1	Collection agency must provide debtor with receipt for payments made in cash or by any other means which does not in and of itself provide evidence of payment. (Check drawn on debtor's bank account would not require receipt.) Receipt must be provided within five working days after payment is received.
		If debtor requests in writing, collection agency must provide at no cost once per year, statement of up to 12 months of payments within ten days of request. Statement must include debtor's name, creditor's name, amounts paid, dates payments were received, allocation of money to principal, interest, court costs, attorneys' fees and other costs. Collection agency may charge no more than $5 for subsequent statements.
GEORGIA	Ga. Compilation Rules & Regs. 120-1-14-.21	Collection agency cannot contact debtor by phone or in person after 10 p.m. or before 5 a.m.
	Ga. Compilation Rules & Regs. 120-1-14-.23	Collection agency cannot claim it has something of value in its possession to lure debtor.
	Ga. Compilation Rules & Regs. 120-1-14-.24	Collection agency cannot seek or obtain statement in which debtor agrees to pay debt discharged in bankruptcy without clearly disclosing nature and consequence of agreement and fact that debtor is not legally obligated to pay debt.
HAWAII	Ha. Rev. Stats. Ann. §443B-19	Collection agency cannot seek or obtain statement in which debtor agrees: • that debt was incurred to pay for necessities of life when debt was not incurred for that purpose • to pay debt discharged in bankruptcy without clearly disclosing nature and consequence of agreement and fact that debtor is not legally obligated to pay debt, and • to pay collection agency's fee for services rendered.
ILLINOIS	225 Ill. Ann. Stat. ¶425/9	Collection agency cannot: • contact debtor's employer unless debt is more than 30 days past due and at least five days before contacting employer agency notifies debtor in writing of intent to contact employer, or • intend or cause mental or physical illness to debtor or family member.
MAINE	Maine Rev. Stat. Ann. §9-A-5-116	Collection agency debt cannot: • communicate with debtor's employer more than twice concerning existence of debt, or • attempt to collect debt that is legally uncollectable.
MASSACHUSETTS	209 Code of Mass. Regulations 18.09	If debtor sends collection agency more than amount due, excess of $1 or more must be refunded to debtor within 30 days after last day of month.
	209 Code of Mass. Regulations 18.13	Collection agency must include phone number and office hours on all communications.

STATE PROTECTIONS AGAINST UNFAIR COLLECTIONS (continued)		
STATE	**CODE SECTION**	**LEGAL REQUIREMENTS**
MASSACHUSETTS (continued)	209 Code of Mass. Regulations 18.15	Collection agency cannot: • communicate with debtor on phone at debtor's home more than twice in seven-day period or at any location other than debtor's home more than twice in 30-day period • visit debtor at home other than "normal waking hours," or if they are not known, before 8 a.m. and after 9 p.m. • visit anyone at debtor's home more than once in a 30-day period unless debtor consents in writing to more frequent visits • enter debtor's home unless expressly invited in • visit debtor at work except to repossess collateral or pick up property including money, or • confront debtor in any public place except courthouse, collection agency's office, debtor's attorney's office, place where conversation between collector and debtor cannot reasonably be overheard, or any other place agreed to by debtor.
		Within 30 days after contacting debtor at work, agency must send debtor notice describing debtor's right not to be contacted at work. As long as debtor does not exercise right not to receive calls at work, agency must send notice every six months.
	209 Code of Mass. Regulations 18.17	Collection agency cannot contact third party for location information more than once in any 12-month period.
	209 Code of Mass. Regulations 18.18	Collection agency cannot: • report information to credit bureau in its own name —must report debt information in name of original creditor • claim it has something of value in its possession to lure debtor.
	209 Code of Mass. Regulations 18.19	Within five days of first contact with debtor, collection agency must provide debtor with: • name and mailing address of collection agency and creditor • description of debt • statement of alleged default • action required to cure default, and • name, address and telephone number of person to be contacted for more information.
MICHIGAN	Mich. Comp. Laws Ann. §339.915	Collection agency cannot: • bring public notice that debtor has not paid debt • violate postal laws, or • fail to implement procedures designed to prevent law violations by employees.
	Mich. Comp. Laws Ann. §339.915a	Collection agency cannot: • hire an attorney to collect debt unless authorized by creditor, or • fail to provide debtor with receipt for cash payments and other payments when specifically requested.
NORTH CAROLINA	Gen. Stats. of N.C. §58-70-70	Collection agency must provide debtor with receipt for all payments made in cash. Receipt must include name, address and permit number of collection agency, name of creditor, amount and date paid and last name of person accepting payment.
	Gen. Stats. of N.C. §58-70-110	Collection agency cannot claim it has something of value in its possession to lure debtor.
	Gen. Stats. of N.C. §58-70-115	Collection agency cannot seek or obtain statement in which debtor agrees to: • pay debt discharged in bankruptcy • pay debt barred by statute of limitations, or • pay collection agency's fee for services rendered.
PENNSYLVANIA	Penn. Admin. Code 303.3	Collection agency cannot: • claim it has something of value in its possession to lure debtor, or • pursue debtor if collector knows or has reason to know another person is attempting to collect same debt.

STATE PROTECTIONS AGAINST UNFAIR COLLECTIONS (continued)		
STATE	**CODE SECTION**	**LEGAL REQUIREMENTS**
PENNSYLVANIA (continued)	Penn. Admin. Code 303.4	Collection agency cannot: • call debtor during seven days following telephone discussion with debtor • visit debtor at home during 30 days following visit with debtor at home • enter or remain on debtor's premises without permission of member of debtor's household • call debtor at work unless collector has been unable to talk with debtor during preceding 30 days and collector does not know or has no reason to know debtor's employer prohibits such calls • send mail to debtor's work unless it is debtor's billing address or debtor consents in writing • visit debtor's work unless debtor requests it in writing, or • confront debtor in public if communication could reasonably be overheard.
TENNESSEE	Tenn. Code Ann. 62-20-111	Collection agency must include address of state agency regulating collection agencies in all written communications.
TEXAS	Tex. Civil Stat. 5069-11.05	Collection agency cannot: • seek or obtain statement in which debtor agrees that debt was incurred to pay for necessaries of life when in fact debt was not incurred for that purpose • claim it has something of value in its possession to lure debtor, or • violate U.S. postal laws.
WASHINGTON	Rev. Code of Wash. Ann. §19.16.250	In all written communications, collection agency must include name, address and license number of agency and name of creditor. In first communication, collection agency must include an itemization showing: • amount owed on original obligation • interest amount, service charges, collection costs and late fees assessed by creditor • interest amount, service charges and collection costs added by collection agency • attorneys' fees, and • any other charges. Collection agency cannot: • threaten debtor with impairment of credit rating if claim is not paid, or • communicate with debtor more than three times in one week or communicate with debtor at work more than once per week.
	Wash. Admin. Code 308-29-070	Collection agency must disclose interest rate charged.
	Wash. Admin. Code 308-29-080	If collection agency reports delinquent debt to credit bureau and debtor later pays, collection agency must notify credit bureau within 45 days that debt has been satisfied.
WEST VIRGINIA	W. Va. Code §§46A-2-127 through 46A-2-128	Collection agency cannot: • communicate with debtor's employer before obtaining court judgment except through court process • communicate with relative of debtor other than those in debtor's household except through court process • claim it has something of value in its possession to lure debtor • seek or obtain statement in which debtor agrees that debt was incurred to pay for necessaries of life when in fact debt was not incurred for that purpose • seek or obtain statement in which debtor agrees to pay debt discharged in bankruptcy without clearly disclosing nature and consequence of agreement and fact that debtor is not legally obligated to pay debt • attempt to collect collection agency's fee for services rendered, or • violate U.S. postal laws.
WISCONSIN	Wisc. Admin. 74.11	Within five days of first communication with debtor, collection agency must notify debtor, in boldface of at least eight-point type, of address of state agency regulating collection agencies.

iii.　If You Can Prove That You Shouldn't Have to Pay Back the Loan

You can defend a student loan lawsuit by arguing that you don't owe the money. One example where this might work is if you are eligible for a loan cancellation because you went to a trade school that ripped you off. (See Chapter 9.) You can then respond to the lawsuit by saying that you shouldn't have to pay any money back because the loan should be canceled by the government. Another argument might be that you owe only some of the money because you withdrew from the school but didn't get a refund or because the agency suing you miscalculated the amount that you owe.

d.　Defenses You Cannot Raise

If you are sued, you are probably trying to figure out what you can do to make the lawsuit go away. Short of fleeing the country or shutting down the Department of Education, there may be very little you can do to stop the slow grinding wheels of the law.

If you explain your situation to a lawyer who is not familiar with the laws that apply to student loans, that person might immediately think that general contract laws and general consumer laws control your rights and responsibilities. They don't. The discussion below can keep you—and any lawyer you hire—from spending the time and money preparing a defense that will fall flat on its face.

i.　Expiration of the Statute of Limitations

The statute of limitations is the length of time a person or agency has to sue you after you default on a loan or cause some type of injury. In general, the federal government has six years to sue after someone defaults on a federal loan, such as a Federal Housing or Small Business Administration loan. There is no time limit for the government to sue on defaulted student loans, however.

ii. Laches

Laches is a legal concept that means that although a lawsuit is not barred by a statute of limitations, the person suing unreasonably delayed in bringing the lawsuit and it would be prejudicial to the person being sued to have to defend the case. In general, you cannot assert the defense of laches against the government. In only one case has a former student defended against a lawsuit claiming laches, but a year after that decision, the same court ruled that laches could no longer be used in student loan cases. The reasoning stated by the court was that when Congress eliminated the statute of limitations defense, its intent was to eliminate all time-related defenses to getting sued. (*U.S. v. Robbins*, 819 F. Supp. 672 (E.D. Mich. 1993).)

iii. Infancy

In this defense, you'd claim that because you were not a legal adult—over 18 in most states—when you signed the loan agreement, you were not competent to enter into a contract. While this defense, called infancy, is generally available with consumer contracts, the infancy defense was eliminated when the statute of limitations defense was repealed in 1991.

iv. Truth-in-Lending Act Violations

The federal Truth in Lending Act (15 U.S.C. § 1638) requires that lenders disclose the terms of a loan, the interest rate and other information related to the loan. Failure is grounds to cancel the loan or sue the lender for damages. While this defense is generally available with consumer contracts, federal law specifically states it is not a defense to actions for failing to pay federal student loans.

C. Collection Efforts on Private and State Loans

Holders of private and state-funded loans must rely on dunning letters (see Section A.1) and lawsuits (see Section B.4) to collect. They will also report your default to credit bureaus and assess collection fees. If the holder of a private or state-funded loan sues you and wins, it is likely to garnish up to 25% of your net wages, as permitted by state law. A few states limit wage garnishments to 10% or to a minimum weekly amount. (The discussion in Section B.4.b.ii on how to respond to post-judgment collection efforts applies.)

Also, if you are sued on a private loan, the defenses you would be prohibited from bringing against the government or a guarantee agency on a federal loan are available to you—such as the expiration of the statute of limitations and truth in lending violations. (See Section B.4.d.)

You will need help to defend against a lawsuit brought by the holder of a private or state loan. (See the resources listed in Section B.4.)

HELP! I'VE ALREADY PAID OFF MY LOAN

In what is becoming a nightmare for some former students, the Department of Education and guarantee agencies sometimes demand payment from people who repaid their loans years ago. The Department or agency claims that the loan was never paid—often the financial institution that originally loaned or collected the money is out of business—and requires former students to prove they paid. This is obviously very difficult, as few people keep bank records.

If you face this problem and the financial institution from which you borrowed or repaid the money is still in business, solicit its help in getting copies of your canceled checks. If you're told that it doesn't keep such old records, ask workers there to check the microfiche and other electronic records.

If the financial institution is out of business or doesn't have your records, contact the federal agency that oversees the type of institution which had your records:

HELP! I'VE ALREADY PAID OFF MY LOAN (Continued)

- **National Banks.** Office of the Comptroller of the Currency, 800-613-6743, http://www.occ.treas.gov
- **Federal Savings and Loans.** Office of Thrift Supervision, 800-842-6929, http://www.ots.treas.gov
- **National Credit Unions.** NCU Administration, 703-518-6300, http://www.ncua.gov
- **State Banks members of the Federal Reserve.** Federal Reserve, 202-452-2631, http://www.bog.frb.fed.us
- **State Banks not members of the Federal Reserve.** Federal Deposit Insurance Corp., 800-934-3342, http://www.fdic.gov

You will also need to contact the Department of Education or guarantee agency and provide whatever evidence you have that you paid the loan in full. Contact the Department of Education, Office of Postsecondary Education, 400 Maryland Avenue, SW, Washington, DC 20202; 800-433-3243. (See Chapter 3, Section A.4, for a list of the guarantee agencies.) Also try contacting the Department of Education's Ombudsman, at 877-557-2575.

Here are some examples of evidence you can use to prove you've paid up.

- If your former spouse or roommate remembers you diligently writing checks every month, have that person sign a sworn statement and send it to the agency.
- Dig up records from lenders for years past for copies of old credit reports listing payments made on the loan.
- Get copies of old tax returns—from the IRS if necessary—showing that you itemized the interest deduction on student loan payments back when that was permitted.
- Contact the school you attended for a report from the Department of Education showing the loan's status.
- Request a copy of the signed promissory note from the last holder of the loan with a summary of the account.

CHAPTER 8

Getting Out of Default

I f you're in default on your student loans, you may be scared— scared of what might happen to you. You might be afraid that you'll lose some money or property, or you might be hit with a lawsuit. Many of those fears are founded. When you are in default, you might lose your tax refund, have your wages garnished or get sued. You'll have a hard time getting a car loan or mortgage. And you may even have trouble landing an apartment.

Default generally occurs when your loan payments are more than 270 days past due and you haven't made any overtures toward paying. If your loan payments are fewer than 270 days late or you've been in touch with the holder of your loan to make arrangements to postpone paying, then your loans are probably considered delinquent, not in default. The most serious consequence of delinquency is that your loan holder will write and possibly call you demanding payment. (See Chapter 7, Section A.1.) If you don't make arrangements to pay, postpone your payments or take other steps to deal with your loans, however, they will quickly go into default.

Being in default on your student loans can be serious. The Department of Education and the guarantee agencies put a lot of time and effort into collecting defaulted federal loans. There are many ways in which their rabid actions can make life difficult for student loan defaulters.

- As long as your are in default on your federal student loans, you risk being subjected to aggressive collection tactics, including having your tax refund intercepted, having 10% of your wages garnished or getting sued.

- You are not entitled to a deferment—that is, postponement of your payments—if you are in default. If you come out of default but cannot afford your student loan payments, you may be eligible for an unemployment deferment if you're not working, financial hardship if your income is very low or several other deferments. (See Chapter 6, Section A.) Being eligible to apply for a deferment is often the most compelling reason to get out of default. Note that you do not have to get out of default to obtain a forbearance.

- You are not eligible for flexible repayment options if you are in default. If you get out of default, you can apply for an extended, graduated or income contingent or income sensitive repayment plan. (See Chapter 5, Section A.)

- You are not eligible for new federal student loans or grants if you are in default. If you want to return to school, you must be out of default before applying for federal money.

- Your credit will be damaged if you are in default. If you are having trouble getting a mortgage, car loan, credit card or other line of credit because of your poor credit history, you can get rid of the default notation on your credit report only by getting out of default.

Until a few years ago, it was virtually impossible to get out of default on federal student loans. Loan balances grew at astronomical rates as guarantee and collection agencies compounded interest and added collection costs. Student loan borrowers often felt overwhelmed and lost about how to proceed—and so frequently did nothing to repay their loans. By the early 1990s, the student loan default rate reached 22.4%.

Congress faced a crisis. While members did not want the guarantee and collection agencies to get soft on borrowers in default, they knew they had to enact legislation that would provide an incentive for student borrowers to repay their loans. And so, since 1992, student borrowers have been able to get out of default by simply making 12 consecutive payments. And clearly, it's working. In 1998, the default rate dropped to 8.6%.

A. Federal Loans

Healthcare loans are not covered by the reasonable and affordable payment plan; there are different rules for how to get out of default on them. (See Section B.) On any other federal student loan, you will be deemed in default only if:

- your loan has entered the repayment period—that is, it is beyond the grace period following your graduation or time you left school

- your loan payments are at least 270 days past due, and

- the Department of Education or a guarantee agency has concluded that you do not intend to repay the loan—for example, you have ignored all requests to get in touch with the holder of your loans or have moved and left no forwarding address.

The four most common ways to get out of default on your federal student loan are discussed in this chapter. The two most popular and the ones you are most likely to use are the reasonable and affordable repayment plan and the consolidation loan plan.

There are other ways to get out of default, including the following:

- Closed School and False Certification Discharges. These programs mainly apply to students who attended private vocational or trade schools . (See Chapter 9.)

- Cancellation or refund for what you owe through a state tuition recovery fund or through a federal program to reimburse you if you dropped out of a school and didn't get a refund. (See Chapter 9.)

- Disability discharge. (See Chapter 6.)

- Bankruptcy. (See Chapter 10.)

GETTING OUT OF ACCIDENTAL DEFAULT

Sometimes, your loans go into default through no fault of your own. For example, you apply for an unemployment deferment on three loans. The holder of your loan misreads your paperwork and grants the deferment on only one loan, while the other two go into default. In such a situation, you must contact a collections supervisor or Department of Education Ombudsman, who has the authority to take your loans out of default.

Be sure to have copies of your original deferment application or other paperwork to show that administrative error, not your inaction, led to the default. You can contact the Department of Education Ombudsman toll-free at 877-557-2575.

1. Repayment Plans

The Higher Education Amendments of 1992 and 1998 provide a way for any student debtor holding federal loans to get out of default. (The 1992 amendments covered Stafford, PLUS and SLS loans; Perkins loans were added in the 1998 amendments.) Under this repayment program, you can make monthly payments you can afford, while still paying for your basic necessities.

A ROSE BY ANY OTHER NAME

To get out of default using the reasonable and affordable repayment plan, you must ask the holder of your loan—the guarantee agency, the Department of Education or a collection agency—for such a plan. (If you want to get out of default on a Perkins Loan, you must also notify your school.) Unfortunately, many people who work for these agencies won't know what you are talking about when you use the phrase reasonable and affordable repayment plan. It seems that representatives of these agencies receive different training about the program. You will most likely get what you're after by making one of the following requests.

- I want a reasonable and affordable repayment plan to renew my eligibility.

- I want to rehabilitate my loan.

- I want to qualify for loan consolidation.

It doesn't matter that you have no interest in applying for a new loan—that is, renewing your eligibility—or consolidating your loans. You have to use this language. And if one request falls on deaf ears, try repeating your request using the other terminology noted above.

If you've been sued. You are eligible for a reasonable and affordable repayment plan even if the Department of Education has sued you and obtained a court judgment. In fact, no matter what types of collection efforts you're being subjected to and no matter what stage they are in, you can always request a reasonable and affordable repayment plan.

The guarantee or collection agency collecting your loan decides what is reasonable and affordable. The agency must consider:

- your disposable income—the amount that remains after mandatory deductions, such as Social Security, taxes, union dues and child support withholdings, and

- your necessary expenses—including housing, utilities, food, medical costs, dependent-care costs, work-related expenses and other student loan repayments.

The Department of Education has not established a formula for deciding what is reasonable and affordable, but the law does have some negotiation guidelines for the guarantee and collection agencies. For example, an agency cannot establish a minimum amount, such as $50 per month, for all former students who want a reasonable and affordable plan. Each repayment plan must be individually negotiated with the former student who requests it.

If your expenses exceed your income, the agency can set a low monthly repayment amount, such as $5. If the agency agrees to an amount of less than $50 per month, however, it must place documentation in your Department of Education file showing why you are entitled to make low payments. Because low payment plans require this extra paperwork, many agencies resist setting payments under $50. But the law is clear that you are obligated to pay only what is reasonable and affordable—and not a penny more. If the person with whom you speak refuses to grant you a low amount, ask to speak with the collections supervisor.

Before you request a reasonable and affordable repayment plan from the guarantee or collection agency holding your loan, gather bills, receipts, court orders and all other papers showing your necessary monthly expenses, as well as pay stubs or receipts of public assistance. The agency may send you a form to complete on which you list your income and expenses. If you completed a budgeting form, you can use the figures on it to complete this form. (See Chapter 4, Section B.3.) Attach a letter or statement pleading your case for an amount no more than you can truly afford. If you're more comfortable and feel you would be more persuasive talking rather than writing, call the agency representative and discuss the matter over the phone. You may still be required to complete a financial form in addition, however.

SAMPLE LETTER REQUESTING REASONABLE AND AFFORDABLE REPAYMENT PLAN

Simone Owens
Rip's Awake Collection Services
690 North Jackson Avenue
Greenville, TX 75000
April 27, 20xx

Re: Social Security # 123-45-6789

Dear Ms. Owens:

The Higher Education Amendments of 1992 and 1998 require guarantee agencies, the Department of Education and collection agencies collecting on their behalf to set up a repayment plan by which a borrower in default can make reasonable and affordable payments to renew his eligibility based upon total financial circumstances. (See 34 C.F.R. §§ 682.200 and 683.401(b)(4).) I am writing to request such a repayment plan to rehabilitate my defaulted student loans.

Currently, I occasionally get work through a temporary agency, and on the average bring home $1,100 per month. My monthly expenses are as follows: $600 (rent); $200 (groceries); $30 (utilities); $40 (phone bill); $35 (transportation); $120 (medical insurance); $25 (clothing) and $25 (miscellaneous)—for a total of $1,075. I can afford to pay no more than $20 per month on my student loans.

Enclosed are copies of pay stubs, receipts and bills verifying my income and expenses. Please confirm in writing that you accept $20 as the monthly amount of my reasonable and affordable repayment plan.

Sincerely,

Walter Harris

The agency will take anywhere from a few weeks to a few months to review your request. Once the agency decides on an amount you must repay each month, it will send you a notice of what it is. If it would be too much of a financial strain to make the payment every month, contact the agency at once. Do not enter into a repayment plan on which you are apt to default. The repayment program is a once-in-a-lifetime opportunity. If you don't live up to your promised payments, the government will not grant you another chance to get out of default this way.

Once you agree on a repayment amount, the agency will send you a confirming letter. The letter will spell out the terms and conditions of the reasonable and affordable repayment program, which are quite extensive.

REPAYMENT PLAN TERMS AND CONDITIONS

The reasonable and affordable repayment plan letter you receive from the guarantee agency, Department of Education or collection agency should state the following conditions.

- Twelve consecutive monthly payments of $_____ must be received timely. According to federal law, a loan may be considered for rehabilitation only after you have made one voluntary reasonable and affordable full payment each of 12 consecutive months; and the payment is received by the guarantee agency or its agent within 15 days of the scheduled date. Should a payment be received untimely (past due) or for less than the agreed amount, this offer becomes null and void.

- After the 12 payments have been applied to your account and your loans have successfully been rehabilitated, your account may be considered for purchase by an eligible lender. You must continue to make your monthly payments, as agreed upon, until you are notified that your loans have been rehabilitated.

- A new repayment schedule will be established by the lender after rehabilitation. Your monthly payments may increase according to the new schedule.

REPAYMENT PLAN TERMS AND CONDITIONS (continued)

- Upon rehabilitation, the major national credit bureaus will be notified to delete any adverse credit rating currently being reported by the guarantee agency in relation to your default.
- Collection costs of 18.5% will be included (capitalized) with the outstanding principal and interest balance due on your account upon rehabilitation. Refusal to agree to the capitalization of collection costs renders you ineligible for participation in this program. Refusal to agree to the capitalized collection costs of 18.5% does not remove the guarantee agency's authority to assess a charge to cover the cost incurred in collecting on your defaulted loans. This charge will be 23% or 25%.

If you are ever unable to make a payment under your new plan, contact the agency at once and ask for an adjustment. If you don't get anywhere with the person who first takes your call, ask to speak with a supervisor to plead your case.

If you make six consecutive reasonable and affordable monthly payments on time—that is, within 15 days of the monthly due date—you will become eligible to apply for new federal student loans or grants if you want to return to school. While you are applying for your new financial aid and even once school begins, you must continue to make the payments under your repayment plan. You must make at least 12 consecutive payments for your loans to come out of default. Once that happens, you can apply for an in-school deferment. (See Chapter 6, Section A.3.)

Even if you do not intend to return to school, the same rules apply. That is, once you make 12 consecutive monthly payments, your loan will no longer be in default. If you are eligible, you can then apply for a deferment—that is, arrange to postpone your payments. (See Chapter 6, Section A.) Continue to make your monthly payments until your deferment is granted.

If you are not eligible for deferment, once you make 12 payments, the guarantee agency or Department of Education can sell your loan back to a company on the secondary market. (See Chapter 3, Section A.2.) This is called loan rehabilitation. Once your loan is rehabilitated, you will be put on a standard ten-year repayment plan. If you've been paying very small amounts for 12 or more months, the new monthly payments probably will increase dramatically. If you can't afford them, you will need to request one of several flexible repayment options available. (See Chapter 5, Section A.)

Once you make the 12 payments—whether you obtain a deferment or your loan is rehabilitated—the guarantee agency or Department of Education must notify the credit bureaus that your loan is no longer in default. The credit bureaus *must* remove the default notation from your credit file. Apparently, until 1998, credit bureaus claimed that removal of the default notation was at their discretion. In 1998, however, the Deaprtment of Education made it clear to the bureaus that the decision to remove or retain the default notation was not theirs—Congress had made it part of the law and they had to follow it. Still, don't assume that the guarantee agency or Department of Education will notify the credit bureaus and that the bureaus will remove the notation. Get a copy of your credit report and check yourself.

Information on obtaining a credit file. *Credit Repair,* by Robin Leonard (Nolo), has all the forms and instructions you need to obtain a copy of your credit report, check it and make sure it's accurate.

NAVIGATING NEGOTIATING ROADBLOCKS

If a private guarantee agency or collection agency won't negotiate a reasonable and affordable repayment plan, or if it insists on a minimum amount or won't let you present evidence of your necessary expenses, you may not be out of luck. The agency is violating the federal Fair Debt Collection Practices Act (FDCPA) by its inflexible behavior. This law prohibits nongovernment debt collectors from making false or deceptive misrepresentations—that is, lying—about a debt. (See Chapter 7, Section B.4.c.)

If your loans are held by a private guarantee agency or a collection agency. You may be able to sue the collector for harassment. You can represent yourself in small claims court or hire an attorney to help you. (See Chapter 11, Section B.) You may be reimbursed for attorneys' fees and court costs if you win. You're entitled to money for actual damages, such as emotional pain and suffering, and up to $1,000 in punitive damages, damages meant to punish the collector for its behavior.

If your loans are held by a collection agency. Contact the Deputy Director of Debt Collection Services for the U.S. Department of Education. Include your name, Social Security number, the name of the collection agency, the name of the particular debt collector, the dates of your conversations and what was said to you. Fax your complaint letter to 202-708-4954. You can call to make sure the Department received your letter and to find out what action the officials there intend to take at 202-708-4766.

Another possible place to go for help is the new student loan Ombudsman within the Office of Student Financial Assistance. This position was created specifically to help student borrowers resolve complaints with lenders, guarantee agencies, the Department of Education and these agencies' collection agencies. To find out more information, visit the website of the Department of Education's Office of Student Financial Assistance at http://www.ed.gov/offices/OSFAP. To contact the Ombudsman, call toll-free 877-557-2575.

NAVIGATING NEGOTIATING ROADBLOCKS (continued)

If your loan is held by a state guarantee agency. You have few recourses. You can contact the state department of education, any public body that oversees the agency or your elected representative to voice your complaint, but unless you have connections, your shouts may fall on deaf ears.

If you are continually stonewalled by a state or private guarantee agency, and it refuses to negotiate with you to set up a reasonable and affordable repayment plan, consider contacting the Policy Development Division, Loans Branch of the U.S. Department of Education. You can fax this office at 202-205-0786 or call it at 202-708-8242. Be aware that the Department of Education has little power over guarantee agencies and may not be able to help you. Nevertheless, Department of Education employees want to know about ongoing problems with guarantee agencies.

2. Consolidating Your Loans

By consolidating, you can combine a number of loans into one package or you may be able to refinance several loans or at least one of your loans to secure a lower interest rate. Consolidating eliminates the old loans on which you were in default in favor of one new arrangement, with new terms and a new loan payback schedule.

There are limitations on consolidating your loans to get out of default. Loan consolidators differ in their requirements. For example, the Student Loan Marketing Association, or Sallie Mae, requires that you first get out of default through 12 consecutive reasonable and affordable payments. That is—Sallie Mae does not consolidate defaulted loans. The federal government and some other lenders will consolidate a defaulted loan, but you may have to shop around to find a willing lender.

There are two main types of consolidation loan programs. One program, FFEL Consolidation, requires you to find a lender who will offer you a consolidated loan. A second, and usually much better program for borrowers, is the Direct Consolidation Loan program which allows you to consolidate your loans directly with the federal government. To qualify for most consolidation loans, you must first make three monthly payments on your defaulted loans. Although these payments can be quite high in some circumstances, they must be reasonable and affordable based on your total financial circumstances. Also, if you are eligible for a direct consolidation loan, you can avoid the three-payment requirement by agreeing to accept what is called an income sensitive payment plan. If your income is low, the payments under this plan will also be very low. The first step in getting a direct loan consolidation is to call the Department of Education at 800-557-7392, or find out more on-line at www.ed.gov/finaid.html.

There are many advantages to loan consolidation. Most importantly, it can get you out of default. This will allow you to become eligible for new loans, grants and even deferments. Also, you will no longer have to deal with threatening collectors who may try to intercept your taxes, garnish your wages, or sue you to collect the loan.

There are some disadvantages too. Consolidation will not completely clean up your credit report. After consolidation, you will no longer be considered in default, but your report will still show that your previous loans had been in default but are now paid in full through the new loan.

Consolidation loans are most useful if you want to qualify for a new loan to go back to school. They can also be easier to get than reasonable and affordable payment plans. But the big advantage to a reasonable and affordable payment plan is that once you make 12 consecutive payments, you will be able to completely clear your credit report of your student loan default. In addition, your payments may be lower than the three payments usually required under the consolidation option. Be sure you understand the pro and cons of consolidating your loans before taking the plunge. (See Chapter 5, Section C).

3. Seeking Compromise of Your Loans

Under little-known Department of Education regulations, a guarantee agency has the authority to compromise what you owe—that is, accept less than the total amount due as full satisfaction of the debt. And this will end your default status. (Standardized Compromise and Write-Off Procedures, approved 12/23/93 by the Director of the U.S. Department of Education, Policy Development Division.) Specifically, a collections supervisor at a guarantee agency can compromise:

- the amount of the collection costs, including the 25% collection fee, if you agree to pay the full amount of the principal and interest owed on defaulted loans

- up to 30% of the principal and interest you owe if you agree to pay the principal and interest on the remaining balance, or

- even more than the 30% of the principal and interest if the situation warrants it and the guarantee agency's director approves the plan.

The guarantee agency will not tell you about these compromise options, and in fact, loans are rarely compromised. If you can afford to pay a substantial lump sum, however, and want to put your student loan indebtedness behind you, contact the guarantee agency and ask about a compromise. You'll probably need to talk with the head of the collections department to find someone who is familiar with the compromise program.

A second compromise program authorizes a guarantee agency to compromise the interest you owe on your loans if you agree to pay the entire principal owed, by certified check, within 30 days of negotiating the compromise with the agency. (Standardized Compromise and Write-Off Procedures, approved 12/23/93 by the Director of the U.S. Department of Education, Policy Development Division.) The agency can exercise this authority only if it judges that the compromise is in the best interests of the government. As you probably guessed, best interest of the government is not easy to define. You may convince the agency to compromise your interest, however, if the only alternative is to sue you, which is fairly expensive for the government, or to take very small monthly payments from you with the risk that you will default again.

While few guarantee agencies exercise this authority, it makes sense to mention the possibility, especially if your loans are very old—you've been in default quite a while and the balance is mostly interest, not principal—and you can easily afford to pay the principal in a lump sum.

4. Requesting a Write-Off of Your Loans

If you believe there is no way you will ever be able to repay your loans and you don't qualify for cancellation (see Chapter 6, Section A) or compromise (see Section A.3), you can ask the guarantee agency or the Department of Education to write off your loans. The agency or Department can permanently eliminate your obligation to repay your loan if:

- the principal balance is $100 or less

- your total balance is $1,000 or less, or

- the balance remaining is for interest, collection costs, court fees and costs other than the principal, no matter what the amount.

In any other situation, the agency can write off your loans by permanently assigning them to the Department of Education and ceasing collection efforts. Or the Department can write off your loans by ending collection efforts. You can receive this type of write-off only if you never again seek federal school loans or grants, however. If you later want to apply for federal money to go back to school, your obligation to pay off your loans will be revived. To qualify for new federal financial aid, you will have to make six payments under a reasonable and affordable repayment plan. (See Section A.1.)

To qualify for any type of write-off, you will have to prove that you cannot repay your loans. You might qualify, for example, if you:

- have been unemployed for a long time and have no prospects for future employment

- have been receiving public assistance, or

- have a chronic illness or disability that makes it impossible for you to work.

A supervisor in charge of collections can write off up to $5,000. To write off between $5,000 and $20,000, the supervisor must obtain approval from the next level of management. Above that amount, the supervisor must get approval from the director of the guarantee agency or from an upper-level manager at the Department of Education. You need to be persistent and provide as much documentation as possible to support your request for a write-off, especially if a large amount is involved.

B. Federal Healthcare Loans

Federal laws governing Health Education Assistance Loans (HEALs), Health Professions Student Loans (HPSLs), Loans for Disadvantaged Students (LDSs) or Nursing Student Loans (NSLs) make it relatively easy to get out of default. As long as your lender or school holds your loan—as opposed to the federal Department of Health and Human Services (DHHS)—you can probably negotiate your way out of default.

Under DHHS regulations, you are in default on a healthcare loan if your payments are more than 120 days past due. But regardless of whether you have simply missed a few payments and are delinquent or are more than 120 days past due and in default, your lender in the case of HEAL loans or your school in the case of HPSL, LDS or NSL loans must contact you in writing and by telephone and offer you ways to get back on track with paying your loans.

Your lender or school may agree to:

- negotiate a repayment plan you can afford

- grant you a graduated repayment plan for the first five years of your payback period (see Chapter 5, Section A.2), or

- place your loans in forbearance—that is, allow you to postpone payments while interest still accrues; unlike forbearance on other federal loans, this forbearance will take you out of default.

If you have a HEAL loan, you have additional routes out of default. In addition to the options mentioned above, your lender may:

- grant you an extended forbearance in which your past due payments are treated as if you had received a forbearance, as long as you repay the balance due over the years remaining on your ten-year payback period

- grant you an income-contingent repayment plan for the first five years of your payback period (see Chapter 5, Section A.4), or

- consolidate your loans for a new 25-year payback period.

If you ignore your lender or school's offers to get you out of default, you are likely to wind up in state court. The lender or school will sue you for breaching, or breaking, your agreement to repay your loans. Once the lawsuit begins, you can still get out of default by taking advantage of one of the above repayment options and paying whatever litigation costs the lender or school incurred.

If you ignore or lose a lawsuit filed by your lender and your lender gets a judgment against your for HEAL loans, the lender will sell the loans to DHHS—at which time you have lost your right to get out of default. If you ignore or lose the lawsuit filed by your school and your school gets a judgment on HPSL, LDS or NSL loans, the school still must try to collect from you. Only after the school concludes that collection is hopeless can it sell the loans back to DHHS.

C. Private and State-Funded Student Loans

It is usually impossible to get out of default on private student loans or loans from a state or university loan fund. As with any type of commercial debt, you are almost always liable for what you owe—regardless of your life circumstances. Still, if you have a private student loan, get in touch with your lender or the current holder of your loan for help. (See Chapter 2, Section B.)

Similarly, if you are in default on a loan from a state or university fund, contact your school's financial aid office or the state student loan office to discuss your options. (See Chapter 2, Section C.)

Before you contact the holder of your loan, take some time to clearly understand why you are doing so. Once you get a willing ear, you don't simply want to babble on about why you haven't been paying your loans. Ideally, you want to get a new agreement, qualify for deferments, obtain new loans if you want to go back to school and get the negative notation removed from your credit file.

If you're able to make payments on your loan—and aren't looking to apply for a deferment or new loan—focus on getting the default out of your credit file. You can make two requests to the holder of your loan.

- Ask that the default notation in your credit file associated with the loan be removed in exchange for full or partial payment. Some loan holders will agree to report your account as nonevaluated—meaning neither good nor bad—rather than as in default or formerly in default. Subsequent creditors tend to ignore nonevaluated accounts.

- If the holder of your loan agrees to put you on a new repayment schedule, ask the loan holder to re-age your loan—making the current month the first repayment month and showing no late payments or default. Sometimes, the loan holder won't re-age the account until you make two or three monthly payments.

HOW TO NEGOTIATE ON PRIVATE AND STATE LOANS

Not all loan holders remove default notations or re-age accounts, but it never hurts to ask. Contact the collections or customer service department and make an offer. Tell the person with whom you speak that you cannot afford to pay more, but that you'd really like to pay a good portion of the bill. Explain your financial problems—be bleak, but never lie.

If your request is denied, ask to speak with a supervisor. Never agree to pay more than you can afford. Once you reach an agreement, get it in writing before sending any money. Send your own confirming letter if need be. If you're uncomfortable negotiating on your own behalf, get help from a debt counseling agency such as Debt Counselors of America (http://www.dca.org) or Consumer Credit Counseling Service (http://www.nfcc.org). (For other tips on negotiating with the holder of your loan, see Chapter 5, Section E.3.)

If You Attended a Trade or Vocational School

Millions of Americans have attended a trade or vocational school—places that offer courses in medical or dental technology, high school equivalency degrees, cosmetology, computer programming or repair, auto mechanics, truck driving or word processing, for example.

Many trade school graduates received good instruction and the opportunity to leave the unemployment lines, public assistance rolls and minimum wage, dead-end jobs.

But for many people—maybe you—the reality of a trade or vocational school program did not measure up to golden expectations. Perhaps you were lured by the promise of job training and placement paid for by the federal government. But when you signed up, you were not told that Uncle Sam was not your Sugar Daddy. In reality, you borrowed thousands of dollars in federal student loans to attend the program, and turned over the money to the school.

If all trade and vocational schools delivered what they promised, owing $5,000 or $6,000 wouldn't be so bad. It wouldn't be that difficult to repay that kind of money within ten years if you landed a good job in a secure field. But many trade or vocational school students do not come away with new skills or a good job—only with a whopping loan debt. Your school may have closed before you completed the course, or the school may not have hired teachers or had the equipment to teach any useful skills. You may have dropped out or been forced out.

EXPANDING FINANCIAL AID FOR TRADE AND VOCATIONAL SCHOOL STUDENTS: THE GOOD, THE BAD AND THE UGLY

When the government-guaranteed student loan program was created in the 1960s, vocational and trade school students were not allowed to participate. Congress changed these rules in the late 1970s so that for the first time, trade school students were eligible for most of the same financial assistance money that other students had been receiving for years. Many legitimate private and non-profit trade schools were able to use this new source of revenue to offer valuable training for needy students.

The bad news is that an entire industry of scam trade schools also opened up. Especially during the 1980s, these schools ripped off countless trade school students by signing them up for federal loans and grants and then offering worthless courses at outrageous prices. The cost of private vocational training was often as much as 40 times what public schools charged. Students who had been promised lucrative job opportunities were left only with huge student loan bills. Many students defaulted on these loans, creating big headaches for the students and costing tax payers millions of dollars. In the meantime, many trade school officials got rich, grabbing money to finance their own expensive cars, extravagant vacations, questionable investments or huge salaries.

Congress initially panicked over the loss of money in the federal coffers, passing legislation that cut back the amount of loan money available to students attending trade and vocational schools. In 1992, however, Congress also passed legislation to help students who were victims of rip-off trade schools. These rights are discussed throughout this chapter.

A. Canceling a Federal Student Loan

To address the burden of repaying loans improperly awarded to trade and vocational school students, Congress enacted the Higher Education Amendment Act of 1992.

If you had a Stafford loan, Supplemental loan, federal direct loan or PLUS loan issued January 1, 1986, or later, it may be canceled if:

- you were unable to complete your program because the school closed (called a closed school discharge or cancellation), or

- school officials falsely certified you as eligible to benefit from the loan (called a false certification discharge or cancellation).

Due to a recent change in the law, Perkins loan borrowers are also eligible to apply for the closed school discharge only.

Closed school and false certification are the two main types of cancellations available to trade school students. But don't forget—even if you don't qualify for one of these cancellations, you may be eligible for a refund (discussed later in this chapter), or for a cancellation due to disability (discussed in Chapter 6) or bankruptcy (discussed in Chapter 10).

If you receive either a closed school or false certification discharge, you will no longer be required to repay the loan or any charges such as interest or collection costs connected to the loan. You will also get reimbursement for any payments you made on the loan and for money taken through tax intercepts or wage garnishments to pay the loan. You will no longer be considered to be in default and will be eligible again for new loans and grant. A cancellation will also wipe out negative marks on your credit report.

There is no deadline for requesting either a closed school or false certification cancellation.

More information on trade school loans. If you need more information on the laws allowing you to cancel a federal student loan if you attended a trade or vocational school, get a copy of "New Relief for Trade School Victims: Discharging Student Loans Based on False Certification of Ability to Benefit," by Alan M. White. It's available from the National Center on Poverty Law, 205 West Monroe Street, 2nd Floor, Chicago, IL 60606. Enclose a check for $15 and request a copy of the April 1996 journal (where the article was published).

In addition, you can request a trade school fact sheet from the Department of Education at 800-256-7346 or on the Department's website at http://www.ed.gov. The fact sheet, specific for your state, will contain most information you need, including how to cancel your loan and obtain a refund and contact information for your state trade school licensing agency.

1. School Closure

You are entitled to cancel a federal Stafford loan, SLS, direct loan, Perkins loan, PLUS or the portion of a consolidation loan used to pay off any of those loans if you were unable to complete your program because the school closed:

- before you began attending classes

- while you were enrolled and attending

- within 90 days of when you left it

- and you left anticipating its closure, or

- if you were still enrolled and unable to return to complete your studies.

If you attended and withdrew from certain correspondence schools, you may be eligible for a closed school cancellation if you withdrew up to a year before the school closed.

The Department of Education has compiled a list of closed schools at which former students may qualify to have their loans canceled. The growing list is updated every Wednesday and now contains thousands of trade and vocational schools from all over the country. In order to get a closed school cancellation, your school must be on the list and you must be able to show that you were an enrolled student or withdrew within 90 days from the date the Department says is the official closure date of the school. The official list will have a school identification number for each closed school. Write down that number because you will need it for the official closed school discharge form.

To find out if your school is on the list, contact the Department of Education at:

U.S. Department of Education
Closed School Section
P.O. Box 23800
L'Enfant Plaza Station
Washington, DC 20026
http://www.ed.gov/offices/osfap/students/closedschool/search.html

Even if your school is not on the list, if you can show the holder of your loan—either the Department of Education or guarantee agency—that you took out a loan, attended the school or attempted to enroll, and that the school's closure prevented you from completing your course, you are entitled to a cancellation. If any former student claims that a school closed down, even if the only proof you have is your own story, the Department will investigate at once.

In a few situations, the Department of Education or guarantee agency might claim that you are not entitled to a cancellation, even if your school is on the closed school list. You are likely to hear this argument if any of the following are true.

- You were offered the opportunity to finish your course of study at another school located within a reasonable commuting distance.

- You earned credits at the closed school that were transferable for credit toward a degree, diploma or certificate in a similar program at another regionally accredited institution.

- You attended and dropped out more than three months before the school closed.

⚠️ **If the Department of Education has the wrong closing date for your school.** You may need to gather evidence of the actual closing date. Help could come from classmates or others you know who were attending the school when it actually closed.

2. False Certification

Before a lender or school makes a loan guaranteed by the federal government, it must certify that the student is eligible to benefit from the loan. This means that the student must meet the minimum qualifications necessary to attend the school.

Example: In your state, beauticians must have a high school diploma or equivalency to obtain a license. You left high school in the tenth grade and do not have your high school equivalency. Nevertheless, Betty's Beautician School admitted you and you received a Stafford loan to finance your way. You were falsely certified as eligible to benefit from the loan.

You are entitled to cancel a federal Stafford loan, SLS, direct loan, PLUS or the portion of a consolidation loan used to pay off one of those loans if you were falsely certified as eligible for the loan. You must have received some or all of the loan after January 1, 1986.

The grounds for a false certification are:

- You could not benefit from the training. (One court has ruled that this requirement conflicts with the statute and is therefore invalid. Jordan v. Riley, _F.3d_ (D.C. Cir 1999).)

- At the time of enrollment, you could not meet the requirements for employment in the field for which you were to receive training.

- Your signature was forged on the loan papers.

a. Inability to Benefit From the Educational Program

Trade and vocational school recruiters often prey on high school drop-outs. They promise job security and advancement, when in truth, many people who didn't complete high school don't have the basic skills to succeed in the programs taught at the schools. The law helps level the playing field by providing that most people who enrolled in a trade school without a high school education can cancel their student loans.

But this cancellation is complicated; you must meet three different tests. The first one depends on when you enrolled in the school and whether or not you had a high school education or equivalency. The second relates to the entrance exam you might have been given to get into the program. The third hoop you have to jump through is to show that you did not find work in the field for which you were supposed to receive training.

i.   Dates of Enrollment

The requirements for this cancellation are slightly different depending on when you enrolled. First, you must have received at least part of the loan after January 1, 1986. Assuming you meet that requirement, your cancellation must be based on one of three grounds:

- If you enrolled before July 1, 1987, you are eligible for this cancellation if the school did not validly determine that you had the ability to benefit from the training.

- If you enrolled on or after July 1, 1987, but before July 1, 1991, you are eligible for this cancellation if you did not have a high school diploma or equivalency at the time you enrolled, and you didn't either pass an approved ability to benefit test or receive a general education diploma before completing the program.

- If you enrolled on or after July 1, 1991, you are eligible for this cancellation if you did not have a high school diploma or equivalency at the time you enrolled, and didn't pass an approved ability to benefit test.

ii.   Entrance Exam

The programs offered at trade and vocational schools are supposed to meet the requirements of state accreditation agencies. One requirement is that a student who does not have a high school diploma or equivalency must pass a school-administered entrance exam, called an ability to benefit (ABT) test, before enrolling. The purpose of the test is to measure whether or not the student has the minimum skills to benefit from the program being taught. Ability to benefit tests often measure English proficiency, math skills and other prerequisites.

Only students without high school diplomas or equivalencies are required to take these tests. This is the government's way of making sure that these students are really capable of benefiting from a particular program. If you have a high school diploma or equivalency, the government automatically assumes that you can benefit.

Although many students lack the basic skills these tests are meant to measure, school officials have been known to enroll students who didn't pass. You are entitled to have your student loan canceled if school officials determined that you had the ability to benefit from the course offered, but made the determination improperly. This may be true, for example, if:

- you were never given a test

- the test you were given bore no relation to the course you were taking

- school officials falsified your answers to the test

- school officials did not use the passing score listed by the course publisher

- school officials administered the test incorrectly—for example, you were given 90 minutes to complete a 12-minute test, given some or all of the answers or permitted to retake the test until you passed it, or

- school officials gave the test in your native language while the course was taught in English or gave you a math test while the course required no math skills.

iii. Lack of Employment

Even if you meet the other requirements, you are not eligible for a false certification cancellation if you were able to find employment in the field for which the training was intended. If you didn't finish the program, you can meet this requirement simply by certifying on the application that you did not find employment. If you completed the program, you must do more. You must show that you made a reasonable attempt to find employment. "Reasonable attempt" means that you tried at least three different times to find a job.

KNOWING YOUR SCORE

It may be possible for you to obtain information about the ability to benefit test you took, including your score. If you enrolled after July 1, 1991, the test was approved by the federal Department of Education, which should still have your test on record. Before that date, your state higher education department may have information.

Start by contacting the state office of higher education. (See Chapter 2, Section C.1.) If you reach someone who can help you, find out the name of the test, the name and address of the publisher of the test and the passing or failing or cut off score for the course you took. Ideally, you will also find your own file to locate the test you took and your score—the custodian of records for the school should have it. If the school has closed, ask for help from your state higher education department.

---

b. Condition Prohibits You From Working in the Field

This is another way to get a false certification cancellation. You can qualify even if you had a high school diploma when you enrolled. You have to show that at the time you enrolled, you were unable to meet the minimum state employment requirements for the field in which you were to receive training.

Every state establishes a few baseline requirements for working in the fields typically taught at trade and vocational schools. To be eligible for a cancellation based on this standard, you first must find out what those requirements were. Then you must show that you couldn't have met them because of any of the following:

• a physical or mental condition—for example, you didn't meet your state's minimum height requirement to become a truck driver, but were admitted to a truck driving program

• your age, if you were under 18, or

• a criminal record which, according to your state's laws, would have prevented you from working in the field.

c. The School Forged Your Signature

You are entitled to have your student loan canceled if your signature was forged or missing on your loan application, the promissory note, the loan check or an electronic fund transfer authorization and you did not receive the proceeds of the loan. To qualify on this ground, it doesn't matter whether you had a high school diploma at the time you enrolled. If you suspect that this happened to you, you will probably need the help of a lawyer to track down the documents. (See Chapter 11, Section B.)

HEY—THAT'S NOT MY SIGNATURE

Although forgery of student loan documents is rare, a number of school officials engage in this out and out fraud. In a typical situation, a student with minimal English skills provides enough information—such as name, address and Social Security number—to school officials who then complete a loan application and forge the borrower's signature. The check is sent directly to the school, where the same school officials forge the student's signature to endorse the check. Rarely is this money used to run the school, buy equipment or pay teachers' salaries. More likely, school officials who orchestrate these charades and don't get caught live in huge estates, drive luxury cars and take in the sun on the beaches of the Mediterranean Sea.

---

3. Applying for a Cancellation

If you are entitled to have your loan canceled because the school closed or you were falsely certified as eligible for the loan, contact the guarantee agency or the Department of Education. (See Section A.1 for contact information.). You can obtain the appropriate application or you can send your own letter. It is better to use the form, because it will have boxes for you to fill in the required information. Sometimes, you will need to keep calling or writing the holder of your loan until you are sent a form. You can add additional pages if you don't have enough room on the form to explain everything you need to support your application.

If you are applying for a closed school discharge, you will need to specify that:

- your school closed

- you were enrolled at the time the school closed or withdrew within 90 days of closure, and

- you did not complete the program.

In some situations, you won't have to send a written application but will be able to apply for a closed school discharge over the phone. You can do this if:

- you are applying for cancellation of a loan and you already received a closed school discharge for a different loan from the same program of study and time period, or

- you qualify for the discharge based on information already in the Department's or guaranty agency's possession.

If you are applying for a false certification discharge, what you need to say depends on the type of cancellation for which you are applying.

- If the school falsely certified your ability to benefit, you must specify that you didn't have a high school diploma or equivalency at the time you enrolled in the course, that you were falsely admitted and that you didn't find employment in the field.

- If you did not meet minimum state requirements for employment, you must show that at the time you enrolled, you had a physical or mental condition or other circumstances and couldn't have met the minimal state requirements for the field.

- If your loan papers were forged, in addition to any other evidence, you must show that the signature on the loan papers was not yours and provide five different samples of your signature.

Send the original completed application or your letter to the Department of Education or the guarantee agency holding your loan. Once the Department or agency receives your paperwork, it must stop all collection efforts. If you send your materials to a guarantee agency, the agency will forward them to the Department. Don't send them directly to the Department yourself if the guarantee agency is trying to collect the loan.

If you do, no one at the agency will know that you've applied for a cancellation and they will keep trying to collect.

You can also send the Department of Education's Collection Office a copy of your application or letter for added assurance that all collection efforts will end. Send the copy to:

U.S. Department of Education
National Payment Center
P.O. Box 4169
Greenville, TX 75403-4169

Once the Department of Education has your application or letter and any documents you submit, it will review them. If officials at the Department agree with your request for cancellation of your loan, they will forward your paperwork to your lender, who is required to issue you a refund for any payments you made. (See Section B.)

Even though guaranty agencies are supposed to respond within 90 days to applications for discharges, they almost never act that quickly. Sometimes it can take years to get a response. This means that you have to be aggressive in pressuring the Department or guaranty agency to respond. Also, be sure to request what is called an administrative forbearance (see Chapter 6) from anyone trying to collect the loan. You are entitled to this forbearance, which keeps the agency from trying to collect the loan while your discharge application is pending.

You can apply for both a false certification and closed school discharge for the same loan if you are eligible for both. But you cannot get double reimbursement.

If your request to cancel your student loan is denied, you can appeal. If no reason was specified as to why you were denied a cancellation, call the Closed School Section at 202-708-6048 and find out. Then, resubmit your application or letter and any new documentation that supports your claim to:

Secretary of Education
U.S. Department of Education
400 Maryland Avenue, SW
Washington, DC 20202
Attn: School Closing Appeals [or]
Attn: False Certification Appeal

REPORTING A TRADE OR VOCATIONAL SCHOOL

If you recently attended a trade or vocational school that you believe is violating the federal school loan program—for example, classes were frequently canceled because of lack of instructors—contact one of the Department of Education's Program Review Offices.

Boston   617-223-9328
Denver   303-844-3675

B. Obtaining a Refund

Many students signed up for courses at trade schools and never showed up for classes, but were still charged for the entire period of the loan. Other students withdrew at later dates but were not granted refunds for the period after they withdrew. If this happened to you, even a long time ago, there are still a number of ways you can try to get reimbursement for a refund that you were entitled to but didn't get.

When you enroll after securing a federal loan to help pay your way, the school is required to give you a written explanation of its refund policy. If you still have any of the loan or school documents, take a look at them. Look specifically at a section entitled Withdrawal From School, or something similar. You may find that you are entitled to a full or partial refund, even if you are not eligible to have your loan canceled. (See Section A.)

Under California law, for example, if you withdraw within the first five class sessions, you are entitled to a 100% reimbursement. If you withdraw after attending five or more classes but any time before completing the full course, the school owes you a partial refund. Usually the school will be long gone by the time you decide you want to pursue this refund money. This is not the end of the story. There are still ways to get that refund.

Collect the refund money from the federal government. As part of the 1998 Higher Education Reauthorization Act, Congress created an unpaid refund discharge that will allow you to get a discharge for all or a portion of a loan if the school failed to pay you the refund you were owed.

You are eligible for this refund if you got your loan on or after January 1, 1986. As of November 1, 1999, it was not exactly clear how the program would work, but the application process should be similar to the closed school and false certification cancellation process. This means that in most cases you will need to submit a written application for the unpaid refund discharge. Under some circumstances, however, you will be able to get the refund without submitting a written application.

The rules will be different if you are applying for a refund from a school that is still open. In that situation, you will be first required to try to get the refund directly from the school.

Collect the money from a state tuition recovery fund. The states listed below have set up tuition recovery funds for students unable to collect from the school. Depending on the state, there are a number of grounds for getting the state money. But almost every state fund reimburses students for unpaid refunds. The catch is that these state funds almost always have deadlines to apply.

Each state has its own set of rules for you to follow, including:

- the schools covered by the fund

- the precise steps you must take against the school before applying to the state fund for reimbursement

- whether the fund covers students owed a refund because of withdrawal, school closure or other circumstance, and

- the deadline you must meet to apply for a refund from the state.

Collect the money from the school's bond company. In most states, vocational schools must post a bond before opening their doors. If you are entitled to a refund, contact the state department of higher education to find out how to apply to the bond company for a refund. (See Chapter 2, Section C, for contact information). If the bond money is all used up, you will have to pursue the school directly, often by filing a lawsuit.

Sue the school or lender. You can try to collect money from the school not only for unpaid refunds, but also for damages you suffered as a result of your experience with the school, and for money to pay back your loans. This is much easier to do if the school is still open. If the school is closed, you can still try to sue, possibly even in your state small claims court, and get a judgment which you may be able to collect, if not from the school, possibly from your state tuition recovery fund. You also might be able to get the lender on the hook for what the school did to you. (See Section C.)

STATE TUITION RECOVERY PROGRAMS

ARIZONA

Student Tuition Recovery
Fund
1400 West Washington,
Suite 250
Phoenix, AZ 85007
602-542-5709

ARKANSAS

Student Protection Fund
612 South Summit
Little Rock, AR 72201
501-683-8000

CALIFORNIA

Student Tuition Recovery
Fund
1027 Tenth Street,
Fourth Floor
Sacramento, CA 95814
916-445-3427

CONNECTICUT

Student Protection Fund
61 Woodland Street
Hartford, CT 06105
860-566-5201

GEORGIA

Tuition Guaranteed Trust
Fund
89 North Lake Pkwy,
Bldg. 10, Suite 100
Tucker, GA 30084
770-414-3300

LOUISIANA

Student Protection Fund
P.O. Box 94064
Baton Rouge, LA 70804-4064

MARYLAND

Guaranteed Student Tuition
Fund
16 Francis Street
Annapolis, MD 21704
410-974-2971

NEBRASKA

Tuition Recovery Cash Fund
301 Centennial Mall South
Lincoln, NE 68509-4987
402-471-4825

STATE TUITION RECOVERY PROGRAMS (continued)

NEVADA

Student Tuition
Indeminification Fund
1820 East Sahara, Suite 111
Las Vegas, NV 89104
702-486-7330

NEW YORK

Tuition Reimbursement
Account
116 West 32nd Street,
14th Floor
New York, NY 10001
212-643-4760

OHIO

Student Tuition Recovery
Authority
35 East Gay Street, Suite 403
Columbus, OH 43215
614-466-2752
http://www.state.oh.us/gov

OREGON

Tuition Protection Fund
255 Capital Street, NE
Salem, OR 97310-0203
503-378-5810, ext. 335
http://www.ode.state.or.us

TENNESSEE

Tuition Guarantee Fund
404 James Robertson Park-
way, Suite 1900
Nashville, TN 37243
615-741-5293

TEXAS

Tuition Protection Fund
101 East 15th Street
Austin, TX 78778
512-936-3253

VIRGINIA

Student Tuition Recovery
Fund
P.O. Box 2120
Richmond, VA 23218
804-225-2848

WASHINGTON

Tuition Recovery Trust Fund
P.O. Box 43105
Olympia, WA 98504-3105
360-753-5673

C. If the Holder of Your Loan Sues You

What's even worse than getting a lousy education and not qualifying to have your loan canceled is getting a lousy education and getting sued for failing to repay the loan. Sadly, however, many former trade or vocational school students get served with a summons and complaint notifying them that they owe thousands of dollars; this is how a lawsuit begins.

If this happens to you, you may feel hopeless. Don't despair. If you received shoddy instruction or were defrauded into attending, you may be able to defend against the lawsuit on that basis. Like most vocational or trade school students, your objection to paying your student loan is because of the conduct of the school, not about the loan itself.

If you are sued. Defending yourself in a lawsuit against your lender or other holder of your loan will almost certainly require the help of a lawyer. (See Chapter 11, Section B.)

In your lawsuit, your lawyer may try to defend you by claiming that you were defrauded—that is lied to or deceived—by school officials, that the school breached or broke the agreement with you or that school officials engaged in other illegal behavior. The holder of your loan is likely to respond by insisting that you borrowed money and must repay it. It is also likely to hide behind the school's skirts, claiming that the complaints you have are with the school, not with the lender that provided the money you borrowed to attend the school or the company that bought your loan from the lender.

Whether you will be allowed to proceed with your defense may depend on the state in which you are sued; cases have come down both ways on the matter. Your strongest argument is that if the school and lender had a close relationship, then the school's fraud can be attributed to the lender, erasing your obligation to repay the loan. This might be the case, for example, if the school filled out the loan application and promissory note on the school premises and you never stepped foot inside a bank.

If you signed your promissory note after January 1, 1994, your lawyer will be in a better position to raise these defenses than if you signed the note earlier. On that date, the Department of Education added a clause to federal loan promissory notes called the holder in due course clause. This clause means that from January 1, 1994, forward, if you have complaints about the school, you are entitled to assert them against anyone who holds your loan.

You may have another way to defend a collection lawsuit if you are eligible for one of the discharges discussed in this chapter but haven't applied for one. You can respond to the lawsuit by claiming that you don't owe the money, or that you only owe part, because your loan should be canceled.

More information on lawsuits. The details on raising school-related defenses are beyond the scope of this book. You or your lawyer could benefit greatly from reading the relevant material in *Unfair and Deceptive Acts and Practices,* published by the National Consumer Law Center. If it's not available at a local law library, call NCLC Publications at 617-523-8089. You'll want to read both the main volume and the most recent supplement.

Bankruptcy and Student Loans

Many former students consider filing for bankruptcy to get rid of, or discharge, their student loans. Unfortunately for most—and despite the cries of bankruptcy lawyers who promise to clear the slate of all your debts—this may be more fantasy than reality. Filing for bankruptcy will seldom get you off the hook for paying your student loans. This is more true than ever now that Congress has eliminated the easiest way to erase student loan debt in bankruptcy. Before October 1998, you could get rid of student loans in bankruptcy if your payments had become due more than seven years prior or if repaying the loans would be a severe hardship for you. Congress eliminated the seven-year rule in 1998. This will make it much more difficult for you to use bankruptcy to eliminate your student loans.

But even if bankruptcy can't erase your student loans, it may be useful in some situations. For example, if you owe a lot of debts—not just your student loans—you can file for bankruptcy to get rid of all or most of your other debts, which might leave you with enough cash each month to repay your student loans.

Or you can include your student loans in a bankruptcy repayment plan. In such a set up, you will generally have to pay off your entire student loan debt during your plan. But the reprieve from collection efforts for those years, during which no additional interest accumulates, may be a great relief.

STUDENT LOANS AND SCHOOL RECORDS

Your school may try to withhold your transcripts if you don't pay back your student loans. Many students need their transcripts to supplement job applications, and virtually all former students need their transcripts to re-enroll in school. One way to get around this problem is to file a bankruptcy and receive a discharge of your loan. In this case, the school can no longer deny you a copy of your transcript. (*Juras v. Aman Collection Service, Inc.*, 829 F.2d 739 (9th Cir. 1987). (Some courts have even held that the school cannot withhold your transcript while your bankruptcy case is pending, even if the court eventually rules your school loan cannot be eliminated in your bankruptcy case. (*In re Gustafson*, 111 B.R. 282 (9th Cir. 1990).)

While it wouldn't make sense to file for bankruptcy just to get a copy of your transcript, if you do need a copy of it and plan to file for bankruptcy, be sure to request a copy before the court decides whether or not your loans are included in the debts that are discharged in bankruptcy.

If you think your student loans may qualify for a discharge in bankruptcy or that bankruptcy might be of help, pay special attention to Section A, which explains the basics of bankruptcy. You'll need to understand those mechanics before reading about the nitty gritty of how bankruptcy applies to student loans, which is covered in Sections B and C.

A. Bankruptcy Basics

Most people think of bankruptcy as a process in which you go to court and get your debts erased. In fact, there are two types of bankruptcies. The more familiar is liquidation, or Chapter 7, bankruptcy, in which most or all of your debts are wiped out completely. The second type is reorganization bankruptcy, in which you partially or fully repay your debts. The reorganization bankruptcy for individuals is called Chapter

13 bankruptcy. There are two other kinds of reorganization bankruptcy: Chapter 11, for businesses and for individuals with debts over $1.2 million, and Chapter 12, for family farmers. The names come from the chapters of the federal Bankruptcy Code that sets out the requirements and procedures for the varieties of bankruptcy.

This book discusses Chapter 7 and Chapter 13 bankruptcies only.

1. Chapter 7 Bankruptcy

To file for Chapter 7 bankruptcy, you fill out a two-page petition and several other forms describing your money, property, expenses, debts and income. Then you file all these papers with the bankruptcy court in your area. The whole process takes from four to six months, costs $200 in fees and commonly requires only one trip to the courthouse.

WHAT CAN YOU KEEP IF YOU FILE FOR CHAPTER 7 BANKRUPTCY?

If you're thinking about Chapter 7 bankruptcy, you probably want to know what property you'll be able to keep if you file. Most states let you keep clothing, household furnishings, an inexpensive car (or an expensive car on which you still owe a bundle), Social Security payments you haven't spent and other basic items. A few states let you keep your house. Items you get to keep when you file for bankruptcy are called exempt property, and the laws that specify what property is exempt are called exemption laws. (See Chapter 7, Section B.4.b.ii.)

Filing for Chapter 7 bankruptcy puts into effect something called the automatic stay. The automatic stay immediately stops your creditors from trying to collect what you owe them. So, at least temporarily, creditors—including the Department of Education or a guarantee agency—cannot garnish your wages, intercept your tax refund, sue you, go after your car, house or other property.

The moment you file your bankruptcy petition, your financial problems are in the hands of the bankruptcy court. It assumes legal control of the debts you owe and the property you own, except for your exempt property, which is yours to keep. Nothing can be sold or paid without the court's consent. You have control, however, of almost all property and income you acquire after you file for bankruptcy.

The court makes certain you obey bankruptcy rules by appointing a person called a bankruptcy trustee. The trustee is mostly interested in what you own and what property you claim as exempt. This is because the trustee's primary duty is to see that your creditors are paid as much as possible on what you owe them. And the more assets the trustee recovers for creditors, the more the trustee is paid.

The trustee goes through the papers you file and asks you questions at a short hearing, called the creditors' meeting, which you must attend. Creditors may attend, too, but rarely do. Most creditors' meetings last no more than five minutes.

After the creditors' meeting, the trustee collects your nonexempt property. You can give the property directly to the trustee, pay the trustee its fair market value or, if the trustee agrees, swap some exempt property of value equal to the nonexempt property. If the property isn't worth very much or would be cumbersome for the trustee to sell, the trustee can abandon the property—which means that you get to keep it. Very few people actually lose any property in Chapter 7 bankruptcy because their property is exempt or the trustee doesn't want it.

If you've pledged property as collateral for a loan, the loan is called a secured debt. The most common examples of collateral are houses and motor vehicles. In most cases, you'll either have to surrender the collateral to the creditor or make arrangements to pay for it during or after bankruptcy. If a creditor has recorded a lien—a public notice in which the creditor claims a financial interest in your property—that debt is also secured. You may be able to wipe out certain liens in bankruptcy.

If you change your mind after you file for Chapter 7 bankruptcy, you can ask the court to dismiss your case. As a general rule, a court will dismiss a Chapter 7 bankruptcy case as long as doing so wouldn't harm your creditors. Usually, you can file again if you want to, although you probably will have to wait 180 days.

At the end of your Chapter 7 bankruptcy case, your debts that qualify are wiped out, or discharged, by the court. You no longer legally owe those creditors. You can't file for Chapter 7 bankruptcy again for another six years from the date you filed your previous petition.

2. Chapter 13 Bankruptcy

In Chapter 13 bankruptcy, you discharge most debts by paying all or a portion of them over a period of time. In most situations, Chapter 7 bankruptcy is a better approach to debt problems than is Chapter 13. But student loans are an exception.

If you have regular income and think you could squeeze out a steady amount each month to make payments on your debts, Chapter 13 bankruptcy may be a good option for you. Instead of having your nonexempt assets sold to pay creditors, as happens in Chapter 7 bankruptcy, you keep your property and use your income to pay all or a portion of the debts over three to five years. The minimum amount you must pay is roughly equal to the value of your nonexempt property. In addition, you must pledge your disposable income—net income less reasonable expenses—over the period during which you are making repayments. The income you use to repay creditors need not be wages. You can use benefits, investment income or money you get working as an independent contractor.

To file for Chapter 13 bankruptcy, you fill out the same forms as in a Chapter 7 bankruptcy, listing your money, property, expenses, debts and income, and file them with the bankruptcy court. The filing fee for Chapter 13 bankruptcy is $185. You must also file a workable plan to repay your debts, given your income and expenses. If the court accepts your plan, you make payments directly to the bankruptcy trustee, who in turn distributes the money to your creditors. As in Chapter 7 bankruptcy, the act of filing for Chapter 13 bankruptcy immediately stops your creditors—including the Department of Education or a guarantee agency—from taking further action against you.

You can file for Chapter 13 bankruptcy at any time, even if you wound up a Chapter 7 bankruptcy the day before or just completed another Chapter 13 repayment plan. If you file more than once, however, you'll be required to pay back a large percentage of your debts. You cannot file for Chapter 13 bankruptcy if your secured debts—those for which you have pledged property as collateral or where the creditor has filed a lien—exceed $807,750 or your unsecured debts exceed $269,250.

Most people file a Chapter 13 bankruptcy case to take care of secured debts, such as mortgages and car loans, and other debts called priority debts, such as taxes. Their unsecured creditors—including the Department of Education or guarantee agency holding a student loan—generally get only the money that is left over.

If for some reason you cannot finish a Chapter 13 repayment plan—for example, you lose your job and can no longer make the payments—the bankruptcy court may modify it. The court can allow you to postpone your payments if the problem looks temporary, reduce your total monthly payments or extend the repayment period. As long as it looks as if you are conscientiously trying to pay off your debts, the court is likely to be accommodating and help you across rocky periods. If it's clear that there's no way you'll be able to complete the plan because of circumstances beyond your control, the court might let you discharge some or all of your debts on the basis of hardship. Examples of hardship would be a sudden plant closing in a one-factory town or a debilitating illness that keeps you from working.

If the bankruptcy court won't let you modify your plan and refuses to give you a hardship discharge, you have two options.

• *You can convert your case to a Chapter 7 bankruptcy.* This is not possible, however, if you received a Chapter 7 discharge within the previous six years.

• *Ask the bankruptcy court to dismiss your Chapter 13 case.* This would leave you in the same position as you were in before you filed it, except you'd owe less because of the payments you've made. Also, if your Chapter 13 bankruptcy is dismissed, your creditors will add to their debts any interest that was suspended during your case.

More information on bankruptcy. This chapter provides an introduction to bankruptcy. For more information, see the following Nolo publications:

• *Bankruptcy: Is It the Right Solution to Your Debt Problems?*, by Robin Leonard.

• *How to File for Chapter 7 Bankruptcy*, a detailed Chapter 7 guide, by Stephen Elias, Albin Renauer and Robin Leonard.

• *Chapter 13 Bankruptcy: Repay Your Debts*, by Robin Leonard.

B. When Student Loans Can Be Discharged

As mentioned earlier, you can no longer wipe out student loans in bankruptcy just because your payments first became due more than seven years ago. This big change in bankruptcy law became effective for all cases filed on or after October 7, 1998. Student loans can be eliminated in a Chapter 7 or a Chapter 13 bankruptcy only if you can show that it would cause you undue hardship to repay the loans.

1. Undue Hardship

The Bankruptcy Code does not define undue hardship, but in general, it means that your present income is inadequate to pay the loan and your future earning potential will not change the situation. It is a very, very difficult standard to meet. In determining undue hardship, bankruptcy courts look to several factors, discussed below. If you can show that all or most factors are present, the court will grant an undue hardship discharge of your student loans. If you show only some of them, however, the court may grant you a partial discharge—even though that is not specifically authorized by law—if reducing your loan balance might help you repay at least a portion of it.

In deciding whether it would be an undue hardship for you to repay your student loans, a bankruptcy court will be most swayed if you can show the following.

- **Poverty.** Based on your current income and expenses, you cannot maintain a minimal living standard and repay the loan. The court must consider your current and future, or your potential, employment and income, education, skills and the marketability of your skills, health and family support obligations.

  Unfortunately for you, it is impossible to predict how any one bankruptcy judge will define poverty. Two different judges can look at nearly the same set of facts and come up with vastly different outcomes.

  In one recent case, for example, a couple who earned $23,500 annually and had four children were not permitted to discharge their student loans because they earned $4,230 a year above the federal poverty level for a family of six. (*In re Reyes,* 154 B.R. 320 (E.D. Okla. 1993).) In another case, however, a couple earned $36,000 a year and had three children. They lived in a mobile home, bought food on sale, shopped for clothing at discount stores and rarely sought medical attention. The court allowed them to discharge $47,000 in student loans because their income wouldn't cover their monthly expenses if they were forced to pay their student loans as well. (*In re Skaggs*, 196 B.R. 865 (W.D. Okla. 1996).)

- **Persistence.** It is not enough that you can't currently make your loan payments. You must also demonstrate to the court that your current financial condition is likely to continue into the indefinite future. To prove this, you'll probably have to show the bankruptcy court that a permanent medical condition keeps you from working at all or from working more hours than you do, or that you have achieved the highest level possible in your career given your education.

- **Good Faith.** The court must conclude that you've made a good faith effort to repay your loans. This means that you've tried to repay them but absolutely cannot afford to or that circumstances beyond your control such as a serious injury have prohibited you from repaying your loans. Someone who files for bankruptcy immediately after getting out of school or just after the payback period begins without ever trying to repay will not likely meet this good faith standard. Nor will someone who hasn't looked extensively for employment.

- **Policy.** Some courts also require that you show that you filed for bankruptcy for a reason other than discharging your student loan— that is, that you have other debts you want to discharge in bankruptcy. Other courts will want to make sure you haven't financially benefited from the education made possible by the loan. This means that a court will probably deny a discharge to someone earning a good living in a field he or she borrowed money to study.

If you want to apply for a hardship discharge, you must file an additional document, called a Complaint to Determine Dischargeability, with the bankruptcy court to begin a formal lawsuit that is a part of your bankruptcy case. This currently costs $120.

In general, you can file your complaint with the court any time after you file for bankruptcy. Some courts may require that you file such lawsuits at a certain time, however, so once you file your bankruptcy case, be sure to check with the court clerk or do some research on the court's local rules.

You must establish a number of things in your court forms.

- *Based on your current income and expenses, you cannot maintain a minimal living standard and repay the loan.* You must include specific information about your current and future employment, your income and income potential, education, skills and the marketability of your skills, health and family support obligations.

- *Your current financial condition is likely to continue for an indefinite period.* You must include specific information about your health—including any life threatening, debilitating or chronic conditions you have.

- *You have made a good faith effort to repay the loans.* For example, you might show evidence of payments you made when you had the money, efforts you made to find work and copies of deferment and forbearance applications you submitted over the years.

- *You have filed for bankruptcy for reasons other than just to discharge your student loans*—for example, to eliminate credit card and medical debts.

Bankruptcy resources. Sample completed forms for filing a complaint to determine the dischargeability of a student loan are in *How to File for Chapter 7 Bankruptcy,* by Stephen Elias, Albin Renauer and Robin Leonard (Nolo). In addition, *Represent Yourself in Court: How to Prepare and Try a Winning Case,* by Paul Bergman and Sara J. Berman-Barrett (Nolo), explains all you need to handle your own case, start to finish, without a lawyer.

Because a student loan hardship discharge case is fairly straightforward—a medical or similar condition is keeping you from working or working enough to pay your student loan—you should have little problem proceeding on your own. Nevertheless, you may find it very stressful to create an adversarial situation where you must prove you own weaknesses. If you think it would be too hard to proceed on your own, consider filing your own bankruptcy case but hiring a lawyer just to handle this procedure. (See Chapter 11, Section B.)

Don't file for bankruptcy if you don't need to. Many former students unnecessarily file for bankruptcy hoping to obtain a hardship discharge of their student loans because of a debilitating, life threatening or chronic illness. If your health keeps you from working and paying your student loans, you may qualify for a loan cancellation directly from the holder of your loan. (See Chapter 6, Section A.2.)

2. Discharging HEAL Loans

The dischargeability of HEAL loans is governed by the federal HEAL Act, not the Bankruptcy Act. Under the HEAL Act, to discharge your student loans, you must show that your first payment became due more than seven years ago and that repaying your student loans would impose an unconscionable burden on your life. (42 U.S.C. § 292f (g).)

The HEAL Act provides no guidance on what is considered unconscionable. Nevertheless, Congress clearly intended to prevent most former health students from getting rid of HEAL loans in bankruptcy. You are apt to succeed only if you can show that you have been unable

to find work in the profession in which you were trained, you're unlikely to find work in the future and that some other factor would make
repaying the loan grossly unfair.

In one case in which a debtor was granted a discharge, the original
loan was $8,000, but it rapidly increased due to compounding interest,
assessed at a very high—but legal—rate. The debtor worked two jobs,
but could not support a family that included an autistic child. (*In re
Lawrence*, No. 94-13092-BKC-AJC (S.D. Fla. 1995).)

3. Loans Not Covered by the Bankruptcy Code

A student loan or an educational benefit, scholarship or stipend cannot
be discharged in bankruptcy if it was either:

- made, insured or guaranteed by a government unit, or

- made under any program funded in whole or in part by a government unit or nonprofit institution.

Many former students, unable to repay their student loans, have
argued to bankruptcy courts—occasionally with success—that their
student loans fall outside the Bankruptcy Code. Don't get your hopes up
too high, as these arguments rarely succeed. Nevertheless, creative and
persistent thinking might lead you—with the help of an experienced
lawyer—to figure out a way around the tight constraints of the federal
Bankruptcy Code.

a. Private Loans

On their faces, loans made with private funds look as if they fall outside
the reach of the federal Bankruptcy Code. Unfortunately for you, however, private loans usually fall under the Bankruptcy Code's exceptions

to the discharge. These loans are also not dischargeable if they were made under a program that provides educational loans and if that program is funded at least in part by a non-profit organization. See (*In re Hammarstrom*, 95 B.R. 160 (N.D. Cal. 1989) and *In re Pilcher*, 149 B.R. 595 (9th Cir. 1993).)

b. Consolidation Loans

As discussed in Chapter 5, it is often a good strategy to consolidate your loans. Consolidation means that you get a new loan that is made up of either one or more of your existing student loans. The new consolidation loan should have better terms for you such as a lower interest rate and lower monthly payments.

If you consolidate your student loans and later are unable to pay, you might be able to eliminate the consolidation loan in bankruptcy even though you wouldn't have been able to get rid of the loans before consolidation. At least one court has supported this idea, ruling that a consolidation loan is not for your education but rather to pay off other debt. (*In re Cobb*, 196 BR 34 (E.D. Va. 1996). A Michigan bankruptcy court ruled similarly, but was reversed on appeal.) This distinction is important because loans that are not for educational purposes can usually be discharged in bankruptcy. The majority of courts don't buy this argument, but it has worked in at least one case and might work for you.

c. Other Loans

Other attempts to discharge student loans in bankruptcy can best be described as shots in the dark. There are no general rules to follow, other than to argue that the Bankruptcy Code—which applies to all debts in which the federal or state government or a nonprofit organization is involved in providing money used as a loan or for an educational benefit—does not apply. In one unusual case, a doctor received a

National Health Service Corps, or NHSC, scholarship that required her
either to work for four years at a location the NHSC designated or repay
the money. Her employer, not one chosen by the NHSC, agreed to lend
her money to repay the NHSC so she could go to work for the employer
immediately. She later filed for bankruptcy and included the loan from
her employer. The bankruptcy court granted the discharge, ruling that
the purpose of the loan was for her employment, not her education. (*In
re Segal,* 57 F.3d 342 (3rd Cir. 1995).)

Even if you come up with a creative argument, not all courts will
agree with you. Here are two examples of cases that did not succeed.

Promissory note for school fees. A student owed his school
$5,000 for tuition, late fees, nursing student malpractice fees and lab
fees. He signed a promissory note with his university when he left
school, and then tried to discharge the note in bankruptcy. The court
refused to let him, finding that the debt was an educational benefit
under the Bankruptcy Code. (*In re Stone,* No. 393-05578 (M.D. Tenn.
1995); see also *In re Renshaw,* 229 B.R. 552 (2d Cir. 1999).)

Loan owed to a credit union. A student borrowed money from a
credit union to pay for school and argued that because the credit union
pays dividends to its members, it is not really a nonprofit institution.
The court disagreed, admitting that the credit union's annual issuance of
dividends to its members was an important part of its business life, but
concluded that the dividends were incidental to the credit union's
principal purpose. Therefore, it did not take away from the credit
union's nonprofit status. (*TI Federal Credit Union v. Delbonis,* 183 B.R. 1
(D. Mass. 1995).)

Help with discharging loans in bankruptcy. If you want to
discharge your loan and don't qualify for hardship discharge, you
probably don't have a case. In unusual situations, however, a lawyer
might be able to argue that the Bankruptcy Code doesn't apply. If your
loans are so overwhelming that you're willing to try anything, call
around until you find a lawyer who specializes in bankruptcy and has
handled student loan cases. (See Chapter 11, Section B.)

C. Filing Chapter 13 Bankruptcy If Your Loans Aren't Dischargeable

If you want to file for bankruptcy but your student loans don't qualify for discharge, you can still use Chapter 13 bankruptcy to repay them. During your Chapter 13 case, interest and collection costs stop accruing and the holder of your loans must stop all collection activities, including wage garnishments, tax refund intercepts and lawsuits.

You have several options for repaying your student loans in a Chapter 13 bankruptcy case. As explained in the beginning of this chapter (Section A.2), you file with the bankruptcy court a proposed Chapter 13 plan in which you specify how your creditors will be paid. In most Chapter 13 cases, unsecured creditors—including the Department of Education or the guarantee agency holding a student loan—are generally paid last with the leftover money.

You may be required to classify your unsecured creditors and specify who gets repaid in full and who gets less. Your natural inclination will be to create two classes of unsecured creditors. One class would be made up of unsecured creditors with debts that can be discharged, such as credit cards and medical bills. That class would not be repaid in full. The other class would be made up of unsecured creditors with debts that cannot discharged, including your student loans. You would be required to repay them in full.

While this scheme will please you, it probably won't please your creditors. Any creditor who feels your classifications unfairly discriminate will object to your Chapter 13 plan. By treating your unsecured creditors differently—repaying one class in full while repaying the other class less—you are discriminating. The bankruptcy court will have to decide if your discrimination is unfair. Most courts will rule against you. Very few bankruptcy courts permit separate classes in Chapter 13 bankruptcy cases for student loans. Courts frown on this because it means your other unsecured creditors get less of the pie.

Probably the best way to deal with your student loans in a Chapter 13 bankruptcy is to propose in your plan to pay all your unsecured creditors the same percentage. If you will pay less than 100%, you will owe a balance on your student loans at the end of your case because these loans are not dischargeable. The balance owed on any dischargeable debts, such as credit cards, is wiped out at the end of a Chapter 13 case.

These are a few of the ways you can avoid owing a balance on your student loans at the end of your Chapter 13 case.

• File Chapter 7 bankruptcy first to eliminate your dischargeable unsecured debts, such as your credit cards. You then might have enough money to put toward your Chapter 13 plan to pay your student loans in full without paying your other unsecured debts.

• Pay your student loans proportionally with your other unsecured debts for three years. At the end of the three years, ask for an extension to pay off the balance on just your student loans. The court will not let you go beyond five years.

• Pay your student loans proportionally with your other unsecured debts during your Chapter 13 plan. At the end of the case, file Chapter 13 again to pay off the balance remaining on your student loans.

You have one other possible option for dealing with your nondischargeable student loans in a Chapter 13 bankruptcy case. The Bankruptcy Code has a special rule for secured debts, such as mortgages. Under this rule, you would pay back the late payments on your student loans through your monthly bankruptcy plan payments at the same time you make your regular payments. You can do this only if the remaining regular payments on your student loans go beyond the length of your Chapter 13 plan. With new options allowing for as many as 25 years to repay, this may not be so difficult.

Example: *You began the ten-year repayment of your student loans in June of 1996. You stopped paying in 1999, with seven years of payments left. You file for bankruptcy in 2000. In your plan, you propose to make up the missed payments while also making your regular payments. The court approves your proposal because your ten-year repayment period ends in 2006, three years after your Chapter 13 case will end. If you had only one or two years of student loan payments remaining, however, you could not use this option to repay your student loans.*

Bankruptcy laws may change. If you're a regular reader of a newspaper or listener to news reports on television or radio, you may know that Congress has considered legislation that would significantly change the bankruptcy laws.

The intent of those who support bankruptcy reform is to make it harder to file for Chapter 7 bankruptcy and increase payments to creditors in both Chapter 7 bankruptcy and Chapter 13 bankruptcy. If you are currently considering filing, you probably want to do so before the law changes.

If you want to follow any legislation, get on the Internet. You can download copies of bills at http://www.thomas.loc.gov. Analyses of the bills and day-by-day news updates are available on the website maintained by the American Bankruptcy Institute at http://www.abiworld.org.

CHAPTER 11

Help Beyond the Book

This book gives you many strategies for taking control of your student loans. But the suggestions outlined here may not be enough. A guarantee agency may refuse to grant you a reasonable and affordable payment plan. A bill collector might continue to contact you even after you tell her to stop. You might be sued. You may want to sue the holder of your loan. You may decide to file for bankruptcy.

This chapter suggest some ways to get more information or advice than this book provides. Before discussing the methods in more detail, here's a general piece of advice: Make all decisions yourself. By reading this book, you've taken the responsibility of getting information necessary to make informed decisions about your student loan problems. If you decide to get help from others, apply this same self-empowerment principle. Shop around until you find an advisor who values your competence and intelligence, and recognizes your right to make your own decisions.

A. Do Your Own Legal Research

Often, you can handle a legal problem yourself if you're willing to do some research. The trick is to know where to turn for the type of information you need. One obvious source is a lawyer. But lawyers aren't the only source for legal help. There's a lot you can do on your own. Both the Internet and law libraries are full of valuable information, such as federal statutes. For example, you could read the Fair Debt Collection Practices Act, find out that harassment by collection agencies is illegal, and then read court cases that have decided what types of behavior constitute harassment by a bill collector.

If you decide to take the library route, you must first to find a law library that's open to the public. You might find such a library in your county courthouse or at your state capitol. Publicly funded law schools generally permit the public to use their libraries, and some private law schools grant access to their libraries—sometimes for a modest fee.

Don't overlook the reference department of the public library if you're in a large city. Many large public libraries have a fairly decent legal research collection. Also, ask about using the law library in your own lawyer's office. Some lawyers, on request, will share their books with their clients.

We don't have space here to show you how to do your own legal research in anything approaching a comprehensive fashion. To go further, get a copy of *Legal Research: How to Find and Understand the Law,* by Stephen Elias and Susan Levinkind (Nolo). This nontechnical book gives easy-to-use, step-by-step instructions on how to find legal information.

1. Federal Statutes and Regulations

Most student loan issues are covered by federal laws—including the Higher Education Act, the Fair Debt Collection Practices Act and the Bankruptcy Code. To find a federal statute, you need to look in a multi-volume set of books known as the United States Code, or U.S. Code, which is organized into 50 numbered titles. Title 20 contains the Higher Education Act. Title 15 contains the Consumer Credit Act, including the Fair Debt Collections Practices Act. Title 11 contains the Bankruptcy Code.

The U.S. Code is published in three different formats. One is simply the U.S. Code itself. The other two, U.S. Code Annotated (published by West Publishing Co.) and U.S. Code Service (published by Lawyers Coop/Bancroft-Whitney), contain the statutes as well as references to materials interpreting the codes, such as cases and legal articles. The statutes are the same in all three publications; however, for research purposes, you will want to use either the U.S. Code Annotated or the U.S. Code Service.

As you might have guessed, statutes are often unclear and incomplete. To clarify them, regulations are passed by federal agencies and departments, such as the Department of Education or Federal Trade Commission. These regulations are all compiled and bound together in a series of books you can find in the library called the Code of Federal Regulations, or C.F.R.

Finding federal regulations you need can be frustrating. The C.F.R. is divided into volumes, and individual regulations are published in the order they were issued, not by subject matter. Regulations also frequently have very long citations. For example, the regulations that authorize the Department of Education to grab your tax refund is found at 26 C.F.R. § 301.6402-6T(b)(1).)

THE HIGHER EDUCATION ACT: NOT BEDTIME READING

Visiting a law library to locate specific student loan laws referred to in this book may turn into a lesson in futility. First, many of the regulations and policies described in this book are found in memos and letters sent by the Department of Education to guarantee agencies. These documents are not found in any published materials located at the law library. Second, a few of the provisions contained in the HEA never took effect due to glitches in congressional funding. If you read the HEA, you may develop false hopes that there are ways to cancel or defer your student loans not described in this book. Finally, even if you locate what you are looking for, you may find the HEA impossible to understand.

If you already have a proper reference to the statute—called the citation—finding it is easy. If you don't have a citation, you can find it by using the General Index to the Code. Once you have the statute citation, locate the title you need and turn to the section number.

Congress passes hundreds of laws a year amending the U.S. Code. Therefore, you need to find out if the section you read has been updated. You can do this by turning to the back of the book. There should be an pamphlet called a pocket part inserted there that contains information available after the hardcover volume was printed. Look for the statute in the pocket part to see if it has been amended or if additional cases interpreting the statute have been decided if you're looking at the U.S. Code Annotated or U.S. Code Service.

2. Secondary Sources

If you want to research a specific student loan issue but don't know where to begin, there are several resources to help you. You might want to read a detailed discussion of a particular law, for example, or learn how different courts have interpreted a particular statute or regulation. Lucky for you, many writers have taken the time and effort to compile good information all in one place. These are often referred to as secondary sources. While these publications are aimed at lawyers, many of them can provide a wealth of information for nonlawyers as well.

Here are some of the best secondary sources you might find in your local law library.

- **National Consumer Law Center Publications.** Two very thorough volumes published by NCLC contain current information about student loans. *Unfair and Deceptive Acts and Practices* is the bible of the few lawyers who handle student loan cases. Also, *Consumer Bankruptcy Law and Practice* contains a thorough discussion of bankruptcy, including the issues related to student loans. If you can't find a library that contains these books, call NCLC at: 617-523-8089.

- **LRP Publications.** LRP's *Discharging Student Loans in Bankruptcy*, by David Light, contains a thorough discussion of discharging student loans, including summaries of significant cases, listed by court. If it's not at your library, you can obtain a copy by sending $30, which includes shipping and handling, to LRP Publications, Dept. 440, 747 Dresher Road, P.O. Box 980, Horsham, PA 19044-0980; to order using a credit card, call 800-341-7874. If you'd like to read a summary of the publication, visit LRP's website at http://www.lrp.com.

- **Law journals.** They contain compilations of articles published by law schools, bar associations and law societies. Most of these contain academic, not practical, material. You may, however, find some practical information in bar association journals. You can look up your topic in the *Index to Legal Periodicals*, available at virtually all law libraries.

3. Court Decisions

Sometimes the answer to a legal question cannot be found in a statute. This happens when court cases and opinions have greatly expanded or explained the statute, taking it beyond its obvious or literal meaning. It might also happen if the law that applies to your question has been made by judges, not legislators. This is unusual with student loan questions, however.

a. Court Decisions That Explain Statutes

Statutes and regulations do not explain themselves. For example, the Higher Education Act allows you to discharge your student loans in bankruptcy if repayment would cause you undue hardship, but the statute doesn't define undue hardship. Chances are, however, that others before you have had the same questions, and they may have come up in the context of a lawsuit. If a judge interpreted the statute and wrote an opinion on the matter, that written opinion, once published, will become "the law" as much as the statute itself. If a higher court (an appellate court) has also examined the question, then its opinion will rule.

To find out if there are written court decisions that interpret a particular statute or ordinance, look in an "annotated code." If you find a case that seems to answer your question, it's crucial to make sure that the decision you're reading is still "good law"—that a more recent opinion from a higher court has not reached a different conclusion. To make sure that you are relying on the latest and highest judicial pronouncement, you must use the library research tool known as *Shepard's*. Nolo's *Legal Research: How to Find and Understand the Law* has a good, easy-to-follow explanation of how to use the *Shepard's* system to expand and update your research.

b. How to Read a Case Citation

If you find a citation to a case that looks important, you may want to read the opinion. You'll need the title of the case and its citation, which is like an address for the set of books, volume and page where the case can be found.

There are several places in which a case may be reported. A case decided by the U.S. Supreme Court can be found in the U.S. Reports (U.S.) or in the Supreme Court Reporter (S.Ct.). Most federal cases decided by a court other than a the U.S. Supreme Court will be in either the Federal Reporter, Second or Third Series (F.2d or F.3d) or the Federal Supplement (F. Supp.) Bankruptcy cases are in the Bankruptcy Reporter (B.R.).

Although it may look about as decipherable as hieroglyphics, once understood, a case citation gives lots of useful information in a small space. It tells you the names of the people or companies involved, the volume of the reporter in which the case is published, the page number on which it begins and the year in which the case was decided. Take, for example, *Juras v. Aman Collection Service, Inc.*, 829 F.2d 739 (9th Cir. 1987).

Juras and Aman Collection Services are the names of the people with the legal dispute. The case is reported in volume 829 of the Federal Reporter, Second Series, beginning on page 739. The Ninth Circuit Court of Appeals issued the decision in 1987.

4. Online Legal Research

If you have access to the Internet, there is a good deal of legal research you can accomplish using your computer. But you can't do it all—not every court decision or statute is available online. Furthermore, unless you know what you are looking for—the case name and citation or the code section—you may have difficulty finding it.

Still, there are four useful sites:

- Nolo.com [http://www.nolo.com]. Nolo's site includes a legal encyclopedia, a dictionary of legal terms, "Ask Auntie Nolo" your legal question, a legal research center, calculators, web forms, guides and books

- Cornell Law School [http://www.law.cornell.edu]. You can find links to extensive federal and state online legal information.

- Findlaw [http://www.findlaw.com]. This address has links to each state's online legal information, such as statutes and cases, as well as links to federal statutes and cases. It also links to many online bankruptcy resources, including government documents, journals, newsletters, articles mailing lists and usenet groups.

- The U.S. House of Representatives Internet Law Library [http://www.law.house.gov]. This site provides the entire Code of Federal Regulations, plus federal statutes, including the Bankruptcy Code.

Specific student loan information is available at a few sites, including the following:

- U.S. Department of Education [http://www.ed.gov]. You can search all Department of Education Web pages for specific text of regulations and policies. At the Department of Education's site, the following specific locations may prove quite helpful:

  — Project EASI (Easy Access for Students and Institutions) [http://easi.ed.gov]. Project EASI's goals include making life easier for anyone who must repay student loans. The site contains information on managing your debt, loan consolidation, avoiding default, deferment and forbearance, what to do if you do default, and loan cancellation. You can download deferment and discharge application forms.

  — Financial Aid for Students [http://www.fafsa.ed.gov]. You can find two excellent publications here—the *Student Guide*, which explains the requirements for loan cancellation and deferment, and the *Guide to Defaulted Student Loans*.

  — Information for Financial Aid Professionals [http://ifap.ed.gov]. IFAP's site is geared toward lenders, schools, guarantee agencies and other players in the student loan world. Included at the site are different federal regulations and correspondence from the Department of Education entitled "Dear Colleague Letters." These letters often include valuable information such as interpretations of regulations, effective dates of programs, changes in collection practices and much more.

  — Direct Loans [http://www.ed.gov/DirectLoan]. Here's the place to go for information on direct loans, including account information and frequently asked questions. You can also find interactive budgets and repayment calculators.

— Proposed Regulations [http://www.ed.gov/legislation/FedRegister/proprule/index.html]. Read proposed regulations from the Department of Education's Office of Postsecondary Education.

— Final Regulations [http://www.ed.gov/legislation/FedRegister/finrule/index.html]. Read final regulations from the U.S. Department of Education's Office of Postsecondary Education.

• National Council of Higher Education Loan Programs [http://www.nchelp.org.] NCHELP's site includes the Common Manual, a reference and operations manual for the Federal Family Education Loan Program (FFELP) offered by 36 guarantee agencies. Prepared for schools and lenders, the manual provides background, describes procedures, cites statutes and regulations and organizes reference materials. NCHELP's site also links to guarantee agencies, student loan servicers, secondary market companies and other student loan-related sites.

• U.S. Department of Labor [http://www.bls.gov/ocohome.htm]. This is the site for the Occupational Outlook Handbook, which provides numbers of job openings, salary ranges and training requirements for Department of Labor job classifications. This information can be useful to evaluate representations made by trade school sales representatives about job placement.

B. Consult With or Hire a Lawyer

As a general rule, consider hiring an attorney if the amount at stake is high enough to justify the legal fees or if there is something the lawyer can do for you that you can't do yourself. For example, if a you owe a large amount on your student loans, say $25,000, and you are trying to negotiate a compromise of your loans under one of the little-known compromise programs, it might well be worth the money to hire a lawyer who will charge you $1,000 to get the job done. If you owe only $2,500, by contrast, and your doctor has written a letter stating that you are totally and permanently disabled, you'd be wasting your money hiring a lawyer to complete your cancellation application.

Of course, you may be exhausted and feeling beat up from handling your student loan problems yourself, so you may want a lawyer to take over for you. That's a perfectly legitimate reason to hire legal help as long as you make sure you get what you pay for and don't turn your life over to the lawyer and become a passive observer of your own case.

1. What Lawyers Can Do for You

There are three basic ways a lawyer can help you.

Consultation and advice. A lawyer can analyze your situation and advise you on your best plan of action. Ideally, the lawyer will explain all of your options so you can make the choice. But keep on your toes. Many lawyers will subtly steer you in the direction they want you to go, often the one that nets them the largest fee. Be wary of any lawyer who recommends that you file for bankruptcy.

Negotiation. The lawyer can help you negotiate with the holder of your loan. Many lawyers excel at negotiating—especially if they use that skill a lot in their practices. If your loan is held by an attorney working for a collection agency, that attorney may be more apt to settle with a lawyer you hire than with you.

Representation. If the holder of your loan sues you or you want to sue a collection agency, you may want to hire a lawyer to represent you. This, however, could get expensive, so be sure about your decision before you hire someone.

FEW LAWYERS HANDLE STUDENT LOAN CASES

If you decide to hire a lawyer to give you advice or to represent you, you may become frustrated in your search for someone who handles student loan cases. Most lawyers have expertise—or at least focus their practices—in just one or a few areas of law. Very few concentrate on handling student loans. Sometimes bankruptcy lawyers handle student loan problems, but often only in the context of a bankruptcy case.

If you find a lawyer who knows little about student loans but is willing to learn, you might mention this book as a resource that contains citations to many other helpful references.

2. How to Find a Lawyer

There are several ways to find a lawyer.

Personal referrals. If you know someone who was pleased with the services of a lawyer, call that lawyer first. If the lawyer doesn't have experience with student loan cases or doesn't want to take your case, ask for another recommendation. Be careful, however, when selecting a lawyer from a personal referral. The fact that a lawyer performed to another person's standard in one situation doesn't guarantee he or she will meet your needs.

Legal Aid. Legal Aid offices are partially funded by the federal Legal Services Corporation and offer legal assistance in many areas. To qualify for Legal Aid, you must have a limited income—that is, your household income cannot exceed 135% of the federal poverty level. Legal Aid lawyers have handled many of the cases pertaining to trade schools and loan cancellation, and many of those lawyers have worked with the Department of Education to draft the trade school regulations. If you have any kind of a trade school loan problem, visiting a Legal Aid office may be your best bet. To find a Legal Aid office, look in your local phone book.

Legal clinic. Many law schools sponsor legal clinics and provide free legal advice to consumers. Some legal clinics have the same income requirements as Legal Aid offices; others offer free services to people who have low or moderate incomes. To find out if there is a legal clinic in your area, contact a local Legal Aid office or law school.

Group legal plans. Some unions, employers and consumer action organizations offer group plans to their members or employees, who can obtain legal assistance free or for low rates. If you're a member of such a plan, check with it first for a lawyer.

Prepaid legal insurance. Prepaid legal insurance plans offer some services for a low monthly fee and charge more for additional work. Beware, however, that participating lawyers may use the plan to snare clients who are attracted by the promise of low-cost, basic services, and then sell them more expensive services. If the lawyer with whom you consult recommends an expensive course of action, get a second opinion. But if a plan offers extensive free advice, or the lawyer will agree to help you negotiate a repayment plan, your membership fee may be worth the cost.

There's no guarantee that the lawyers available through these plans are of the best caliber. Check out the plan carefully before signing up. Ask about the plan's complaint system, whether you get to choose your lawyer and whether or not the lawyer will represent you in court.

Consumer organizations. A local consumer organization might be able to recommend an attorney who handles student loan cases. In some large urban areas, advocate groups publish guides of legal organizations and lawyer referrals. If you call a local consumer organization, you'll probably talk with someone who can help you find the right organization or lawyer for you.

Lawyer referral panels. Most county bar associations will give out the names of attorneys who practice locally. But bar associations rarely screen the attorneys they list, which means those who participate may not be the most experienced or competent.

3. What to Look for in a Lawyer

No matter what approach you take to finding a lawyer, here are several suggestions on how to make sure you have the best possible working relationship.

First, fight the urge you may have to surrender your will and be intimidated. You should be the one who decides what you feel comfortable doing about your legal affairs. Keep in mind that you're hiring the lawyer to perform a service for you; shop around if the price or personality isn't right.

Second, you must be as comfortable as possible with any lawyer you hire. When you talk with the lawyer, ask some specific questions. Do you get clear, concise answers? If not, try someone else. If the lawyer says little except to agree to take over your problem—with a substantial fee—watch out. You're talking with someone who doesn't know the answer and won't admit it, or someone who is likely to be paternalistic or pushy with you. Don't be a passive client or hire a lawyer who wants you to be one. If the lawyer admits he or she doesn't know an answer, that isn't necessarily bad. In most cases, the lawyer must do some research to find out how to best handle your specific situation.

Also, pay attention to how the lawyer responds to the fact that you have considerable information about the law. If you've read this book, you're better informed about student loans than most clients—and many lawyers. Many lawyers are threatened when the client knows a lot.

After your initial meeting, think about the lawyer's suggestions. If they don't make sense or you have reservations, call another lawyer.

Finally, keep in mind that the lawyer works for you. Once you hire a lawyer, you have the absolute right to switch to another—or to fire the lawyer and handle the matter yourself—at any time, for any reason.

4. How Much Lawyers Charge

The single most common area in which lawyers and clients have misunderstandings is over legal fees. Enter any relationship with a lawyer knowing that. You can help eliminate the chance of a fee dispute if you have a clear agreement in writing, signed by both of you. If the lawyer doesn't mention a written fee agreement, ask about one. If you hire a lawyer to help you with a debt problem, you don't want the financial arrangement to be misunderstood so that the lawyer's fee just becomes another debt you can't pay.

If all you want is a consultation with an attorney to find out where you stand and what options you have, the lawyer should not charge more than $100 per hour. Some charge as little as $75 an hour, while others charge as much as $175 an hour or more. But any lawyer willing to work with people with debt problems is taking advantage of a debtor by charging much more than $100 per hour.

If you want the lawyer to do some negotiating, the fee could pile up. A letter doesn't take that long to write, however, and as long as you are clear about what you want the lawyer to do and not do, you can keep the bill low.

If you're sued by the Department of Education and hire a lawyer to represent you, the lawyer's fee will probably add up fast. A few lawyers might represent you for a flat fee, for example $500, but most charge by the hour. If you enter into an hourly arrangement, it's best to add a cap beyond which the lawyer shouldn't work without your permission.

If you plan to hire a lawyer to help you file for bankruptcy, expect to pay between $350 to $1,000. Many bankruptcy attorneys let you pay in installments. Also, the attorney must report the fee to the bankruptcy court for approval. The court can make the attorney justify the fee if it's high. This rarely happens, however, because most attorneys know what local bankruptcy judges will allow and set their fees accordingly.

If you are unhappy with your lawyer. If you hire a lawyer and are dissatisfied with the service you receive, see *Mad at Your Lawyer,* by Tanya Starnes (Nolo).

C. Contact a Debt or Credit Counseling Agency

Credit and debt counseling agencies are nonprofit organizations funded primarily by major creditors, such as department stores, credit card companies and banks, who can work with you to help you repay your debts and improve your financial picture.

To use a credit or debt counseling agency to help you pay your debts, you must have some disposable income. A counselor contacts your creditors to let them know that you've sought assistance and need more time to pay. Based on your income and debts, the counselor, with your creditors, decides on how much you pay. You then make one payment each month to the counseling agency, which in turn pays your creditors. The agency asks the creditors to return a small percentage of the money received to the agency office to fund its work. This arrangement is generally referred to as a debt management program.

Some creditors will make overtures to help you when you're on a debt management program. For example, Citicorp waives minimum payment and late charges—and may freeze interest assessments—for customers undergoing credit counseling. But few creditors will make interest concessions, such as waiving a portion of the accumulated interest to help you repay the principal. More likely, you'll get late fees dropped and the opportunity to reinstate your credit if you successfully complete a debt management program.

The combination of high consumer debt and easy access to information (the Internet) has led to an explosion in the number of credit and debt counseling agencies ready to offer you help. Some provide limited services, such as budgeting and debt repayment, while others offer a range of services, from debt counseling to financial planning. Some counseling agencies will not negotiate with the holders of student loans because the government does not return a percentage collected to the counseling agency's office. But if you find an agency that will negotiate with the government, or if your student loan is one of many debts, you might find a counseling agency to be very helpful.

Participating in a credit or debt counseling agency's debt management program is a little bit like filing for Chapter 13 bankruptcy. (See Chapter 10.) Working with a credit or debt counseling agency has one advantage: no bankruptcy will appear on your credit record.

But a debt management program also has two disadvantages when compared to Chapter 13 bankruptcy. First, if you miss a payment, Chapter 13 protects you from creditors who would start collection actions. A debt management program has no such protection and any one creditor can pull the plug on your plan. Also, a debt management program plan usually requires that your debts be paid in full. In Chapter 13 bankruptcy, you're required to pay the value of your nonexempt property, which can mean that you pay only a small fraction of your unsecured debts.

Critics of credit and debt counseling agencies point out that they get most of their funding from creditors. (Some offices also receive grants from private agencies such as the United Way and federal agencies including the Department of Housing and Urban Development.) Nevertheless, critics claim that counselors cannot be objective in counseling debtors to file for bankruptcy if they know the office won't receive any funds.

In response to this and other consumer concerns, credit and debt counseling agencies accredited by the National Foundation for Consumer Credit (the majority of agencies are) reached an agreement with the Federal Trade Commission to disclose the following to consumers:

- that creditors fund a large portion of the cost of their operations

- that the credit agency must balance the ability of the debtor to make payments with the requirements of the creditors that fund the office, and

- a reliable estimate of how long it will take a debtor to repay his or her debts under a debt management program.

QUESTIONS TO ASK A CREDIT OR DEBT COUNSELING AGENCY

Debt Counselors of America suggests that you ask the following questions before using any counseling agency.

1. **Will you send me information on your agency and programs?** There is no reason you should be required to provide account numbers and balances or any information other than a name and mailing address before an agency will agree to send you information about itself. Some agencies require account numbers and balances to see if you have enough debt for them to be interested in helping you. If an agency won't provide you with information about its programs, consider that a warning sign.

2. **Do you pay referral fees?** No agency should pay referral fees to outside parties or pay agents to enroll consumers into a debt management program. This may be a warning signal that the agency is simply interested in placing as many consumers as possible into a repayment program, rather than providing educational assistance.

3. **What should I do if I cannot afford the minimum payment?** A good agency will not quickly dismiss you or tell you to file bankruptcy simply because you cannot meet their minimum debt management program payment. Ask about hardship programs.

QUESTIONS TO ASK A CREDIT OR DEBT COUNSELING AGENCY (continued)

4. **What kind of training do you have that makes you qualified to assist me?** A home study course or a few hours of class are not sufficient training. A good counseling agency provides its counselors with regular training from lawyers, Certified Financial Planners and other experts.

5. **What kind of security measures do you take to protect my information?** It is important that the agency you select has sufficient security in place to protect your confidential information.

6. **Can I get up-to-date, regular reports of the status of my accounts?** If access is by telephone only, will a knowledgeable person be available when you call to give you the information you need?

7. **Will you answer my general questions, even if I am not in your repayment program?** Ask any agency you are considering for advice if it can assist you with information even if you are not going to enroll in its debt management program.

8. **What kinds of educational programs and services do you provide?** Educational seminars are great but you might need some hard and fast answers about your situation without having to wait for the next seminar.

9. **Is there a minimum amount of debt I have to have in order to work with you?** The answer should always be "no." If an agency is there to help, it should not turn you away because you do not have enough debt.

10. **Will you help me with all my debts?** Some agencies offer little assistance for secured debts like car payments or mortgages, or government debts like taxes and student loans. Make sure you'll receive full service.

11. **Is there a mandatory up-front fee?** Some agencies charge a mandatory up-front fee for their debt management program—as much as $250 or more. These fees may be so high that they prevent you from getting assistance.

QUESTIONS TO ASK A CREDIT OR DEBT COUNSELING AGENCY (continued)

12. **Will you sell my name or address to outside parties?** Be sure you know the agency's privacy policy. Ask before your name and address appears on a mailing list sold to outside organizations.

13. **How often do you pay creditors?** Although your creditors will be paid only once a month, make sure the agency sends payments out at least weekly. Your payment should not sit at the agency for a month waiting for the next payment cycle.

1. Consumer Credit Counseling Service

Consumer Credit Counseling Service (CCCS) is the oldest credit or debt counseling agency in the country. Actually, CCCS isn't one agency. CCCS is the primary operating name of many credit and debt counseling agencies affiliated with the National Foundation for Consumer Credit (NFCC).

CCCS may charge you a small monthly fee (an average of about $9) for setting up a repayment plan. CCCS also helps people make monthly budgets, and sometimes charges a one-time fee of about $20. If you can't afford the fee, CCCS will waive it. In most CCCS offices, the primary service offered is a debt management program. A few offices have additional services, such as helping you save money toward buying a house or reviewing your credit report.

CCCS has more than 1,100 offices, located in every state. Look in the phone book to find the one nearest you or contact the main office at 8611 Second Avenue, Suite 100, Silver Spring, MD 20910, 800-388-2227 or http://www.nfcc.org.

2. Debt Counselors of America

Debt Counselors of America (DCA) offers budgeting and debt management programs, like other debt and credit counseling agencies. But unlike most other agencies, DCA has a financial planning department with Certified Financial Planners and a Crisis Relief Team to assist consumers who are turned away by other credit or debt counseling agencies or who have very complex problems. DCA is also the first credit or debt counseling agency that is a registered investment advisor. Each week, DCA broadcasts a live call-in radio show over its Internet site, where you can also find numerous publications on a range of money issues.

DCA has only one office. That's because DCA offers its services via phone, fax, email and the Internet. You can contact DCA at 1680 East Gude Drive, Rockville, MD 20850, 800-680-3328 or http://www.dca.org.

3. Other Credit and Debt Counseling Agencies

Surf the Internet and you'll find many other credit and debt counseling agencies offering a variety of services. Be sure to ask questions about their services before signing up.

Three agencies with national recognition are as follows:

Genus Credit Management
10500 Little Patuxent Parkway
Columbia, MD 21044
888-793-4368
http://www.genus.org

Genus offers a debt management program, with payments deducted automatically from your checking or savings account. Genus also provides mortgage repayment assistance, publications, videos, a monthly newsletter and workshops.

Money Management International
4600 Gulf Freeway, Suite 500
Houston, TX 77023
800-762-2271
http://www.moneymanagementbymail.org

MMI provides credit counseling, debt management and economic education information by telephone, email, fax and mail, 24 hours a day, seven days a week. MMI's Internet site includes a debt counseling application and message board where you can send your money questions to "Letters to Susan and Co."

The Center for Debt Management
Family Debt Arbitration and Counseling Services, Inc.
P.O. Box 99
Candia, NH 03034
603-483-0593
http://members.aol.com/DebtRelief/index.html

CDM offers several services on its Internet site:

- debt counseling—answers to your questions

- debt management—repayment plan

- publications—topics include bankruptcy, debt consolidation, credit cards, credit bureaus, credit repair, collection agencies, student loans, financial aid, government programs, law and more.

- words of wisdom—words of inspiration and noteworthy quotations analogous to debt, and

- consumer information—consumer alerts and links to consumer protection agencies and other sites of interest.

Glossary

Your confusion over your student loans may be compounded by your encounter with unfamiliar terminology. This section contains definitions of words and concepts you are likely to come across in dealing with your loans. Many of these terms aren't in this book, but may be used by the government and loan company representatives with whom you speak.

Accrued Interest

The interest charged to your loan over time. Typically, you are responsible for paying all accrued interest. If you have a subsidized loan, however, the federal government pays any interest that accrues while you are in school and during any other authorized periods of deferment.

Amortization

Repaying and reducing your debt through regular (usually monthly) installments of principal and interest calculated over a set period of time. For example, most student loans are amortized to be repaid over ten years, in 120 equal monthly payments.

Annual Percentage Rate

The total cost of your loan (including interest and any other fees) as calculated on an annual basis.

Cancellation

Relieving yourself of your obligation to repay your loan by meeting certain, carefully specified requirements.

Capitalized Interest

Accrued interest that is added to the principal balance of your loan while you are not making payments or your payments are insufficient to cover both the principal and interest due. When this happens, you end up paying interest on interest, sometimes called "negative amortization."

Comaker, Cosigner or Codebtor

Anyone who has guaranteed a debt. This person is fully responsible for repaying the debt, including accrued interest, late fees or collection costs, in the event the borrower defaults. Most student loans do not have a comaker.

If the borrower defaults, the holder of the loans can attempt to collect from the comaker without first trying to collect from the borrower. If the loan is in default, that notation will appear in the comaker's credit report.

Compounded Interest

The frequency with which interest and fees are computed and added to the principal balance of your loan. If your promissory note states that the interest on your loan will be compounded monthly, your loan holder will calculate and add interest on the outstanding balance at the start of each month.

Consolidation Loan

A loan that allows you to combine many loans into a single new loan, or to refinance just one loan. When you consolidate, you typically extend your repayment period and lower your monthly payments, thereby increasing the overall cost of your loan.

Cost of Attendance/Cost of Education

The total amount it costs you to go to school each year. Your cost of attendance is determined using rules established by Congress. It typically includes tuition, fees, room and board, books, supplies, transportation, loan fees, dependent care, costs related to disability and miscellaneous expenses.

Credit Bureau

Credit bureaus are profit-making companies that gather and sell information about your credit history. They sell credit files to banks, mortgage lenders, credit unions, credit card companies, department stores, insurance companies, landlords and even a few employers. These companies and individuals use the credit files to supplement applications for credit, insurance, housing and employment. The three major credit bureaus are Equifax, Experian and Trans Union.

Default

Failure to repay a loan according to the terms you agreed to when you signed a promissory note coupled with the holder of your loan concluding that you do not intend to repay. Default may also result from failure to submit timely requests for cancellation, deferment or forbearance.

Deferment/Deferral

A temporary postponement of your loan payments. If you have a subsidized loan, the federal government pays the interest that accrues during any authorized period of deferment.

Deferred Interest

Interest that has accrued but does not need to be paid immediately. Deferred interest is often capitalized.

Direct Loan

A federal Stafford, PLUS or consolidation loan that comes directly from the U.S. Department of Education, rather than through a financial institution. The loans are made through the William D. Ford Federal Direct Loan Program. They have slightly different repayment terms than loans obtained through the Federal Family Education Program (FFEL loans).

Disbursement

The time at which your lender makes your loan available to you.

Disclosure Statement

The notice you receive when your loan is made. This notice should include the costs of your loan, including the interest rate and any additional fees.

Discretionary Income

Your federal adjusted gross income minus the poverty level defined by the Department of Health and Human Services for your family size.

Disposable Income

Money left over when your necessary expenses (housing, food, medical care, clothing, transportation and the like) are deducted from your net income.

Due Diligence

Procedures the federal government requires lenders to use to try to collect student loans, such as calling and writing to request payments, offer new payment terms and reporting late payments to credit bureaus, before the lender is permitted to sell the loans back to the government.

Exit Interview

A counseling session required by federal law. If you have federally guaranteed loans, a school financial aid officer must speak with you about loan repayment and debt management before you graduate or leave school.

Federal Family Education Loans

A federally guaranteed loan obtained through the Federal Family Education Program. These are Stafford, PLUS, SLS or federal consolidation loans obtained from financial institutions. They have slightly different repayment terms than those obtained through the federal Direct Loan Program.

Forbearance

A temporary postponement or reduction of your loan payments, or an extension of your time to pay. Forbearances are typically granted at the discretion of the holder of your loan. Interest continues to accrue during all forbearance periods.

Grace Period

A period of time following your graduation or departure from school during which you are not required to make payments on your loan. If you have a subsidized loan, the federal government pays the interest that accrues during your grace period.

Graduated Repayment

A loan repayment plan where your payments are low in the beginning and then gradually "step-up" over time. Graduated payment plans are not based on your income.

Guarantee Agency

A state or private nonprofit company that is essentially an insurance company. Guarantee agencies insure your loans and pay off the holder if you default, and receive reinsurance money from the federal Department of Education.

Guarantee Fee

A percentage of your loan withheld by your lender to cover the costs of administering and insuring your loan.

Half-Time

For schools that measure progress by credit hours and semesters, trimesters or quarters, half-time enrollment is at least six semester hours or quarter hours per term. For schools that measure progress by credit hours without using semesters, trimesters or quarters, half-time enrollment is at least 12 semester hours or 18 quarter hours per year. For schools measuring progress by clock hours, half-time enrollment is at least 12 hours per week. Schools, however, may choose to set higher requirements for half-time enrollment.

Holder

The owner of your loan or company hired by the owner of your loan to service it. This company or agency is entitled to receive your payments. Your loan holder may be your lender or a company that has purchased your loan from the lender.

Income Contingent Repayment

A loan repayment plan for borrowers who have federal direct loans. This plan is based on your annual income, family size and loan amount. As your income rises and falls, so do your payments.

Income Sensitive Repayment

A loan repayment plan for borrowers who obtained their federally guaranteed loans through a financial institution. Like the income contingent repayment plan, your payments are based on your income.

Independent Student

A student who is over 24 years of age or who is:

- married
- enrolled in a graduate a professional school program
- responsible for legal dependents other than a spouse
- an orphan or ward of the court (or had been an orphan or ward of the court up until the age or 18), or
- a veteran of the U.S. Armed Forces.

Insurance Fee

A percentage of your loan withheld by your lender to cover the costs of administering and insuring (guaranteeing) your loan.

Interest

A commission you pay a bank, your school or the government for lending you money. Anyone who buys your loan from the original lender is entitled to assess the same interest the original lender was entitled to tack on. An interest rate represents the annual percentage tacked on to a loan. This means that if your loans are at 8%, the holder of your loan adds 8% to the remaining balance each year. (It's a little more complex than that. In actuality, each day 1/365th of 8% is added to the balance existing that day. For example, you are ready to pay off your loan in full. If you called today for the payoff amount, it will be slightly less than if you call tomorrow, which will have one more day of interest tacked on).

Lender

The institution from which you obtain your loan. This may be a bank, savings and loan, credit union, your school or the federal government.

Loan Period

The period of study for which you obtain a loan. For example, you may receive a Stafford loan to cover a loan period of one academic year.

Origination Fee

A percentage of your loan withheld by your lender to cover the costs of processing and administering your loan.

Perkins Loan

A federally guaranteed, low interest loan made to students by their schools from a combination of school and federal government funds. Formerly known as National Direct Student Loans and National Defense Student Loans.

PLUS Loan

A federally guaranteed, non-need based loan made to parents who want to borrow money to finance the education of their dependent children.

Principal

The total amount you borrowed, not including any capitalized fees or interest.

Private Loan

A loan not guaranteed by the federal government and made by a financial institution.

Promissory Note

The legal document you sign when you get your student loan. Your promissory note lists the conditions under which you're borrowing the money and the terms under which you agree to pay it back. The document also includes your interest rate, information about other costs, and your options for cancellation, deferment and forbearance.

Rehabilitation

Getting out of default on your student loans.

Repayment Period

The total amount of time you have to repay your loan.

Satisfactory Repayment Arrangement

A student loan repayment schedule acceptable to the holder of your loan, negotiated by you and the holder. Often, you can avoid aggressive collection efforts (such as an interception of your tax refund or a wage garnishment) by entering into a satisfactory repayment arrangement.

Secondary Market

The place where lenders sell loans that are not in default if they don't want to collect the loans themselves.

Servicer

A company hired by either your lender or a company on the secondary market—whoever holds your loan—to receive and process your payments, to process requests for postponement or cancellation, and to handle other requests or correspondence.

Stafford Loan

The most common type of student loan, made by the federal government and financial institutions. Stafford loans may be subsidized or unsubsidized. Subsidized Stafford loans are need-based; the federal government pays the interest while you are in school or during other authorized periods of deferment. Unsubsidized Stafford loans are not need based; you are responsible for all interest that accrues to your loan. Stafford loans were previously known as Guaranteed Student Loans and Federal Insured Student Loans.

Subsidized Loan

If you have a subsidized loan, someone other than you (usually the federal government) pays the interest while you are in school or during other authorized periods of deferment.

Supplemental Loan For Students (SLS)

A federally guaranteed, non-need based loan made to independent students prior to July 1, 1994. These have been replaced by unsubsidized Stafford loans. They were previously known as Auxiliary Loans to Assist Students (ALAS) and Student PLUS Loans.

Term

The total amount of time you have to repay your loan.

Terms

The rules that apply to your loan, including how you get it and how it must be repaid. It also refers to loan costs, such as interest and other fees.

Unsubsidized Loan

If your loan is unsubsidized, you must pay all interest as it accrues or be subject to interest capitalization.

Variable Interest Rate

An interest rate that fluctuates according to a certain pre-determined interest rate, such as the prime rate or the rate of Treasury bills (T-bills).

Wage Garnishment

A sum of money deducted from your net pay by your employer to and sent to the holder of your loan. For most consumer loans, if you default, the only way the creditor can garnish your wages is to sue you and get a judgment against you. If you're in default on federal student loans, however, the holder of your loan can garnish up to 10% of your net wages without first suing you.

Write-Off

The buying back of a student loan by the federal government (Department of Education, for most loans or Department of Health and Human Services, for healthcare loans). The federal government writes off loans only when it concludes that collection is hopeless. It is still possible to get out of default ("rehabilitate" your loans) if they are held by the Department of Education. Rehabilitated loans are usually turned over to guarantee agencies or resold to a company on the secondary market.

Appendix

STUDENT LOAN INFORMATION

_____

(Type of Loan)

_____

(Account Number)

Repayment Information
Amount Borrowed: _____

Interest Rate: _____

Payment Amount: _____

Repayment Start Date: _____

Payment Due Date: _____

Loan Holder
Name: _____

Address: _____

_____

Telephone: _____

Fax: _____

Loan Servicer
Name: _____

Address: _____

_____

Telephone: _____

Fax: _____

Notes: _____

_____

_____

STUDENT LOAN PHONE LOG

_____   _____
(Type of Loan)   (Account Number)

_____   _____
(Loan Holder/Servicer's Name)   (Loan Holder/Servicer's Phone Number)

Date	Subject of Conversation	Contact Person	Advice Given	Action Taken

DAILY EXPENSES

Sunday's Expenditures	Cost	Monday's Expenditures	Cost	Tuesday's Expenditures	Cost	Wednesday's Expenditures	Cost
Daily Total:		**Daily Total:**		**Daily Total:**		**Daily Total:**	

Thursday's Expenditures	Cost	Friday's Expenditures	Cost	Saturday's Expenditures	Cost	Other Expenditures	Cost
Daily Total:		**Daily Total:**		**Daily Total:**		**Weekly Total:**	

MONTHLY INCOME FROM ALL SOURCES

1 Source of income		2 Amount of each payment	3 Period covered by each payment	4 Amount per month
A. Wages or Salary				
Job 1:	Gross Pay, including overtime			
	Subtract:			
	Federal taxes			
	State taxes			
	Self-employment taxes			
	Other mandatory deductions (specify):			
	_____			
	Subtotal	$_____	_____	_____
Job 2:	Gross Pay, including overtime			
	Subtract:			
	Federal taxes			
	State taxes			
	Self-employment taxes			
	Other mandatory deductions (specify):			
	_____			
	Subtotal	$_____	_____	_____
Job 3:	Gross Pay, including overtime			
	Subtract:			
	Federal taxes			
	State taxes			
	Self-employment taxes			
	Other mandatory deductions (specify):			
	_____			
	Subtotal	$_____	_____	_____

1 Source of income		2 Amount of each payment	3 Period covered by each payment	4 Amount per month
B. Self-Employment Income				
Job 1:	Gross Pay, including overtime			
_____	Subtract:			
	Federal taxes			
	State taxes			
	Self-Employment taxes			
	Other mandatory deductions (specify):			
	_____			
	Subtotal	$_____	_____	_____
Job 2:	Gross Pay, including overtime			
_____	Subtract:			
	Federal taxes			
	State taxes			
	Self-employment taxes			
	Other mandatory deductions (specify):			
	_____			
	Subtotal	$_____	_____	_____
C. Other Sources				
	Bonuses			
	Dividends and interest			
	Rent, lease or license income			
	Royalties			
	Note or trust income			
	Alimony or child support you receive			
	Pension or retirement income			
	Social Security			
	Other public assistance			
	Other (specify):			
	_____			
	_____			
	_____			
	Total monthly income			$_____

MONTHLY BUDGET

EXPENSE CATEGORY	proj.	Aug.	Sept.	Oct.	Nov.	Dec.	Jan.	Feb.	Mar.	April	May	June	July
HOME													
FOOD													
EDUCATION													
WEARING APPAREL													
SELF CARE													

EXPENSE CATEGORY	proj.	Aug.	Sept.	Oct.	Nov.	Dec.	Jan.	Feb.	Mar.	April	May	June	July
HEALTHCARE													
TRANSPORTATION													
ENTERTAINMENT													
GIFTS & CARDS													
PERSONAL BUSINESS													
SAVINGS													

STUDENT LOAN PAYMENTS

Federal Loans	Amount Borrowed	Monthly Payments	Total Interest Paid	Total Loan Payments	Number of Payments
Totals for Federal Loans					
Private Loans	**Amount Borrowed**	**Monthly Payments**	**Total Interest Paid**	**Total Loan Payments**	**Number of Payments**
Totals for Private Loans					
Other Loans	**Amount Borrowed**	**Monthly Payments**	**Total Interest Paid**	**Total Loan Payments**	**Number of Payments**
Totals for Other Loans					
	Amount Borrowed	**Monthly Payments**	**Total Interest Paid**	**Total Loan Payments**	**Number of Payments**
Grand Totals for all Loans					

REQUEST FOR REVIEW

| Name | Social Security number | | |
| Current Address | City | State | Zip Code |

If you object to offset against your refund for the student loan described in the Loan Statement or notice, you can use this form to request a review or hearing. If you object ONLY because you believe you cannot afford to pay this debt, but you wish to arrange payment terms, **DO NOT USE THIS FORM. INSTEAD**, write or call the Contact listed on the Loan Statement.

Important: You should request and review copies of the records evidencing your loan before you complete this statement. See the Notice of Proposal Offset of Federal Income Tax Refund for instructions on how to request these records.

I.	**Check <u>ONLY ONE</u> of the following:**
a. ❏	I want a review of my objection based on this written statement and the records in my loan file. **COMPLETE PARTS II AND IV OF THIS FORM.**
b. ❏	I want an in-person hearing in the city shown on the Loan statement to present my objection. I understand that I must pay my own expenses to appear for this hearing. **COMPLETE PARTS II, III, and IV OF THIS FORM.** Provide a telephone number where you can be reached during the day: ( )_____
c. ❏	I want a hearing by telephone. **COMPLETE PARTS II, III, and IV OF THIS FORM.** Provide a telephone number where you can be reached during the day: ( )_____

II.	**Check the objections that apply. <u>ENCLOSE</u> the documents described below.** (If you do not enclose documents; ED will consider your objections based on the information on this form and the records in ED's file on this loan.)
1. ❏	I do not owe the full amount shown because I repaid some or all of this loan. **ENCLOSE** copies of the front and back of all checks, and copies of all money orders and receipts showing payments made to the holder of the loan.
2. ❏	I am making payments on this loan as required under the repayment agreement I reached with the holder of the loan. **ENCLOSE** copies of repayment agreement and front and back of checks by which you paid on the agreement.
3. ❏	I filed for bankruptcy and my case is still open. **ENCLOSE** copies of **ANY** document **FROM THE COURT** that shows the name of the court and your case number.
4. ❏	This loan was discharged in bankruptcy. **ENCLOSE** copies of discharge order and the schedule of debts filed with the court.
5. ❏	I am totally and permanently disabled—unable to work and earn money because of an impairment that is expected to continue indefinitely or result in death.
6. ❏	This is not my Social Security number, **AND** I do not owe this loan. **ENCLOSE** copy of your Driver's License or other identification issued by a government agency, and a copy of your Social Security card.
7. ❏	I believe that this loan is not an enforceable debt in the amount stated because: (**EXPLAIN** any other reason you object to the collection of this loan amount by offset against your refund. Be specific as possible. **ENCLOSE** any records that support your reasons.)

_____

_____

_____

_____

_____

(over)

8. ☐ I used this loan to enroll in _____ (school) on or about ___/___/___, and withdrew from school on or about ___/___/___. I believe that I am owed, but have not been paid, a refund from the school of $_____. **ENCLOSE** any records you have showing your withdrawal.

9. ☐ This loan is a guaranteed student loan that I used to attend _____ (school), which closed on or about ___/___/___, and I was unable to complete my education because the school closed.

10. ☐ This loan is a guaranteed student loan that I used to attend _____ (school). I was admitted to the school based on my ability to benefit from the training offered. I believe that the school improperly determined my ability to benefit from the training offered, **AND** I was unable to obtain employment in the field for which the school's program was intended to provide training.

11. ☐ I believe that_____ (school) signed my name without authorization on the loan application or promissory note or endorsed my loan check or authorization for electronic funds transfer (EFT) without my authorization with respect to all or a portion of the loan proceeds.

(If you check No. 5, No. 9, No. 10, or No.11, you will be asked to provide additional information in order to avoid refund offset.)

III.	If you want an in-person or telephone hearing; you _must_ complete the following:

The loan records and documents I submitted to support my statement in Part II do not show all the material (important) facts about my objection to collection of this loan. I need a hearing to explain the following important facts about this loan: (**EXPLAIN** here the additional facts that you believe make a hearing necessary. Use a separate sheet of paper if necessary. If you have already fully described these facts in your response in Part II, **WRITE HERE** the number of the objection in which you described these facts _____.)

Note: If ED does not offer you an in-person or telephone hearing, ED will consider your objection based on the information and documents you supply with this form and the records in the ED's file on this loan.

IV.	I state under penalty of perjury that the statements I have made on the request are true and accurate to the best of my knowledge.

Signature

Date

REQUEST FOR HEARING OR EXEMPTION

In RE:

Student Loan Dept of

_____, **DEBTOR**

Name	Social Security number
Address	Home Phone # ( )
City, State, Zip	Work Phone # ( )

Use this form to request a hearing or claim exemption from wage withholding. If you wish to enter into a repayment agreement in order to prevent wage withholding, **DO NOT USE THIS FORM.** Instead, contact the _____ Collections Department at the telephone number listed on the Notice Prior to Wage Withholding.

REQUEST FOR HEARING
(Check the Appropriate box)

❑   I want a hearing based on my written statement and the records in my loan file. I do not believe I owe this debt or I dispute the amount of this debt because: (Explain here your basis for disputing the existence or amount of the debt. Be as specific as possible and enclose any documents that support your position. Please note that failure to complete your education, dissatisfaction with your school or inability to obtain employment in the field for which the school prepared you does not diminish or excuse your obligation to repay the loan(s). Use a separate sheet of paper if necessary.)

❏   I want a hearing by telephone. (Provide a telephone number where you can be reached during the day):
(   ) _____

❏   I want an in-person hearing in _____.
I understand that I must pay my own expenses to appear at this hearing.

IF YOU WANT A TELEPHONE OR AN IN-PERSON HEARING, YOU MUST COMPLETE THE FOLLOWING:

I request a telephone or in-person hearing for the following reason(s):   (You may check more than one)

❏   I dispute the amount of this debt. (Please enclose with this form any proof you have that the debt amount indicated on the Notice Prior to Wage Withholding is incorrect)

❏   I dispute the existence of this debt. (Please enclose with this form any proof you have that this debt has been paid in full or that the debt does not exist on any other grounds.)

❏   I wish to be heard regarding the terms of my repayment schedule.

❏   Other. (Explain here additional or other facts or reasons why you believe a telephone or in-person hearing is necessary. Please note that failure to complete your education, dissatisfaction with your school or inability to obtain employment in the field for which the school prepared you does not diminish or excuse your obligation to repay your loan(s). Use a separate sheet of paper if necessary.)

❏ I am exempt from wage withholding because I was involuntarily separated from employment and have not been reemployed continuously for twelve (12) months.

My previous employer was:

Company Name
Address
City, Sate, Zip
Date of Separation:
Phone #:

My present employer is:

Company Name
Address
City, Sate, Zip
Date of Hire:
Phone #:

If you are covered under a State's unemployment program, you must submit this form along with documents from the _____ Employment Commission (or a similar agency in another state) indicating your entitlement to unemployment compensation and a statement from your present employer indicating the date you began work at your present job. If you are not covered under a State's unemployment program (even if involuntarily separated from employment), you must provide a statement to that effect from the state unemployment agency.

I STATE UNDER PENALTY OF PERJURY THAT THE STATEMENTS I HAVE MADE ON THIS REQUEST FOR HEARING OR EXEMPTION ARE TRUE AND ACCURATE TO THE BEST OF MY KNOWLEDGE.

Signature   Date

Printed Name

Return This Form To: _____

_____

_____

_____

IN-SCHOOL DEFERMENT REQUEST

Federal Family Education Loan Program

OMB No. 1845-0005
Form Approved
Exp. Date 06/30/2002

SCH

WARNING: Any person who knowingly makes a false statement or misrepresentation on this form or on any accompanying documents shall be subject to penalties which may include fines, imprisonment or both, under the U.S. Criminal Code and 20 U.S.C. §1097.

SECTION 1: BORROWER IDENTIFICATION

Please correct or, if information is missing, enter below. If a correction, check this box: ❏

SSN | | | | – | | | – | | | | |

Name _____
Address _____
City, State, Zip _____
Telephone - Home ( ) _____
Telephone - Other ( ) _____

SECTION 2: DEFERMENT REQUEST

Before answering any questions, carefully read the entire form, including the instructions and other information in Sections 5 and 6.

■ I meet the qualifications for the deferment checked below and request that my loan holder defer repayment of my loan(s):

  ❏ While I am enrolled at an eligible school as a **FULL-TIME STUDENT**. (For borrowers with any FFEL Program loan.)

  ❏ While I am enrolled at an eligible school as a **LESS THAN FULL-TIME BUT AT LEAST HALF-TIME STUDENT**. (For borrowers who, on the date they signed the promissory note, did not have an outstanding balance on a FFEL Program loan made before July 1, 1987.)

NOTE: Your promissory note or other loan documents may state that a borrower with an outstanding balance on a FFEL Program loan made prior to July 1, 1993 must receive another loan in order to qualify for a half-time student deferment. This requirement was eliminated by the Higher Education Amendments of 1998. Effective October 1, 1998, no FFEL Program borrower who is eligible for a deferment based on enrollment as at least a half-time student is required to receive another loan in order to qualify for this deferment.

SECTION 3: BORROWER UNDERSTANDINGS AND CERTIFICATIONS

■ **I understand that: (1)** Principal payments will be deferred, but if I have an unsubsidized loan, I am responsible for paying the interest that accrues. **(2)** I have the option of making interest payments on my unsubsidized loan(s) during my deferment. I may choose to make interest payments by checking the box below; unpaid interest that accrues will be capitalized by my loan holder.

  ❏ I wish to make interest payments on my unsubsidized loan(s) during my deferment.

(3) My deferment will begin on the date the deferment condition began, but no more than six months before the date my loan holder receives this request. **(4)** My deferment will end on the earlier of the date that establishes my deferment eligibility ends or the certified deferment end date. **(5)** My loan holder will not grant this deferment request unless all applicable sections of this form are completed and any required additional documentation is provided. **(6)** If my deferment does not cover all my past due payments, my loan holder may grant me a forbearance for all payments due before the begin date of my deferment or — if the period for which I am eligible for a deferment has ended — a forbearance for all payments due at the time my deferment request is processed. **(7)** If I am eligible for a post-deferment grace period on loans made before October 1, 1981, my loan holder may grant me a forbearance on my other loans for this period so that I can begin repayment of all my loans at the same time. I understand that my loan holder may capitalize the interest that accrues on my other loans during the six-month period and that this will increase the principal balance of my other loans. **(8)** My loan holder may grant me a forbearance on my loans for up to 60 days, if necessary, for the collection and processing of documentation related to my deferment request. Interest that accrues during the forbearance will not be capitalized.

■ **I certify that: (1)** The information I provided in Sections 1 and 2 above is true and correct. **(2)** I will provide additional documentation to my loan holder, as required, to support my deferment status. **(3)** I will notify my loan holder immediately when the condition(s) that qualified me for the deferment ends. **(4)** I have read, understand, and meet the eligibility criteria of the deferment for which I have applied.

Borrower's Signature _____ **Date** _____

SECTION 4: AUTHORIZED OFFICIAL'S CERTIFICATION

NOTE: As an alternative to completing this section, the school may attach its own enrollment certification report listing the required information.

I certify, to the best of my knowledge and belief, that the borrower named above:

(1) is/was enrolled as (check the appropriate box)   ❏ a full-time student   ❏ at least a half-time student

during the academic period from | | | – | | | – | | | | to | | | – | | | – | | | | and

(2) is reasonably expected to complete his/her program requirements on | | | – | | | – | | | | .

Name of Institution _____   OPE-ID _____
Address _____   City, State, Zip _____
Name/Title of Authorized Official _____   Telephone ( ) _____
Authorized Official's Signature _____   **Date** _____

Page 1 of 2

SECTION 5: INSTRUCTIONS FOR COMPLETING THE FORM

Type or print using dark ink. Report dates as month-day-year (MM-DD-YYYY). For example, 'January 1, 1999' = '01-01-1999'. An authorized school official must either (A) complete Section 4, or (B) attach the school's own enrollment certification report listing the required information. If you need help completing this form, contact your loan holder.

Return the completed form and any required documentation to the address shown in Section 7.

SECTION 6: DEFINITIONS FOR IN-SCHOOL DEFERMENT REQUEST

Definitions

- The **Federal Family Education Loan (FFEL) Program** includes Federal Stafford Loans (both subsidized and unsubsidized), Federal Supplemental Loans for Students (SLS), Federal PLUS Loans, and Federal Consolidation Loans.

- A **deferment** is a period during which I am entitled to postpone repayment of the principal balance of my loan(s). The federal government pays the interest that accrues during an eligible deferment for all subsidized Federal Stafford Loans and for Federal Consolidation Loans for which the Consolidation loan application was received by my loan holder **(1)** on or after January 1, 1993 but before August 10, 1993, **(2)** on or after August 10, 1993, if it includes *only* Federal Stafford Loans that were eligible for federal interest subsidy, or **(3)** on or after November 13, 1997, for that portion of the Consolidation loan that paid a subsidized Federal Stafford Loan or a Federal Direct Stafford/Ford (Direct Subsidized) Loan. I am responsible for the interest that accrues during this period on all other FFEL Program loans.

- **Forbearance** means permitting the temporary cessation of payments, allowing an extension of time for making payments, or temporarily accepting smaller payments than previously scheduled. I am responsible for paying the interest on my loan(s) during a forbearance.

- The **holder** of my FFEL Program loan(s) may be a lender, guaranty agency, secondary market, or the U.S. Department of Education.

- **Capitalization** is the addition of unpaid interest to the principal balance of my loan. This will increase the principal and the total cost of my loan.

- An **authorized certifying official** for an In-School Deferment is an authorized official of the school where I am/was enrolled as a full-time or at least half-time student.

SECTION 7: WHERE TO SEND THE COMPLETED DEFERMENT REQUEST

RETURN THE COMPLETED DEFERMENT REQUEST AND ANY REQUIRED DOCUMENTATION TO:
(IF NO ADDRESS IS SHOWN, RETURN TO YOUR LOAN HOLDER)

SECTION 8: IMPORTANT NOTICES

Privacy Act Disclosure Notice

The Privacy Act of 1974 (5 U.S.C. §552a) requires that we disclose to you the following information:

The authority for collecting this information is §421 *et seq.* of the Higher Education Act of 1965, as amended (the HEA) (20 U.S.C. §1071 to 1087-2). The principal purpose for collecting this information is to determine whether you are eligible for a deferment on your loan(s) under the Federal Family Education Loan (FFEL) Program.

We ask that you provide the information requested on this deferment request on a voluntary basis. However, you must provide all of the requested information so that the holder(s) of your loan(s) can determine whether you qualify for a deferment.

The information in your file may be disclosed to third parties as authorized under routine uses in the Privacy Act notices called "Title IV Program Files" (originally published on April 12, 1994, *Federal Register*, Vol. 59, p. 17351) and "National Student Loan Data System" (originally published on December 20, 1994, *Federal Register*, Vol. 59, p. 65532). Thus, this information may be disclosed to parties that we authorize to assist us in administering the federal student aid programs, including contractors that are required to maintain safeguards under the Privacy Act. Disclosures may also be made for verification of information, determination of eligibility, enforcement of conditions of the loan or grant, debt collection, and the prevention of fraud, waste, and abuse and these disclosures may be made through computer matching programs with other federal agencies. Disclosures may be made to determine the feasibility of entering into computer matching agreements. We may send information to members of Congress if you ask them in writing to help you with federal student aid questions. If we are involved in litigation, we may send information to the Department of Justice (DOJ), a court, adjudicative body, counsel, or witness if the disclosure is related to financial aid and certain other conditions are met. If this information, either alone or with other information, indicates a potential violation of law, we may send it to the appropriate authority for consideration of action and we may disclose to DOJ to get its advice related to the Title IV, HEA programs or questions under the Freedom of Information Act. Disclosures may be made to qualified researchers under Privacy Act safeguards. In some circumstances involving employment decisions, grievances, or complaints or involving decisions regarding the letting of a contract or making of a grant, license, or other benefit, we may send information to an appropriate authority. In limited circumstances, we may disclose to a federal labor organization recognized under 5 U.S.C. Chapter 71.

Because we request your social security number (SSN), we must inform you that we collect your SSN on a voluntary basis, but section 484(a)(4) of the HEA (20 U.S.C. §1091(a)(4)) provides that, in order to receive any grant, loan, or work assistance under Title IV of the HEA, a student must provide his or her SSN. Your SSN is used to verify your identity, and as an account number (identifier) throughout the life of your loan(s) so that data may be recorded accurately.

Paperwork Reduction Notice

According to the Paperwork Reduction Act of 1995, no persons are required to respond to a collection of information unless it displays a currently valid OMB control number. The valid OMB control number for this information collection is 1845-0005. The time required to complete this information collection is estimated to average 0.16 hours (10 minutes) per response, including the time to review instructions, search existing data resources, gather and maintain the data needed, and complete and review the information collection. *If you have any comments concerning the accuracy of the time estimate(s) or suggestions for improving this form, please write to:*

U.S. Department of Education, Washington, DC 20202-4651.

If you have any comments or concerns regarding the status of your individual submission of this form, write directly to the address shown in Section 7.

ECONOMIC HARDSHIP DEFERMENT REQUEST

Federal Family Education Loan Program

USE THIS FORM ONLY IF **ALL** OF YOUR OUTSTANDING FEDERAL FAMILY EDUCATION LOAN PROGRAM LOANS
WERE MADE ON OR AFTER JULY 1, 1993.

HRD

WARNING: Any person who knowingly makes a false statement or misrepresentation on this form or on any accompanying documents
shall be subject to penalties which may include fines, imprisonment or both, under the U.S. Criminal Code and 20 U.S.C. §1097.

OMB No. 1845-0716
Form Approved
Exp. Date 06/30/2002

SECTION 1: BORROWER IDENTIFICATION

Please correct or, if information is missing, enter below. If a correction,
check this box: ☐

SSN ☐☐☐ – ☐☐ – ☐☐☐☐

Name _____

Address _____

City, State, Zip _____

Telephone - Home ( ) _____

Telephone - Other ( ) _____

SECTION 2: DEFERMENT REQUEST

Before answering any questions, carefully read the entire form, including the instructions and other information in Sections 4, 5, and 6.

■ I meet the qualifications stated in Section 6 for the Economic Hardship Deferment checked below and request that my loan holder defer repayment of my
loan(s) beginning ☐☐ – ☐☐☐☐. To qualify, I must meet **one** of the conditions listed below and must provide the required
documentation, as described in Section 6, for only that condition. ***Check one:***

(1) ☐ I have been granted an economic hardship deferment under the William D. Ford Federal Direct Loan (Direct Loan) Program or the Federal Perkins
Loan Program for the same period of time for which I am requesting this deferment. **I have attached documentation of the deferment.**

(2) ☐ I am receiving or received payments under a federal or state public assistance program, such as Aid to Families with Dependent Children (AFDC),
Supplemental Security Income (SSI), Food Stamps, or state general public assistance. **I have attached documentation of these payments.**

(3) ☐ I am serving as a Peace Corps volunteer. **I have attached documentation certifying my period of service in the Peace Corps.**

(4) ☐ I work full-time *and* my total monthly gross income does not exceed the **larger of** (A) the Federal Minimum Wage Rate, or (B) the Poverty Line
income for a family of two for my state (regardless of my actual family size), as listed below. **I have attached documentation of this income.**

My total monthly gross income is $ _____.

(A) Federal Minimum Wage Rate (monthly amount, based on $5.15 an hour) $ 892.66

(B) Poverty Lines for a Family of Two (monthly amounts)
- All states and the District of Columbia (except Alaska and Hawaii) $ 921.67
- Alaska $1,153.33
- Hawaii $1,060.83

(5) ☐ I do **not** work full-time *and* my total monthly gross income does not exceed the **larger of** (A) **two times** the Federal Minimum Wage Rate, or
(B) **two times** the Poverty Line income for a family of two for my state (regardless of my actual family size), as listed above under condition (4).
In addition, after deducting the total monthly payments that I am making on all of my federal education debts from my total monthly gross
income, the amount remaining does not exceed the **larger of** (A) the Federal Minimum Wage Rate, or (B) the Poverty Line income for a family of
two for my state, as listed above under condition (4). My total monthly federal education debt payments must be adjusted, if necessary, to reflect
a minimum 10-year repayment period. **I have attached documentation of my total monthly gross income and my federal education loan debt.**

NOTE: *A worksheet to help you determine whether you meet this condition is available from your loan holder. Completion of the worksheet
is optional. Your loan holder will determine whether you qualify based on the income and education debt information that you provide below.*

My total monthly gross income is $ _____.

The total amount I borrowed for all of my federal education loans now in repayment (including loans for which I am requesting this deferment)
is $ _____.

(6) ☐ I work full-time *and* the total amount of my annual payments on all of my federal education loans in repayment is equal to or larger than 20%
of my adjusted gross income. In addition, after deducting the total amount of my annual payments on my federal education loans in repayment
from my adjusted gross income, the amount remaining must be less than 220% of the **larger of** (A) the Federal Minimum Wage rate, or (B) the
Poverty Line income for a family of two for my state (regardless of my actual family size), as listed below. My total annual federal education loan
payments must be adjusted, if necessary, to reflect a minimum 10-year repayment period. **I have attached documentation of my adjusted gross
income and my federal education loan debt.**

NOTE: *A worksheet to help you determine whether you meet this condition is available from your loan holder. Completion of the worksheet is
optional. Your loan holder will determine whether you qualify based on the income and education debt information that you provide below.*

My adjusted gross income is $ _____.

The total amount I borrowed for all of my federal education loans now in repayment (including loans for which I am requesting this deferment)
is $ _____.

(A) Federal Minimum Wage Rate (annual amount, based on $5.15 an hour) $10,712.00

(B) Poverty Lines for a Family of Two (annual amounts)
- All states and the District of Columbia (except Alaska and Hawaii) $11,060.00
- Alaska $13,840.00
- Hawaii $12,730.00

SECTION 3: BORROWER INTEREST SELECTION AND CERTIFICATION

■ Principal payments will be deferred, but if I have an unsubsidized loan, I am responsible for paying the interest that accrues. I have the option of making
interest payments on my unsubsidized loan(s) during my deferment. I may choose to make interest payments by checking the box below; unpaid interest
that accrues will be capitalized by my loan holder.

☐ I wish to make interest payments on my unsubsidized loan(s) during my deferment.

■ **I certify that** the information I provided in Sections 1 and 2 above is true and correct, and that I have read, understand, and meet the terms and conditions
and eligibility criteria of the deferment for which I have applied, as explained in Section 6.

Borrower's Signature _____ **Date** _____

SECTION 4: INSTRUCTIONS FOR COMPLETING THE FORM

Type or print using dark ink. Report dates as month-day-year (MM-DD-YYYY). For example, 'January 1, 1999' = '01-01-1999'. Include your name and social security number (SSN) on any documentation that you are required to submit with this form. If you need help completing this form, contact your loan holder.

Return the completed form and any required documentation to the address shown in Section 7.

SECTION 5: DEFINITIONS

■ The **Federal Family Education Loan (FFEL) Program** includes Federal Stafford Loans (both subsidized and unsubsidized), Federal Supplemental Loans for Students (SLS), Federal PLUS Loans, and Federal Consolidation Loans.

■ The **William D. Ford Federal Direct Loan (Direct Loan) Program** includes Federal Direct Stafford/Ford (Direct Subsidized) Loans, Federal Direct Unsubsidized Stafford/Ford (Direct Unsubsidized) Loans, Federal Direct PLUS (Direct PLUS) Loans, and Federal Direct Consolidation (Direct Consolidation) Loans.

■ The **holder** of my FFEL Program loan(s) may be a lender, guaranty agency, secondary market, or the U.S. Department of Education.

■ A **deferment** is a period during which I am entitled to postpone repayment of the principal balance of my loan(s). The federal government pays the interest that accrues during an eligible deferment for all subsidized Federal Stafford Loans and for Federal Consolidation Loans for which the Consolidation loan application was received by my loan holder **(1)** on or after January 1, 1993 but before August 10, 1993, **(2)** on or after August 10, 1993, if it includes **only** Federal Stafford Loans that were eligible for federal interest subsidy, or **(3)** on or after November 13, 1997, for that portion of the Consolidation loan that paid a subsidized Federal Stafford Loan or a Federal Direct Stafford/Ford (Direct Subsidized) Loan. I am responsible for the interest that accrues during this period on all other FFEL Program loans.

■ **Monthly gross income** is the amount of my monthly income from my employment (either full-time or part-time) or any other source before taxes and other deductions.

■ **Adjusted gross income** means the amount recorded on my Federal Income Tax Return as adjusted gross income.

■ **Full-time** employment is defined as working at least 30 hours per week in a position expected to last at least three consecutive months.

■ Eligible **federal education loans** that may be included in determining the total amount I borrowed for deferment conditions (5) and (6) in Section 2 are listed below. I may include defaulted loans only if I have made satisfactory repayment arrangements with the holder of those loans.

· All **FFEL Program** loans listed above	· National Direct Student Loans (NDSL)	· Health Professions Student Loans (HPSL)
· All **Direct Loan Program** loans listed above	· National Defense Student Loans (NDSL)	· Loans for Disadvantaged Students (LDS)
· Guaranteed Student Loans (GSL)	· Auxiliary Loans to Assist Students (ALAS)	· Primary Care Loans (PCL)
· Federal Insured Student Loans (FISL)	· Parent Loans for Undergraduate Students (PLUS)	· Nursing Student Loans (NSL)
· Federal Perkins Loans	· Health Education Assistance Loans (HEAL)	

■ **Minimum 10-year repayment period** (for deferment conditions (5) and (6) in Section 2) refers to the period that is 10 years from the date I entered repayment, regardless of the actual length of my repayment schedule. If the length of my repayment schedule is more than 10 years, my payment amounts must be adjusted to show the estimated monthly or annual amount that I would owe if my loan were scheduled to be repaid in fixed installments within a 10-year period.

■ **Forbearance** means permitting the temporary cessation of payments, allowing an extension of time for making payments, or temporarily accepting smaller payments than previously scheduled. I am responsible for paying the interest on my loan(s) during a forbearance.

■ **Capitalization** is the addition of unpaid interest to the principal balance of my loan. This will increase the principal and the total cost of my loan.

SECTION 6: ELIGIBILITY CRITERIA / TERMS AND CONDITIONS FOR ECONOMIC HARDSHIP DEFERMENT

■ If **ALL** of my outstanding FFEL Program loans were made **on or after July 1, 1993**, I may defer repayment of my loan(s) while I meet one of the economic hardship conditions listed in Section 2.

■ If my economic hardship deferment eligibility is based on condition (1), as described in Section 2, I must provide my loan holder with documentation of the deferment that has been granted under the Direct Loan Program or the Federal Perkins Loan Program (for example, correspondence from my loan holder showing that I have been granted a deferment).

■ If my economic hardship deferment eligibility is based on condition (2), as described in Section 2, I must provide my loan holder with documentation confirming that I am receiving or received payments under a federal or state public assistance program.

■ If my economic hardship deferment eligibility is based on condition (3), as described in Section 2, I must provide my loan holder with documentation which certifies the beginning and anticipated ending dates of my service in the Peace Corps and which is signed and dated by an authorized Peace Corps official.

■ If my economic hardship deferment eligibility is based on condition (4), as described in Section 2, I must provide my loan holder with documentation of my most recent monthly gross income from all sources, such as pay stubs.

■ If my economic hardship deferment eligibility is based on condition (5) or condition (6), as described in Section 2, I must provide my loan holder with:

· documentation of my most recent total monthly gross income from all sources, such as pay stubs (for condition 5 only);

· documentation of my adjusted gross income (a copy of my Federal Income Tax Return — for condition 6 only); and

· documentation of the total amount I borrowed for all federal education loans that are now in repayment, such as disclosure statements or current repayment schedules. This must include the monthly payment amount, beginning loan balance, and repayment terms.

· If my total federal education loan debt includes defaulted loans, I must provide documentation that I have made satisfactory repayment arrangements with the holder of the defaulted loans.

■ If my economic hardship deferment eligibility is based on conditions (4), (5), or (6), as described in Section 2, and I am applying for an additional period of economic hardship deferment that begins less than one year after the end of my previous period of economic hardship deferment, I must provide my loan holder with a copy of my latest federal income tax return (if one was filed within the preceding eight months), in addition to the other documentation required for these conditions.

■ If my economic hardship deferment eligibility is based on conditions (4), (5), or (6), as described in Section 2, and I am not currently residing in the United States, I will use the Poverty Line amounts for my last state of residence in the United States.

Section 6 continued on Page 3.

SECTION 6 *(Continued)*

■ I will provide additional documentation to my loan holder, as required, to support my deferment status.

■ I will notify my loan holder immediately when the condition that qualified me for the deferment ends.

■ My deferment will begin on the date the deferment condition began, but no more than six months before the date my loan holder receives this request.

■ My deferment will end on the earlier of the date that the condition that establishes my deferment eligibility ends or the certified deferment end date.

■ My maximum cumulative eligibility for an economic hardship deferment is 36 months. Except for a deferment based on condition (3), as described in Section 2, I must reapply every 12 months if I continue to meet the criteria for an economic hardship deferment.

■ My loan holder will not grant this deferment request unless all applicable sections of this form are completed and any additional required documentation is provided.

■ If my deferment does not cover all my past due payments, my loan holder may grant me a forbearance for all payments due before the begin date of my deferment. If the period for which I am eligible for a deferment has ended, my loan holder may grant me a forbearance for all payments due at the time my deferment request is processed.

■ My loan holder may grant me a forbearance on my loans for up to 60 days, if necessary, for the collection and processing of documentation related to my deferment request. Interest that accrues during the forbearance will not be capitalized.

SECTION 7: WHERE TO SEND THE COMPLETED DEFERMENT REQUEST

RETURN THE COMPLETED DEFERMENT REQUEST AND ANY REQUIRED DOCUMENTATION TO:
(IF NO ADDRESS IS SHOWN, RETURN TO YOUR LOAN HOLDER)

SECTION 8: IMPORTANT NOTICES

Privacy Act Disclosure Notice

The Privacy Act of 1974 (5 U.S.C. §552a) requires that we disclose to you the following information:

The authority for collecting this information is §421 *et seq.* of the Higher Education Act of 1965, as amended (the HEA) (20 U.S.C. §1071 to 1087-2). The principal purpose for collecting this information is to determine whether you are eligible for a deferment on your loan(s) under the Federal Family Education Loan (FFEL) Program.

We ask that you provide the information requested on this deferment request on a voluntary basis. However, you must provide all of the requested information so that the holder(s) of your loan(s) can determine whether you qualify for a deferment.

The information in your file may be disclosed to third parties as authorized under routine uses in the Privacy Act notices called "Title IV Program Files" (originally published on April 12, 1994, *Federal Register*, Vol. 59, p. 17351) and "National Student Loan Data System" (originally published on December 20, 1994, *Federal Register*, Vol. 59, p. 65532). Thus, this information may be disclosed to parties that we authorize to assist us in administering the federal student aid programs, including contractors that are required to maintain safeguards under the Privacy Act. Disclosures may also be made for verification of information, determination of eligibility, enforcement of conditions of the loan or grant, debt collection, and the prevention of fraud, waste, and abuse and these disclosures may be made through computer matching programs with other federal agencies. Disclosures may be made to determine the feasibility of entering into computer matching agreements. We may send information to members of Congress if you ask them in writing to help you with federal student aid questions. If we are involved in litigation, we may send information to the Department of Justice (DOJ), a court, adjudicative body, counsel, or witness if the disclosure is related to financial aid and certain other conditions are met. If this information, either alone or with other information, indicates a potential violation of law, we may send it to the appropriate authority for consideration of action and we may disclose to DOJ to get its advice related to the Title IV, HEA programs or questions under the Freedom of Information Act. Disclosures may be made to qualified researchers under Privacy Act safeguards. In some circumstances involving employment decisions, grievances, or complaints or involving decisions regarding the letting of a contract or making of a grant, license, or other benefit, we may send information to an appropriate authority. In limited circumstances, we may disclose to a federal labor organization recognized under 5 U.S.C. Chapter 71.

Because we request your social security number (SSN), we must inform you that we collect your SSN on a voluntary basis, but section 484(a)(4) of the HEA (20 U.S.C. §1091(a)(4)) provides that, in order to receive any grant, loan, or work assistance under Title IV of the HEA, a student must provide his or her SSN. Your SSN is used to verify your identity, and as an account number (identifier) throughout the life of your loan(s) so that data may be recorded accurately.

Paperwork Reduction Notice

According to the Paperwork Reduction Act of 1995, no persons are required to respond to a collection of information unless it displays a currently valid OMB control number. The valid OMB control number for this information collection is 1845-0716. The time required to complete this information collection is estimated to average 0.16 hours (10 minutes) per response, including the time to review instructions, search existing data resources, gather and maintain the data needed, and complete and review the information collection. *If you have any comments concerning the accuracy of the time estimate(s) or suggestions for improving this form, please write to:*

U.S. Department of Education, Washington, DC 20202-4651.

If you have any comments or concerns regarding the status of your individual submission of this form, write directly to the address shown in Section 7.

ECONOMIC HARDSHIP DEFERMENT
WORKSHEET A

Use this worksheet to determine if you are eligible for an economic hardship deferment based on condition (5) in Section 2 of the Economic Hardship Deferment Request form. Completion of this worksheet is optional — if you check condition (5), your loan holder will determine your eligibility based on the income and federal education debt documentation that you provide.

DO NOT RETURN THIS WORKSHEET WITH THE DEFERMENT REQUEST — KEEP IT FOR YOUR RECORDS.

STEP 1

Are you working full-time?

❏ Yes   You do not qualify for an economic hardship deferment based on condition (5). Do not continue with this worksheet.

❏ No   Go to Step 2.

STEP 2

(1) Line 1. Enter the amount listed below for your state: $ _____

(2) Line 2. $ _____1,785.32_____

(3) Line 3. Enter the **larger** of Line 1 or Line 2: $ _____

(4) Line 4. Enter your **TOTAL MONTHLY GROSS INCOME**: $ _____

(5) Is the amount on Line 4 **larger** than the amount on Line 3?

❏ Yes   You do not qualify for an economic hardship deferment based on condition (5). Do not continue with this worksheet.

❏ No   Go to Step 3.

Amounts for Line 1, above:

$1,843.34   (if you live in any state or the District of Columbia, *except* Alaska or Hawaii)

$2,306.66   (if you live in Alaska)

$2,121.66   (if you live in Hawaii)

NOTE: *If you are not currently living in the United States, use the amount for your last state of residence in the United States.*

STEP 3

Determine the total amount you borrowed in federal education loans that are now in repayment by adding together the amounts owed for the federal education loans listed below. You may include defaulted loans only if you have made satisfactory repayment arrangements with the holder of the loans.

Loan Type	Total Amount You Owed When Your Loans Entered Repayment
Federal Stafford Loans (subsidized and unsubsidized)	$ _____
Direct Subsidized and Direct Unsubsidized Loans	+ $ _____
Federal PLUS Loans	+ $ _____
Direct PLUS Loans	+ $ _____
Federal SLS Loans	+ $ _____
Federal Consolidation Loans	+ $ _____
Direct Consolidation Loans	+ $ _____
Federal Perkins Loans and/or National Direct Student Loans	+ $ _____
Other eligible federal education loans listed in Section 5	+ $ _____
TOTAL AMOUNT BORROWED:	= $ _____

Worksheet A continued on Page 2.

Worksheet A
Page 1 of 2

ECONOMIC HARDSHIP DEFERMENT

WORKSHEET A (Continued)

STEP 4

(1) Circle the current interest rate for your FFEL Program loan(s) in the chart below. If your exact interest rate is not listed, choose the next highest interest rate. If you have loans with different interest rates, circle the rate for the loan with the highest interest rate.

Interest Rate	7.0%	7.25%	7.43%	7.5%	7.75%	8.0%	8.25%	8.38%	8.5%	8.75%	9.0%
Constant Multiplier	.0116108	.0117401	.0118337	.0118702	.0120011	.0121328	.0122653	.0123345	.0123986	.0125237	.0126676

(2) Multiply the **TOTAL AMOUNT BORROWED** from Step 3 by the constant multiplier listed directly below the interest rate that you circled in the chart above:

TOTAL AMOUNT BORROWED (from Step 3)   **Constant multiplier** (from the chart above)   **ESTIMATED MONTHLY PAYMENT***

$ _____   X   _____   = $ _____

* This is an estimate of the amount that you would pay each month on your federal education loans if all of your loans were scheduled to be repaid in fixed installments over a 10-year period, regardless of the actual repayment period for your loans.

STEP 5

(1) Line 1. Enter your **TOTAL MONTHLY GROSS INCOME** (from Step 2): $ _____

(2) Line 2. Enter your **ESTIMATED MONTHLY PAYMENT** (from Step 4): $ _____

(3) Line 3. Subtract Line 2 from Line 1: $ _____

(4) Line 4. Enter the amount listed below for your state: $ _____

(5) Line 5. $ 892.66

(6) Line 6. Enter the **larger** of Line 4 or Line 5: $ _____

(7) Line 7. Enter the amount from Line 3: $ _____

(8) Is the amount on Line 7 larger than the amount on Line 6?

     ❐   Yes   You do not qualify for an economic hardship deferment based on condition (5).

     ❐   No   You meet the qualifications for an economic hardship deferment based on condition (5). Check the box for condition (5) in Section 2 of the deferment request.

Amounts for Line 4, above:

   $ 921.67 (if you live in any state or the District of Columbia, *except* Alaska or Hawaii).

   $1,153.33 (if you live in Alaska)

   $1,060.83 (if you live in Hawaii)

   NOTE: *If you are not currently living in the United States, use the amount for your last state of residence in the United States.*

ECONOMIC HARDSHIP DEFERMENT
WORKSHEET B

Use this worksheet to determine if you are eligible for an economic hardship deferment based on condition (6) in Section 2 of the Economic Hardship Deferment Request form. Completion of this worksheet is optional — if you check condition (6), your loan holder will determine your eligibility based on the income and federal education debt documentation that you provide.

DO NOT RETURN THIS WORKSHEET WITH THE DEFERMENT REQUEST — KEEP IT FOR YOUR RECORDS.

STEP 1

Are you working full-time?

❑ Yes   Go to Step 2.

❑ No   You do not qualify for an economic hardship deferment based on condition (6). Do not continue with this worksheet.

STEP 2

Determine the total amount you borrowed in federal education loans that are now in repayment by adding together the amounts owed for the federal education loans listed below. You may include defaulted loans only if you have made satisfactory repayment arrangements with the holder of the loans.

Loan Type	Total Amount You Owed When Your Loans Entered Repayment
Federal Stafford Loans (subsidized and unsubsidized)	$ _____
Direct Subsidized and Direct Unsubsidized Loans	+ $ _____
Federal PLUS Loans	+ $ _____
Direct PLUS Loans	+ $ _____
Federal SLS Loans	+ $ _____
Federal Consolidation Loans	+ $ _____
Direct Consolidation Loans	+ $ _____
Federal Perkins Loans and/or National Direct Student Loans	+ $ _____
Other eligible federal education loans listed in Section 5	+ $ _____
TOTAL AMOUNT BORROWED:	= $ _____

STEP 3

(1) Circle the current interest rate for your FFEL Program loan(s) in the chart below. If your exact interest rate is not listed, choose the next highest interest rate. If you have loans with different interest rates, circle the rate for the loan with the highest interest rate.

Interest Rate	7.0%	7.25%	7.43%	7.5%	7.75%	8.0%	8.25%	8.38%	8.5%	8.75%	9.0%
Constant Multiplier	.0116108	.0117401	.0118337	.0118702	.0120011	.0121328	.0122653	.0123345	.0123986	.0125237	.0126676

(2) Multiply the **TOTAL AMOUNT BORROWED** from Step 3 by the constant multiplier listed directly below the interest rate that you circled in the chart above:

TOTAL AMOUNT BORROWED (from Step 3)   **Constant multiplier** (from the chart above)   **Estimated monthly payment**

$ _____   X   _____   = $ _____

(3) Multiply the estimated monthly payment (from the line above) by 12:

Estimated monthly payment   **ESTIMATED ANNUAL PAYMENT** *

$ _____   X   12   = $ _____

* This is an estimate of the amount that you would pay each year on your federal education loans if all of your loans were scheduled to be repaid in fixed installments over a 10-year period, regardless of the actual repayment period for your loans.

Worksheet B continued on Page 2.

Worksheet B
Page 1 of 2

ECONOMIC HARDSHIP DEFERMENT
WORKSHEET B (Continued)

STEP 4

(1) Line 1. Enter your adjusted gross income: $ _____

(2) Line 2. Multiply the amount on Line 1 by .20 (= 20%): $ _____

(3) Line 3. Enter your **ESTIMATED ANNUAL PAYMENT** (from Step 3): $ _____

(4) Is the amount on Line 3 **equal to or larger than** the amount on Line 2?

    ❏ Yes   Go to Step 5.

    ❏ No   You do not qualify for an economic hardship deferment based on condition (6). Do not continue with this worksheet.

STEP 5

(1) Line 1. Enter your adjusted gross income: $ _____

(2) Line 2. Enter your **ESTIMATED ANNUAL PAYMENT** (from Step 3): $ _____

(3) Line 3. Subtract Line 2 from Line 1: $ _____

(4) Line 4. Enter the amount listed below for your state: $ _____

(5) Line 5. $ ___23,566.00___

(6) Line 6. Enter the **larger** of Line 4 or Line 5: $ _____

(7) Line 7. Enter the amount from Line 3: $ _____

(8) Is the amount on Line 7 **less than** the amount on line 6?

    ❏ Yes   You meet the qualifications for an economic hardship deferment based on condition (6). Check the box for condition (6) in Section 2 of the deferment request.

    ❏ No   You do not qualify for an economic hardship deferment based on condition (6).

Amounts for Line 4, above:

$24,332.00 (if you live in any state or the District of Columbia, *except* Alaska or Hawaii)

$30,448.00 (if you live in Alaska)

$28,006.00 (if you live in Hawaii)

NOTE: *If you are not currently living in the United States, use the amount for your last state of residence in the United States.*

Worksheet B
Page 2 of 2

EDUCATION RELATED DEFERMENT REQUEST

Federal Family Education Loan Program

OMB No. 1845-0005
Form Approved
Exp. Date 06/30/2002

EDU

WARNING: Any person who knowingly makes a false statement or misrepresentation on this form or on any accompanying documents shall be subject to penalties which may include fines, imprisonment or both, under the U.S. Criminal Code and 20 U.S.C. §1097.

SECTION 1: BORROWER IDENTIFICATION

Please correct or, if information is missing, enter below. If a correction, check this box: ☐

SSN | | | | – | | | – | | | | |

Name _____

Address _____

City, State, Zip _____

Telephone - Home (   ) _____

Telephone - Other (   ) _____

SECTION 2: DEFERMENT REQUEST

Before answering any questions, carefully read the entire form, including the instructions and other information in Sections 5 and 6.

■ I meet the qualifications stated in Section 6 for the deferment checked below and request that my loan holder defer repayment of my loan(s):

For all FFEL Program borrowers:

☐ While I am engaged in a full-time course of study in a **GRADUATE FELLOWSHIP** program.

☐ While I am engaged in a full-time **REHABILITATION TRAINING** program.

For borrowers with an outstanding balance on at least one FFEL Program loan that was made before July 1, 1993:

☐ While I am engaged in an **INTERNSHIP/RESIDENCY*** program at the following type of institution (check the appropriate box):

    ☐ Institution of higher education, hospital, or health care facility.

    ☐ Any other institution or organization. Name of Internship/Residency program _____ .

* Federal PLUS Loans qualify for INTERNSHIP/RESIDENCY deferments only if they were made **before August 15, 1983.**

☐ While I am teaching in a designated **TEACHER SHORTAGE AREA.****

** Only Federal Stafford and SLS borrowers whose first loans were made **on or after July 1, 1987 and before July 1, 1993** are eligible for TEACHER SHORTAGE AREA deferments.

SECTION 3: BORROWER UNDERSTANDINGS AND CERTIFICATIONS

■ **I understand that: (1)** Principal payments will be deferred, but if I have an unsubsidized loan, I am responsible for paying the interest that accrues. **(2)** I have the option of making interest payments on my unsubsidized loan(s) during my deferment. I may choose to make interest payments by checking the box below; unpaid interest that accrues will be capitalized by my loan holder.

☐ I wish to make interest payments on my unsubsidized loan(s) during my deferment.

(3) My deferment will begin on the date the deferment condition began, but no more than six months before the date my loan holder receives this request. **(4)** My deferment will end on the earlier of the date that the condition that establishes my deferment eligibility ends or the certified deferment end date. **(5)** My loan holder will not grant this deferment request unless all applicable sections of this form are completed and any required additional documentation is provided. **(6)** If my deferment does not cover all my past due payments, my loan holder may grant me a forbearance for all payments due before the begin date of my deferment or — if the period for which I am eligible for a deferment has ended — a forbearance for all payments due at the time my deferment request is processed. **(7)** If I have used all 24 months allowed for an INTERNSHIP/RESIDENCY Deferment, I can apply for a forbearance for up to 12 months at a time for the remainder of my internship/residency program. **(8)** If I am eligible for a post-deferment grace period on loans made before October 1, 1981, my loan holder may grant me a forbearance on my other loans for this period so that I can begin repayment of all my loans at the same time. I understand that my loan holder may capitalize the interest that accrues on my other loans during the six-month period and that this will increase the principal balance of my other loans. **(9)** My loan holder may grant me a forbearance on my loans for up to 60 days, if necessary, for the collection and processing of documentation related to my deferment request. Interest that accrues during the forbearance will not be capitalized.

■ **I certify that: (1)** The information I provided in Sections 1 and 2 above is true and correct. **(2)** I will provide additional documentation to my loan holder, as required, to support my deferment status. **(3)** I will notify my loan holder immediately when the condition(s) that qualified me for the deferment ends. **(4)** I have read, understand, and meet the eligibility criteria of the deferment for which I have applied, as explained in Section 6.

Borrower's Signature _____ **Date** _____

SECTION 4: AUTHORIZED OFFICIAL'S CERTIFICATION

I certify, to the best of my knowledge and belief, that the borrower named above is/was engaged in the program/teaching service indicated in Section 2, and that the borrower and the borrower's program/teaching service meet all of the eligibility requirements specified in Section 6. The borrower's program/teaching service begins/began on | | | – | | | – | | | | | and is expected to end/ended on | | | – | | | – | | | | | .

Teacher Shortage Area Deferment Only

The borrower is/was teaching in (area/curriculum) _____ , which is a shortage area designated by the U.S. Secretary of Education for the state of _____ for the school year beginning on | | | – | | | – | | | | | and ending on | | | – | | | – | | | | | . The borrower is/was teaching grade level _____ .

Name of Institution _____ OPE-ID (if applicable) _____

Address _____ City, State, Zip _____

Name/Title of Authorized Official _____ Telephone (   ) _____

Authorized Official's Signature _____ **Date** _____

Page 1 of 3

SECTION 5: INSTRUCTIONS FOR COMPLETING THE FORM

Type or print using dark ink. Report dates as month-day-year (MM-DD-YYYY). For example, 'January 1, 1999' = '01-01-1999'. An authorized official must complete Section 4. If you need help completing this form, contact your loan holder.

Return the completed form and any required documentation to the address shown in Section 7.

SECTION 6: DEFINITIONS / ELIGIBILITY CRITERIA FOR EDUCATION RELATED DEFERMENT REQUEST

Definitions

■ The **Federal Family Education Loan (FFEL) Program** includes Federal Stafford Loans (both subsidized and unsubsidized), Federal Supplemental Loans for Students (SLS), Federal PLUS Loans, and Federal Consolidation Loans.

■ A **deferment** is a period during which I am entitled to postpone repayment of the principal balance of my loan(s). The federal government pays the interest that accrues during an eligible deferment for all subsidized Federal Stafford Loans and for Federal Consolidation Loans for which the Consolidation loan application was received by my loan holder **(1)** on or after January 1, 1993 but before August 10, 1993, **(2)** on or after August 10, 1993, if it includes **only** Federal Stafford Loans that were eligible for federal interest subsidy, or **(3)** on or after November 13, 1997, for that portion of the Consolidation loan that paid a subsidized Federal Stafford Loan or a Federal Direct Stafford/Ford (Direct Subsidized) Loan. I am responsible for the interest that accrues during this period on all other FFEL Program loans.

■ **Forbearance** means permitting the temporary cessation of payments, allowing an extension of time for making payments, or temporarily accepting smaller payments than previously scheduled. I am responsible for paying the interest on my loan(s) during a forbearance.

■ The **holder** of my FFEL Program loan(s) may be a lender, guaranty agency, secondary market, or the U.S. Department of Education.

■ **Capitalization** is the addition of unpaid interest to the principal balance of my loan. This will increase the principal and the total cost of my loan.

■ **Authorized certifying officials**:

- Authorized Graduate Fellowship Program Official
- Rehabilitation Training Program Official
- Internship/Residency Program Official (for all internships and residencies)
- State Licensing Official (for internships required to begin professional practice or service)*
- Chief School Administrator (for borrowers teaching in teacher shortage areas; additional certification may be required if the Chief State School Office has not provided a list of approved shortage areas to school administrators)
- * **NOTE**: Certification by a state licensing official, if required, must be provided on a separate statement attached to this form.

Eligibility Criteria

GRADUATE FELLOWSHIP and REHABILITATION TRAINING Deferments

I may defer repayment of my loan(s) while I am:

■ Engaged in a full-time course of study in a **GRADUATE FELLOWSHIP** program. To qualify: **(1)** My graduate fellowship program must **(a)** provide sufficient financial support to allow for full-time study for a period of at least six months; **(b)** require, prior to the awarding of financial support, a written statement from each applicant which explains the applicant's objectives; **(c)** require a graduate fellow to submit periodic reports, projects, or other evidence of the graduate fellow's progress, and **(d)** in the case of a course of study at a foreign university, accept the course of study for completion of the fellowship program. **(2)** I must **(a)** hold at least a Bachelor's Degree conferred by an institution of higher education, and **(b)** have been accepted or recommended by an institution of higher education for acceptance into the graduate fellowship program on a full-time basis. **(3)** If I am in a medical internship or residency program, I am not eligible for this deferment.

■ Engaged in a full-time **REHABILITATION TRAINING** program. To qualify, **(1)** My training program must: **(a)** be licensed, approved, certified or recognized as providing rehabilitation training to disabled individuals by the Department of Veterans Affairs or a state agency responsible for vocational rehabilitation, drug abuse treatment, mental health services, or alcohol abuse treatment programs; **(b)** provide services under a written individualized plan that specifies the date the services are expected to end; and **(c)** be structured in a way that requires a substantial commitment by me to my rehabilitation. ("Substantial commitment" means a commitment of time and effort that would normally prevent a person from being employed 30 or more hours per week in a position expected to last at least three months.) **(2)** I must be either receiving, or scheduled to receive, these rehabilitation services.

INTERNSHIP/RESIDENCY and TEACHER SHORTAGE AREA Deferments

To qualify:

■ I must have an outstanding balance on at least one FFEL Program loan which was made **before July 1, 1993**. If I am a Federal PLUS Loan borrower, **(1)** I am eligible for the INTERNSHIP/RESIDENCY Deferment only on PLUS loans made **before August 15, 1983**, and **(2)** I am not eligible for the TEACHER SHORTAGE AREA Deferment. I am eligible for the TEACHER SHORTAGE AREA deferment only if I am a Federal Stafford or SLS loan borrower whose first FFEL Program loan was made **on or after July 1, 1987 and before July 1, 1993**.

I may defer repayment of my loan(s) while I am:

■ Engaged in an **INTERNSHIP/RESIDENCY** program. (Maximum eligibility is two years; borrowers may request forbearance for the remainder of a medical or dental internship/residency program. Dental Interns/Residents are encouraged to apply for an IN-SCHOOL Deferment.) To qualify: **(1)** I must have been accepted into a medical or dental internship/residency program which must **(a)** be a supervised training program, and **(b)** require that I hold at least a Bachelor's Degree before acceptance into the program. **(2)** In addition, my program must either **(a)** lead to a degree or certificate from an institution of higher education, a hospital, or a health care facility that offers postgraduate training, or **(b)** be required before I may be certified for professional practice or service. **(3) If my program does not lead to a degree or certificate, but is required before I may be certified for professional practice or service, I must also provide (attached to this form) a separate statement from the appropriate state licensing agency certifying this requirement, in addition to the Authorized Official's Certification in Section 4.**

■ Teaching in a designated **TEACHER SHORTAGE AREA**. (Maximum eligibility is three years; borrowers must reapply each school year.) To qualify, I must teach full-time in a public or non-profit private elementary or secondary school in a geographic region, grade level, academic, instructional subject matter or discipline classified shortage area as defined by the U.S. Department of Education. (I will contact my Chief School Administrator or Chief State School Officer for a list of my state's shortage areas.) I may reapply for a continuation of this deferment even if my teaching area is no longer classified as a shortage area.

SECTION 7: WHERE TO SEND THE COMPLETED DEFERMENT REQUEST

RETURN THE COMPLETED DEFERMENT REQUEST AND ANY REQUIRED DOCUMENTATION TO:
(IF NO ADDRESS IS SHOWN, RETURN TO YOUR LOAN HOLDER)

SECTION 8: IMPORTANT NOTICES

Privacy Act Disclosure Notice

The Privacy Act of 1974 (5 U.S.C. §552a) requires that we disclose to you the following information:

The authority for collecting this information is §421 *et seq.* of the Higher Education Act of 1965, as amended (the HEA) (20 U.S.C. §1071 to 1087-2). The principal purpose for collecting this information is to determine whether you are eligible for a deferment on your loan(s) under the Federal Family Education Loan (FFEL) Program.

We ask that you provide the information requested on this deferment request on a voluntary basis. However, you must provide all of the requested information so that the holder(s) of your loan(s) can determine whether you qualify for a deferment.

The information in your file may be disclosed to third parties as authorized under routine uses in the Privacy Act notices called "Title IV Program Files" (originally published on April 12, 1994, *Federal Register*, Vol. 59, p. 17351) and "National Student Loan Data System" (originally published on December 20, 1994, *Federal Register*, Vol. 59, p. 65532). Thus, this information may be disclosed to parties that we authorize to assist us in administering the federal student aid programs, including contractors that are required to maintain safeguards under the Privacy Act. Disclosures may also be made for verification of information, determination of eligibility, enforcement of conditions of the loan or grant, debt collection, and the prevention of fraud, waste, and abuse and these disclosures may be made through computer matching programs with other federal agencies. Disclosures may be made to determine the feasibility of entering into computer matching agreements. We may send information to members of Congress if you ask them in writing to help you with federal student aid questions. If we are involved in litigation, we may send information to the Department of Justice (DOJ), a court, adjudicative body, counsel, or witness if the disclosure is related to financial aid and certain other conditions are met. If this information, either alone or with other information, indicates a potential violation of law, we may send it to the appropriate authority for consideration of action and we may disclose to DOJ to get its advice related to the Title IV, HEA programs or questions under the Freedom of Information Act. Disclosures may be made to qualified researchers under Privacy Act safeguards. In some circumstances involving employment decisions, grievances, or complaints or involving decisions regarding the letting of a contract or making of a grant, license, or other benefit, we may send information to an appropriate authority. In limited circumstances, we may disclose to a federal labor organization recognized under 5 U.S.C. Chapter 71.

Because we request your social security number (SSN), we must inform you that we collect your SSN on a voluntary basis, but section 484(a)(4) of the HEA (20 U.S.C. §1091(a)(4)) provides that, in order to receive any grant, loan, or work assistance under Title IV of the HEA, a student must provide his or her SSN. Your SSN is used to verify your identity, and as an account number (identifier) throughout the life of your loan(s) so that data may be recorded accurately.

Paperwork Reduction Notice

According to the Paperwork Reduction Act of 1995, no persons are required to respond to a collection of information unless it displays a currently valid OMB control number. The valid OMB control number for this information collection is 1845-0005. The time required to complete this information collection is estimated to average 0.16 hours (10 minutes) per response, including the time to review instructions, search existing data resources, gather and maintain the data needed, and complete and review the information collection. *If you have any comments concerning the accuracy of the time estimate(s) or suggestions for improving this form, please write to:*

U.S. Department of Education, Washington, DC 20202-4651.

If you have any comments or concerns regarding the status of your individual submission of this form, write directly to the address shown in Section 7.

TEMPORARY TOTAL DISABILITY DEFERMENT REQUEST

Federal Family Education Loan Program

OMB No. 1845-0005
Form Approved
Exp. Date 06/30/2002

USE THIS FORM ONLY IF YOU HAVE AN OUTSTANDING BALANCE ON A FEDERAL FAMILY EDUCATION LOAN PROGRAM LOAN THAT WAS MADE BEFORE JULY 1, 1993.

TDIS

WARNING: Any person who knowingly makes a false statement or misrepresentation on this form or on any accompanying documents shall be subject to penalties which may include fines, imprisonment or both, under the U.S. Criminal Code and 20 U.S.C. §1097.

SECTION 1: BORROWER IDENTIFICATION

Please correct or, if information is missing, enter below. If a correction, check this box: ☐

SSN ☐☐☐ – ☐☐ – ☐☐☐☐

Name _____

Address _____

City, State, Zip _____

Telephone - Home ( ) _____

Telephone - Other ( ) _____

SECTION 2: DEFERMENT REQUEST

Before answering any questions, carefully read the entire form, including the instructions and other information in Sections 5 and 6. A representative may complete and sign this form on your behalf if you are unable to do so because of your disability.

■ I meet the qualifications stated in Section 6 on the following page for a Temporary Total Disability Deferment and request that my loan holder defer repayment on my loans while I am **TEMPORARILY TOTALLY DISABLED** or while I am unable to secure employment because I am caring for a spouse or dependent who is **TEMPORARILY TOTALLY DISABLED**. Check the appropriate box:

☐ I am disabled.   ☐ I am taking care of my spouse or dependent who is disabled. (For spouse or dependent disability, provide the information requested below.)

Name of Spouse or Dependent _____ Relationship to Borrower _____

SECTION 3: BORROWER AUTHORIZATION, UNDERSTANDINGS AND CERTIFICATIONS

■ **I authorize** any physician, hospital, or other institution having records about the disability for which I am requesting a deferment of loan payments to make information from these records available to the holder of my loans.

■ **I understand that: (1)** Principal payments will be deferred, but if I have an unsubsidized loan, I am responsible for paying the interest that accrues. **(2)** I have the option of making interest payments on my unsubsidized loan(s) during my deferment. I may choose to make interest payments by checking the box below; unpaid interest that accrues will be capitalized by my loan holder.

☐ I wish to make interest payments on my unsubsidized loan(s) during my deferment.

(3) My deferment will begin on the date the deferment condition began, but no more than six months before the date my loan holder receives this request. **(4)** My deferment will end on the earlier of the date that the condition that establishes my deferment eligibility ends or the certified deferment end date. **(5)** My deferment will last no more than six months after the date my physician certifies this request. **(6)** My loan holder will not grant this deferment request unless all applicable sections of this form are completed. **(7)** If my deferment does not cover all my past due payments, my loan holder may grant me a forbearance for all payments due before the begin date of my deferment or — if the period for which I am eligible for a deferment has ended — a forbearance for all payments due at the time my deferment request is processed. **(8)** If I am eligible for a post-deferment grace period on loans made before October 1, 1981, my loan holder may grant me a forbearance on my other loans for this period so that I can begin repayment of all my loans at the same time. I understand that my loan holder may capitalize the interest that accrues on my other loans during the six-month period and that this will increase the principal balance of my other loans. **(9)** My loan holder may grant me a forbearance on my loans for up to 60 days, if necessary, for the collection and processing of documentation related to my deferment request. Interest that accrues during the forbearance will not be capitalized. **(10)** If I am a veteran, the certification by a physician on this form is only for the purposes of establishing my eligibility to receive a deferment of a FFEL Program loan and is not for purposes of determining my eligibility for or the extent of my eligibility for Department of Veterans Affairs benefits.

■ **I certify that: (1)** The information I provided in Sections 1 and 2 above is true and correct. **(2)** I will provide additional documentation to my loan holder, as required, to support my deferment status. **(3)** I will notify my loan holder immediately when the condition(s) that qualified me for the deferment ends. **(4)** I have read, understand, and meet the eligibility criteria of the deferment for which I have applied, as explained in Section 6.

Signature of Borrower or Borrower's Representative _____ Date _____

Name of Borrower's Representative (if applicable) _____ Relationship to Borrower _____

Address of Borrower's Representative _____

SECTION 4: PHYSICIAN'S CERTIFICATION

Instructions for physician: You are being asked to complete and sign this form to certify that the borrower or the borrower's spouse or dependent identified in Section 2 is temporarily totally disabled. You may complete this form **only** if you are a **doctor of medicine or osteopathy** legally authorized to practice. Sign the certification only if the disabled person's condition meets the definition of Temporary Total Disability in Section 6. Provide all requested information (you may attach additional pages). Report dates as month-day-year (MM-DD-YYYY).

■ The disabled person became unable to work and earn money or attend school, or required continuous nursing or similar care on ☐☐ – ☐☐ – ☐☐☐☐ . The disabling condition or care is expected to continue until ☐☐ – ☐☐ – ☐☐☐☐ .

■ Diagnosis of the disabled person's present medical condition:

■ If different from the date provided above, when did the disabled person's injury or illness begin? ☐☐ – ☐☐ – ☐☐☐☐

■ I certify that, in my best professional judgment, the borrower identified in Section 2 is unable to work and earn money or attend school for at least 60 days because of a medically determinable impairment, or the borrower's spouse or dependent identified in Section 2 requires continuous nursing or similar care for a period of at least 90 days. I am a **doctor of medicine or osteopathy** legally authorized to practice.

Physician's Signature _____ Date _____

Physician's Name (printed) _____ Telephone ( ) _____

Address _____ City, State, Zip _____

Page 1 of 3

SECTION 5: INSTRUCTIONS FOR COMPLETING THE FORM

Type or print using dark ink. Report dates as month-day-year (MM-DD-YYYY). For example, 'January 1, 1999' = '01-01-1999'. A doctor of medicine or osteopathy legally authorized to practice must complete Section 4. If you need help completing this form, contact your loan holder.

Return the completed form and any required documentation to the address shown in Section 7.

SECTION 6: DEFINITIONS / ELIGIBILITY CRITERIA FOR TEMPORARY TOTAL DISABILITY DEFERMENT REQUEST

Definitions

- The **Federal Family Education Loan (FFEL) Program** includes Federal Stafford Loans (both subsidized and unsubsidized), Federal Supplemental Loans for Students (SLS), Federal PLUS Loans, and Federal Consolidation Loans.

- A **deferment** is a period during which I am entitled to postpone repayment of the principal balance of my loan(s). The federal government pays the interest that accrues during an eligible deferment for all subsidized Federal Stafford Loans and for Federal Consolidation Loans for which the Consolidation loan application was received by my loan holder **(1)** on or after January 1, 1993 but before August 10, 1993, **(2)** on or after August 10, 1993, if it includes *only* Federal Stafford Loans that were eligible for federal interest subsidy, or **(3)** on or after November 13, 1997, for that portion of the Consolidation loan that paid a subsidized Federal Stafford Loan or a Federal Direct Stafford/Ford (Direct Subsidized) Loan. I am responsible for the interest that accrues during this period on all other FFEL Program loans.

- **Forbearance** means permitting the temporary cessation of payments, allowing an extension of time for making payments, or temporarily accepting smaller payments than previously scheduled. I am responsible for paying the interest on my loan(s) during a forbearance.

- The **holder** of my FFEL Program loan(s) may be a lender, guaranty agency, secondary market, or the U.S. Department of Education.

- **Capitalization** is the addition of unpaid interest to the principal balance of my loan. This will increase the principal and the total cost of my loan.

- The **physician** who completes Section 4 of this form must be a doctor of medicine or osteopathy legally authorized to practice.

- **Temporary Total Disability**: The disabled borrower must, because of injury or illness, be unable to work and earn money or go to school for at least 60 days in order to recover. If the disabled person is the borrower's spouse or dependent, the disabled person must require at least 90 days of continuous nursing or similar care from the borrower. An uncomplicated pregnancy is **not** a qualifying condition for a pregnant borrower, or for a borrower caring for a spouse or dependent with an uncomplicated pregnancy.

Eligibility Criteria

- To qualify for a Temporary Total Disability Deferment, I must have an outstanding balance on at least one FFEL Program loan which was made **before July 1, 1993**.

- I may defer repayment of my loan(s) while I am, or my spouse or dependent is, **TEMPORARILY TOTALLY DISABLED**. (Maximum eligibility is three years. Eligibility must be recertified every six months). To qualify:

  (1) I must be unable to work and earn money or go to school for at least 60 days in order to recover from an injury or illness.

  (2) I must not be requesting this deferment based on a condition that existed before I applied for my loan(s) (underlying loan(s) in the case of a Consolidation loan), unless my condition has since substantially deteriorated, and I am now temporarily totally disabled.

  (3) I must not be requesting this deferment based on an uncomplicated pregnancy (either my pregnancy, or my spouse's or dependent's uncomplicated pregnancy).

  (4) If I am requesting this deferment based on the disability of my spouse or dependent, my spouse or dependent must have an injury or illness that requires at least 90 days of continuous nursing or similar care from me, which prevents me from securing full-time employment of at least 30 hours per week in a position expected to last at least three months.

  (5) I understand that my physician (or my spouse's or dependent's physician) must recertify this condition every six months to continue this deferment.

SECTION 7: WHERE TO SEND THE COMPLETED DEFERMENT REQUEST

RETURN THE COMPLETED DEFERMENT REQUEST AND ANY REQUIRED DOCUMENTATION TO:
(IF NO ADDRESS IS SHOWN, RETURN TO YOUR LOAN HOLDER)

SECTION 8: IMPORTANT NOTICES

Privacy Act Disclosure Notice

The Privacy Act of 1974 (5 U.S.C. §552a) requires that we disclose to you the following information:

The authority for collecting this information is §421 *et seq.* of the Higher Education Act of 1965, as amended (the HEA) (20 U.S.C. §1071 to 1087-2). The principal purpose for collecting this information is to determine whether you are eligible for a deferment on your loan(s) under the Federal Family Education Loan (FFEL) Program.

We ask that you provide the information requested on this deferment request on a voluntary basis. However, you must provide all of the requested information so that the holder(s) of your loan(s) can determine whether you qualify for a deferment.

The information in your file may be disclosed to third parties as authorized under routine uses in the Privacy Act notices called "Title IV Program Files" (originally published on April 12, 1994, *Federal Register*, Vol. 59, p. 17351) and "National Student Loan Data System" (originally published on December 20, 1994, *Federal Register*, Vol. 59, p. 65532). Thus, this information may be disclosed to parties that we authorize to assist us in administering the federal student aid programs, including contractors that are required to maintain safeguards under the Privacy Act. Disclosures may also be made for verification of information, determination of eligibility, enforcement of conditions of the loan or grant, debt collection, and the prevention of fraud, waste, and abuse and these disclosures may be made through computer matching programs with other federal agencies. Disclosures may be made to determine the feasibility of entering into computer matching agreements. We may send information to members of Congress if you ask them in writing to help you with federal student aid questions. If we are involved in litigation, we may send information to the Department of Justice (DOJ), a court, adjudicative body, counsel, or witness if the disclosure is related to financial aid and certain other conditions are met. If this information, either alone or with other information, indicates a potential violation of law, we may send it to the appropriate authority for consideration of action and we may disclose to DOJ to get its advice related to the Title IV, HEA programs or questions under the Freedom of Information Act. Disclosures may be made to qualified researchers under Privacy Act safeguards. In some circumstances involving employment decisions, grievances, or complaints or involving decisions regarding the letting of a contract or making of a grant, license, or other benefit, we may send information to an appropriate authority. In limited circumstances, we may disclose to a federal labor organization recognized under 5 U.S.C. Chapter 71.

Because we request your social security number (SSN), we must inform you that we collect your SSN on a voluntary basis, but section 484(a)(4) of the HEA (20 U.S.C. §1091(a)(4)) provides that, in order to receive any grant, loan, or work assistance under Title IV of the HEA, a student must provide his or her SSN. Your SSN is used to verify your identity, and as an account number (identifier) throughout the life of your loan(s) so that data may be recorded accurately.

Paperwork Reduction Notice

According to the Paperwork Reduction Act of 1995, no persons are required to respond to a collection of information unless it displays a currently valid OMB control number. The valid OMB control number for this information collection is 1845-0005. The time required to complete this information collection is estimated to average 0.16 hours (10 minutes) per response, including the time to review instructions, search existing data resources, gather and maintain the data needed, and complete and review the information collection. *If you have any comments concerning the accuracy of the time estimate(s) or suggestions for improving this form, please write to:*

U.S. Department of Education, Washington, DC 20202-4651.

If you have any comments or concerns regarding the status of your individual submission of this form, write directly to the address shown in Section 7.

UNEMPLOYMENT DEFERMENT REQUEST
Federal Family Education Loan Program

OMB No. 1845-0005
Form Approved
Exp. Date 06/30/2002

UNEM

WARNING: Any person who knowingly makes a false statement or misrepresentation on this form or on any accompanying documents shall be subject to penalties which may include fines, imprisonment or both, under the U.S. Criminal Code and 20 U.S.C. §1097.

SECTION 1: BORROWER IDENTIFICATION

Please correct or, if information is missing, enter below. If a correction, check this box: ☐

SSN |___|___|___| – |___|___| – |___|___|___|___|

Name _____

Address _____

City, State, Zip _____

Telephone - Home (   ) _____

Telephone - Other (   ) _____

SECTION 2: DEFERMENT REQUEST

Before answering any questions, carefully read the entire form, including the instructions and other information in Sections 4, 5, and 6.

■ I meet the qualifications stated in Section 6 for an Unemployment Deferment and request that my loan holder defer repayment of my loan(s).
To document eligibility, complete the following:

(A) TO BE COMPLETED BY ALL BORROWERS:

I became unemployed or began working less than 30 hours per week on |___|___| – |___|___| – |___|___|___|___| . My deferment begins on this date (but no more than 6 months before the date my loan holder receives this request) unless I request my deferment to begin on the following later date: |___|___| – |___|___| – |___|___|___|___| .

(B) IF YOU ARE ELIGIBLE FOR UNEMPLOYMENT BENEFITS, CHECK THIS BOX AND ATTACH THE REQUIRED DOCUMENTATION:

☐ I am eligible for unemployment benefits. I have attached documentation of my eligibility for these benefits. The documentation includes my name, address, social security number, and the effective dates of my eligibility to receive unemployment benefits.

If you checked this box, skip to Section 3 ("Borrower Interest Selection and Certification"). Do not complete items (C) and (D).

(C) IF YOU ARE NOT ELIGIBLE FOR UNEMPLOYMENT BENEFITS, OR IF YOUR ELIGIBILITY HAS EXPIRED, CHECK THE APPROPRIATE BOX BELOW AND PROVIDE THE REQUESTED INFORMATION:

☐ I registered with the following public or private employment agency on |___|___| – |___|___| – |___|___|___|___| .

Name of Employment Agency _____

Address (Street, City, State, Zip Code) _____ Telephone (   ) _____

NOTE: School placement offices and "temporary" agencies do not qualify as public or private employment agencies.

☐ I am not registered with an employment agency because there is not one within 50 miles of my permanent or temporary address. If I am not residing at my permanent address, my temporary address is:

Street, City, State, Zip Code _____ Telephone (   ) _____

(D) COMPLETE THIS ITEM ONLY IF (1) YOU ARE REQUESTING AN EXTENSION OF AN EXISTING UNEMPLOYMENT DEFERMENT AND (2) YOU ARE NOT ELIGIBLE FOR UNEMPLOYMENT BENEFITS. IF THIS IS YOUR FIRST UNEMPLOYMENT DEFERMENT REQUEST, OR IF YOU ARE ELIGIBLE FOR UNEMPLOYMENT BENEFITS, SKIP TO SECTION 3 ("BORROWER INTEREST SELECTION AND CERTIFICATION").

In the last six months, I have attempted to secure full-time employment (see Section 5: Definitions) with the following six employers:

1. Employer _____	2. Employer _____	3. Employer _____
Street _____	Street _____	Street _____
City _____ State _____ Zip _____	City _____ State _____ Zip _____	City _____ State _____ Zip _____
Contact (Name or Title) _____	Contact (Name or Title) _____	Contact (Name or Title) _____
Telephone ( ) _____	Telephone ( ) _____	Telephone ( ) _____

4. Employer _____	5. Employer _____	6. Employer _____
Street _____	Street _____	Street _____
City _____ State _____ Zip _____	City _____ State _____ Zip _____	City _____ State _____ Zip _____
Contact (Name or Title) _____	Contact (Name or Title) _____	Contact (Name or Title) _____
Telephone ( ) _____	Telephone ( ) _____	Telephone ( ) _____

SECTION 3: BORROWER INTEREST SELECTION AND CERTIFICATION

■ Principal payments will be deferred, but if I have an unsubsidized loan, I am responsible for paying the interest that accrues. I have the option of making interest payments on my unsubsidized loan(s) during my deferment. I may choose to make interest payments by checking the box below; unpaid interest that accrues will be capitalized by my loan holder.

☐ I wish to make interest payments on my unsubsidized loan(s) during my deferment.

■ I certify that the information I have provided in Sections 1 and 2 above is true and correct, and that I have read, understand, and meet the eligibility criteria and terms and conditions of the deferment for which I have applied, as explained in Section 6.

Borrower's Signature _____ **Date** _____

Page 1 of 3

SECTION 4: INSTRUCTIONS FOR COMPLETING THE FORM

Type or print using dark ink. Report dates as month-day-year (MM-DD-YYYY). For example, 'January 1, 1999' = '01-01-1999'. If you need more space to provide any of the information requested in Section 2, continue on separate sheets of paper attached to this form. Indicate the number of the item for which you are providing information, and include your name and social security number (SSN) on all attached sheets. If you need help completing this form, contact your loan holder.

Return the completed form and any required documentation to the address shown in Section 7.

SECTION 5: DEFINITIONS

■ The **Federal Family Education Loan (FFEL) Program** includes Federal Stafford Loans (both subsidized and unsubsidized), Federal Supplemental Loans for Students (SLS), Federal PLUS Loans, and Federal Consolidation Loans.

■ A **deferment** is a period during which I am entitled to postpone repayment of the principal balance of my loan(s). The federal government pays the interest that accrues during an eligible deferment for all subsidized Federal Stafford Loans and for Federal Consolidation Loans for which the Consolidation loan application was received by my loan holder **(1)** on or after January 1, 1993 but before August 10, 1993, **(2)** on or after August 10, 1993, if it includes *only* Federal Stafford Loans that were eligible for federal interest subsidy, or **(3)** on or after November 13, 1997, for that portion of the Consolidation loan that paid a subsidized Federal Stafford Loan or a Federal Direct Stafford/Ford (Direct Subsidized) Loan. I am responsible for the interest that accrues during this period on all other FFEL Program loans.

■ **Forbearance** means permitting the temporary cessation of payments, allowing an extension of time for making payments, or temporarily accepting smaller payments than previously scheduled. I am responsible for paying the interest on my loan(s) during a forbearance.

■ The **holder** of my FFEL Program loan(s) may be a lender, guaranty agency, secondary market, or the U.S. Department of Education.

■ **Capitalization** is the addition of unpaid interest to the principal balance of my loan. This will increase the principal and the total cost of my loan.

■ **Full-time** employment is defined as working at least 30 hours per week in a position expected to last at least three months.

SECTION 6: ELIGIBILITY CRITERIA / TERMS AND CONDITIONS FOR UNEMPLOYMENT DEFERMENT

■ I may defer (postpone) repayment of my loans while I am unemployed. I must reapply every six months. If my first loans were made **before July 1, 1993**, my maximum cumulative eligibility for Unemployment Deferments is 24 months. If my first loans were made **on or after July 1, 1993**, my maximum cumulative eligibility is 36 months.

■ To qualify:

(1) I must be conscientiously seeking but unable to find full-time employment in the United States in any field or at any salary or responsibility level. (The United States includes the 50 states, the District of Columbia, Puerto Rico, American Samoa, Guam, the Trust Territory of the Pacific Islands, the Virgin Islands, the Commonwealth of the Northern Mariana Islands, and U.S. military bases and embassy compounds in a foreign country.)

(2) I must provide documentation establishing that I am eligible for unemployment benefits. This documentation must include my name, address, social security number, and the effective dates of my eligibility to receive unemployment benefits.

OR

(3) If I am not eligible for unemployment benefits, I must be registered with a private or public employment agency if there is one within 50 miles of my permanent or temporary address (school placement offices and "temporary" agencies do not qualify as public or private employment agencies). If I am not eligible for unemployment benefits and I am requesting an extension of an existing unemployment deferment, I must provide my loan holder with documentation of my conscientious search for full-time employment in the preceding six months by completing Item (D) in Section 2 of this form.

■ I will provide additional documentation to my loan holder, as required, to support my deferment status.

■ I will notify my loan holder immediately when the condition(s) that qualified me for the deferment ends.

■ **My deferment will begin on the date the deferment condition began, but no more than six months before the date my loan holder receives this request.**

■ My deferment will end on the earlier of the date that the condition that establishes my deferment eligibility ends or the certified deferment end date.

■ My deferment will last for no more than six months after the date I sign the deferment request.

■ My loan holder will not grant this deferment request unless all applicable sections of this form are completed and any required additional documentation is provided.

■ If my deferment does not cover all my past due payments, my loan holder may grant me a forbearance for all payments due before the begin date of my deferment or — if the period for which I am eligible for a deferment has ended — a forbearance for all payments due at the time my deferment request is processed.

■ If I am eligible for a one-time post-deferment grace period on loans made before October 1, 1981, my loan holder may grant me a forbearance on my other loans for this period so that I can begin repayment of all my loans at the same time. I understand that my loan holder may capitalize the interest that accrues on my other loans during the six-month period and that this will increase the principal balance of my other loans.

■ My loan holder may grant me a forbearance on my loans for up to 60 days, if necessary, for the collection and processing of documentation related to my deferment request. Interest that accrues during the forbearance will not be capitalized.

SECTION 7: WHERE TO SEND THE COMPLETED DEFERMENT REQUEST

RETURN THE COMPLETED DEFERMENT REQUEST AND ANY REQUIRED DOCUMENTATION TO:
(IF NO ADDRESS IS SHOWN, RETURN TO YOUR LOAN HOLDER)

SECTION 8: IMPORTANT NOTICES

Privacy Act Disclosure Notice

The Privacy Act of 1974 (5 U.S.C. §552a) requires that we disclose to you the following information:

The authority for collecting this information is §421 *et seq.* of the Higher Education Act of 1965, as amended (the HEA) (20 U.S.C. §1071 to 1087-2). The principal purpose for collecting this information is to determine whether you are eligible for a deferment on your loan(s) under the Federal Family Education Loan (FFEL) Program.

We ask that you provide the information requested on this deferment request on a voluntary basis. However, you must provide all of the requested information so that the holder(s) of your loan(s) can determine whether you qualify for a deferment.

The information in your file may be disclosed to third parties as authorized under routine uses in the Privacy Act notices called "Title IV Program Files" (originally published on April 12, 1994, *Federal Register*, Vol. 59, p. 17351) and "National Student Loan Data System" (originally published on December 20, 1994, *Federal Register*, Vol. 59, p. 65532). Thus, this information may be disclosed to parties that we authorize to assist us in administering the federal student aid programs, including contractors that are required to maintain safeguards under the Privacy Act. Disclosures may also be made for verification of information, determination of eligibility, enforcement of conditions of the loan or grant, debt collection, and the prevention of fraud, waste, and abuse and these disclosures may be made through computer matching programs with other federal agencies. Disclosures may be made to determine the feasibility of entering into computer matching agreements. We may send information to members of Congress if you ask them in writing to help you with federal student aid questions. If we are involved in litigation, we may send information to the Department of Justice (DOJ), a court, adjudicative body, counsel, or witness if the disclosure is related to financial aid and certain other conditions are met. If this information, either alone or with other information, indicates a potential violation of law, we may send it to the appropriate authority for consideration of action and we may disclose to DOJ to get its advice related to the Title IV, HEA programs or questions under the Freedom of Information Act. Disclosures may be made to qualified researchers under Privacy Act safeguards. In some circumstances involving employment decisions, grievances, or complaints or involving decisions regarding the letting of a contract or making of a grant, license, or other benefit, we may send information to an appropriate authority. In limited circumstances, we may disclose to a federal labor organization recognized under 5 U.S.C. Chapter 71.

Because we request your social security number (SSN), we must inform you that we collect your SSN on a voluntary basis, but section 484(a)(4) of the HEA (20 U.S.C. §1091(a)(4)) provides that, in order to receive any grant, loan, or work assistance under Title IV of the HEA, a student must provide his or her SSN. Your SSN is used to verify your identity, and as an account number (identifier) throughout the life of your loan(s) so that data may be recorded accurately.

Paperwork Reduction Notice

According to the Paperwork Reduction Act of 1995, no persons are required to respond to a collection of information unless it displays a currently valid OMB control number. The valid OMB control number for this information collection is 1845-0005. The time required to complete this information collection is estimated to average 0.16 hours (10 minutes) per response, including the time to review instructions, search existing data resources, gather and maintain the data needed, and complete and review the information collection. *If you have any comments concerning the accuracy of the time estimate(s) or suggestions for improving this form, please write to:*

U.S. Department of Education, Washington, DC 20202-4651.

If you have any comments or concerns regarding the status of your individual submission of this form, write directly to the address shown in Section 7.

PUBLIC SERVICE DEFERMENT REQUEST

Federal Family Education Loan Program

USE THIS FORM ONLY IF YOU HAVE AN OUTSTANDING BALANCE ON A FEDERAL FAMILY EDUCATION LOAN PROGRAM LOAN THAT WAS MADE BEFORE JULY 1, 1993.

WARNING: Any person who knowingly makes a false statement or misrepresentation on this form or on any accompanying documents shall be subject to penalties which may include fines, imprisonment or both, under the U.S. Criminal Code and 20 U.S.C. §1097.

OMB No. 1845-0005
Form Approved
Exp. Date 06/30/2002

PUB

SECTION 1: BORROWER IDENTIFICATION

Please correct or, if information is missing, enter below. If a correction, check this box: ❏

SSN | | | | – | | | – | | | | |

Name _____

Address _____

City, State, Zip _____

Telephone - Home ( ) _____

Telephone - Other ( ) _____

SECTION 2: DEFERMENT REQUEST

Before answering any questions, carefully read the entire form, including the instructions and other information in Sections 5 and 6.

■ I meet the qualifications stated in Section 6 for the deferment checked below and request that my loan holder defer repayment of my loan(s) while I am:

❏ On active duty in the **ARMED FORCES** of the United States.*

❏ Serving full time as an officer in the Commissioned Corps of the **PUBLIC HEALTH SERVICE.** *

❏ Serving in the **PEACE CORPS.** *

❏ A full-time paid volunteer in the **ACTION PROGRAMS.** *

❏ A full-time paid volunteer for a **TAX-EXEMPT ORGANIZATION.** *

   * Federal PLUS Loans made **on or after August 15, 1983** do **not** qualify for the Armed Forces, Public Health Service, Peace Corps, ACTION Programs, and Tax-Exempt Organization Deferments.

❏ On active duty in the **NATIONAL OCEANIC AND ATMOSPHERIC ADMINISTRATION (NOAA).** * *

   * * The NOAA Deferment is available **only** to Federal Stafford and SLS loan borrowers whose first loans were made **on or after July 1, 1987 and before July 1, 1993.**

SECTION 3: BORROWER UNDERSTANDINGS AND CERTIFICATIONS

■ I understand that: **(1)** Principal payments will be deferred, but if I have an unsubsidized loan, I am responsible for paying the interest that accrues. **(2)** I have the option of making interest payments on my unsubsidized loan(s) during my deferment. I may choose to make interest payments by checking the box below; unpaid interest that accrues will be capitalized by my loan holder.

❏ I wish to make interest payments on my unsubsidized loan(s) during my deferment.

(3) My deferment will begin on the date the deferment condition began, but no more than six months before the date my loan holder receives this request. **(4)** My deferment will end on the earlier of the date that the condition that establishes my deferment eligibility ends or the certified deferment end date. **(5)** My loan holder will not grant this deferment request unless all applicable sections of this form are completed and any required additional documentation is provided. **(6)** If my deferment does not cover all my past due payments, my loan holder may grant me a forbearance for all payments due before the begin date of my deferment or — if the period for which I am eligible for a deferment has ended — a forbearance for all payments due at the time my deferment request is processed. **(7)** If I am eligible for a post-deferment grace period on loans made before October 1, 1981, my loan holder may grant me a forbearance on my other loans for this period so that I can begin repayment of all my loans at the same time. I understand that my loan holder may capitalize the interest that accrues on my other loans during the six-month period and that this will increase the principal balance of my other loans. **(8)** My loan holder may grant me a forbearance on my loans for up to 60 days, if necessary, for the collection and processing of documentation related to my deferment request. Interest that accrues during the forbearance will not be capitalized.

■ I certify that: **(1)** The information I provided in Sections 1 and 2 above is true and correct. **(2)** I will provide additional documentation to my loan holder, as required, to support my deferment status. **(3)** I will notify my loan holder immediately when the condition(s) that qualified me for the deferment ends. **(4)** I have read, understand, and meet the eligibility criteria of the deferment for which I have applied, as explained in Section 6.

Borrower's Signature _____ **Date** _____

SECTION 4: AUTHORIZED OFFICIAL'S CERTIFICATION

I certify, to the best of my knowledge and belief, that the borrower named above is/was engaged in the service indicated in Section 2, and that the borrower and the borrower's service meet all the eligibility requirements specified in Section 6.

The borrower's service began on | | | – | | | – | | | | | and is expected to end/ended on | | | – | | | – | | | | | .

Name of Organization _____

Address _____ City, State, Zip _____

Name/Title of Authorized Official _____ Telephone ( ) _____

Authorized Official's Signature _____ **Date** _____

Page 1 of 3

SECTION 5: INSTRUCTIONS FOR COMPLETING THE FORM

Type or print using dark ink. Report dates as month-day-year (MM-DD-YYYY). For example, 'January 1, 1999' = '01-01-1999'. An authorized official must complete Section 4. If you need help completing this form, contact your loan holder.

Return the completed form and any required documentation to the address shown in Section 7.

SECTION 6: DEFINITIONS / ELIGIBILITY CRITERIA FOR PUBLIC SERVICE DEFERMENT REQUEST

Definitions

■ The **Federal Family Education Loan (FFEL) Program** includes Federal Stafford Loans (both subsidized and unsubsidized), Federal Supplemental Loans for Students (SLS), Federal PLUS Loans, and Federal Consolidation Loans.

■ A **deferment** is a period during which I am entitled to postpone repayment of the principal balance of my loan(s). The federal government pays the interest that accrues during an eligible deferment for all subsidized Federal Stafford Loans and for Federal Consolidation Loans for which the Consolidation loan application was received by my loan holder **(1)** on or after January 1, 1993 but before August 10, 1993, **(2)** on or after August 10, 1993, if it includes *only* Federal Stafford Loans that were eligible for federal interest subsidy, or **(3)** on or after November 13, 1997, for that portion of the Consolidation loan that paid a subsidized Federal Stafford Loan or a Federal Direct Stafford/Ford (Direct Subsidized) Loan. I am responsible for the interest that accrues during this period on all other FFEL Program loans.

■ **Forbearance** means permitting the temporary cessation of payments, allowing an extension of time for making payments, or temporarily accepting smaller payments than previously scheduled. I am responsible for paying the interest on my loan(s) during a forbearance.

■ The **holder** of my FFEL Program loan(s) may be a lender, guaranty agency, secondary market, or the U.S. Department of Education.

■ **Capitalization** is the addition of unpaid interest to the principal balance of my loan. This will increase the principal and the total cost of my loan.

■ **Authorized certifying officials:**

  • Commanding or Personnel Officer (Armed Forces Deferment)

  • Authorized Official of the U.S. Public Health Service (Public Health Service Deferment)

  • Authorized Official of the Peace Corps (Peace Corps Deferment)

  • Authorized Official of the ACTION Program (ACTION Program Deferment)

  • Authorized Official of the Volunteer Program (Tax-Exempt Organization Deferment)

  • Authorized Official of the NOAA Corps (NOAA Deferment)

Eligibility Criteria

■ To qualify for any of the deferments listed in Section 2 of this form:

  • I must have an outstanding balance on at least one FFEL Program loan which was made **before July 1, 1993**. If I am a Federal PLUS Loan borrower, **(1)** I am not eligible for the NOAA Deferment, and **(2)** I am eligible for the Armed Forces, Public Health Service, Peace Corps, ACTION Programs, and Tax-Exempt Organization Deferments only if my first loan was made **before August 15, 1983**. I am eligible for the NOAA Deferment only if I am a Federal Stafford or SLS loan borrower whose first loan was made **on or after July 1, 1987 and before July 1, 1993**.

■ I may defer repayment of my loan(s) while I am:

  • On active duty in the **ARMED FORCES** of the United States. (Maximum eligibility is three years; this is a combined limit with Public Health Service and NOAA deferments.) To qualify, I must: **(1)** be on active duty in the Army, Navy, Air Force, Marine Corps or Coast Guard, and **(2)** provide my loan holder with copies of my military identification and orders or have my commanding or personnel officer certify Section 4 on the front of this form. **NOTE:** Borrowers enlisted in a reserve component of the Armed Forces or the National Guard (while on active duty status in the Army or Air Force Reserves) may qualify for this deferment only if: (1) serving full-time for a period expected to last at least one year, or (2) serving under an order for national mobilization.

  • Serving full-time as an officer in the Commissioned Corps of the **PUBLIC HEALTH SERVICE**. (Maximum eligibility is three years; this is a combined limit with Armed Forces and NOAA deferments.)

  • Serving in the **PEACE CORPS**. (Maximum eligibility is three years.) To qualify, I must have agreed to serve for a period of at least one year.

  • A full-time paid volunteer in the **ACTION PROGRAMS**. (Maximum eligibility is three years.) To qualify, I must have agreed to serve for a period of at least one year.

  • A full-time paid volunteer for a **TAX-EXEMPT ORGANIZATION**. (Maximum eligibility is three years.) To qualify, I must: **(1)** be serving full-time in an organization that has a tax exemption under Section 501(c)(3) of the Internal Revenue Code of 1986; **(2)** assist low income people and their communities in eliminating poverty and poverty-related human, social, and environmental conditions; **(3)** not earn more than the federal minimum wage; however, I may receive fringe benefits like those received by other employees of the organization; **(4)** not engage in religious instruction, proselytizing, fund-raising to support religious activities, or conduct worship services as part of my duties; and **(5)** have agreed to serve for a period of at least one year.

  • On active duty in the **NATIONAL OCEANIC AND ATMOSPHERIC ADMINISTRATION (NOAA)**. (Maximum eligibility is three years; this is a combined limit with Armed Forces and Public Health Service Deferments.)

SECTION 7: WHERE TO SEND THE COMPLETED DEFERMENT REQUEST

RETURN THE COMPLETED DEFERMENT REQUEST AND ANY REQUIRED DOCUMENTATION TO:
(IF NO ADDRESS IS SHOWN, RETURN TO YOUR LOAN HOLDER)

Page 2 of 3

SECTION 8: IMPORTANT NOTICES

Privacy Act Disclosure Notice

The Privacy Act of 1974 (5 U.S.C. §552a) requires that we disclose to you the following information:

The authority for collecting this information is §421 *et seq.* of the Higher Education Act of 1965, as amended (the HEA) (20 U.S.C. §1071 to 1087-2). The principal purpose for collecting this information is to determine whether you are eligible for a deferment on your loan(s) under the Federal Family Education Loan (FFEL) Program.

We ask that you provide the information requested on this deferment request on a voluntary basis. However, you must provide all of the requested information so that the holder(s) of your loan(s) can determine whether you qualify for a deferment.

The information in your file may be disclosed to third parties as authorized under routine uses in the Privacy Act notices called "Title IV Program Files" (originally published on April 12, 1994, *Federal Register*, Vol. 59, p. 17351) and "National Student Loan Data System" (originally published on December 20, 1994, *Federal Register*, Vol. 59, p. 65532). Thus, this information may be disclosed to parties that we authorize to assist us in administering the federal student aid programs, including contractors that are required to maintain safeguards under the Privacy Act. Disclosures may also be made for verification of information, determination of eligibility, enforcement of conditions of the loan or grant, debt collection, and the prevention of fraud, waste, and abuse and these disclosures may be made through computer matching programs with other federal agencies. Disclosures may be made to determine the feasibility of entering into computer matching agreements. We may send information to members of Congress if you ask them in writing to help you with federal student aid questions. If we are involved in litigation, we may send information to the Department of Justice (DOJ), a court, adjudicative body, counsel, or witness if the disclosure is related to financial aid and certain other conditions are met. If this information, either alone or with other information, indicates a potential violation of law, we may send it to the appropriate authority for consideration of action and we may disclose to DOJ to get its advice related to the Title IV, HEA programs or questions under the Freedom of Information Act. Disclosures may be made to qualified researchers under Privacy Act safeguards. In some circumstances involving employment decisions, grievances, or complaints or involving decisions regarding the letting of a contract or making of a grant, license, or other benefit, we may send information to an appropriate authority. In limited circumstances, we may disclose to a federal labor organization recognized under 5 U.S.C. Chapter 71.

Because we request your social security number (SSN), we must inform you that we collect your SSN on a voluntary basis, but section 484(a)(4) of the HEA (20 U.S.C. §1091(a)(4)) provides that, in order to receive any grant, loan, or work assistance under Title IV of the HEA, a student must provide his or her SSN. Your SSN is used to verify your identity, and as an account number (identifier) throughout the life of your loan(s) so that data may be recorded accurately.

Paperwork Reduction Notice

According to the Paperwork Reduction Act of 1995, no persons are required to respond to a collection of information unless it displays a currently valid OMB control number. The valid OMB control number for this information collection is 1845-0005. The time required to complete this information collection is estimated to average 0.16 hours (10 minutes) per response, including the time to review instructions, search existing data resources, gather and maintain the data needed, and complete and review the information collection. *If you have any comments concerning the accuracy of the time estimate(s) or suggestions for improving this form, please write to:*

U.S. Department of Education, Washington, DC 20202-4651.

If you have any comments or concerns regarding the status of your individual submission of this form, write directly to the address shown in Section 7.

PLWM

PARENTAL LEAVE / WORKING MOTHER DEFERMENT REQUEST

Federal Family Education Loan Program

USE THIS FORM ONLY IF YOU HAVE AN OUTSTANDING BALANCE ON A FEDERAL FAMILY EDUCATION LOAN PROGRAM LOAN THAT WAS MADE BEFORE JULY 1, 1993.
WARNING: Any person who knowingly makes a false statement or misrepresentation on this form or on any accompanying documents shall be subject to penalties which may include fines, imprisonment or both, under the U.S. Criminal Code and 20 U.S.C. §1097.

OMB No. 1845-0005
Form Approved
Exp. Date 06/30/2002

SECTION 1: BORROWER IDENTIFICATION

Please correct or, if information is missing, enter below. If a correction, check this box: ❑

SSN | | | | – | | | – | | | | |

Name _____
Address _____
City, State, Zip _____
Telephone - Home (   ) _____
Telephone - Other (   ) _____

SECTION 2: DEFERMENT REQUEST

Before answering any questions, carefully read the entire form, including the instructions and other information in Sections 5 and 6.

■ I meet the qualifications stated in Section 6 for the deferment checked below and request that my loan holder defer repayment of my loan(s) beginning
| | | – | | | – | | | | | while I am (check one):

❑ On **PARENTAL LEAVE**.

NOTE: For a Parental Leave Deferment, the beginning deferment date listed above must be within six months of the date you were last enrolled in school at least half-time. **Federal PLUS Loan borrowers are not eligible for Parental Leave Deferments.**

❑ A **WORKING MOTHER**.

NOTE: Federal PLUS Loan borrowers are not eligible for Working Mother Deferments. Additional conditions apply — see Section 6.

SECTION 3: BORROWER UNDERSTANDINGS AND CERTIFICATIONS

■ **I understand that: (1)** Principal payments will be deferred, but if I have an unsubsidized loan, I am responsible for paying the interest that accrues. **(2)** I have the option of making interest payments on my unsubsidized loan(s) during my deferment. I may choose to make interest payments by checking the box below; unpaid interest that accrues will be capitalized by my loan holder.

❑ I wish to make interest payments on my unsubsidized loan(s) during my deferment.

(3) My deferment will begin on the date the deferment condition began, but no more than six months before the date my loan holder receives this request. **(4)** My deferment will end on the earlier of the date that the condition that establishes my deferment eligibility ends or the certified deferment end date. **(5)** My loan holder will not grant this deferment request unless all applicable sections of this form are completed and any required additional documentation is provided. **(6)** If my deferment does not cover all my past due payments, my loan holder may grant me a forbearance for all payments due before the begin date of my deferment or — if the period for which I am eligible for a deferment has ended — a forbearance for all payments due at the time my deferment request is processed. **(7)** If I am applying for a Parental Leave Deferment and am in my grace period, I agree to waive up to one month of my grace period so that my deferment begins within six months of the date I was last enrolled in school at least half-time. **(8)** If I am eligible for a post-deferment grace period on loans made before October 1, 1981, my loan holder may grant me a forbearance on my other loans for this period so that I can begin repayment of all my loans at the same time. I understand that my loan holder may capitalize the interest that accrues on my other loans during the six-month period and that this will increase the principal balance of my other loans. **(9)** My loan holder may grant me a forbearance on my loans for up to 60 days, if necessary, for the collection and processing of documentation related to my deferment request. Interest that accrues during the forbearance will not be capitalized.

■ **I certify that: (1)** The information I provided in Sections 1 and 2 above is true and correct. **(2)** I will provide additional documentation to my loan holder, as required, to support my deferment status. **(3)** I will notify my loan holder immediately when the condition(s) that qualified me for the deferment ends. **(4)** I have read, understand, and meet the eligibility criteria of the deferment for which I have applied, as explained in Section 6.

Borrower's Signature _____ Date _____

SECTION 4: AUTHORIZED OFFICIAL'S CERTIFICATION

Required for Parental Leave Deferments only.

I certify, to the best of my knowledge and belief, that the borrower named above was last enrolled at least half-time on:
| | | – | | | – | | | | | .

Name of Institution _____ OPE-ID _____
Address _____ City, State, Zip _____
Name/Title of Authorized Official _____ Telephone (   ) _____
Authorized Official's Signature _____ **Date** _____

SECTION 5: INSTRUCTIONS FOR COMPLETING THE FORM

Type or print using dark ink. Report dates as month-day-year (MM-DD-YYYY). For example, 'January 1, 1999' = '01-01-1999'. If you are applying for a Parental Leave Deferment, an authorized official must complete Section 4. If you need help completing this form, contact your loan holder.

Return the completed form and any required documentation to the address shown in Section 7.

SECTION 6: DEFINITIONS / ELIGIBILITY CRITERIA FOR PARENTAL LEAVE / WORKING MOTHER DEFERMENT REQUEST

Definitions

- The **Federal Family Education Loan (FFEL) Program** includes Federal Stafford Loans (both subsidized and unsubsidized), Federal Supplemental Loans for Students (SLS), Federal PLUS Loans, and Federal Consolidation Loans.

- A **deferment** is a period during which I am entitled to postpone repayment of the principal balance of my loan(s). The federal government pays the interest that accrues during an eligible deferment for all subsidized Federal Stafford Loans and for Federal Consolidation Loans for which the Consolidation loan application was received by my loan holder **(1)** on or after January 1, 1993 but before August 10, 1993, **(2)** on or after August 10, 1993, if it includes *only* Federal Stafford Loans that were eligible for federal interest subsidy, or **(3)** on or after November 13, 1997, for that portion of the Consolidation loan that paid a subsidized Federal Stafford Loan or a Federal Direct Stafford/Ford (Direct Subsidized) Loan. I am responsible for the interest that accrues during this period on all other FFEL Program loans.

- **Forbearance** means permitting the temporary cessation of payments, allowing an extension of time for making payments, or temporarily accepting smaller payments than previously scheduled. I am responsible for paying the interest on my loan(s) during a forbearance.

- The **holder** of my FFEL Program loan(s) may be a lender, guaranty agency, secondary market, or the U.S. Department of Education.

- **Capitalization** is the addition of unpaid interest to the principal balance of my loan. This will increase the principal and the total cost of my loan.

- **Full-time** employment is defined as working at least 30 hours per week in a position expected to last at least three months.

- An **authorized certifying official** for the Parental Leave Deferment is an authorized official from the school where I was enrolled at least half-time within the six-month period preceding this deferment.

Eligibility Criteria

- To qualify for a Parental Leave / Working Mother Deferment:
  - I must have an outstanding balance on at least one FFEL Program loan which was made **before July 1, 1993**. If I am a Federal PLUS Loan borrower, I am not eligible for the Parental Leave or Working Mother Deferments. I am eligible for the Working Mother Deferment only if I am a Federal Stafford or SLS loan borrower whose first FFEL Program loan was made **on or after July 1, 1987 and before July 1, 1993**.

- I may defer repayment of my loan(s) while I am:
  - On **PARENTAL LEAVE**. (Maximum eligibility is six months per occurrence.) To qualify:

    (1) I must:
    (a) be pregnant, caring for my newborn child (a child less than six months of age), or caring for my newly adopted child;
    (b) not be working full-time or attending school during the deferment period; and
    (c) have been enrolled in school at least half-time within the six-month period preceding this deferment (an authorized school must certify my enrollment in Section 4).

    (2) I must provide my loan holder with:
    (a) a statement from my physician documenting my pregnancy, if I am requesting this deferment due to my pregnancy; or
    (b) a copy of my newborn child's birth certificate; or
    (c) a statement from the adoption agency documenting my newly adopted child's placement and the placement date.

  - A **WORKING MOTHER**. (Maximum eligibility is 12 months.) To qualify:

    (1) I must:
    (a) have entered or reentered the workforce within one year preceding this deferment;
    (b) be working full-time in a position earning not more than $1 per hour above the federal minimum wage; and
    (c) be the mother of a preschool-age child who has not yet enrolled in the first grade or a higher grade in elementary school.

    (2) I must provide my loan holder with documentation of:
    (a) my rate of pay, such as a pay stub; and
    (b) the age of my preschool-age child, such as a birth certificate.

SECTION 7: WHERE TO SEND THE COMPLETED DEFERMENT REQUEST

RETURN THE COMPLETED DEFERMENT REQUEST AND ANY REQUIRED DOCUMENTATION TO:
(IF NO ADDRESS IS SHOWN, RETURN TO YOUR LOAN HOLDER)

SECTION 8: IMPORTANT NOTICES

Privacy Act Disclosure Notice

The Privacy Act of 1974 (5 U.S.C. §552a) requires that we disclose to you the following information:

The authority for collecting this information is §421 *et seq.* of the Higher Education Act of 1965, as amended (the HEA) (20 U.S.C. §1071 to 1087-2). The principal purpose for collecting this information is to determine whether you are eligible for a deferment on your loan(s) under the Federal Family Education Loan (FFEL) Program.

We ask that you provide the information requested on this deferment request on a voluntary basis. However, you must provide all of the requested information so that the holder(s) of your loan(s) can determine whether you qualify for a deferment.

The information in your file may be disclosed to third parties as authorized under routine uses in the Privacy Act notices called "Title IV Program Files" (originally published on April 12, 1994, *Federal Register*, Vol. 59, p. 17351) and "National Student Loan Data System" (originally published on December 20, 1994, *Federal Register*, Vol. 59, p. 65532). Thus, this information may be disclosed to parties that we authorize to assist us in administering the federal student aid programs, including contractors that are required to maintain safeguards under the Privacy Act. Disclosures may also be made for verification of information, determination of eligibility, enforcement of conditions of the loan or grant, debt collection, and the prevention of fraud, waste, and abuse and these disclosures may be made through computer matching programs with other federal agencies. Disclosures may be made to determine the feasibility of entering into computer matching agreements. We may send information to members of Congress if you ask them in writing to help you with federal student aid questions. If we are involved in litigation, we may send information to the Department of Justice (DOJ), a court, adjudicative body, counsel, or witness if the disclosure is related to financial aid and certain other conditions are met. If this information, either alone or with other information, indicates a potential violation of law, we may send it to the appropriate authority for consideration of action and we may disclose to DOJ to get its advice related to the Title IV, HEA programs or questions under the Freedom of Information Act. Disclosures may be made to qualified researchers under Privacy Act safeguards. In some circumstances involving employment decisions, grievances, or complaints or involving decisions regarding the letting of a contract or making of a grant, license, or other benefit, we may send information to an appropriate authority. In limited circumstances, we may disclose to a federal labor organization recognized under 5 U.S.C. Chapter 71.

Because we request your social security number (SSN), we must inform you that we collect your SSN on a voluntary basis, but section 484(a)(4) of the HEA (20 U.S.C. §1091(a)(4)) provides that, in order to receive any grant, loan, or work assistance under Title IV of the HEA, a student must provide his or her SSN. Your SSN is used to verify your identity, and as an account number (identifier) throughout the life of your loan(s) so that data may be recorded accurately.

Paperwork Reduction Notice

According to the Paperwork Reduction Act of 1995, no persons are required to respond to a collection of information unless it displays a currently valid OMB control number. The valid OMB control number for this information collection is 1845-0005. The time required to complete this information collection is estimated to average 0.16 hours (10 minutes) per response, including the time to review instructions, search existing data resources, gather and maintain the data needed, and complete and review the information collection. *If you have any comments concerning the accuracy of the time estimate(s) or suggestions for improving this form, please write to:*

U.S. Department of Education, Washington, DC 20202-4651.

If you have any comments or concerns regarding the status of your individual submission of this form, write directly to the address shown in Section 7.

PLUS

PLUS BORROWER WITH DEPENDENT STUDENT DEFERMENT REQUEST

Federal Family Education Loan Program

USE THIS FORM ONLY IF YOU HAVE AN OUTSTANDING BALANCE ON A FEDERAL FAMILY EDUCATION LOAN PROGRAM LOAN THAT WAS MADE BEFORE JULY 1, 1993.

WARNING: Any person who knowingly makes a false statement or misrepresentation on this form or on any accompanying documents shall be subject to penalties which may include fines, imprisonment or both, under the U.S. Criminal Code and 20 U.S.C. §1097.

OMB No. 1845-0005
Form Approved
Exp. Date 06/30/2002

SECTION 1: BORROWER IDENTIFICATION

Please correct or, if information is missing, enter below. If a correction, check this box: ☐

SSN |___|___|___| - |___|___| - |___|___|___|___|

Name _____

Address _____

City, State, Zip _____

Telephone - Home ( ) _____

Telephone - Other ( ) _____

SECTION 2: DEFERMENT REQUEST

Before answering any questions, carefully read the entire form, including the instructions and other information in Sections 5 and 6.

■ I meet the qualifications stated in Section 6 for this deferment and request that my loan holder defer repayment of my loan(s) while the student (named below) for whom I borrowed a PLUS loan is dependent and is (check one):

☐ Enrolled full-time at an eligible school.

☐ Enrolled at least half-time at an eligible school (additional conditions apply — see Section 6).

☐ Engaged full-time in a rehabilitation training program.

Student's Name _____ Student's SSN |___|___|___| - |___|___| - |___|___|___|___|

SECTION 3: BORROWER UNDERSTANDINGS AND CERTIFICATIONS

■ **I understand that: (1)** Principal payments will be deferred. I am responsible for paying the interest that accrues. **(2)** I have the option of making interest payments during my deferment. I may choose to make interest payments by checking the box below; unpaid interest that accrues will be capitalized by my loan holder.

☐ I wish to make interest payments on my loan(s) during my deferment.

(3) My deferment will begin on the date the deferment condition began, but no more than six months before the date my loan holder receives this request. **(4)** My deferment will end on the earlier of the date that the condition that establishes my deferment eligibility ends or the certified deferment end date. **(5)** My loan holder will not grant this deferment request unless all applicable sections of this form are completed and any required additional documentation is provided. **(6)** If my deferment does not cover all my past due payments, my loan holder may grant me a forbearance for all payments due before the begin date of my deferment or — if the period for which I am eligible for a deferment has ended — a forbearance for all payments due at the time my deferment request is processed. **(7)** If I am eligible for a post-deferment grace period on loans made before October 1, 1981, my loan holder may grant me a forbearance on my other loans for this period so that I can begin repayment of all my loans at the same time. I understand that my loan holder may capitalize the interest that accrues on my other loans during the six-month period and that this will increase the principal balance of my other loans. **(8)** My loan holder may grant me a forbearance on my loans for up to 60 days, if necessary, for the collection and processing of documentation related to my deferment request. Interest that accrues during the forbearance will not be capitalized.

■ **I certify that: (1)** The information I provided in Sections 1 and 2 above is true and correct. **(2)** I will provide additional documentation to my loan holder, as required, to support my deferment status. **(3)** I will notify my loan holder immediately when the condition(s) that qualified me for the deferment ends. **(4)** I have read, understand, and meet the eligibility criteria of the deferment for which I have applied, as explained in Section 6.

Borrower's Signature _____ **Date** _____

SECTION 4: AUTHORIZED OFFICIAL'S CERTIFICATION

I certify, to the best of my knowledge and belief, that the dependent student named above is/was enrolled at an eligible institution or engaged in the program indicated in Section 2, and that the dependent student and (if applicable) the dependent student's program meet all the eligibility requirements specified in Section 6 on the following page.

☐ Is/was enrolled as (check the appropriate box) ☐ a full-time student ☐ at least a half-time student

during the academic period from |___|___| - |___|___| - |___|___|___|___| to |___|___| - |___|___| - |___|___|___|___|

and is reasonably expected to complete his/her program requirements on |___|___| - |___|___| - |___|___|___|___| .

☐ Is/was engaged full-time in a rehabilitation training program that began on |___|___| - |___|___| - |___|___|___|___|

and will end/ended on |___|___| - |___|___| - |___|___|___|___| .

Name of Institution/Facility _____ OPE-ID (if applicable) _____

Address _____ City, State, Zip _____

Name/Title of Authorized Official _____ Telephone ( ) _____

Authorized Official's Signature _____ **Date** _____

Page 1 of 3

SECTION 5: INSTRUCTIONS FOR COMPLETING THE FORM

Type or print using dark ink. Report dates as month-day-year (MM-DD-YYYY). For example, 'January 1, 1999' = '01-01-1999'. An authorized school/program official must complete Section 4. If you need help completing this form, contact your loan holder.

Return the completed form and any required documentation to the address shown in Section 7.

SECTION 6: DEFINITIONS / ELIGIBILITY CRITERIA FOR PLUS BORROWER WITH DEPENDENT STUDENT DEFERMENT REQUEST

Definitions

- The **Federal Family Education Loan (FFEL) Program** includes Federal Stafford Loans (both subsidized and unsubsidized), Federal Supplemental Loans for Students (SLS), Federal PLUS Loans, and Federal Consolidation Loans.

- A **deferment** is a period during which I am entitled to postpone repayment of the principal balance of my loan(s). The federal government pays the interest that accrues during an eligible deferment for all subsidized Federal Stafford Loans and for Federal Consolidation Loans for which the Consolidation loan application was received by my loan holder **(1)** on or after January 1, 1993 but before August 10, 1993, **(2)** on or after August 10, 1993, if it includes *only* Federal Stafford Loans that were eligible for federal interest subsidy, or **(3)** on or after November 13, 1997, for that portion of the Consolidation loan that paid a subsidized Federal Stafford Loan or a Federal Direct Stafford/Ford (Direct Subsidized) Loan. I am responsible for the interest that accrues during this period on all other FFEL Program loans.

- **Forbearance** means permitting the temporary cessation of payments, allowing an extension of time for making payments, or temporarily accepting smaller payments than previously scheduled. I am responsible for paying the interest on my loan(s) during a forbearance.

- The **holder** of my FFEL Program loan(s) may be a lender, guaranty agency, secondary market, or the U.S. Department of Education.

- **Capitalization** is the addition of unpaid interest to the principal balance of my loan. This will increase the principal and the total cost of my loan.

- **Authorized certifying officials**:
  - Authorized School Official (for dependent students enrolled full-time or at least half-time at an eligible institution)
  - Authorized Rehabilitation Training Program Official

Eligibility Criteria

To qualify:

- To receive a deferment based on my dependent student's full-time or at least half-time enrollment at an eligible school, I must have an outstanding balance on a Federal Stafford, SLS, FISL, PLUS, or Consolidation loan made **on or after July 1, 1987 and before July 1, 1993**. To receive a deferment based on my dependent student's full-time engagement in a rehabilitation training program, I must have had an outstanding balance on a Federal Stafford, SLS, FISL, PLUS, or Consolidation loan **on June 30, 1993**.

- I may defer repayment of my loan(s) while the student for whom I borrowed a Federal PLUS Loan is dependent and is:
  - Enrolled full-time at an eligible school.
  - Enrolled at least half-time at an eligible school. In addition, the dependent student must have an outstanding balance on a Federal Stafford, SLS, FISL, PLUS, or Consolidation loan made **on or after July 1, 1987**.
  - Engaged full-time in a rehabilitation training program. To qualify: **(1)** The training program must **(a)** be licensed, approved, certified or recognized as providing rehabilitation training to disabled individuals by the Department of Veterans Affairs or a state agency responsible for vocational rehabilitation, drug abuse treatment, mental health services, or alcohol abuse treatment programs; **(b)** provide services under a written individualized plan that specifies the date the services are expected to end; and **(c)** be structured in a way that requires a substantial commitment by the student to his/her rehabilitation. ("Substantial commitment" means a commitment of time and effort that would normally prevent a person from being employed 30 or more hours per week in a position expected to last at least three months.) **(2)** The dependent student must be either receiving, or scheduled to receive, these rehabilitation services.

SECTION 7: WHERE TO SEND THE COMPLETED DEFERMENT REQUEST

RETURN THE COMPLETED DEFERMENT REQUEST AND ANY REQUIRED DOCUMENTATION TO:
(IF NO ADDRESS IS SHOWN, RETURN TO YOUR LOAN HOLDER)

SECTION 8: IMPORTANT NOTICES

Privacy Act Disclosure Notice

The Privacy Act of 1974 (5 U.S.C. §552a) requires that we disclose to you the following information:

The authority for collecting this information is §421 *et seq.* of the Higher Education Act of 1965, as amended (the HEA) (20 U.S.C. §1071 to 1087-2). The principal purpose for collecting this information is to determine whether you are eligible for a deferment on your loan(s) under the Federal Family Education Loan (FFEL) Program.

We ask that you provide the information requested on this deferment request on a voluntary basis. However, you must provide all of the requested information so that the holder(s) of your loan(s) can determine whether you qualify for a deferment.

The information in your file may be disclosed to third parties as authorized under routine uses in the Privacy Act notices called "Title IV Program Files" (originally published on April 12, 1994, *Federal Register*, Vol. 59, p. 17351) and "National Student Loan Data System" (originally published on December 20, 1994, *Federal Register*, Vol. 59, p. 65532). Thus, this information may be disclosed to parties that we authorize to assist us in administering the federal student aid programs, including contractors that are required to maintain safeguards under the Privacy Act. Disclosures may also be made for verification of information, determination of eligibility, enforcement of conditions of the loan or grant, debt collection, and the prevention of fraud, waste, and abuse and these disclosures may be made through computer matching programs with other federal agencies. Disclosures may be made to determine the feasibility of entering into computer matching agreements. We may send information to members of Congress if you ask them in writing to help you with federal student aid questions. If we are involved in litigation, we may send information to the Department of Justice (DOJ), a court, adjudicative body, counsel, or witness if the disclosure is related to financial aid and certain other conditions are met. If this information, either alone or with other information, indicates a potential violation of law, we may send it to the appropriate authority for consideration of action and we may disclose to DOJ to get its advice related to the Title IV, HEA programs or questions under the Freedom of Information Act. Disclosures may be made to qualified researchers under Privacy Act safeguards. In some circumstances involving employment decisions, grievances, or complaints or involving decisions regarding the letting of a contract or making of a grant, license, or other benefit, we may send information to an appropriate authority. In limited circumstances, we may disclose to a federal labor organization recognized under 5 U.S.C. Chapter 71.

Because we request your social security number (SSN), we must inform you that we collect your SSN on a voluntary basis, but section 484(a)(4) of the HEA (20 U.S.C. §1091(a)(4)) provides that, in order to receive any grant, loan, or work assistance under Title IV of the HEA, a student must provide his or her SSN. Your SSN is used to verify your identity, and as an account number (identifier) throughout the life of your loan(s) so that data may be recorded accurately.

Paperwork Reduction Notice

According to the Paperwork Reduction Act of 1995, no persons are required to respond to a collection of information unless it displays a currently valid OMB control number. The valid OMB control number for this information collection is 1845-0005. The time required to complete this information collection is estimated to average 0.16 hours (10 minutes) per response, including the time to review instructions, search existing data resources, gather and maintain the data needed, and complete and review the information collection. *If you have any comments concerning the accuracy of the time estimate(s) or suggestions for improving this form, please write to:*

U.S. Department of Education, Washington, DC 20202-4651.

If you have any comments or concerns regarding the status of your individual submission of this form, write directly to the address shown in Section 7.

Index

CATALOG

...more from nolo.com

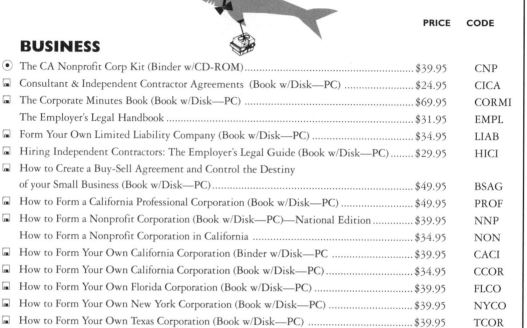

	PRICE	CODE

BUSINESS

⦿ The CA Nonprofit Corp Kit (Binder w/CD-ROM)	$39.95	CNP
▣ Consultant & Independent Contractor Agreements (Book w/Disk—PC)	$24.95	CICA
▣ The Corporate Minutes Book (Book w/Disk—PC)	$69.95	CORMI
The Employer's Legal Handbook	$31.95	EMPL
▣ Form Your Own Limited Liability Company (Book w/Disk—PC)	$34.95	LIAB
▣ Hiring Independent Contractors: The Employer's Legal Guide (Book w/Disk—PC)	$29.95	HICI
▣ How to Create a Buy-Sell Agreement and Control the Destiny of your Small Business (Book w/Disk—PC)	$49.95	BSAG
▣ How to Form a California Professional Corporation (Book w/Disk—PC)	$49.95	PROF
▣ How to Form a Nonprofit Corporation (Book w/Disk—PC)—National Edition	$39.95	NNP
How to Form a Nonprofit Corporation in California	$34.95	NON
▣ How to Form Your Own California Corporation (Binder w/Disk—PC	$39.95	CACI
▣ How to Form Your Own California Corporation (Book w/Disk—PC)	$34.95	CCOR
▣ How to Form Your Own Florida Corporation (Book w/Disk—PC)	$39.95	FLCO
▣ How to Form Your Own New York Corporation (Book w/Disk—PC)	$39.95	NYCO
▣ How to Form Your Own Texas Corporation (Book w/Disk—PC)	$39.95	TCOR
How to Write a Business Plan	$24.95	SBS
The Independent Paralegal's Handbook	$29.95	PARA
Legal Guide for Starting & Running a Small Business, Vol. 1	$24.95	RUNS
▣ Legal Guide for Starting & Running a Small Business, Vol. 2: Legal Forms (Book w/Disk—PC)	$29.95	RUNS2
Marketing Without Advertising	$19.00	MWAD
▣ Music Law (Book w/Disk—PC)	$29.95	ML
Nolo's California Quick Corp (Quick & Legal Series)	$19.95	QINC
⦿ Open Your California Business in 24 Hours (Book w/CD-ROM)	$24.95	OPEN
▣ The Partnership Book: How to Write a Partnership Agreement (Book w/Disk—PC)	$34.95	PART
Sexual Harassment on the Job	$18.95	HARS
Starting & Running a Successful Newsletter or Magazine	$24.95	MAG
Take Charge of Your Workers' Compensation Claim (California Edition)	$29.95	WORK
Tax Savvy for Small Business	$29.95	SAVVY
Trademark: Legal Care for Your Business and Product Name	$34.95	TRD

▣ Book with disk
⦿ Book with CD-ROM

CALL 800-992-6656 OR USE THE ORDER FORM IN THE BACK OF THE BOOK

	PRICE	CODE
How to Mediate Your Dispute	$18.95	MEDI
How to Seal Your Juvenile & Criminal Records (California Edition)	$24.95	CRIM
How to Sue For Up to $25,000...and Win!	$29.95	MUNI
Mad at Your Lawyer	$21.95	MAD
Represent Yourself in Court: How to Prepare & Try a Winning Case	$29.95	RYC

HOMEOWNERS, LANDLORDS & TENANTS

	PRICE	CODE
▣ Contractors' and Homeowners' Guide to Mechanics' Liens (Book w/Disk—PC)	$39.95	MIEN
The Deeds Book (California Edition)	$24.95	DEED
Dog Law	$14.95	DOG
▣ Every Landlord's Legal Guide (National Edition, Book w/Disk—PC)	$34.95	ELLI
Every Tenant's Legal Guide	$26.95	EVTEN
For Sale by Owner in California	$24.95	FSBO
How to Buy a House in California	$24.95	BHCA
The Landlord's Law Book, Vol. 1: Rights & Responsibilities (California Edition)	$34.95	LBRT
The Landlord's Law Book, Vol. 2: Evictions (California Edition)	$34.95	LBEV
Leases & Rental Agreements (Quick & Legal Series)	$18.95	LEAR
Neighbor Law: Fences, Trees, Boundaries & Noise	$17.95	NEI
Renters' Rights (National Edition—Quick & Legal Series))	$15.95	RENT
Stop Foreclosure Now in California	$29.95	CLOS
Tenants' Rights (California Edition)	$21.95	CTEN

HUMOR

	PRICE	CODE
29 Reasons Not to Go to Law School	$9.95	29R
Poetic Justice	$9.95	PJ

IMMIGRATION

	PRICE	CODE
How to Get a Green Card: Legal Ways to Stay in the U.S.A.	$24.95	GRN
U.S. Immigration Made Easy	$44.95	IMEZ

MONEY MATTERS

	PRICE	CODE
▣ 101 Law Forms for Personal Use (Quick & Legal Series, Book w/disk—PC)	$24.95	SPOT
Bankruptcy: Is It the Right Solution to Your Debt Problems? (Quick & Legal Series)	$15.95	BRS
Chapter 13 Bankruptcy: Repay Your Debts	$29.95	CH13
Credit Repair (Quick & Legal Series)	$15.95	CREP
▣ The Financial Power of Attorney Workbook (Book w/disk—PC)	$24.95	FINPOA
How to File for Chapter 7 Bankruptcy	$26.95	HFB
IRAs, 401(k)s & Other Retirement Plans: Taking Your Money Out	$21.95	RET
Money Troubles: Legal Strategies to Cope With Your Debts	$19.95	MT
Nolo's Law Form Kit: Personal Bankruptcy	$16.95	KBNK
Stand Up to the IRS	$24.95	SIRS
Take Control of Your Student Loans	$19.95	SLOAN

▣ Book with disk

◉ Book with CD-ROM

PATENTS AND COPYRIGHTS

RESEARCH & REFERENCE

SENIORS

SOFTWARE

Call or check our website at www.nolo.com for special discounts on Software!

Special Upgrade Offer

Get 35% off the latest edition off your Nolo book

It's important to have the most current legal information. Because laws and legal procedures change often, we update our books regularly. To help keep you up-to-date we are extending this special upgrade offer. Cut out and mail the title portion of the cover of your old Nolo book and we'll give you 35% off the retail price of the NEW EDITION of that book when you purchase directly from us. For more information call us at 1-800-992-6656. This offer is to individuals only.

Order Form

Name

Address

City

State, Zip

Daytime Phone

E-mail

Our "No-Hassle" Guarantee

Return anything you buy directly from Nolo for any reason and we'll cheerfully refund your purchase price. No ifs, ands or buts.

☐ Check here if you do not wish to receive mailings from other companies

Item Code	Quantity	Item	Unit Price	Total Price

Method of payment

☐ Check ☐ VISA ☐ MasterCard
☐ Discover Card ☐ American Express

Subtotal	
Add your local sales tax (California only)	
Shipping: RUSH $8, Basic $3.95 (See below)	
"I bought 3, Ship it to me FREE!"(Ground shipping only)	
TOTAL	

Account Number

Expiration Date

Signature

Shipping and Handling

Rush Delivery-Only $8

We'll ship any order to any street address in the U.S. by UPS 2nd Day Air* for only $8!

* Order by noon Pacific Time and get your order in 2 business days. Orders placed after noon Pacific Time will arrive in 3 business days. P.O. boxes and S.F. Bay Area use basic shipping. Alaska and Hawaii use 2nd Day Air or Priority Mail.

Basic Shipping—$3.95

Use for P.O. Boxes, Northern California and Ground Service.

Allow 1-2 weeks for delivery. U.S. addresses only.

For faster service, use your credit card and our toll-free numbers

Order 24 hours a day

Online	www.nolo.com
Phone	1-800-992-6656
Fax	1-800-645-0895
Mail	Nolo.com
950 Parker St.
Berkeley, CA 94710

Visit us online at
www.nolo.com

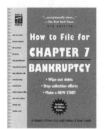

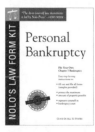

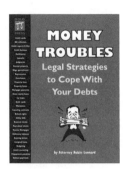

Take 2 minutes & Give us your 2 cents

Your comments make a big difference in the development and revision of Nolo books and software. Please take a few minutes and register your Nolo product—and your comments—with us. Not only will your input make a difference, you'll receive special offers available only to registered owners of Nolo products on our newest books and software. Register now by:

PHONE
1-800-992-6656

FAX
1-800-645-0895

EMAIL
cs@nolo.com

or **MAIL** us
this registration card

REMEMBER:
Little publishers have big ears. We really listen to you.

fold here

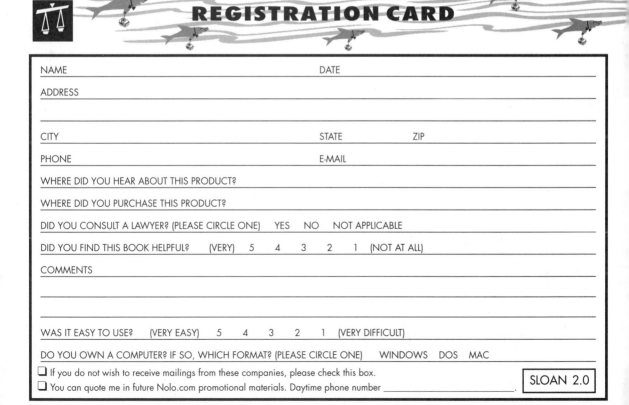

NAME	DATE
ADDRESS	
CITY	STATE ZIP
PHONE	E-MAIL

WHERE DID YOU HEAR ABOUT THIS PRODUCT?

WHERE DID YOU PURCHASE THIS PRODUCT?

DID YOU CONSULT A LAWYER? (PLEASE CIRCLE ONE)   YES   NO   NOT APPLICABLE

DID YOU FIND THIS BOOK HELPFUL?   (VERY)   5   4   3   2   1   (NOT AT ALL)

COMMENTS

WAS IT EASY TO USE?   (VERY EASY)   5   4   3   2   1   (VERY DIFFICULT)

DO YOU OWN A COMPUTER? IF SO, WHICH FORMAT? (PLEASE CIRCLE ONE)   WINDOWS   DOS   MAC

❏ If you do not wish to receive mailings from these companies, please check this box.
❏ You can quote me in future Nolo.com promotional materials. Daytime phone number _____.

SLOAN 2.0

NOLO IN THE *NEWS*

"Nolo helps lay people perform legal tasks without the aid—or fees—of lawyers."

—USA TODAY

Nolo books are ..."written in plain language, free of legal mumbo jumbo, and spiced with witty personal observations."

—ASSOCIATED PRESS

"...Nolo publications...guide people simply through the how, when, where and why of law."

—WASHINGTON POST

"Increasingly, people who are not lawyers are performing tasks usually regarded as legal work... And consumers, using books like Nolo's, do routine legal work themselves."

—NEW YORK TIMES

"...All of [Nolo's] books are easy-to-understand, are updated regularly, provide pull-out forms...and are often quite moving in their sense of compassion for the struggles of the lay reader."

—SAN FRANCISCO CHRONICLE

fold here

nolo.com
950 Parker Street
Berkeley, CA 94710-9867

Attn: SLOAN 2.0